PRISMATIC REFLECTIONS ON SPANISH GOLDEN AGE THEATER

Ibérica

A. Robert Lauer
General Editor

Vol. 44

This book is a volume in a Peter Lang monograph series.
Every volume is peer reviewed and meets
the highest quality standards for content and production.

PETER LANG
New York • Bern • Frankfurt • Berlin
Brussels • Vienna • Oxford • Warsaw

PRISMATIC REFLECTIONS ON SPANISH GOLDEN AGE THEATER

ESSAYS IN HONOR OF MATTHEW D. STROUD

EDITED BY
Gwyn E. Campbell and
Amy R. Williamsen

PETER LANG
New York • Bern • Frankfurt • Berlin
Brussels • Vienna • Oxford • Warsaw

Library of Congress Cataloging-in-Publication Data

Prismatic reflections on Spanish Golden Age theater:
essays in honor of Matthew D. Stroud /
edited by Gwyn E. Campbell, Amy R. Williamsen.
pages cm. — (Ibérica; vol. 44)
Includes bibliographical references and index.
1. Spanish drama—Classical period, 1500–1700—History and criticism.
2. Theater—Spain—History—16th century. 3. Theater—Spain—History—17th century.
I. Campbell, Gwyn Elizabeth, editor. II. Williamsen, Amy R., editor.
III. Stroud, Matthew D., honouree.
PQ6105.P68   862'.309—dc23   2015010729
ISBN 978-1-4331-3008-3 (hardcover)
ISBN 978-1-4539-1604-9 (e-book)
ISSN 1056-5000

Bibliographic information published by **Die Deutsche Nationalbibliothek**.
Die Deutsche Nationalbibliothek lists this publication in the "Deutsche
Nationalbibliografie"; detailed bibliographic data are available
on the Internet at http://dnb.d-nb.de/.

Cover image: Gwyn E. Campbell, "Prismatic Reflections," quilt.

The paper in this book meets the guidelines for permanence and durability
of the Committee on Production Guidelines for Book Longevity
of the Council of Library Resources.

Preludio

*In loving tribute to my first source of inspiration, my late parents,
Colin Kydd Campbell and Vivian Gwyn Norval Campbell*

—G.E.C.

*To all the **comediantes** we have loved and lost*

—A.R.W

Reconocimientos

Any *Festschrift* is a labor of love, made possible by the generosity of all those involved. Although we cannot possibly mention everyone, we would like to offer our thanks to Michael Boglovits, who helped in the very initial stages of this project, and our heartfelt gratitude to Molly Reininger, who provided indispensable editorial support throughout the majority of the process. During the final stages of production, we have been fortunate to work with a talented and experienced editor, A. Robert Lauer, a treasured friend of the *comedia*.

We would also like to extend our sincere appreciation for the grant received from Washington and Lee University's Lenfest Subvention Fund to help defray publishing costs. In addition, we thank the University of North Carolina Greensboro for its support of this project.

As always, we are indebted to *comediantes*, past and present, for their inspiration and guidance.

Table of Contents

Matthew D. Stroud

Dedicatoria a nuestro "autor"

Among the many rich traditions shared by *comediantes* is the honoring of those who have helped shape the lives of others through their scholarship, teaching, research and more. We dedicate this volume to celebrating the career of our esteemed colleague and cherished friend, Dr. Matthew D. Stroud. Matt has served, in many senses, as the *"autor"* in that he has inspired this project, as well as countless others, through his impressive mastery of diverse fields of inquiry, supplemented by his illuminating spectrum of relationships in *academia* and beyond.

Born on October 4, 1950, in Hillsboro, Texas, Matt grew up in Amarillo, his early years giving little indication that he would spend his adult life immersed in the study of Spanish literature. It was in the 9th grade, at Austin High School, that he took his first Spanish course, then continuing with language courses at Tascosa High School—because they were required. His own history is a powerful example of the impact that individual teachers can have on a student's life; Patricia Harnett, Rosemary Patterson and Allie Grillo, in particular, instilled in him an avid interest in the cultures of Mexico, Spain, and Argentina.

After graduating as valedictorian in 1968, Matt continued on to the University of Texas at Austin, the only university to which he applied, although his path to a major was less straightforward. Forays into mathematics, computer sciences (he earned the Computer Science Creativity Award), and education did little to pique his interest. The one constant through all of these experiences was a deepening and broadening interest in Spanish literature under such notable professors as Ricardo Guillén, George Schade, Beverly Gibbs, and Virginia Higginbotham. Matt completed his BA in Spanish in short order, graduating in 1971, but without ever having taken a course in Spanish literature before 1700.

After a one-year hiatus from studies, at a time when the economy was in a slump, the best job Matt could find was as Assistant Manager at the Woolworth's in San Angelo, Texas. Fortunately, with his prodigious acumen, he enrolled for one semester at West Texas State University (now West Texas A & M) in order both to complete his second major in French and to investigate graduate schools. His decision about which graduate school to attend was in part determined by the weather: a heavy snowfall in Urbana, Illinois, the week the choice needed to be made led him to the west coast and the University of Southern California. There, Matt reveled in the total immersion in Spanish language, culture, and literature—and beyond—of Los Angeles during the mid 1970s. His first semester as a graduate student finally introduced him to Early Modern Spanish literature: *Don Juan* with Dr. Ted Sackett, and *Don Quijote* with Dr. James A. Parr. Nonetheless, Matt's affinity was more for Latin American literature and philology, given that Latin became his doctoral minor. It was again fortuitous that USC did not have the resources to offer a Ph.D. in philology, and that Matt felt at home where he was. His off-the-cuff remark to the department Chair, that his interests were so broad that he could *even* consider specializing in the Golden Age, led him to an influential conversation with Jim Parr, and the rest is history, as it were. Moreover, for Matt, the best part of the story is that the more he delved into the history, culture, and literature of the Golden Age, the more he loved the period and his area of studies.

In 1977, Matt accepted a position at Trinity University. He has shared his love of Spanish literature with generations of students there ever since, as well as inspiring his colleagues at Trinity and around the world. The official university introduction clarifies: "His area of specialization is 16th- and 17th-century Spain, but he considers every aspect of his academic life from the point of view of the humanities in the broadest sense: what does it mean to be human, and how do we relate to each other?" In his teaching, he underscores that education is a transformative process for all involved since we learn as much from our students as they do from us. He finds that "students are often amazed at the relevance to today's world of the issues that arise in the discussion of the Spanish epic, *El poema de Mio Cid*, Lope de Vega's play, *Fuenteovejuna*, 19th-century Spanish history, and even Spanish grammar." It is no surprise that in 1999 he was awarded the prestigious Dr. and Mrs. Z. T. Scott Faculty Fellowship for Outstanding Teaching and Advising, and more recently, the Trinity University Distinguished Achievement Award for Scholarship as well.

The impact that Matt has had on our field is profound. Throughout his career, he has practiced a unique brand of intellectual alchemy, exploring ways to combine his disparate interests. Once at Trinity, he revolutionized the teaching of languages, developing over twenty-two instructional online programs in Spanish, French and Latin, a task that, in the seventies, required that he program them on the mainframe. He also creatively incorporated technology while engaging students in a hands-on research experience as they created their own online editions. In one such course, Matt had his students create an anthology of the one hundred best Spanish lyric poems; the project, of course, included discussions of what makes a poem good. The students undertook all the editing themselves, and each received a copy of the volume at the end of the course. Beyond his home campus, his ground-breaking work developing websites and electronic editions of classical Spanish texts still benefit students and specialists around the globe. Matt's pioneering contributions as one of the four original founders of the Association of Hispanic Classic Theater, and his active decades-long management of the AHCT web presence, including the reformatting of over two thousand files, represent an invaluable legacy.

A true Renaissance scholar, he also delved into the musical realm, serving as a creative consultant for various productions. The grandest of these is, without question, his 1981 staging of *Celos aun del aire matan* [*Even Baseless Jealousy Can Kill*]. For this ambitious project, the first presentation in 250 years of Calderón de la Barca and Juan Hidalgo's only fully sung three-act play for which the music still exists, he supervised every aspect of the seven performances. From editing the libretto to serving as language coach, creating publicity and producing the video- and audio-taped versions, he did it all. The visual aspect of the spectacle proved so stunning that the *Museo del Barrio* of New York dedicated an exhibit to the costumes that same year.

Although he has officially taught more undergraduates than graduate students, his mentoring has touched many lives. In fact, he was instrumental in launching the careers of several of the contributors to this volume. Whether in the classroom, at conferences or through his participation as an expert outside reader of dissertations and grant proposals, he simultaneously challenges and inspires those who work with him.

Matt's innovative spirit continually leads him to deviate from established scripts, refracting, reframing and reshaping ideas and disciplines along the way, although he insists that he did not necessarily set out to blaze any trails. He stumbled across Serrano y Sanz's edition and study of women writers, which led to his early work on Zayas and Caro. His friendship with Dr. Henry W. Sullivan took him down the path toward Lacan, and his participation in the 1989 Paris Lacan Seminar, the first offered in English. Matt's unique combination of language skills enabled him to follow the trail of the *comedia* to Amsterdam and beyond. Grounded in philosophical and theoretical considerations and his own personal experiences as a gay man, his exemplary work in the nascent field of queer studies blazed paths that freed others to explore exciting new critical avenues. All told, he has published three single-authored monographs; created over half a dozen editions and translations; written almost fifty journal articles and book chapters; and delivered countless presentations. There is no question, at least in *comedia* circles, that Matt's colleagues rue being scheduled in a session concurrent with his: Matt's room is packed to the proverbial rafters, with few potential audience members for the rest.

His unflinching insistence on intellectual rigor and his dogged commitment to precision may, at times, be misperceived as unyieldingness when, in fact, it underscores his resolute integrity. His unabashed directness and his forthright honesty combine with his candid openness to engender fierce loyalty across generations of scholars—his remarks, prepared and spontaneous, often serve as the catalyst for watershed moments. Matt's razor sharp wit and singular laugh have graced many a session or exchange. Best known as an encouraging mentor who generously shares both time and knowledge, he is also a fierce competitor on and off the racquetball courts. Because of his erudition, his perspicacity, and his own compelling performances, he commands the respect and admiration of audiences from across our profession. He often quips that he is a legend in his own mind; yet, in fact, his irreverent brilliance radiates, unchecked and uncensored.

Matt has also been actively involved in community engagement, long before that term became an administrative commonplace serving, for example, as President of a nonprofit arts organization (Festival Calderón) in San Antonio. His civic activism and persistence have sparked meaningful dialogue and prompted significant change. He has especially worked to alleviate the suffering of others and to better our world by advocating for the marginalized. To this end, he has been involved, directly or indirectly, in every advance of inclusion of LGBT members of the Trinity University community: from being recognized as gay, to having his beloved partner (now spouse, Tom Davis) invited to University functions, first as a "guest," then by name; from a decade-long work with his home institution's benefits committee to eliminate discrimination on the basis of sexual orientation and HIV status, to a university-wide non-discrimination policy, and a recognition of domestic partners, with full medical benefits. Not a bad record, he believes, for a country boy at a Presbyterian university, deep in the heart of Texas!

Loa

En la que hablan las editoras

Every editing project requires multiple decisions. Throughout this process, we have tried to make information accessible to the specialist and the non-specialist alike. Thus, quotations from *comedia* texts are followed by English translations; any published translations used by the individual contributors are included in the references. If a specific translation is not referenced, that means that the authors supplied their own translations. Because of the metrical complexities of Spanish versification in the *comedia*, few of the translations attempt to capture the meaning within rhyming verse. Nonetheless, the division by virgules of the renditions in English prose roughly approximates the respective verse length in the original. The format that we have chosen to document verses quoted from the *comedias* strives to provide as much information as possible to facilitate finding the verses in the editions used and beyond. Thus, wherever feasible, we have indicated the details as follows: I.1203–05, 71; that is, Act [I], verse [1203–05], and page [71]; if no page number was readily available, as in the case of many electronic editions, we limit the citation to Act and verse [I.1203–05]. For editions lacking line numbers, the citations will read Act, page [I, 71]. An attempt has been made to standardize certain spellings and terms across all articles.

The most difficult decision we encountered during the final stages of assembling this volume was how to handle the consequences of the untimely and unexpected death of our cherished friend and colleague, Kathleen Regan. Kate fervently wished to contribute to this homage volume as a way of showing her respect and admiration for Matt, given her immense gratitude for all the ways he supported and encouraged her throughout her career. Ever since he served as a reader for her doctoral dissertation, completed at the University

of Chicago, he assumed a pivotal role as mentor and friend. Equally important, Kate was among the scholars named by Matt as those whose presence
in the collection would be meaningful to him. Although she was unable to
complete the revisions she had planned for her article, we could not conceive
of this volume without her presence. While remaining faithful to the original
version she submitted, we have made any necessary small corrections and
minor stylistic revisions. In this way, we respect Kate's intellectual property,
and honor both Matt and her memory. Although in recent years she had
moved away from more traditional scholarship to produce digital documentaries exploring various facets of Spain's socio-cultural heritage, poignantly,
her contribution to this project brings her journey full circle, as she returns to
her first academic passion—the *comedia* and its fascinating women characters.

Dramatis personae

ISAAC BENABU is Associate Professor of Theater Studies at Hebrew University (Jerusalem). His areas of specialization, with numerous publications, include the public theater in Renaissance Europe, Spanish tragedy, Performance Theory, Early-Medieval Spanish lyric and the *comedia*. He is the author of *Reading for the Stage: Calderón and His Contemporaries*, and his current projects include *The Problematics of Performance in Renaissance Theater*.

WILLIAM R. BLUE is Professor of Spanish at the Pennsylvania State University. In addition to numerous articles on Early Modern Spanish theater, he is the author of three books: *The Development of Imagery in Calderón's Comedias*, *Comedia: Art and History*, and *Spanish Comedy and Historical Contexts in the 1620s*.

GWYN E. CAMPBELL is Professor of Spanish at Washington and Lee University. She has published or presented on numerous 17th-century dramatists, including Calderón, Lope, Tirso, Azevedo, Vélez de Guevara, Zayas, and Mira de Amescua. The co-founder of *GEMELA*, her co-edited volumes include: *Zayas and Her Sisters: An Anthology of novelas by 17th-century Spanish Women Writers*, *Zayas and Her Sisters, II: Essays on novelas by 17th-century Spanish Women Writers*, and a critical edition of Leonor de Meneses's *El desdeñado más firme*. Her most recent articles appear in *Bulletin of the Comediantes*.

CATHERINE CONNOR-SWIETLICKI is Professor of Spanish at the University of Vermont. Her many articles have appeared in such journals as *Bulletin of the Comediantes*, *Cervantes*, *Comedia Performance*, and *Latin American Theater Review*. Her recent book is entitled *Spanish Christian Cabala: The Works of Luis de León, Santa Teresa de Jesús and San Juan de la Cruz*, while her monograph in progress is *Performance and Neuroscience: Enacting Embodied Cognition On-Stage and Off*.

MANUEL DELGADO is Professor of Spanish at Bucknell University. His approach to Spanish Golden Age literature is grounded in the fields of philosophy, religion, ethics, political issues, and the history of ideas. Publishers of his numerous articles include: *Bulletin of the Comediantes, Bulletin Hispanique, Hispanic Review*, Juan de la Cuesta, the Modern Language Association, *Ediciones* Cátedra; and he is co-editor of *The Calderonian Stage: Body and Soul*.

EZRA ENGLING is Professor of Spanish at Eastern Kentucky University. His scholarship includes a critical edition of Calderón's *La aurora en Copacabana* and articles and reviews published in *Bulletin of the Comediantes, Romance Quarterly, Afro-Hispanic Review*, and *Moroccan Cultural Studies Journal*.

SUSAN M. FISCHER is Professor *Emerita* of Spanish and Comparative Literature at Bucknell University. Author of more than 75 studies on Calderón, Lope, Tirso and Shakespeare, her most recent monograph is *Reading Performance: Spanish Golden Age Theater and Shakespeare on the Modern Stage*.

BALTASAR FRA-MOLINERO is Professor of Spanish at Bates College. In addition to his many articles, he is author of *La imagen de los negros en el teatro del Siglo de Oro*, editor of a double issue on *Don Quijote* and race in *Annals of Scholarship: Don Quixote's Racial Other*, and is currently finishing a co-edition and translation of the *Vida* of Sor Teresa Juliana de Santo Domingo.

EDWARD H. FRIEDMAN is Gertrude Conaway Vanderbilt Professor of Spanish, Professor of Comparative Literature, and Director of the Robert Penn Warren Center for the Humanities at Vanderbilt University. Editor of the *Bulletin of the Comediantes*, and past President of the Cervantes Society of America, he has published numerous articles on Early Modern Spanish literature and *Wit's End: An Adaptation of Lope de Vega's La dama boba* (Lang, 2000). His most recent book is *The Labyrinth of Love*.

KATRINA M. HEIL is Associate Professor of Spanish at East Tennessee State University. Her recent scholarship has focused on the tragedies of Miguel de Unamuno and Antonio Buero Vallejo, and tragedy as a literary genre in general. Recent articles have appeared in *Anales de la literatura española contemportánea*, *Estreno* and *Redes América*.

DAVID J. HILDNER is Professor of Hispanic literature at the University of Wisconsin-Madison. A specialist in the Renaissance and Baroque theater and poetry of Spain, in addition to numerous publications he is author of *Reason and the Passions in the Comedias of Calderón* and *Poetry and Truth in the Spanish Works of Fray Luis de León*.

ROBERT M. JOHNSTON is Professor *Emeritus* of Spanish at Northern Arizona State University. A past President of the Association of Hispanic Classical Theater, he has published articles on Medieval and Golden Age Spanish literature including *El libro de buen amor*, *El poema de mío Cid*, Cervantes's *Novelas ejemplares*, and Calderón's *dramas de honor*.

CATHERINE LARSON is Professor of Spanish at Indiana University. In addition to numerous article-length studies on Spanish and Spanish American theater, she is the author of two monographs: *Games and Play in the Theater of Spanish American Women* and *Language and the Comedia: Theory and Practice*. She has also co-edited *Latin American Women Dramatists: Theater, Texts and Theories* and *Brave New Words: Studies in Spanish Golden Age Literature*, and translated Zayas's *La traición en la amistad* for a bilingual edition of the *comedia*.

DONALD R. LARSON is Professor *Emeritus* of Spanish at the Ohio State University. In addition to numerous articles and book chapters on Spanish Golden Age literature and the plays of Lope de Vega in particular, he is author of *The Honor Plays of Lope de Vega*, co-editor of *The Comedia in English: Translation and Performance*, and co-compiler/annotator of *Lope de Vega Studies, 1937–62: A Critical Survey and Annotated Bibliography*. His current book-length project studies visual aspects of the Spanish *comedia* in the 17th century.

MARYRICA ORTIZ LOTTMAN is Associate Professor of Spanish at the University of North Carolina-Charlotte. She specializes in the representation of gardens and landscapes in Early Modern Hispanic literature. Her many articles and interviews focus on the Spanish *comedia* and have appeared in such journals as *Bulletin of the Comediantes*, *Cervantes*, *Comedia Performance*, and *Romance Quarterly*.

BARBARA MUJICA is Professor of Spanish and Associated Faculty in the Department of Performing Arts at Georgetown University and Director of *El Retablo* Theater Group. She has published and lectured widely on Spanish theater, and her latest books are *A New Anthology of Early Modern Spanish Theater: Play and Playtext*, and *Shakespeare and the Spanish Comedia: Translation, Interpretation, Performance*. She is founder and editor of *Comedia Performance*, and an award-winning novelist.

THOMAS A. O'CONNOR is Distinguished Professor of Spanish at Binghamton University. He has published extensively on Spanish Golden Age literature, specializing in the dramatic works of Calderón and Salazar y Torres. He is author of *Myth and Mythology in the Theater of Calderón*, *Love in the "corral": Conjugal Spirituality and Anti-theatrical Polemic in Early Modern Spain* (Lang, 2000), and, at present, he is editing the *Complete Works of Salazar* for Edition Reichenberger.

SUSAN PAUN DE GARCÍA is Professor of Spanish and Associate Provost at Denison University. Her articles have focused on María de Zayas, the 17th-century Spanish *comedia*, and the post-Baroque *comedia* of Cañizares and the early 18th century. The current President of the Association of Hispanic Classical Theater, she has co-edited *The Comedia in English: Translation and Performance* and is currently co-editing *Remaking the Comedia*.

KATHLEEN REGAN was Professor of Spanish at the University of Portland. Recipient of the US Professor of the Year Teaching Award (2000), she published articles on gender identity in the *comedia*. Her final research projects focused on the production of documentaries on the Sephardic legacy of Medieval Spain, the Sephardic musical tradition in the diaspora, and *Don Quijote*.

BARBARA SIMERKA is Associate Professor of Spanish at Queen's College-CUNY where she specializes in Early Modern Spanish literature. She has published widely in the areas of the *comedia*, women writers, postcolonial studies and cognitive theory. The editor of three anthologies of scholarly articles, her books include *Discourses of Empire* and *Knowing Subjects: Cognitive Cultural Studies and Early Modern Spanish Literature*.

HENRY W. SULLIVAN is Professor of Golden Age Spanish literature at Tulane University. In addition to his extensive array of published articles, his books include: *Juan del Encina, Tirso de Molina and the Drama of the Counter Reformation, Calderón in the German Lands, Grotesque Purgatory: A Study of Cervantes's* Don Quixote, *Part II*, and *Hispanic Essays in Honor of Frank P. Casa* (Lang, 1997, 1999). His current book-length monograph, *When Two Golden Worlds Collide: Bohemia & The Fall of the Spanish European Empire (1576–1700)*, is a micro-history of cultural relations between Spain and the Kingdom of Bohemia.

RONALD E. SURTZ is Professor of Medieval and Golden Age Spanish literature at Princeton University. In addition to numerous articles, he is author of *The Birth of a Theater: Dramatic Convention in the Spanish Theater from Juan del Encina to Lope de Vega, The Guitar of God: Gender, Power and Authority in the Visionary World of Mother Juana de la Cruz*, and *Writing Women in Late Medieval and Early Modern Spain: The Mothers of Saint Teresa de Avila*.

PETER E. THOMPSON is Associate Professor of Spanish at Queen's University (Canada). He has written extensively and published on the Spanish Golden Age actor, Juan Rana. His books include *The Triumphant Juan Rana: A Gay Actor in Spanish Golden Age Theater* and *The Outrageous Entremeses of Juan Rana: An Annotated and Bilingual Selection of Plays Written for the Spanish Golden Age Actor*. His current monograph treats the *entremesista*, Jerónimo Cáncer y Velasco.

SHARON D. VOROS is Professor *Emerita* of Spanish and French at the United States Naval Academy. Her many articles include studies of Ana Caro, Zayas, Lope, Calderón, and Cueva y Silva. Author of *Petrarch and Garcilaso: A Linguistic Approach to Style*, she has also published a translation of Jeanne Guyon's prison memoirs: *Bastille Witness: The Prision Autobiography of Madame Guyon (1648–1717)*. Current research includes a comparative study of Teresa de Jesús and Guyon.

CHRISTOPHER WEIMER is Professor of Spanish at Oklahoma State University. His essays on Hispanic theater, prose and film have appeared in such journals as *Anuario de estudios cervantinos, Bulletin of the Comediantes, Caliope, Hispanic Review, Hispanófila, Latin American Theater Review* and *Modern Drama*. He is co-editor of *Echoes and Inscriptions: Comparative Approaches to Early Modern Spanish Literatures*, and founder of *Laberinto: An Electronic Journal of Early Modern Hispanic Literatures and Cultures*.

BARBARA F. WEISSBERGER is Professor *Emerita* of Spanish at the University of Minnesota. She has published extensively on ideologies of gender and ethnicity in late Medieval and Early Modern Spain. Her award-winning books include *Isabel Rules: Constructing Queenship, Wielding Power*. A past editor of *Medieval Encounters: Jewish, Christian and Muslim in Confluence and Dialogue*, she was co-President of the Ibero-Medieval Association of North America.

KERRY WILKS is Associate Professor of Spanish and Associate Dean of the Graduate School at Wichita State University. Past publications cover a wide variety of topics, including the 20th-century Spanish novel, *comedia* performances studies, political readings of the *comedia* and the dramatic figure of Circe. She is currently working on an edition of a play by Funes y Villalpando, and a pedagogy/translation project on Juan del Encina's carnival eclogue.

AMY R. WILLIAMSEN is Professor of Spanish at the University of North Carolina Greensboro. Her specializations include Early Modern Spanish literature, Hispanic women writers, theater and performance, contemporary literary theory, and Cognitive Science. The co-founder of *GEMELA*, her most recent article appears in *Cervantes*. In addition to her book *Co(s)mic Chaos: Exploring* Los trabajos de Persiles y Sigismunda, her co-edited volumes include: *Critical Reflections: Essays on Spanish Golden Age Literature in Honor of James A. Parr, Engendering the Early Modern Stage: Women Playwrights in the Spanish Empire, Ingeniosa Invención: Studies in Honor of Professor Geoffrey Stagg*, and *María de Zayas: The Dyamics of Discourse*.

Setting the Stage: An Introduction

The current volume is organized in five major acts to reflect Dr. Matthew D. Stroud's myriad scholarly contributions to the study of Early Modern Spanish theater. Each essay engages directly with his work; each essay also marks an original contribution to our field.

Act One: Uxoricide Unleashed

In Stroud's seminal study of the wife-murder plays, *Fatal Union: A Pluralistic Approach to the Spanish Wife-Murder Comedias,* his analysis of this corpus considers the moral, ethical and legal backdrop of uxoricide, and the public and private concepts of guilt and shame, and the varying secular and religious tenets in play. Stroud convincingly argues that this "disparate and often contradictory group of plays" (141) defies a single epistemological truth with which to interpret them. At the heart of this ambiguity of interpretation lie the Baroque dichotomy of appearances versus reality, the socio-literary Spanish code of honor, and the wife-murder play as a dramatic representation subject to audience interpretation.

For David J. Hildner, the occasional deflection from bloody vengeance against allegedly unfaithful wives to differing forms of revenge, or even pardon, in select *comedias* by Lope and Tirso points to the need for a closer examination of the mental faculty of prudence in the offended noblemen in question. His study shows the differing degrees of this virtue that allow for an outcome other than uxoricide, while at the same time revealing the barriers to thought beyond which the minds of these *galanes* are unwilling to explore. Susan L. Fischer's article furthers the study of honor, and the concepts of guilt and shame in her consideration of two Calderonian wife-murder plays alongside the canonical *El caballero de Olmedo* [*The Knight from Olmedo*] and

Sor Juana's *Los empeños de una casa* [*House of Trials*]. Drawing on speech-act theory, the prevalent precepts on the education of women, and the ethics of secrecy, Fischer re-examines the motif of silence and silencing in domestic relationships, and the manner in which they effect thought processes, perception and communication in honor-driven plots, and the (im)perfect repercussions that result. Katrina M. Heil further explores Aristotelian poetics in her approximation to Calderón's *El médico de su honra* [*The Surgeon of His Honor*]. Through a close examination of the "morally shocking" vengeful husband, and the morally ambiguous King, Heil carefully crafts the case for the murdered wife as the true Aristotelian tragic hero of the play. The innocent Mencía, characterized by her moral clarity, reflects a new type of tragic hero that brings into question, for the spectator, the very values of the honor code and the monarchy themselves.

While the murdered wife typically represents the actual victim of the uxoricide play, Ezra Engling considers the two murderous husbands of Calderón's *El médico de su honra* and *El pintor de su deshonor* [*The Painter of His Dishonor*] as victims as well. Focusing on the Aristotelian precept of tragedy, Engling highlights the inherent tragedy of both Gutierre and Juan Roca, who must first kill their respective wives, only to then be compelled to accept the new life forced upon each by the play's monarch. Calderón, he concludes, reveled in the dramatic possibilities occasioned by the rigid *código de honor* [code of honor]. As William R. Blue aptly notes, the audience's reception of Calderón's *El médico* is ambiguous at best, and runs the gamut from fascination to repulsion. In light of what Stroud terms the "epistemological haze" that serves to create layers of blame, Blue investigates jealousy, and the crises of interpretations it spawns, as the dramatic mainspring of the fog of this play. Moreover, the chiastic phrases that result from the tense atmosphere of this emotion are reflected, in addition, in the play's structure in which parallel scenes both replicate and differentiate actions, further contributing to the hall of mirrors that the spectator has entered.

Turning to Lope's *El castigo sin venganza* [*Punishment Without Revenge*], Manuel Delgado focuses on the perversion of love, in its intimate sense and in the broader context of human relationships. In particular, he centers his study on incest in this play, including its sociological and psycho-pathological perspectives, the Early Modern concept of Natural Law, and the intellectual and cardinal virtues of prudence and justice. Delgado, then, considers the incestuous relationship not as the cause of instability in the play, but as a symptom of the moral disorder in the palace at Ferrara. For Gwyn E. Campbell, Mira's somewhat frenetic *La adúltera virtuosa* [*The Virtuous Adulteress*], a potential wife-murder play, offers a moralizing precept on chivalry and honor itself.

Through an examination of the multiple levels of chaos that permeate plot, setting, and characters, including the leitmotif of the biblical Susanna split between two noblewomen, Campbell notes the stark counterpoint between nefarious *desafíos* [rivalrous challenges] and the solemn *duelo* [formal duel]: multiple dishonors must be resolved. Nonetheless, a lack of true resolution in the primary plot further delineates the code of honor as distinct from the essence of what it means to be honorable.

Act Two: Reflections and Refractions: Cognitive Play(s) in the Mirror

Stroud's explorations of the meaningful intersections of psychoanalytic theory and *comedia*, as reflected in *The Play in the Mirror: Lacanian Perspectives on Spanish Baroque Theater*, opened up a fruitful branch of discovery that helped lay the groundwork for cognitive approaches to the *comedia*. His insightful interrogation of identity and desire continues in *Plot Twists and Critical Turns: Queer Approaches to Early Modern Spanish Theater*. The studies in this section each simultaneously claim and wrestle with aspects of this critical legacy.

Christopher Weimer's essay argues that Ovidian allusions in Tirso point spectators and readers toward the structural and thematic importance of specific myths as interpretative touchstones. He focuses on the *Metamorphoses* as the nexus of the classical references underpinning *Don Gil de las calzas verdes* [*Don Gil of the Green Breeches*], a play text that includes relatively few mythological references by *comedia* standards, thus highlighting those that are present: the suggestive cluster of Hermaphroditus, Narcissus, and Adonis, along with Achilles and Argos. All of these Ovidian narratives provide intertextual relations to *Don Gil*'s plot developments, foregrounding the confusions of gender and its customary norms, which Stroud has discerned in Juana's "enormous fluidity of identity and sexuality." Barbara F. Weissberger builds upon Stroud's use of Freudian and Lacanian psychoanalytic theory as a critical lens by drawing upon feminist revisions of Freud and Lacan in order to analyze the representation of Queen Isabel I of Castile in two plays by Lope de Vega. Both *El niño inocente de La Guardia* [*The Innocent Child of La Guardia*] (c. 1597) and *El mejor mozo de España* [*The Best Boy in Spain*] (1611) are striking for their interest in Isabel's unconscious. In the opening scene of each play, Isabel falls asleep and dreams. The few scholars who have dealt with these dreams see them as justifying the Queen's gender role transgressions, relieving her of responsibility for them, and thus ultimately reinforcing her passive femininity. In contrast, Weissberger convincingly argues that from the perspective of feminist psychoanalytic criticism, the dreams can be seen as true points of resistance to patriarchal constructs.

Cognitive theory has emerged as the newest psychological paradigm to be incorporated into literary analysis. Where Lacan (and Freud) use the mirror as a metaphor for the ways that the human mind understands its own individual subjectivity, studies of the mirror neuron network provide new insights concerning social interaction. In her essay, Barbara Simerka examines *privanza* drama (the relationship between Kings and their *privados* [favorite ministers]), in order to study the ways in which plays such as Mira de Amescua's *La adversa fortuna de don Alvaro de Luna* [*The Fall of Don Alvaro de Luna*] represent the complex social interactions among courtiers, with a focus on Theory of Mind. She employs these insights to trace the connections between psychological processes and Early Modern culture, following the model set by Stroud's Lacanian analyses in *The Play in the Mirror* and in *Plot Twists and Critical Turns*. Insights from cognitive science also inform Robert M. Johnston's consideration of the affective responses dramatists might elicit from *comedia* audiences. Recent discoveries in neuroscience show that emotions govern human cognitive processes to a much greater extent than most of us imagine. In fact, the aesthetic dynamic of vicarious identification, essential to both political campaigning and theatrical performance, closes the link between primal instincts, emotions, and spectator response. He employs Calderón's *El alcalde de Zalamea* [*The Mayor of Zalamea*] as a case study of this notion, proposing that the experience of the play as understood in these terms can be essentially the same for modern audiences as it was for audiences in Calderón's time.

In her contribution, Catherine Connor-Swietlicki focuses on two key factors that complicate body-mind relations portrayed in the plays of María de Zayas and Ana Caro de Mallén. She indicates how their dramatic works anticipate 20th- and 21st-century discoveries proving, first of all, that categories of sexual identity are always necessarily individualized, and secondly, that spectators see less with their eyes and more with their personal experiences in the "symbolic order." Building upon current biological research that demonstrates that narrow classifications of "male" and "female" body parts are drastic simplifications that societies develop for survival, she argues that the performativity of gender and sexuality *does matter* in life and in art, as discussed by Judith Butler and *comedia* scholars like Stroud. Her study, informed by performance and spectator studies as well as scientific findings regarding the bio-cultural development of sex and gender in bodies and minds, examines the critical consequences of the weighty new evidence for *comedia* scholarship.

Act Three: Gender Games: Plotting Women

Stroud's work, throughout the many years of his career, has consistently returned to the topics of women, gender and identity. He has studied various stock-types of women characters, from the *mujer esquiva* [disdainful woman], to the *mujer varonil* [manly woman] in Vélez de Guevara and his contemporary dramatists. Stroud's works includes woman as victim in the *comedia*, the gendered gaze, and Biblical women in such authors as Mira de Amescua and Tirso. Too, he has contributed numerous articles and papers on such canonical women dramatists as Caro, Zayas, and Sor Juana, opening pathways to future investigation along the way.

Edward H. Friedman first establishes the paradoxical status of women in comic drama, contrasting the power that this marginalized social group wields in theater, yet which eludes them in the "real" world. With particular attention to Cervantes's *El laberinto de amor*, Friedman furthers the argument that writing an adaptation, such as his own *The Labyrinth of Love* (2013), is both a critical reading and a Bloomsian confrontation between tradition and the literary/cultural past. Through his select focus on the application of the conventions of characterization, Friedman explores how Cervantes, his contemporaries and subsequent playwrights portray women and how the resulting depiction of society is revealing, concealing, and, ultimately, an exhibition of irony. Next, Baltasar Fra-Molinero analyzes Enciso's *Juan Latino* as a study in the formation of Early Modern consciousness. In particular, his close reading focuses on the learned female lead who must choose between two "monsters" as the objects of her desire: a Black slave, or a *morisco* [Muslim converted to Christianity], who represents both a religious and a political enemy to the status quo. Her choices both negative, Ana de Carlobal thus embodies Early Modern *melancholia* [melancholy] and the ultimate dilemma of freedom as choice between always imperfect objects. For Kathleen Regan, *Antona García* further exemplifies Tirso's heightened interest in the female character in particular, as it underscores his dynamic vision of female identity itself. Far from a parody of the *mujer varonil* convention, Regan shows the manner in which Tirso uses this loosely-based historical character to subvert the prevalent gender norms of patriarchal society. In addition, her analysis examines the humour employed by Tirso, with the resulting "masculine" woman character that resonates even with contemporary audiences.

In her article, Susan Paun de García further explores the character of Antona García in plays by Tirso, Lope, and, the 18th-century playwright Cañizares. With particular attention to the largely identical full song sung in these plays, García examines their respective historical contexts, united by differing external threats posed, and the manner in which the sung refrain progressively takes on greater meaning, while sending messages of xenophobia, patriotism, the worthiness of wife and Queen, and the effectiveness of women as defenders of hearth or homeland. In her analysis, Sharon D. Voros foregrounds the creative work of women dramatists as she explores the relationship between two accomplished *dramaturgas* [women dramatists] and a canonical male author. She employs two critical models, Helmut Bonheim's notion of the "scenic narreme" to analyze narrative aspects of dramatic structure, and Gerald Prince's notion of "disnarrated" plot lines that are expected to take place, but do not in the end. She considers Leonor de la Cueva y Silva's *La firmeza en la ausencia* [*Steadfastness in Absence*], Tirso's *El amor y el amistad* [*Love and Friendship*], and Madame de Villedieu's *Le favori* [*The Favourite*] (1665). Common to all three plays is the "master narreme" of the Court favorite who falls from grace and is subjected to a series of tests. While all ends well in these three works, trials, revelation scenes, and judgments provide the dénouement and keys to a "true" understanding of the stagecraft of these three dramatists.

Act Four: Performative Possibilities: From Actors to Audiences

In addition to his theoretically grounded scholarship, Stroud was also a pioneer in foregrounding the importance of performance in *comedia* studies. His active participation in international theater festivals informed both his research and his teaching. Never content to remain on the sidelines, he delved into one of the most challenging directing experiences possible—staging Calderón's *Celos aun del aire matan* [*Even Baseless Jealousy Can Kill*]. The articles in this section also bridge the gap between dramatist and actors, between page and stage.

Barbara Mujica's study opens up the world of the women actors, more public and more literate than their "real" counterparts, as professional women required to attend to their bodies in non-traditional ways. As Mujica details the physical demands that resulted from the two-level *corrales* [public theaters] and the stage machinery in vogue, and the reality of roles that demanded a woman portray a man, she highlights the situations which demanded great athleticism of this select group. These women actors, Mujica shows, not only challenged the status quo of prescribed social norms, but in their transformation into thinking, feeling subjects, they largely defied objectification. Amy R. Williamsen focuses on how staged acts of passing (involving intersections of gender, sexuality, social rank, religion and ethnicity) in the *comedia* challenge notions of social stability, with special attention to Lope's *Los melindres de Belisa* [*Belisa's Whims*] (1606–1608). Passing, in these plays, coincides with heightened meta-theatricality. Not only are the players playing roles within their roles (and, at times, a series of roles), dramatic asides on theatrical, literary, and social conventions abound. At every turn, the works foreground the performativity of identity—and its inherent instability. Her analysis reveals that these works anticipate the theoretical formulations of Butler, Stroud and others as they attempt to frame and reframe categories of meaning, thereby highlighting the very impossibility of "fixing" an individual's illusive/illusory identity through intangible terms. In his study, Peter E. Thompson explores the impact of Juan Rana, one the most famous actors of the Spanish Golden Age specializing in the *entremés*, on the genre. Many of the most well-known *entremesistas* [writers of theatrical interludes] of the Golden Age took full advantage of Juan Rana's queerness and otherness to subvert implicitly and explicitly the social norms of sexual and gender identity that are still questioned today. The fame and notoriety of the actor himself influenced the work of the *entremesistas*. Thompson then confronts the challenges inherent in translating selected Juan Rana *entremeses*, including "El parto de Juan Rana" ["The Birth of Juan Rana"], "Juan Rana mujer" ["Juan Rana, Woman"] and "El guardainfante I y II" ["Hoopskirt: Part I and II"].

Maryrica Ortiz Lottman considers how the directors of three contemporary productions of *El condenado por desconfiado* [*Damned by Despair*] (Teatro del Valle's 2003 Afro-Colombian version, Spain's Centro Nacional de Teatro Clásico 2010 staging, and the 2012 London's National Theater English adaptation) attempt to render this highly theological play more accessible for modern audiences by transforming the character of the Devil. In the original, the Devil appears only briefly; yet, he quickly claims center stage as his appearances involve dramatic special effects. Each contemporary director refashioned the devil as a comic character, often greatly expanding the role. While all three productions portray the Devil as androgynous, the director of the London production explores the rich performative possibilities created by casting a woman in the role. Catherine Larson further interrogates the complicated relationships between translation and adaptation, theory and practice, and the *comedia* in print and as staged performance. She demonstrates that it has become ever more imperative to bridge the gap separating scholars and theater practitioners as we strive to transform the printed word into embodied practice onstage. Her study offers four possible models for analysis in order to better "come to terms" with the adaptation of the Spanish classics for modern, English-speaking audiences. In the end, the final product—the staged adaptation—no matter where it lies along the continuum of transformed texts, becomes the site from which future adaptations and performances emerge.

Act Five: Contours and Contexts: Crossing (Temporal/Spatial/Political) Boundaries

Stroud's ground-breaking research has always pushed at the edges of traditional scholarship or delved into the margins of *comedia* scholarship. The studies included in this section involve the same dynamic interrogation across established boundaries that characterizes his pioneering work on the Dutch translations of *comedias*.

In his epistemological study, Henry W. Sullivan returns to prolific dramatist, Fray Gabriel Téllez, unique amongst his contemporaries for the pseudonym under which he chose to write. Sullivan carefully studies the varied and various reasons that contributed to the chosen first and surname, Tirso de Molina. Then, Isaac Benabu considers the performative potential of the honor code in Calderón's *El médico de su honra*. The concept of honor in Spanish literature as a whole, and in the 17th-century Spanish *comedia* in particular, differs from European treatments which are often related to moral questions and questions of integrity. Lope de Vega, father of the *comedia*, recommends honor as a powerful motif because it moves spectators deeply, but he does not explain why this should be so. On the stage, some 200 years after the Expulsion, what we see, especially in the tragedies, is that the honor theme was exploited as an effective theatrical metaphor to represent a society governed by an oppressive social code, not a moral one, concerned with *limpieza de sangre* [purity of bloodlines], one which both limits and ultimately defeats the individual.

Ronald E. Surtz's article examines the early dramatic piece, *Aucto del peccado de Adán* [*Play of Adam's Sin*] and the peculiar features that arise from its dramatization of the Book of Genesis. In particular, Surtz considers the allegorical companions assigned to Lucifer in Eden, Eve's initial resistance to the serpent's flattery, the non-traditional motive—pleasing his mate—that leads Adam to taste the forbidden fruit, and the suggestion of a future happy ending, grounded in God's mercy, as the pair are expelled from Paradise. Too, Surtz ponders the twin motifs of clothing and nudity, together with contrasting modes of music, and the ramifications of these on any staging of the work. In her essay, Kerry Wilks reflects back to the beginning of Stroud's career with the groundbreaking edition of Calderón's *Celos aun del aire matan*; in addition, it also pays tribute to Stroud's work on Calderón's *teatro palaciego* [*comedias* for the Court] with its strong musical component. Her archival research, conducted over the last ten years in the Biblioteca Nacional de España, has led to the clear identification of a *refundición* [adaptation] of Calderón's one-act *zarzuela, El golfo de las sirenas* [*The Sirens' Abyss*] (1685). She explores Funes's intertextuality with Calderón's work, including the detailed stage directions found within the manuscript. The play and its accompanying *teatro menor* [short theatrical works] provide a fascinating case study for the seldom explored theater of this time period in addition to the general topic of *refundiciones*.

Thomas A. O'Connor's detailed examination of two *refundiciones* of Salazar y Torres's *Los juegos olímpicos* [*The Olympic Games*] takes us to the late 18th century. As he documents the musical grafts needed to modernize the Baroque score of this *zarzuela*, written 100 years early, O'Connor considers the serious attention given to the popular Italian operatic forms added to *Juegos*; then, in counterpoint, he juxtaposes the loss of respect for the inherent dramatic logic of Salazar's work and the ensuing audience reception of these adaptations. Donald R. Larson, in turn, considers an even later adaptation, of sorts, of a *comedia* in 20th-century Nazi Germany. In particular, he concludes the influence of Calderón's *El sitio de Bredá* [*The Siege of Breda*], not to mention Velázquez's painting on the subject, on the *libretto, Friedenstag* [*Day of Peace*], penned by Richard Strauss in collaboration with Joseph Gregor, and premiered in Munich, 1938. While he articulates the differences between source play and operatic adaptation, Larson details the theme of brotherhood and (re)conciliation espoused by Strauss and Calderón alike.

To conclude these introductory remarks and allow the entertainment to begin, in the words so frequently recited at the start of a performance during the *Siglo de Oro Festival*, at the Chamizal National Memorial, in El Paso, Texas: ¡Favor de divertirse! [Please enjoy!].

Act One

Uxoricide Unleashed

Wife-Murder Deflected:
How Stage Husbands' Prudence and
Ingenuity Lead to Differing Outcomes

DAVID J. HILDNER
University of Wisconsin-Madison

In his wide-ranging study of Spanish Baroque *comedias* that include wife murder (*Fatal Union*), Matthew Stroud not only points out the variety of forms
and motives that these bloody acts assume on stage, but also mentions that, in
a certain number of plays, the ultimate vengeance is deflected to other forms
of revenge or to pardon (73–74). Among the works in this category, we find
several whose titles highlight the husbands' "prudence" or "intelligence."
Given that the husbands in the best-known wife-murder plays call on these
same mental faculties, it behooves critics to examine whether there are detect-
able differences between the prudence that leads to killing and that which
allows offended noblemen to avoid it. Three early 17th-century *comedias* from
Stroud's list of "non-lethal" plays will be used as case studies in the following
pages: Tirso de Molina's *El celoso prudente* [*Prudent in Jealousy*], Lope de
Vega's *El castigo del discreto* [*The Clever Man's Revenge*], and the same playwright's *El cuerdo en su casa* [*Wise in His Own Home*].

At the outset it should be stated that the husbands in these three plays do
not spare their wives because of a fundamental repugnance to wife-murder.
In other words, they necessarily start from an attitude similar in some ways to
that of Calderonian characters like Don Gutierre (*El médico de su honra* [*The
Surgeon of His Honor*]) or Don Lope de Almeida (*A secreto agravio, secreta
venganza* [*Secret Revenge for Secret Insult*]). William Fichter, in his edition of
what he considers to be an exceptional play, *El castigo*, summarizes Lope's
general tendency: "There is no comedia among the many by Lope de Vega
that I have examined in which the husband fails to decide on death as the only

punishment for the wife he believes unfaithful" (69). All three protagonists in our plays contemplate killing their wives at some point, but not all with the same intensity or determination. Don Sancho de Urrea (*El celoso prudente*) declares his wife to be worthy of execution, but delays his plan several times in order to warn her and to carry out his design without publicity. In *El castigo*, although Ricardo claims to have renounced the desire for execution ("... verás de qué modo / quito a Casandra el amor / sin matarla ..." (II, 130) [... you'll see how / I'll cure Casandra of her love / without killing her ...])[1], he exclaims, upon seeing his wife gaze lovingly on the young Felisardo:

RICARDO: ¡Ojos de traiciones llenos,
              ya sé que venís tras él;
              pero yo haré que amor tanto
              os cueste sangre por llanto! (II, 149)

[Oh, eyes full of treachery, / I know you follow him eagerly; / but I will make your great desire / pay for its tears with blood!]

In truth, this last declaration is not necessarily a call for execution, since the punishment that the wife receives is a severe beating, which, as we know from *Don Quijote* and other Early Modern comic narratives, can involve loss of blood. However, in calling spontaneously for "blood," Ricardo is following the pattern of countless other stage husbands.

The *letrado* [jurist] Leonardo (in *El cuerdo en su casa*) discovers a man in his wife's bedroom, and runs to take up weapons, but calls first on his neighbor of low estate, Mendo, for help in executing the plan:

Salto y vístome, aunque mal;
tomé mi espada y mi rodela,
y queriendo ejecutar
el castigo de la ofensa,
imaginé que sería
mejor, cerrando las puertas,
llamaros, porque no puedan
escaparse ni romperlas. (III, 583a)

[I jumped out of bed and hastily got dressed; / I took up my sword and buckler, / and, as I was about to carry out / the punishment of the offense, / I thought that it would be / better to lock the doors / and call on you, so that the pair could not / escape or break them down.]

The use of the plural *no puedan escaparse* indicates that Leonardo has the intention, or at least wants to appear to have the intention, of killing both suspected adulterers. However, Mendo cleverly avoids bloodshed by allowing the entrapped *galán* to escape and substituting a servant, who convinces everyone that he had entered the house to visit his "promised bride," the servant Leonor, and had found himself in the wrong bedroom.

Thus, Donald Larson's view that the early honor plays of Lope de Vega contain "a propensity ... to regard the actions of the offenders as partially excusable" (24) needs to be qualified. Over the whole genre of Baroque *comedia*, the almost automatic urge to execute the wife when she is presumed guilty seldom relaxes, except in some plays of peasant or pseudo-peasant honor. There we find, if not a stated moral repugnance, at least a "gut-level" repugnance to carry out the act, as well as a greater capacity to perceive the wife's possible or probable innocence, despite the appearance of dishonor.

The hero of Lope's *Peribáñez y el comendador de Ocaña* [*Peribáñez and the Comendador of Ocaña*], when his suspicions first arise during a visit to Toledo, pronounces a soliloquy in which he half laments that, being a commoner, he married an extraordinarily beautiful woman, yet, as he prepares to return home, he is willing to broach the subject in conversation with his Casilda and even feels embarrassed to bring it up: "Cuanto me ayuda me daña; / pero hablaré con mi esposa, / aunque es ocasión odiosa / pedirle celos también" (*Peribáñez* II, 76) [What helps me, harms me. / Yet I'll tell Casilda, / Even if my words / stir bitter jealous thoughts (trans. Lloyd 163)]. Such reluctance could originate either in his confidence in her innocence or in the fear that speaking openly about his suspicions would give them more substance, as several Calderonian husbands believe. As he reaches the outskirts of Ocaña, he hears one of the reapers in his fields sing about Casilda's heroic rejection of the advances of the local *comendador*. These words are enough to dispel his jealousy, at least partially. Nevertheless, his disquiet is not completely resolved, because any talk about Casilda among the inhabitants of Ocaña, whether favorable or unfavorable, is bound to be harmful: "porque honor que anda en canciones / tiene dudosa opinión" (II, 80) [Since honour that a laborer sings about / Must put my reputation all in doubt (trans. Lloyd 169)]. This ambiguity in attitude leads Steven Wagschal to state first that Peribáñez is "far from thinking of murdering his wife" (47), but later that, if the protagonist had not felt jealous and had not dallied in the fields, he "might have hurried straight home, perhaps to murder his innocent wife for the sake of honor" (47). In any case, this character repeatedly shows a greater openness to dispel his jealousy and never really forms an explicit plan to punish Casilda.

In the figure of García del Castañar in Rojas Zorrilla's *Del rey abajo ninguno* [*None Beneath the King*] we only have a pseudo-commoner, since the audience discovers early on that he is really a high-ranking nobleman who, to hide from his political enemies, has lived as a *labrador rico* [wealthy farmer] in a secluded hamlet. Thus, his attitude is a curious mixture of that of honorable, but non-obsessed, peasants like Peribáñez with that of the code-bound husbands of urban and courtly *comedias*. When he discovers a man (whom he takes to be the King) invading his bedroom balcony, but manages to force the intruder to retire without violence, he initially feels obliged to kill Blanca to restore his honor, since he cannot take vengeance against a member of the royal family. He recognizes that his motivation is *not* jealousy, but an external obligation of every nobleman. He soliloquizes: "Perdóname, Blanca mía, / que, aunque de culpa te absuelvo, / sólo por razón de Estado, / a la muerte te condeno" (II, 749) [Forgive me, dearest Blanca, / since, though I absolve you from guilt, / I must condemn you to death / only for 'reasons of state']. Yet when later that night he tries to raise his hand against Blanca, he is so conflicted that he plans to kill himself after stabbing her. In fact, before he can deliver the blow, he faints and plummets to the floor.

By contrast, in the case of most aristocratic husbands in the *comedia*, prudence or *discreción* does not lead them to re-think the morality of taking the wife's life. It is true that several Calderonian males, mostly in lighter plays, do state that they would prefer not be required to avenge, such as in the following passage of Calderón's *Las manos blancas no ofenden* [*White Hands Can Never Offend*]:

> FEDERICO: porque nunca está mejor
> aquél que se desagravia
> con la venganza que toma,
> que dejando de tomarla;
> porque no hay venganza como
> no haber menester venganza. (*Obras* III, 1116b)

> [for those who wish to restore their honor / by taking vengeance are / never more fortunate / than when they desist; / for there is no better revenge than / having no need to take it.]

Yet, statements like this, rather than promoting the view that vengeance in itself is optional, appear to affirm that the best course of action is to avoid placing oneself in the position of being obliged to seek vengeance.

Thus, the various shades of *prudencia* and *discreción* evident in *comedia* husbands, whether the latter end up committing uxoricide or sparing their wives, share a common factor: they all start from unexamined premises about honor and its cure, about female nature, and about the relationship between inner dishonor and others' knowledge or suspicions about an affront. As Stroud describes the husbands' epistemological procedures, in contrast to the Stoic ideal of knowledge, "[t]he consequences of this dependence on prior information are that one bases much of one's judgment on prejudice and pre-conception" (118). Furthermore, "[the] establishment of 'the truth' based only on necessarily partial evidence, when combined with the individual creativity involved in seeking the truth, implies that truth is a function of will" (120). This insight is reinforced by Wagschal's use of the term "instrumental rationality," derived from philosophers of emotion such as Peter Goldie and Ronald de Sousa, to characterize the thoughts and acts of a large number of jealous *comedia* characters (11–12).

On one hand, Calderón's Don Gutierre can assume that his mere pronunciation of the word *celos* [jealousy], even when no one else is present, constitutes a diminution of honor. He also sets up his own supposition about Doña Mencía as an absolute criterion, disregarding any arguments in her favor. On the other hand, characters like Don Sancho can believe their honor is restored once their suspicions are dispelled. Yet, in this last case, as long as his conviction of her guilt remains, he does not question the wisdom of executing her. The husbands' wise or foolish reasoning builds on these premises, but does not penetrate beyond a certain level of analysis. Even Sancho's impassioned outburst, "¡Ay leyes fieras del mundo, / de las de Dios embarazo!" (III, 1141b) [Oh, cruel laws of the world / which hinder those of God!], although it recognizes a realm of being higher than that of honor, implies nevertheless that, in the social world he inhabits, avenging one's honor is a law to be complied with.

Such a reluctance to question shows certain parallels, according to Wagschal, to the seldom-questioned need for a *príncipe* or "head" of state to lead nations. "[T]he representation of jealousy in mass theater … promoted the alleged necessity of the King, who, at one extreme of the political spectrum, sanctioned specific violent outbursts of jealousy" (190–91). Furthermore, according to the same critic, the similarities between the King as a "father" of his subjects, who at times needs to execute traitors or enemies, and the avenging *paterfamilias* of a specific household made both privileges appear more "natural" or divinely instituted.

What, then, deters certain husbands from murder? The answer contains at least two parts. In the first place, they are generally more responsive to extenuating circumstances and contrary evidence than the Calderonian husbands, for whom the determination of guilt and dishonor is an almost purely internal process. Don Gutierre confesses to his wife that an iota of jealousy, even illusory jealousy, would be enough to dishonor him: "Que yo no sé qué son, ¡viven los cielos!; / porque si lo supiera, / y celos … /… llegar pudiera / a tener … ¿qué son celos? / átomos, ilusiones, desvelos" (*Médico,* II, 170) [I have not got the least idea (of jealousy). But if / I *had* … the slight inkling— / Or felt the slightest twinge— (trans. Campbell 55; emphasis in original)]. Given such an attitude, the only field left for the operation of *prudencia* and *discreción* lies in the method of execution. In the plays under consideration, however, the husbands' intellect and imagination keep open the possibility of a *desagravio* (a removal of dishonor) by less drastic means; they are willing to be convinced that they were mistaken. Ricardo makes a distinction, derived from "law" and from the "will of Kings," between offenses that deserve death and those that do not; the letter he has intercepted from his wife to Felisardo falls into the second category: "que no permiten las leyes / su muerte por un papel, / que por dolor más crüel / dieron licencia los reyes" (II, 126) [since the laws do not permit her / to die for a letter; / Kings have only allowed it / for a graver offense]. Don Sancho, on his part, feels glad, at the end of Act III, to have regained his honor by discovering that his suspicions were false:

> Hablen los otros maridos
> en su afrenta y vituperio;
> que hasta agora nadie sabe
> sino el cielo y yo mis celos
> que, en mi honra averiguados,
> del alma alegre los echo. (III, 1155a)

> [Let other husbands speak aloud / their affront and humiliation; / for as yet no one, / except Heaven and I, knows of my jealousy, / which, dispelled to my greater honor, / I happily banish from my soul.]

Aside from wise judgment and restraint in determining guilt or innocence, the main field of operation for these three husbands' practical reasoning involves the manner of punishing or of refraining from punishment. Just as for many wife-murderers, the avoidance of public disclosure of both the *agravios* and their punishment is important: in fact, it can be the central consideration. Tirso's play carries in most editions the alternative title *Al buen callar llaman Sancho*, [*Keeping Silent is Known as "Sancho"*] which plays on the popular saying "Al buen callar llaman santo" (Correas 35) [Wisely keeping quiet is akin to holiness]. The need for secrecy arises in the husbands' minds either through their implicit knowledge of social conventions or from the specific experiences of others. Critics have recognized, for example, as a practical certainty that *El celoso prudente* provided Calderón with a good part of his material for *A secreto agravio, secreta venganza* (Valbuena Briones xxxvi–xcii). One of the most striking similarities is the inclusion in both plays of an incident, narrated by another character, in which a public vengeance or a public recognition of innocence does more to reveal a man's dishonor than to re-establish his honor in the eyes of society. In Tirso's play, the anecdote is about an anonymous tailor whom the judicial system orders to be whipped through the streets at night, but who, having demonstrated his innocence to the judge, is publicly exonerated during the daytime. Nevertheless, all of the spectators during this second event keep referring to him as "el azotado" (III, 1142a–b) [the whipping victim]. The story is far removed from the nobility and its conjugal honor, and it is clothed in an almost humorous tone, yet it brings home to Sancho that he must keep secret his plans and their execution. In the case of Calderón's Don Lope de Almeida, we witness the tragic incident of his friend, Don Juan de Silva, whose monologue shows that he has accomplished nothing by challenging his rival to a duel: "… que mil veces, / por vengarse uno atrevido, / por satisfacerse honrado / publicó su agravio mismo, / porque dijo la venganza / lo que la ofensa no dijo" (*A secreto agravio* III, 78) [For however much, however often, / a man of pride and daring / avenge the insult done him, / by so much and so often / does he publicize that insult. / For his vengeance must reveal / what the insult may conceal (trans. Honig 54)].

Ricardo hears the same lesson, not through the experience of another, but through the direct advice of his comic servant, Pinabel:

> y si fuesses tan discreto
> que sin sangre lo alcançasses
> no dudes de que enseñasses
> a castigar con secreto.
> El matar una muger,
> puesto que al honor deleyte,
> es hazer la sangre azeyte
> y la deshonra estender. (II, 129)

[and if you were clever enough / to attain your goal without shedding blood, / you would surely teach a lesson / in secret punishment. / Killing one's wife, / though it may satisfy honor, / turns her blood into oil / which spreads the dishonor.]

This speech, although meant seriously, casts the advice in the homely metaphor of oil, which, when not properly contained, oozes out and spreads, as well as making its whole surroundings "slippery." Leonardo, portrayed as rather unwise in the ways of the world, has to learn the lesson from the mouth of his rustic neighbor, Mendo, who in the dénouement turns out be the genuine *cuerdo en su casa* because he recognizes that the shedding of blood does not necessarily cancel out an affront to honor.

Another factor which distinguishes the protagonists of these dramas from those of the canonical wife-murder plays is that their circumstances, behavior, and social standing, before and during their trials of honor, often reduce their *gravitas* and turn them partly into figures of amusement or even scorn.

Sancho de Urrea, a descendent of Aragonese royalty, is the most illustrious of the three, so much so that the King of Bohemia proposes him to the aged courtier Fisberto as a suitable groom for his older daughter Diana. He is thus the closest in standing to Calderonian figures like Don Gutierre, who are closely allied, by blood or official post, to the royal Court. However, the playwright makes Sancho an inadvertent victim in an elaborate ruse to allow Fisberto's other daughter, Lisena, to marry the King's son. The audience knows much earlier than Sancho that his suspicions are baseless, since the cunning young Prince pretends to be in love with and to visit Diana rather than Lisena, while at the same time feigning to accept as his bride the foreign Princess whom his father has chosen for him. When Diana and Sancho are married, the former does not break off the ruse, since its object is to make her sister Queen of Bohemia, a goal for which she is willing to sacrifice much. It is not until the very last scene that Sancho finds out that the Prince's letters and visits to Diana were only a subterfuge. While it is true that Sancho does not participate in some of the more comic scenes in which Lisena disguises herself as the intended foreign bride, he is still woefully misled and thus falls partially into the class of characters that in the *Poetics* are designated as the "baser" sort. In fact, the original adjective that Aristotle uses (*phauloi*) can refer simply to a loss of *gravitas* (cf. Hildner 1991). Furthermore, although the two alternative titles of the work refer unambiguously to Sancho, he does not appear in the action until the beginning of the second act, so that the main intrigue is well under way long before he enters the life of Diana's and Lisena's family.

Ricardo, although designated as a *cavallero* in the list of characters, falls into a special kind of *vileza* [baseness] after surviving an ambush by three armed men in the street: he is so impressed with the conduct of the young man who defended him that he cannot seem to stop talking about his rescuer in the presence of his wife. He even draws attention to the physical attractiveness of the *galán*: "¡Qué talle! ¡Qué gallardía! / ¡Qué buena presencia de hombre!" (I, 90) [What a form! What dash! / Such a fine figure of a man!]. Pinabel comments to another servant on his surprise that his master should repeatedly praise another, younger man in Casandra's hearing. In fact, contrary to the servant's characterization of his master as generally *discreto*, Ricardo himself recognizes in the middle of Act II that he has been foolish and resolves to change course: "Mas ya que no fuy discreto / en alabar a mi amigo, / ser discreto en el castigo / a todo el cielo prometo" (II, 126) [But since I showed scant wit / in praising my friend, / I promise to high Heaven / to be cleverer in my punishment].

In Leonardo's case, Lope de Vega has intentionally made him a much less impressive figure, as Yvonne Yarbro-Bejarano has described in detail (222–31);

from the title onward, he is implicitly characterized, not as *el cuerdo en su casa*, but as *el loco en la ajena* [the foolish man in another's house]. This comes about through his insistence that Mendo frequent his house and that he try to attain, if not *hidalgo* [minor nobleman] status by blood, at least the appearance of a noble lifestyle. In parallel fashion, he tries to oblige his wife Elvira to receive Mendo's wife as a visitor on equal social terms. Mendo's (and his wife Antona's) constant rejoinder is that they are content to live as they always have lived, and that *villanos* [peasants] of their standing were not meant either to rise socially or to mix with *hidalgos*, beyond the neighborly help that Mendo ends up providing to the inept Leonardo. Lope's dénouement bears them out: Mendo really gains nothing from Leonardo's friendship but a lesson on what to avoid in his own conduct. Furthermore, the playwright has injected several speeches that satirize the life and occupation of *letrados* in general. In Act I, having lost his way and two of his dogs in the woods during a hunting expedition (a pastime that he is not accustomed to), Leonardo asks help of Mendo and his shepherds. Gilote, one of these rustics, comments: "Y echad de ver esta historia / en que ha perdido los perros, / que son, para tales yerros, / entendimiento y memoria" (I, 549a–b) [And you can see in this story / that he has lost two dogs, / which are, in his great foolishness, / his understanding and his memory]. Gilote's mini-allegory portrays Leonardo as a learned man who, being unsuited for the noble pursuit of hunting, has lost two "dogs," i. e., his reason and his memory. The same character, in a later scene, places Leonardo among the various types of *tontos* that he catalogues for his mistress Antona. According to him, *letrados* are intrinsically vulnerable to criticism:

> Mil estudiantes sutiles[,]
> de ingenio a la ciencia atento,
> tienen corto entendimiento
> para las cosas civiles. (II, 567a)

> [A thousand subtle scholars, / with their minds intent on knowledge, / have little understanding / for practical or lowly matters.]

In short, the deluded neighbor is guilty of trying to govern another's household while neglecting his own, thus becoming almost a *figurón* or stock character of ridicule, like Ruiz de Alarcón's liar Don García (*La verdad sospechosa* [*The Truth Can't Be Trusted*]) or Calderón's pretentious *hidalgo* Don Toribio de Cuadradillos (*Guárdate del agua mansa* [*Beware of Still Waters*]).

Finally, the audience's view of Leonardo at the end must be affected by the fact that the solution to his dishonor, engineered by Mendo, is illusory and farcical. There really was an unauthorized young man in Elvira's bedroom and the latter participated in, or at least did not deter, his plans for an assignation. Furthermore, the neighbors are aware that there have been illicit goings-on in Leonardo's house. In Act III, Mendo mentions to Gilote that two young unmarried noblemen have been frequenting it and, although he nominally admits that "... todo / puede ser santo" (III, 580a) [... it / may all be above board], he also states that he would never permit such familiarity in his own house.

In summary, in comparison to the wife-murderers analyzed by Stroud and especially to the "canonical" protagonists of Calderón's honor dramas, the three husbands described here are deflected from killing their wives by the following factors:

1) Their *prudencia* and *discreción*, which in other protagonists do not allow for a possible verdict of "not guilty" or for a non-lethal remedy to dishonor, operate from the premise that dishonor is more easily cured by a willingness to allow for error, by not taking rash action, or by limiting oneself to a punishment that does not bring further dishonor.

2) Apart from any epistemological considerations, Lope and Tirso place the husbands on the edges of, or securely within, a lighter sub-genre of the *comedia* in which such murders would be out of place. This is accomplished by lowering or canceling the influence of their court status or illustrious birth, and by displacing their centrality to the action. Thus for all three, in varying degrees, the decision not to take revenge is made more acceptable to the audience by the fact that either they have been the pitiable victims of repeated misdirection (Sancho in *El celoso prudente*), or they have partially brought on their wife's suspicious behavior (Ricardo in *El castigo del discreto*), or they have a set of other ridiculous defects (Leonardo in *El cuerdo en su casa*).

Note

1. All translations from the Spanish are my own, unless otherwise indicated.

Works Cited

Calderón de la Barca, Pedro. *A secreto agravio, secreta venganza*. Ed. Ángel Valbuena Briones. Madrid: Espasa-Calpe, 1967. Print. Clásicos Castellanos 141.

———. *Las manos blancas no ofenden*. *Obras completas*. Ed. Ángel Valbuena Briones. Vol. 2. Madrid: Aguilar, 1960. 1077–126. Print.

————. *El médico de su honra.* Ed. D. W. Cruickshank. Madrid: Castalia, 1989. Print. Clásicos Castalia 112.

————. *Secret Vengeance for Secret Insult. Six Plays of Calderón de la Barca.* Trans. Edwin Honig. New York: Institute for Advanced Studies in the Theatre Arts, 1993. 1–68. Print.

————. *The Surgeon of His Honour.* Trans. Roy Campbell. Madison: Wisconsin UP, 1960. Print.

Correas, Gonzalo. *Vocabulario de refranes y frases proverbiales.* Madrid: Jaime Ratés, 1906. Print.

Fichter, William. Introduction. *El castigo del discreto.* By Lope de Vega. New York: Instituto de las Españas en los Estados Unidos, 1925. 9–74. Print.

Hildner, David J. "Calderonian Comedy and Aristotelian *Phaulotes.*" *Texto y espectáculo: nuevas dimensiones críticas de la Comedia.* Ed. Arturo Pérez-Pisonero and Ana Semidey. El Paso, TX: UTEP Department of Languages and Linguistics, 1991. 71–78. Print.

Larson, Donald. *The Honor Plays of Lope de Vega.* Cambridge, MA: Harvard UP, 1977. Print.

Rojas Zorrilla, Francisco de. *Del rey abajo ninguno. Diez comedias del Siglo de Oro.* Ed. José Martel and Hymen Alpern. Rev. Leonard Mades. 2nd ed. Prospect Heights, IL: Waveland, 1985. 701–73. Print.

Stroud, Matthew D. *Fatal Union: A Pluralistic Approach to the Spanish Wife-Murder Comedias.* Lewisburg, PA: Bucknell UP, 1990. Print.

Tirso de Molina (Gabriel Téllez). *El celoso prudente. Obras dramáticas completas.* Ed. Blanca de los Ríos. Vol. 1. Madrid: Aguilar, 1946. 1093–155. Print.

Valbuena Briones, Ángel. Prólogo. *A secreto agravio, secreta venganza.* Madrid: Espasa-Calpe, 1967. xi–civ. Print.

Vega, Lope de. *El castigo del discreto.* Ed. William Fichter. New York: Instituto de las Españas en los Estados Unidos, 1925. Print.

————. *El cuerdo en su casa. Obras de Lope de Vega publicadas por la Real Academia Española (Nueva edición).* Vol. 11. Madrid: Galo Sáez, 1929. 547–86. Print.

————. *Peribáñez and the Comendador of Ocaña.* Trans. James Lloyd. *Hispanic Classics: Golden Age Drama.* Warminster, UK: Aris & Phillips, 1990. Print.

————. *Peribáñez y el comendador de Ocaña. Cuatro comedias.* Ed. John M. Hill and Mabel Margaret Harlan. New York: W. W. Norton, 1941. 1–177. Print.

Wagschal, Steven. *The Literature of Jealousy in the Age of Cervantes.* Columbia: Missouri UP, 2006. Print.

Yarbro-Bejarano, Yvonne. *Feminism and the Honor Plays of Lope de Vega.* West Lafayette, IN: Purdue UP, 1994. Print. Purdue Studies in Romance Literatures 4.

"Nada me digas": Silencing and Silence in Comedia Domestic Relationships

Susan L. Fischer
Bucknell University

"Nada me digas ... Ya sé que querrás decirme" (III.2825, 2827) [Not another word ... I know exactly what you're thinking (Johnston and Boswell 113)] states a confidently unaware Don Luis, silencing his son Don Álvaro and presumptuously projecting his own thoughts onto him when the latter attempts to explain "todo el suceso" (III.2823), the whole matter, in Calderón's *El pintor de su deshonra* [*The Painter of His Dishonour*].[1] This "infelicitous" performative that "misfires," to use J. L. Austin's terminology in *How to Do Things with Words*, is hardly unexpected if we have been reading the signifieds in the protuberating stories of the *gracioso* or "fool," Juanete, which were either hushed or fell upon deaf ears throughout the action (see Fischer, "Function"). We all know the inevitable outcome of that lapse in communication dictated by received social constraints of reputation and a practice of silencing those who are presumed not to be in the know: a wife murder lauded by the authorities-that-be, because the husband's imagined (or "painted") (dis)honor is arguably restored in a final and inevitable spectacle of deafness and silence.

Let us look at this scene-in-performance, since we have Laurence Boswell's English language production of *The Painter of Dishonour* with the Royal Shakespeare Company (1995–1996) as a point of reference (see Fischer, *Reading* 179–202). Here is Calderón's dramatic text, along with the actors' performance text:

DON ÁLVARO: (*Ap.* ¡Ay de mí! todo lo sabe,
                    pues dice que no es posible

de su enemigo vengarle.
No sin mucha ocasión, ¡cielos!,
conmigo llegó a enojarse.
Desdichas, no me matéis.
Pues ya, ¡ay Dios! que él llega a hablarme
hoy tan claro, bien será
que yo de mano le gane,
y cuente todo el suceso
tratando de disculparme.)
Señor, si ...

DON LUIS: ... *Nada me digas,*
que es en vano consolarme.
Ya sé que querrás decirme
que es necia fineza darme
por entendido en desdicha
en que no puedo ampararle,
pues dél ni de su enemigo
ni de su esposa se sabe
desde el día que robada
faltó ... (III.2814–35; emphasis added)

[A: (*Aside*: He knows exactly what I've done, / but is helpless to do anything / because I'm his son. He can't kill me. / But that's why he's been so angry... / It would be best now to confess, / to make a clean breast of everything.) / Father, please ... / L: ... *Not another word.* / There's nothing you can say or do. / *I know exactly what you're thinking:* / why waste my time? I know you're right. / It's madness to think I can help / when I've no idea where he is / or who might have kidnapped his wife. (Johnston and Boswell 112–13; emphasis added)]

In this encounter between father and son, the dramatic irony seems all the more powerful because "the discrepant awareness exists within the play and not just in the theatre" (Muecke 81). The exchange reveals several misfiring performatives: if Don Álvaro assumes fallaciously (in an aside) that his father knows that *he, Álvaro,* has abducted the wife of his friend Don Juan, Álvaro has it all wrong, as revealed when Don Luis assumes that he knows full well what his son wants to say. In performance, Álvaro's (Douglas Henshall) query— "You don't know?" and his well-timed aside—"My heart was frozen, / and I was shaking like a leaf" (Johnston and Boswell 113) [(*Ap.* Mejoróse el lance. / Alentemos, corazón; / que ya es el recelo en balde) (III.2835–37)]— made the audience patently aware of Don Luis's (Clifford Rose) ignorance that his son was responsible for his "sadness" and "distraction" over his friend's misfortune. The actor's antithetic style was in some sense "halfway between thought and feeling," as John Barton remarks in *Playing Shakespeare* (120), at once humorous and deadly serious. The brief exchange between father and son on stage underscored the failure of characters in *The Painter* to communicate despite all of their eloquence; as Barry Ife aptly put it in his critique of the production, "The constant thought, 'if only you'd said …' is answered, 'if only you'd listened'" (16).

Ironically, the only one who listened throughout the production, and in silence, was an interpolated Masque (Peter Holdway) covered in blood red and funereal black and dubbed "Death" in the Programme, though he did not belong to the Calderonian cast of characters (Fischer, *Reading* 186). His voyeuristic presence was felt, for example, as Don Luis reasoned soon thereafter, in response to Serafina's father's inquiry with respect to his daughter's whereabouts, that it was better to hold back:

> (*Ap.* ¡Duda grave!
> Pues decirlo y no decirlo
> es a su honor importante.
> Mas menor inconveniente
> es que lo dude y lo calle;
> que en materias del honor
> hablar sin pensado examen
> es muy difícil, aunque
> a muchos parece fácil.) (III.2885–93)

> [*Aside*: Grave doubt: to speak or not to speak, / for on it depends his honour, / and without a chance to think it through, / I am unable to decide; / it's better, then, to say nothing, / no matter how easy compassion / impels me to dispel his doubts. (Johnston and Boswell 115)]

That Don Luis has again chosen silence over speech will have catastrophic results.

***

Socio-cultural issues of shame and guilt and epistemological concerns of appearance and reality are at the heart of these relatively unexplored domestic moments, in which infelicitous performatives misfire and patterns of "if only you'd said / if only you'd listened" are played out.[2] *Comedias*, however, do not fall neatly into shame-based or guilt based categories; certainly, Juan Roca may be seen (by himself and by his peers) to be both shamed and guilty of murder. Similarly, in Calderón's *El médico de su honra* [*The Surgeon of Honour*], Doña Mencía is a woman of self-referential shame and honor in her domestic existence in home and garden: "… Tuve amor / y tengo honor …" (I.573) [I cannot love, / I must obey (Edwards 21)], she tells her servant, having already uttered the proverbial "Yo soy quien soy" (I.133) [Knowing who I am (Edwards 7)].[3] This implies that what one is obliged to do one does not want to do: "a discontinuity between what one is to the external world (reputation, obligations) and what one is internally (compassionate, subject to emotion)" (Stroud 106–07). Mencía's actions also connect her to the guilt-based system: she has often been judged imprudent for having urged her former admirer, Prince Enrique, to hear her reasons for marrying, and for having written a letter asking him to remain, so as to avoid the appearance of adultery and hence an "… afrenta / pública …" (III.2396–97), a public offense. "If Mencía was not guilty, she had nothing to fear from honesty," notes Matthew D. Stroud, but "to promote open communication as part of prudence completely ignores the shame-based system, in which concealment and deception are prudent" (110).

Misogyny is also at the root of Don Luis's dilemma whether to listen or not to listen, or to speak or not to speak, and of Doña Mencía's conflict between love and honor wherein she is not entitled to feel her own emotions ("ni para sentir soy mía" [I.139]) [not even my feelings are my own]. The following representation of it, though proverbial, is useful for its succinctness:

> Misogyny leaves no doubt about the moral lessons it depicts. Women are every-where inferior, untrustworthy, sinful, and dangerous; even their good points, such as beauty, are perverted into causes of disorder and chaos. According to the literature of misogyny, wives are duly punished for two reasons: they are evil, and they are weak. At one and the same time, wives are powerless (eas-ily tempted, weak-willed, passive) and powerful (bad, dangerous, threatening). Although some wives are willfully adulterous, others succumb because they are easily tempted and therefore incapable of maintaining the primacy of reason in their daily conduct. Taken together, these contradictory characteristics are played off each other so that wives cannot win: they are damned for their activity and for their passivity, for their strength and their weakness, for their desirability to their husbands and their seductive power over other men. (Stroud 38–39)

The subject of the woman as repository of a man's honor, with its misogynis-tic repercussions of silencing and silence, requires a *sortie*, however potentially redundant, into Pauline dicta and their impact on the education of a Christian woman in the Early Modern (Hispanic) world. Here is the apostle Paul's familiar proscription of "*Mulieres in ecclesia taceant*," taken from The First Letter to the Corinthians: "Let your wives be silent in church, for it is not permitted them to speak, but to be subject, as the law commands. If they wish to learn anything, let them ask their husbands at home" (I Cor. 14:34–35). Similarly, in The First Letter to Timothy, Paul is reputed to have written: "Let a woman learn in silence with all subjection. I do not permit a woman to teach or to have authority over her husband, but she is to remain silent" (I Tim. 2:11–12). These Scriptural sources formed the essential ground for Juan Luis Vives's (1492/3–1540) conduct manual, *De institutione feminae*

Christinanae [*The Education of the Christian Woman*] (1523/1538); in fact, he cites the above Biblical passages in the chapter "on the instruction of young girls" (I.29, Fantazzi 72; see Howe, "Let" 124–25).[4] The Pauline dicta at the forefront of Vives's manual, however, were not collectively accepted, as revealed, for example, in the selective reinterpretations by Santa Teresa (1515–1582) and Sor Juana Inés de la Cruz (1561–1595), in whose writings the proscriptions first appeared to be accepted but then were recast in more favorable terms (Howe, *Education* 65–68, 178–80). If Vives's discourse on the education of Christian women became the model for other treatises on this and related subjects, and if it is "rooted in a Spanish reality" (Bergmann 127), there were also disparities between the "ideal" and the "real" according to social class (Kamen 158; Casey 204–05).[5]

In traditional Early Modern culture, as in the cultures of antiquity, chastity was considered woman's primordial virtue, in contrast to courage, generosity, leadership, or rationality, which were seen as virtues attributed to men. Chastity assured prospective husbands of the legitimacy of their line, and it also kept women physically at home, silenced them, segregated them, and guaranteed their ignorance. If Vives was virtually obsessed with feminine chastity and recommended "draconian strictures" to limit women's movements in public and private (Howe, *Education* 100),[6] he also explains, for example in *De officio mariti* (*De los deberes del marido*) [*On the Duties of the Husband*] (1528), that "the woman may become better and be able to control her passions with education and manners, though not eradicate them totally from herself, in the same way that she cannot cease to be a woman or, in fact, an individual human being" (I.1276b, translation mine). Nevertheless, the kind of education a woman received would perforce differ from that of a man:

> [M]any things are required of a man: wisdom, eloquence, knowledge of political affairs, talent, memory, some trade to live by, justice, liberality, magnanimity ... If some of these are lacking, he seems to have less blame as long as some are present. But in a woman, no one requires eloquence or talent or wisdom or professional skills or administration of the republic or justice or generosity; no one asks anything of her but chastity. If that one thing is missing, it is as if all were lacking to a man. (I.44; Fantazzi 85)

Vives invokes the Pauline dicta explicitly with respect to a woman's learning and the study of letters: she must not (rashly) follow her own judgment, lest she "mistake false for true, harmful for salutary, foolish and senseless for serious and commendable"; she is to remember that "it was not without reason that Saint Paul forbade women the faculty of teaching or speaking in church, that they should be subject to men and *silently* learn what it behooves them to learn" (I.35; Fantazzi 78; emphasis added). Women must have a sense of shame or *pudor*, for no one who lacks a sense of shame can be chaste. Vives states:

> The inseparable companions of chastity are a sense of propriety and modest behavior ... Chastity is a kind of veil placed over our face, for when nature and reason covered the corrupt body and the sinful flesh because of the shame caused by the first sin but left the face open and free of coverings that we wear, they did not deny its cloak, namely shame ... Not only is shame considered to ennoble our face, but it is essential to it, so that the words countenance, face, and brow, have become synonymous with shame and modesty (I.83; Fantazzi 116–17).

Seen in the light of Vives's proscriptions, Otavio's pronouncement with respect to the "appropriate conduct" for his daughters in *La dama boba* [*A Woman of Little Sense*] seems all the more critical of "vulnerable women caught between traditional paternalism and striving male egos" (Johnston 6):[7]

> Está la discreción de una casada
> amar y servir a su marido;
> en vivir recogida y recatada,
> honesta en el hablar y en el vestido;
> en ser de la familia respetada,
> en retirar la vista y el oído,
> y en enseñar los hijos, cuidadosa
> preciada más de limpia que de hermosa. (I.225–32)
>
> [Intelligence, of course, serves a certain purpose, / But a wife's intelligence lies in love and service, / and in that loving and serving, she is complete. / Her realm is domestic, her modesty plain to see, / her concern for children, her world her family; / her thought is private; her grooming's her real beauty. / Learned conceits to a good woman are baubles. (Johnston 17–18)]

"Need I recount the universal hatred and wrath that caused daughters to be slaughtered by their parents, sisters by their brothers, wards by their guardians, kinsmen by kinsmen?" Thus spake Vives to young women, married women, and widows alike about "victims of a detestable and savage love" (I.42; Fantazzi 84). Vives's detailed account of the psychological and physiological effects of a "crime" of love on a woman and a "crime" of sullied reputation, whether real or imagined, vividly depicts the ensuing anguish:

> She will fear and be terrified of herself and will find no peace either by day or by night, constantly goaded by her conscience, inflamed as if by burning torches. She will not suffer anyone to gaze at her intently without suspecting that he knows something of her misdeed and that it now occurs to his mind. No one will speak in hushed tones without her thinking that he is speaking of her misconduct. She will not hear talk of wicked women without suspecting that it may be referring to her. She will not hear the name of her seducer even in some other regard without fearing that she is being referred to indirectly. No one will give

voice to secret complaints but that she will be afraid that her crime has been discovered and her punishment is nigh. She must be the slave of those whom she suspects as suspecting. She must have to behave humbly and abjectly for fear that if she says anything rather freely or acts a little arrogantly, her disgrace will be immediately thrown in her face. She will live always in a state of confusion, lifeless, or, rather, she will not live at all, but will be deprived of physical death while undergoing moral death many times over. (I.43; Fantazzi 85)

Would not this harrowing passage constitute background for the actress who prepared to play the roles of Doña Mencía in *El médico* and/or of Serafina in *El pintor*? One thinks of the second garden scene when Mencía awakens suddenly, seems to recognize Don Gutierre's voice "en el mudo silencio / de la noche" (II.1861–62) [still night wrapped in silence (Edwards 62)], but then utters the fatal words "tu Alteza" (II.1931) [His Highness] and replays the Prince's earlier invasion of her space. In this moment she is "constantly goaded by her conscience," as Vives would surely have it, but more dramatically, perhaps, by Gutierre's desperate, if ignoble, impersonation of His Highness's voice (II.1936–63). And the parallel reaction of Serafina when she awakens startled from a dream, imagines her death at the hands of her husband, and falls into Don Álvaro's open arms: "¡No me mates No me mates! / ... Nunca fueron / tus brazos más agradables" (III.966–72) [spare me, I beg ... never / have your arms been of such comfort (Johnston and Boswell 121)]. "The rest is silence," in the voice of Horatio (*Hamlet*, V.2.310).

* * *

To read an honor drama such as *El médico de su honra,* and conduct literature as exemplified by *De institutione feminae Christinanae*, intertextually—both with and against each other—is hardly meant to turn Calderón's play into a slavish dramatization of Vives's 16th-century proscriptions with respect to female chastity, male jealousy, and silence in the name of prudence as required by shame-based domestic relationships. Rather, its emergent purpose is to permit a kind of historicizing of the *querelle des femmes* [women's quarrel] sparked by Christine de Pisan (1364–1430) in her major defense, *The City of Women* (1404)—notwithstanding the reactive nature of the *querelle* discourse, and the intellectual "battle of the pens" imposed by class privilege (Kelly 27–28). Here, however, the emphasis is on silencing and silence as it pervades the honor play and is reified in the emblematical verse, "tienen los celos pasos de ladrones" (II.1896) [jealousy / Must have the silent step of thieves (Edwards 63)]. Calderón relates the idea of "unworthy underhanded behavior both to the immediate need for *silent* movement and to the insidious progress of jealousy itself," as Daniel Rogers observed almost half a century ago (283; emphasis added). What follows, then, is a revisiting of certain moments in *El médico* against the horizon of selected references to *De institutione* in order to buttress the play's *un*orthodox, if not contesting, representation of silence and silencing as it interfaces with love, jealousy, and honor (reputation radically dependent on female chastity) within a particular literary-historical tradition.[8]

As already noted, Doña Mencía *qua* married woman affirms her identity by saying, "Yo soy quien soy" (1.133) [knowing who I am (Edwards 7)]: she knows her personal, social, and religious obligations of obedience which she intends to uphold, as Leo Spitzer put it iconically some sixty-five years ago. In discussing "What thoughts should occupy the mind of a woman when she marries," Vives cites Scripture to underscore that "Because of her, man will leave father and mother and will cleave to his wife and they shall be two in one flesh (Gen II: 23–24)" (2.1; Fantazzi 175). These thoughts inform the conventional view of stage honor that impels Mencía to suppress her feelings ("'Aquí fue amor'" [I.131]) [Here was love! (Edwards 7)], instead of "… dar voces, / y romper con el silencio / cárceles de nieve, donde / está aprisionado el fuego" (I.125–28) [… shattering the icy silence of / the prison where [her] passion lies / In chains (Edwards 7)]. As Vives states categorically: "A husband is not to be loved as we love a friend or a twin brother, where only love is required. A great amount of respect and veneration, obedience, and compliance must be included. Not only the traditions and institutions of our ancestors, but all laws, human and divine, and nature itself, proclaim that a woman must be subject to a man and obey him" (II.3, 24; Fantazzi 193).

Mencía *qua* woman, however, breaks the silence that is her due Christian education when she speaks her mind to defend her reputation in a "private" exchange with Prince Enrique: if before marriage she had behaved as she should in rejecting her lover's favors, she will do no less as a wife: "pues soy para dama más, / lo que para esposa menos" (I.305–06) [Am I worth more as a mistress / but less as a wife]. In her "public" conversation with Gutierre and Enrique, fraught with *double entendre*, she demonstrates "spirit and quick wit" (Fox 6). She urges a formula of communication and conversation in seeking an explanation from the "friend" who has apparently won the heart of the Prince's beloved, as opposed to one of silencing and silence, which will surely result if he succumbs to the emotions of jealousy and anger: "… Dejo / aparte celos, y digo / que aguardéis a vuestro amigo, / hasta ver si se disculpa" (I.409–12) [… Leave / jealousy aside and wait for your friend / to see if he apologizes]. And what goes for the male friend goes for the woman in question: Enrique should solicit her version of the story, because it may be a case of "fuerza, y no mudanza" (I.422): "the imposition of another will" rather than "a change of heart" (Edwards 16).

Mencía has often been judged imprudent and rash for proffering such—rational—advice (hearkening back to A. A. Parker's oft-reassessed view of the moral responsibility of individual characters in determining their fate); nevertheless, her resolution to ask for what is arguably a simple explanation underscores the vulnerability of those who seek good human contact in the face of irrational social codes. Mencía's daring, if couched, invitation flies in the face of Vives's notion of "how [an unmarried young woman] will behave in public": it seems that anything she says, or any way she comports herself, will be an occasion for "corruption and misconduct" and risk a slur on her reputation from the man's point of view (I.93; Fantazzi 125).[9] The obvious solution? To "live in seclusion and not be known to many," because it is "a sign of imperfect chastity and of uncertain reputation to be known by a great number of people" (I.94; Fantazzi 126). Vives insists that "all of the books should be read by every class of woman"—unmarried (Book 1), wives (Book 2), and widows (Book 3)—insofar as "the moral formation of women can be imparted with very few precepts ... A woman's only care is chastity" (Pref.3; Fantazzi 46, 47).

If Mencía must be chaste, she demands—however uncharacteristically for a Christian woman educated à la Vives—the same behavior of her husband, boldly insinuating that he wishes to travel to Seville not so much to pay homage to the King as to see his former betrothed, Doña Leonor: "¡O qué tales sois los hombres! / ¡Hoy olvido, ayer amor, / ayer gusto, y hoy rigor!" (I.517–19) [Because you men are as you are! / Today's love forgotten tomorrow. / Today's pleasure, tomorrow's sorrow! (Edwards 20)]. Has Mencía dared to broach the subject of "female jealousy"? Has she forgotten that, as Vives reminds his (fe)male readers, "human laws do not require the same chastity of the man as they do of the woman"; that "in all aspects of life, the man is freer than the woman"; that "[m]en have to look after many things [whereas] women are responsible only for their chastity" (II.79; Fantazzi 232)? Mencía voices this proscription when she breaks her silence and speaks self-consciously to her servant about her conflict: "La mano a Gutierre di, / volvió Enrique, y en rigor, / tuve amor, y tengo honor" (I.570–73) [I gave my hand to Gutierre / Enrique returned, strictly speaking / I had love, now I have honor]; if her father gave her in marriage to Gutierre, she can no longer love Enrique because she must "*obey*," as the word *honor* (Edwards 21; emphasis added) is pointedly rendered in translation.

When she awakens to find Enrique in her garden, Mencía voices her precarious position, querying who would dare risk destroying the reputation of a lady and offending the honor of a loyal subject. If she was "guilty" of suggesting that the Prince seek an explanation of her "agravios," of her offense against his love (II.1095), and if she is to absolve herself of blame in his eyes, her first thoughts are of her good name and reputation in accordance with her honor (II.1099). If Vives's cautions heretofore formed the ground of her reflections, they are now patently figural. Hardly has she invoked the metaphor of the heron who knows its fate *vis à vis* the predatory hawk, with its implications for the wife who knows who will be responsible for her death (II.1129–35), when Gutierre appears as if on cue to suspect her chastity and suffer pangs of jealousy. Vives puts it all too poignantly:

> [N]either should evil be done nor that which has the *appearance* of evil. 'This is a difficult task,' you say, '*for who can control suspicions?*' ... If you are chaste and you have a jealous husband, hope that he will put away that disturbance of the mind in a short time. But if you are unchaste, know for certain that not only will it not be destroyed, but it will grow stronger with each passing day. (III.76; Fantazzi 231; emphasis added)

Mencía's plight captures that of woman caught in a system in which silence rather than "contactful" communication dominates human relationships: if the innocent woman is made to suffer so, what must the woman feel if she is afraid because she is really guilty (II.1167–70)? Vives could well have penned his next warning with Mencía's husband in mind (or was Calderón in some way dramatizing Vives's assertion, however critically?): "I warn women often, and they must be given this warning very often, more than men, not to be deceived into thinking that it does not matter whether you actually do something or *seem* to do something" (III.77; Fantazzi 231; emphasis added).[10]

Mencía tries to dispel Gutierre's suspicions before they occur by actively announcing the presence of a man in her room, thereby resorting to the Baroque trope of deceiving with truth (*engañar con la verdad*); this ruse almost works because Gutierre recalls that detail, however fleetingly, in seeking to rationalize his wife's innocence: "... fue / la que me avisó ella mesma" (II.1621–22) [... did not / My wife (inform) me of it (Edwards 56)]. Had Gutierre but communicated even some of the thoughts and suspicions he voices in a soliloquy of 132 verses, thereby flying in the face of the social norms operant in cases of conventional dishonor—whether real or imagined— the tragic outcome might have been averted, however intrinsic it is to the play's dénouement. Once again, Vives seems to have anticipated the moral *huis-clos* in which Mencía finds herself:

> [T]he discreet woman with utmost vigilance and instinctive sagacity will ferret out whether her husband harbors any suspicions against her or any seeds of anger or hatred, some remnant of distrust. If such exist, she will devote her energies to dispel them *before they take root*. These increase for the slightest reason and become fatal. She will rid his mind of these gently and make amends to her

husband. Undetected and hidden diseases gain strength and kill more quickly than those that manifest themselves externally. (III.70; Fantazzi 225; emphasis added)

And, of course, Mencía eventually seals her fate by communicating her thoughts in writing, lest Enrique's sudden departure implicate her chastity and good name publicly (III.2394–99). She knows the move is fraught with danger, for any test of honor is a dangerous one (III.2408); not surprisingly, Vives warns that a woman should "neither send nor receive letters without the knowledge of her husband" (III.77; Fantazzi 231).

Gutierre does stop momentarily to admit that all the evidence points to his wife's innocence; both know "who they are" in relation to society's pro-scriptions: "Y así acortemos discursos, / pues todos juntos se cierran / en que Mencía es quien es, / y soy quien soy" (II.1647–50) [Let's dispense with speeches / for everything leads to the conclusion that / Mencía is who she is / and I am who I am (translation mine)]. But then he is propelled, as if Vives's voice were echoing in his head, into expressing concern for the health of his "honor" whose existence is a living death, in that it is a woman who gives it vital breath: "... en vuestro sepulcro / vivís: puesto que os alienta / la mujer ..." (II.1661–63) [... in your tomb / you live since she who gives you breath / is woman]. In his self-imposed role as *el médico de su honra*, he prescribes a "... dieta / del silencio ..." (II.1674–75) [a goodly dose / Of silence (Edwards 58)] to be effected in "... el mudo silencio / de la noche ..." (II.1861–62) [the still night, wrapped in silence (Edwards 82)]; until he diagnoses "... qué malicia tiene / el mal ..."—the cause of the malady—he will not speak of his pain but conceal and dissimulate (II.1689ff.). The moment jealousy comes into his awareness, and the instant he pronounces the word, there is no longer an easy cure; science will not suffice ("... faltará la ciencia" [II.1710]). The surgeon of his honor will resort to the draconian remedy of surgical excision that will lead to the radical silencing of his beloved wife. This is the *husband's* tragedy too, something that Vives's conduct manual fails to address.

If Mencía's tragedy, undoubtedly more horrific, is due to accidental occurrences, it is also born of her authentic though futile attempts to break with the strictures imposed on her sex by the norms of conduct as codified in the instructive manuals of the time—norms which burden woman with the guilt of original sin and champion the chauvinist virtues of chastity, silence, and obedience—pluralism and historicity notwithstanding. Therefore, we cannot but query the potentially totalizing assumption—valid, perhaps, with a director's particular performance reading in mind, yet susceptible to that bugbear of subjectivity—that "the innocent Mencía, like Desdemona before her, is not the principal focus for tragedy at the play's closing (and this despite the dramatic discovery of Mencía's body on the stage in the closing scene), but that instead the murdering husband is the one to engage the spectator's attention, both visually and emotionally" (Benabu 36).

* * *

"Hasta saber cómo vino / ... / ¿cómo quieres que suponga / culpa en Leonor? ..." (II.5, 663b) [Not until I know how she got here ... how can I blame Leonor? (Boyle 59)] reasons Don Carlos about the suspicious presence of his beloved in a strange man's house in Sor Juana Inés de la Cruz's *Los empeños de una casa* [*House of Desires* or *The Trials of a Noble House*].[11] He will project neither suspicions nor accusations until he knows the facts: "Que es muy bajo quien sin causa, / de la dama a quien adora, / se da a entender que le ofende" (II.5, 663b) [It takes a very low man / to assume without reason / that the woman he loves / has betrayed him (Boyle 59)]. "Que en las dolencias de honor / no todas veces son buenos, / si bastan solo süaves, / los medicamentos recios, / que antes suelen hacer daño" (III.13, 694a) [In affairs of honor, harsh medicine / is not always the best remedy: / mild medicine is often the swiftest cure (Boyle 103)], counsels Leonor's father, Don Rodrigo, with equal "rationality." His discourse provides an antidote to the drastic remedy a helplessly jealous Gutierre adopts with his proverbial "dieta del silencio": "[P]ues cuando está mal un miembro, / el experto cirujano / no luego le aplica el hierro / y corta lo dolorido / sino que aplica primero / los remedios lenitivos" (III.13, 694a) [If a limb is damaged / the expert surgeon does not / immediately apply the knife / and cut it off, / but first applies gentle remedies (Boyle 103)]. Sor Juana's play provides a refreshing alternative (despite comedic genre distinctions, and considering authorial gender markings), when both the honor-driven suitor and the honor-driven father stop to consider that they may not have all of the constatives before undertaking to perform a significant action—before engaging in a speech act that will have "infelicitous" repercussions.

One cannot but speculate what might have happened if the wretched personages reinscribed here had been able to enact what Sor Juana's characters exemplify, and what Barbara Mujica proposes so aptly if also with tongue-in-cheek in her historical novel, *I Am Venus*, which deals with the mysterious identity of the model who posed for Velázquez's painting, *The Rokeby Venus*, completed between 1647 and 1651. In a single sentence, Mujica captures the *modus operandi* of that lapse in communication dictated by received social constraints regarding reputation as it plays itself out on the page and on stage: "Rather than sneak around and spy on his wife like a cuckold in a *comedia*,

Velázquez decided to do what characters in plays never did: *he would simply ask Juana to explain what happened"* (186; emphasis added). Alas, the tradeoff of that seductively simple solution would be to silence certain tragic plots of domesticity in which the containment and/or excision of the wife's subjectivity can be historicized, not least *El médico de su honra*, which the consummate British theatre critic Michael Billington once described, in reviewing a production of Gwynne Edwards's translation at the Drama Centre (London) in 1988, as "one of the most disquieting plays in all world drama, ... a dark masterpiece."

Notes

1. References in Spanish to *El pintor de su deshonra* are to A. K. G. Paterson's bilingual edition and are given by Act and verse. References in English, given by page number, are to David Johnston and Laurence Boswell's translation intended for Boswell's production of the play with the Royal Shakespeare Company in 1995.
2. Matthew D. Stroud deftly teases apart the intricate workings of these matters in *Fatal Union: A Pluralistic Approach to the Spanish Wife-Murder* Comedias (1990), which appeared, however paradoxically, in the heyday of deconstructive criticism. Drawing on generic situations in some thirty-one *comedias*, he arrives at the pluralistic conclusion that "social and moral systems based on guilt and shame have many tenets in common, but ... differ significantly in such matters as the importance of secrecy, the threat to individual identity, and the distribution of justice" (142).
3. References in Spanish to *El médico de su honra* are to D. W. Cruickshank's edition and are given by Act and verse. References in English, given by page number, are to Gwynne Edward's (Edwards) translation intended for performance.
4. Commissioned by Queen Catherine of Aragon seemingly for Princess Mary's education, the manual was intended for a larger audience, given its proliferation in the 16th century in some forty editions throughout Europe in the original Latin and in vernacular languages, and its possible influence on Fray Luis de León's (1527–1591) *La perfecta casada* [*The Perfect Wife*] (1583) (Howe, Introducción 21).
5. On the differences between "the ideal woman championed by men like Vives and Fray Luis and the lives of actual Spanish women," Allyson M. Poska writes: "[R]ecent research reveals that although sexual purity might have been applauded by the clerics, intellectuals, and the male members of aristocratic families, for many women it was only haphazardly pursued" (7). See also Scott K. Taylor's revisionary study of honor and violence, which takes into account, among other things, how "criminal records were produced and what role the justice system played in the rhetoric of honor" (15–16).
6. Vives's *De institutione* has been read by historian Fredrik Charpentier Ljungqvist in terms of categories taken from anthropological research: gender order, restrictions on women's physical freedom of movement, regulations and instructions regarding women's clothing, and various rules for women's outward conduct (140). While it is hardly the case that the chastity code in *De institutione* "has not been subjected

to closer examination" (141), the above categories serve to systematize Vives's proscriptive view that "in a woman, chastity is the equivalent of all virtues" (I.44; Fantazzi 85).

7. References in Spanish to *La dama boba*, given by Act and verse, are to Alonso Zamora Vicente's edition. References in English, given by page number, are to David Johnston's (Johnston) translation commissioned for Boswell's production, which was staged at the Ustinov Studio, Theatre Royal Bath (UK) as part of the Spanish Golden Age Season that ran from 12 September to 21 December 2013. (In November 2013, the Association for Hispanic Classical Theater and Out of the Wings jointly organized an international symposium in Bath—"The *Comedia*: Translation and Performance"—to coincide with the Spanish Season.)

8. Georgina Dopico-Black offers a historicized reading of Fray Luis de León's *La perfecta casada* both *with* and *against* the horizon of honor plays, raising questions about "how adultery and illegibility in Fray Luis in some sense anticipates the illegibility of adultery in Calderón"; or about "how questions concerning wifely illegibility invariably become entangled with an inquisitorial hermeneutic and how, in this entanglement, the question of the wife's will either becomes or is made to seem a threat that must somehow be contained" (13). For Dopico-Black, the debates concerning honor can be expressed as a "series of at times opposing, at times overlapping positions" (15). Honor "as the site, localizable on the wife's body, through which the husband's subjectivity is vulnerable to the wife's will," is key to her approach, especially the question of whether a woman "can possess or manifest honor or whether she is a mere receptacle for her husband's honor" (16).

9. Vives constrains woman's no-win behavior thus: "If you speak a little in public, you are thought to be uneducated, if you speak a lot, you are light-headed; unlearnedly, you are accounted ignorant; learnedly, you are malicious; if you are slow in responding, you are haughty and ill-mannered; ready with an answer, a little push will make you stumble; if you sit with composed mien, then you are a dissembler; if you gesticulate, you are stupid by nature; if you look at something, that means your mind is drawn there; if you laugh when someone else laughs, even if your attention was directed elsewhere, your smile has betrayed you; if you listen to a man, it means you approve of what he says and you will be an easy conquest" (I.93; Fantazzi 125).

10. There is no question about what one actually sees (or hears); the problem arises when one presumes to know the "ultimate truth" or "the meaning of what I see" (Stroud 128). The proverbial "¿Qué es esto que miro?" [I can't believe what I am seeing (Edwards 5)] is uttered repeatedly by various characters, most significantly by Don Gutierre when he realizes that the dagger he has found in his house is a companion piece to Prince Enrique's sword (II.1533), with the (erroneous) supposition that he has been dishonored by the actions of his wife (see also Blue).

11. References in Spanish to *Los empeños de una casa*, given by Act and page number, are to the *Obras completas*. References in English, given by page number, are to Catherine Boyle's (Boyle) translation intended for Nancy Meckler's production of the play with the Royal Shakespeare Company in 2004. One thinks, too, of Don Pedro's confession in Lope's *El caballero de Olmedo* [*The Knight from Olmedo*] that, had his daughter but confided in him the true state of her feelings regarding the marriage he had arranged, he never would have persisted (III.2547–50). This serves as another instance of the defective functioning of a speech act, of its im-perfect or tardy application.

Works Cited

Austin, J. L. *How to Do Things with Words.* Cambridge, MA: Harvard UP, 1962. Print.

Barton, John. *Playing Shakespeare.* London: Methuen. 1984. Print.

Benabu, Isaac. *Reading for the Stage: Calderón and His Contemporaries.* Woodbridge, Suffolk, UK: Tamesis, 2003. Print.

Bergmann, Emilie. "The Exclusion of the Feminine in the Cultural Discourse of the Golden Age: Juan Luis Vives and Fray Luis de León." *Religion, Body and Gender in Early Modern Spain.* Ed. Alain Saint-Saëns. San Francisco: Mellen Research UP, 1991. 124–36. Print.

Billington, Michael. *The Surgeon of Honour. The Guardian* [London]. 20 March 1988. Print.

Blue, William R. "'¿Qué es esto que miro?' Converging Sign Systems in *El médico de su honra.*" *Bulletin of the Comediantes* 30 (1978): 83–96. Print.

Calderón de la Barca, Pedro. *El médico de su honra.* Ed. Don W. Cruickshank. 2nd ed. Madrid: Castalia, 1989. Print.

———. *The Painter of His Dishonour* [*El pintor de su deshonra*]. Ed. Alan K. G. Paterson. Warminster, UK: Aris & Phillips, 1991. Print.

———. *The Painter of Dishonour.* Trans. David Johnston and Laurence Boswell. Bath, UK: Absolute Classics, 1996. Print.

Casey, James. *Early Modern Spain: A Social History.* London: Routledge, 1999. Print.

Dopico-Black, Georgina. *Perfect Wives, Other Women: Adultery and Inquisition in Early Modern Spain.* Durham, NC and London: Duke UP, 2001. Print.

Edwards, Gwynne, trans. *Calderón: Plays One: The Surgeon of Honour.* London: Methuen, 1991. Print.

Fischer, Susan L. "The Function and Significance of the *Gracioso* in Calderón's *El pintor de su deshonra.*" *Romance Notes* 14.2 (1972): 334–40. Print.

———. *Reading Performance: Spanish Golden Age Theatre and Shakespeare on the Modern Stage.* Woodbridge, Suffolk, UK: Boydell & Brewer (Tamesis), 2009. Print.

Fox, Dian. Introduction. *The Physician of His Honour* [*El médico de su honra*]. By Pedro Calderón de la Barca. Trans. Dian Fox with Donald Hindley. Warminster, UK: Aris & Phillips, 1997. 1–23. Print.

Howe, Elizabeth Teresa. *Education and Women in the Early Modern Hispanic World.* Surrey, UK: Ashgate, 2008. Print.

———. Introducción. *Instrucción de la mujer cristiana.* Trans. Juan Justiniano. Ed. Elizabeth Teresa Howe. Madrid: Fundación Universitaria Española, 1995. 7–23. Print.

———. "'Let Your Women Keep Silence': The Pauline Dictum and Women's Education." *Women's Literacy in Early Modern Spain and the New World.* Ed. Anne J. Cruz and Rosilie Hernández. Surrey, UK: Ashgate, 2011. 123–37. Print.

Ife, B. W. "Locating the seat of honour in Spanish Golden Age drama." *Times Literary Supplement* [London] 23 August 1995: 16–17. Print.

Johnston, David. Translator's Note. *The Lady Boba: A Woman of Little Sense.* Trans. David Johnston. London: Oberon, 2013. Print.

Juana Inés de la Cruz. *Festejo de los empeños de una casa. Obras completas.* Mexico City: Editorial Porrúa, 1985. Print.

———. *House of Desires or The Trials of a Noble House.* Trans. Catherine Boyle. London: Oberon, 2004. Print.

Kamen, Henry. *Early Modern European Society.* London: Routledge, 2000. Print.

Kelly, Joan. "Early Feminist Theory and the *Querelle des Femmes*, 1400–1789." *Signs: Journal of Women in Culture and Society* 8.1 (1982): 4–28. Print.

Ljungqvist, Fredrik Charpentier. "Female Shame, Male Honor: The Chastity Code in Juan Luis Vives's *De institutione feminae Christianae.*" *Journal of Family History* 37.2 (2012): 139–54. Print.

Muecke, D. C. *Irony and the Ironic.* 2nd ed. London: Methuen, 1982. Print.

Mujica, Bárbara. *I Am Venus.* New York: Overlook P, 2013. Print.

Poska, Allyson M. *Women and Authority in Early Modern Spain: The Peasants of Galicia.* Oxford: Oxford UP, 2006. Print.

Rogers, Daniel. "'Tienen los celos pasos de ladrones': Silence in Calderón's *El médico de su honra.*" *Hispanic Review* 33 (1965): 273–89. Print.

Spitzer, Leo. "Soy Quien Soy." *Nueva Revista de Filología Hispánica* 1.2 (1948): 113–27. Print.

Stroud, Matthew D. *Fatal Union: A Pluralistic Approach to the Spanish Wife-Murder Comedias.* London and Toronto: Associated UP, 1990. Print.

Taylor, Scott K. *Honor and Violence in Golden Age Spain.* New Haven, CT: Yale UP, 2008. Print.

Vega Carpio, Lope Félix de. *La dama boba.* Ed. Diego Marín. Madrid: Cátedra, 2001. Print.

Vives, Juan Luis. *The Education of a Christian Woman: A Sixteenth-Century Manual.* Ed. and trans. Charles Fantazzi. Chicago and London: U of Chicago P, 2000. Print.

———. *De officio mariti* [*De los deberes del marido*]. *Obras completas.* Vol. 1. Ed. Lorenzo Riber. Madrid: Aguilar, 1947. 1259–1352. Print.

Mencía as Tragic Hero in Calderón's El médico de su honra

Katrina M. Heil
East Tennessee State University

Calderón de la Barca's *El médico de su honra* [*The Surgeon of His Honor*], one of the most widely studied wife-murder dramas of the Spanish Golden Age, seems to pose more questions than it answers. Does the play condone or condemn the honor code, which leads to the gruesome murder of Mencía? Are we to admire the "surgeon" Gutierre's astuteness in carrying out the murder in such a way as to leave his honor untainted? Or is there an inherent criticism of his behavior that lies precisely in its cold-hearted and premeditated nature? Golden Age scholars have not reached a consensus on this point (Trubiano 431). Matthew Stroud, in his exhaustive study of thirty-one Spanish uxoricide dramas of the late 16th and 17th centuries, *Fatal Union: A Pluralistic Approach to the Spanish Wife-Murder Comedias*, points out that, "the existing criticism of these plays provides little help and, in fact, could not be more contradictory" (13). Some, such as Roberta Thiher, argue that Calderón carefully and *intentionally* presents a murky view of the morality of the honor code in *The Surgeon of His Honor*, which she describes as "the most ambiguous of [his] dramas" (237). This disparity of opinion among the critics points to a flaw in their approach, which Stroud, following Wayne C. Booth, identifies as a "methodology of monism, [which] leads us to hunt for something hidden that will be revealed ... a 'secret key' to understanding a work" (16). However, Stroud also rejects the other extreme, which posits that, because there may be no unitary meaning to a text, there is no meaning at all. Stroud's approach, therefore, is to recognize the plurality of meanings and interpretations in these wife-murder dramas, and he adds that, "[t]he presentation in a text of contradictory but equally compelling "truths" creates works that are both thematically and dramatically more interesting, more ironic, more unstable" (21). This can certainly be said of *The Surgeon of His Honor.*

In addition to the questions raised concerning how best to interpret Calderón's judgment of the morality of the honor code, this play also evades easy classification into a dramatic genre. Should it be considered a tragedy? Critics such as Alexander A. Parker and Duncan Moir argue that *The Surgeon of His Honor* is fundamentally compatible with classical tragedy—in the Aristotelian sense—with some modifications and even enhancements, which contribute to the evolution of tragedy as a literary genre (MacCurdy 6–7). Others, such as M. Gordon and Raymond MacCurdy, use the precepts of Aristotelian tragedy to show why this play should *not* be considered a "true" tragedy. Mario Trubiano argues that *The Surgeon of His Honor* is at once a tragedy and an anti-tragedy, depending on the astuteness of the spectator in his or her reaction to the figure of Gutierre. Robert ter Horst, on the other hand, argues that Calderón is the creator of a completely new kind of tragedy, which is derived from comedy. I would argue that, just as this play contains a plurality of meanings, it also contains a plurality of dramatic plots, the principle ones being possible Aristotelian tragedies that, when considered together, help explain the vast disparity of interpretations of this work. While many studies have considered whether or not this play can be considered a tragedy in the classical sense, they do not take up the issue under the assumption that Mencía, and not her murderous husband Gutierre, would be its tragic hero.[1] However, of all characters in this play, Mencía most closely represents Aristotle's description of a tragic hero and her fate, that of a classical tragic plot. An analysis of Mencía as tragic hero, in comparison with two other key figures in this play, Gutierre and King Pedro, reveals a complexity of plot in *The Surgeon of His Honor* that helps elucidate the wide-ranging reactions to and interpretations of this most intriguing *comedia.*

While the question of whether or not this play *is* a tragedy in the classical sense has been cause for much debate, it is less difficult to show that *The Surgeon of His Honor* contains a tragedy within. In order to do this, it is necessary to briefly reconsider exactly what Aristotle was describing in the *Poetics*. There are some, such as Friedrich Nietzsche, who reject Aristotle altogether and claim that the only true tragedies were Greek tragedies, particularly those of Aeschylus. Others, such as George Steiner, who are willing to include the likes of Shakespeare and Racine in the exclusive list of true tragedians, concludes that tragedy has been all but impossible in the Modern world, in part because tragedy is fundamentally incompatible with the predominant and utopic view that governs most attempts at tragedy since the fall of Athens: Christianity.

According to Steiner, a just and loving God who sets things right in the end is antithetical to tragedy since, "tragedies end badly" (8). Critics who are quick to condemn all dramas that do not closely resemble paradigm tragedies such as *Oedipus Tyrranus* to be somehow *less* than a "true" tragedy, however, suffer a similar "methodology of monism" that Stroud identifies in many studies of the *comedia*. While this topic is too large to be argued out here, it is important to remember that Ancient Greece produced a plurality of plays that were called tragedies, including many that had happy endings (White 231). In the *Poetics*, Aristotle was describing what he observed to be the main elements of the tragedies that he knew, almost as if he were writing a technical how-to manual for would-be tragedians. Walter Kaufmann, in his *Tragedy and Philosophy*, provides a very complete study of the numerous misinterpretations of the *Poetics*, all of which have the tendency to reduce the field of "true Aristotelian tragedies" so drastically that many plays of even Aeschylus, Sophocles, and Euripides would find themselves excluded.[2] My approach to the *Poetics* and to tragedy as a literary genre instead wishes to keep an open mind about the wide variety of tragedies in Ancient Greece and to avoid the temptation to view tragedy as irreducibly mysterious and unattainable, residing only in the unknowable realms of a lost and ancient world.

In order to see Mencía as a "proper" tragic hero, we must first examine the most fundamental element of Aristotelian tragedy, which is the arousal and subsequent catharsis of terror, or fear, and pity. Starting with Plato, the study of tragedy has dealt, in part, with the effects on the spectator of watching tragedy. Aristotle's famous suggestion that tragedy produces a catharsis of the emotions of fear and pity, which is considered beneficial to the spectator, is precisely the point at which he counters Plato's claim that watching tragedy is bad for us.[3] Aristotle defines tragedy as, "a representation of a serious, complete action which has magnitude, in embellished speech, with each of its elements [used] separately in the various parts [of the play]; [represented] by people acting and not by narration; accomplishing by means of pity and terror the catharsis of such emotions" (*Poetics* VI, 1449b22–28). For Aristotle, the extent to which a tragedy arouses pity and terror lies in the most important component of tragic drama: the *mythos* or plot. All of the specific elements of plot that Aristotle discusses, *peripeteiai* or reversals, *anagnoriseis* or recognitions, and *hamartia* or error, are essential to the plot for the extent to which they aid in the arousal of these tragic emotions. The other elements of tragedy discussed in the *Poetics*, such as the use of verse, music and spectacle, should be considered secondary. Furthermore, Aristotelian "rules" such as the action occurring within a twenty-four hour period are, in my opinion, descriptive of what was most common in Greek tragedy rather than prescriptive of what all tragedy must be. It is certainly hard to argue that nothing fearful nor pitiable could occur in a period of time longer than twenty-four hours.

In chapter 13 of the *Poetics*, Aristotle discusses three types of plots that are unsuitable for tragedy, and a fourth that is. The fault of the first three plots is that they do not elicit pity or terror and are therefore untragic.[4] The first, which portrays "decent men" suffering a reversal from good to misfortune, is not tragic but simply "shocking." The second, which has "wicked men" moving from misfortune to good fortune, is the most untragic of all, since it is neither morally satisfying nor provokes fear and pity. The third, which shows a "thoroughly villainous person" falling from good to misfortune, while morally satisfying, is also untragic, because it provokes neither pity nor terror (XIII, 1452b32–1453a5). We see here that all three of these plots are considered to be untragic, even though the third does provide moral satisfaction, and therefore that the arousal of fear and pity seems to be most central to Aristotle's concept of what is tragic. To illustrate the point even further, let's consider Aristotle's fourth plot, which is indeed tragic. The fourth plot "involves a change not from misfortune to good fortune, but conversely, from good fortune to misfortune, not because of wickedness but because of a great error ... by a better person rather than a worse one" (XIII, 1453a13–17). The fourth plot is remarkably similar to the first, however, with the addition of the *hamartia* or error committed by the tragic hero. The presence of the error is what prevents the tragedy from being simply "shocking," as with the first plot. It is important to note that the error is also central to how modern classicists understand Aristotle's conception of catharsis, which is achieved as the spectator is able to *understand* the cause of the tragedy, whether that cause—the error—can be assigned moral blame or not.[5]

Classicist Stephen White analyzes what Aristotle meant with his insistence that the tragic hero be "a better person rather than a worse one." These characters should not be perfect, but they should be "better than us." "[Aristotle] sets an upper limit on virtue, as well as a lower one, and the *Poetics* disapproves of showing what the *Ethics* finds best. The 'finest' plays are not about paragons of virtue responding nobly to adversity, because it interferes with the tragic effect if the characters are too bad or too good" (228). It is important to feel that the characters are like us in order to feel fear and pity for them. "It is 'fine' when a paragon of virtue handles misfortune well, but also when people more like us manage to do the same, and noble actions in adversity are admirable no matter who performs them" (228). Fear and pity, which have "the decisive role in the distinctively tragic pleasure" (229), are better aroused by characters that respond admirably to adversity. We ought to remember Aristotle's claim that in order to feel pity for the characters, we must feel their suffering is undeserved. White clarifies this point; we do not have to feel that the characters are entirely innocent, but we must feel they deserve better. The more nobly the characters behave, the better we will feel they deserve. Likewise, in order to feel fear for the character, we must feel they are like us; we will feel no fear for a character that we feel to be very different from us. For this reason, the characters must not be too good or too bad. "For a story to arouse our fear and pity, then, it must make us morally 'involved'; unless we care about what happens to its characters and how they fare, *their* actions and fortunes can hardly affect *our* feelings, or cause *us* to suffer fear or pity *for them*" (229).

Given the nature of an Aristotelian tragic hero as described above, it becomes clear that Mencía most appropriately fits the bill, especially when compared to Gutierre and King Pedro.[6] While all three characters suffer their own downfall, which can be attributed to an identifiable flaw or error, Mencía's response to her downfall is the most admirable, especially when contrasted with the moral ambiguity of King Pedro or the moral "wretchedness" of Gutierre. The coexistence of three possible tragic plots in *The Surgeon of His Honor* contributes greatly to its complexity, characteristic of the Spanish Baroque, and creates a hybrid plot, which explains the mixed emotional and moral responses that many spectators are left with as the final curtain falls. Ter Horst claims of all Calderonian drama that, "Calderón is the fabricator of a fundamentally hybrid kind of theatre, a *monstruo* [monster], to use his favorite term" (200). Gordon asserts that, "[w]hat Calderón changes is not the *comedia*'s concern with moral issues but the degree of complexity with which such issues are explored" (339). At first glance, it would seem that the protagonist and tragic hero, if this play has one, would be Gutierre. The play's title, after all, refers to this character, and the final lines of the play are spoken by him (III.2950–53). Assuming that Calderón wishes to roundly affirm the values of the honor code, then Gutierre's situation is indeed unfortunate. His downfall arises with the return of Prince Enrique and in the reality that he and his wife continue to have romantic feelings towards one another, in spite of Mencía's physical fidelity to her husband. The remaining action of the play would then be seen as dictated by a just code of honor, which demands Gutierre's eventual murder of his wife. The fact that Gutierre's fortune is eventually restored by the King's seeming approval of his actions and the acquisition of a new wife, Leonor, would not necessarily mean that Gutierre's saga could not be considered a tragedy. As has been previously noted, many Greek tragedies also had happy endings. White makes clear in his study of Aristotle's favorite tragedies that, "[p]rovided a story involves some serious misfortune, whether actual and ultimate or only prospective, it can end either happily or sadly" (231). A very superficial reading of *The Surgeon of His Honor* seems to affirm that this is so.

However, it does not take very deep penetration to see that this play is not so simple. The figure of Gutierre is portrayed time and again as deeply flawed, far beyond what would be admissible for a proper tragic hero. Before the action of the play begins, we learn that Gutierre has already committed a possible crime against Leonor, destroying her honor by refusing to marry her, led only by his irrational jealousy. We see repeatedly that Gutierre tries in vain to control his jealousy, which he insists must be separate from the cool reasoning of a true surgeon seeking to restore his honor. The most conspicuous example of Gutierre's jealousy is when he explodes at the end of Act II, shouting to Mencía that he does not feel jealousy, but that if he did, "a pedazos sacara con mis manos / el corazón, y luego / envuelto en sangre, desatado en fuego, / el corazón comiera / a bocados, la sangre me bebiera, / el alma le sacara, / y el alma, ¡vive Dios!, despedazara" (II.2024–30) [I would tear the heart to pieces / with my own hands, and then, / wrapped in blood and undone in fire, / I would eat that heart morsel by morsel, / I would drink up its blood, / I would tear out its soul and, / by God!, I would rip it to shreds].

It is hard to imagine that Calderón would include this explosion, which Gutierre himself later regrets, if the main goal were to portray him as a sympathetic and admirable character who responds nobly to his own misfortune. Furthermore, what is most striking about *The Surgeon of His Honor* is not that Gutierre kills his wife, but the *way* he kills her, bleeding her to death slowly and methodically. In addition, after Gutierre has murdered his wife, whom some spectators may conclude he has good reason to suspect, he also intends to kill the entirely innocent phlebotomist Ludovico, who was forced at knife-point to bleed his wife. Gutierre is only stopped in this action when he realizes that King Pedro and Don Diego are watching him. By the play's end, Mencía's blood is literally dripping from his hands. The image is simply too arresting to suppose that Gutierre could be a tragic hero. His character is portrayed as too deeply flawed, so much so that it has lead Trubiano to consider this play an example of *teatro de crueldad* [theater of cruelty] in which Gutierre uses the honor code to justify a cold-blooded murder instigated by his uncontrollable jealousy (438). It does seem most likely that, rather than upholding the honor code, Calderón highlights the extent to which Gutierre is fuelled by jealousy in order to question an honor code for which, according to Gordon, he has an extreme distaste (339). If Gutierre is instead to be considered a "wicked man," as he is by many spectators, his final reversal from the misfortune of nearly being dishonored to the good fortune of being pardoned for murder by the King and remarried, far from a tragedy, instead resembles Aristotle's second plot, which is–it must be remembered—the "most untragic of all."

Most of the criticism taking up the question of whether or not *The Surgeon of His Honor* should be classified as a tragedy does not consider the possibility of King Pedro as a tragic hero. However, it is necessary to investigate this possibility briefly here for one main reason: the figure of Pedro most closely resembles the types of tragic heroes found in Ancient Greece, as a historical figure whose eventual downfall captured the public's imagination over hundreds of years in manifold tales and songs. Indeed, within the context of this particular play, the cause of Pedro's downfall is given a new interpretation. It is Pedro's unfortunate error—one that he immediately recognizes and regrets—in allowing Gutierre to overhear his confrontation with Enrique that leads to the misunderstanding between the brothers. While Pedro is not murdered and succeeded by his brother within the action of this play, the audience is keenly aware of how this story will end. It seems then that Pedro's fate follows Aristotle's fourth plot in the *Poetics* quite neatly, in which the character suffers a reversal from good fortune to misfortune, "not because of wickedness but because of a great error" (XIII, 1453a13–17). Where King Pedro falls short as an Aristotelian hero is not in his fate, however, but in his moral ambiguity. In this play he bears both nicknames that history has given him: *el justiciero* [the Just] and *el cruel* [the Cruel].

There has been a great deal of research dedicated to Pedro's conflicted portrayal in this play, and it is not possible to explore all aspects of it here. Nevertheless, it is important to highlight a few key points. First, we must remember that in the less studied precursor to Calderón's *The Surgeon of His Honor*, which bears the same title and is attributed to Lope de Vega, Pedro's character is simply portrayed as "the just" (Fox 19). Juan Pedro Sánchez Sánchez gives a complete structural comparison of both versions of this play, with the greatest deviation of the second being that, in Calderón's version, Pedro is ambiguous, incompetent, and morally problematic. Gordon notes that the audience is led to question Pedro as a "valid moral arbiter" and that, even though the ending of this play seems closed, "with all the ends neatly tied up in the best *comedia* tradition … the King's justice does not so much solve a problem as pose one" (342). It is in the King's final advice to Gutierre where his vacillations as supreme justice are most evident. Clearly seeing Gutierre as the one responsible for the horrendous murder of Mencía, he at first seems to reproach him for not having used better judgment and prudence. However, as Gutierre recounts the many incidents that fed his suspicions, the King is at a loss to tell Gutierre how he should have behaved differently. In the end, he says the best remedy is the one Gutierre has chosen, "… sangrarla" (III.2929)

[... to bleed her]. His final insistence that Gutierre now give his hand to Leonor, likewise, does not seem based on a clear sense of justice so much as it is a matter of expediency for the King. He has promised to help Leonor restore her honor and to resolve the issue between Mencía and Gutierre. With this new marriage, Pedro is killing two birds with one stone. Given the King's ambiguous moral character, which is a decided addition to the second version of this play, Pedro fails to match the Aristotelian description of a tragic hero. While we do not get to witness his response to his own downfall, it is hard to imagine that *this* Pedro will respond in an unequivocally admirable manner.

We are left now with the third possible tragic hero, Mencía. While concluding that *The Surgeon of His Honor* is not an Aristotelian tragedy, Gordon asserts that, "[i]f there is a tragedy at the heart of *El médico de su honra*, it is surely the immolation of the innocent Mencía on the altar of her society's obsession with honor" (343). Yet when we review Aristotle's description of a tragic plot and hero, it is hard to see where Mencía and her destiny come up short as a *bona fide* tragedy. First, while she is undoubtedly innocent of adultery, she *does* commit an error. Her flaw, that she still loves Enrique in spite of being married to Gutierre, is perhaps beyond her control. Because he is royalty, she was not able to marry Enrique, and for her honor she refused to be his mistress. She summarizes her position quite succinctly when she explains to Jacinta that, "tuve amor, y tengo honor. / Esto es cuanto sé de mí" (I.573–74) [I once had love, and I now have honor. / That is all I know about myself]. Mencía's continued love for Enrique seems to lead to her great error, which occurs when she tells the Prince—in front of her husband no less, who assumes Enrique is speaking of another woman—that she still loves him and can explain why she is now married: "cuanto a la dama, quizá / fuerza, y no mudanza fue; / oídla vos, que yo sé / que ella se disculpará" (I.421–24) [as for the lady, perhaps / it was by force, and not a change of heart; / hear her out, / for I know she will excuse herself]. This statement prompts Enrique to later seek out Mencía's explanation, by sneaking into her house when Gutierre is away, which is the catalyst for the unfolding of her tragic fate. Mencía later recognizes this error when, upon her outrage at Enrique's presence in her house, he reminds her of what she had said. "Es verdad, la culpa tuve" (II.1096) [It's true, I am to blame]. As a woman in Medieval or even 17th-century Spain, Mencía certainly was not afforded the kind of autonomy that allows for the same level of blame and responsibility as men may have, which is perhaps why she is more often seen as an innocent victim than as an instigator of her own tragedy. However, Calderón includes this exchange, and it is hard to imagine he would have done so for no reason. He could just as easily have had Enrique sneak into Mencía's house *without* her having suggested it. Mencía's acceptance of guilt here, in addition to a guilty conscience generally for still harboring feelings for Enrique, helps explain her overly culpable behavior with Gutierre later in the same act, which only serves to increase his suspicions.

The question of whether or not Mencía responds nobly to her downfall is impossible to answer without taking into account how very limited she was by her position in society. She frustrates many readers for never properly defending herself to Gutierre and instead trying to conceal everything from him. However, given Gutierre's exceedingly jealous nature, it is most natural that she wanted to avoid revealing to him her past relationship with Enrique, which any defense would have necessarily required. Nevertheless, within the constraints of her society and its honor code, Mencía certainly makes every attempt to do the right and honorable thing. Before the play's beginning, she had chosen the path of honor by refusing to be Enrique's mistress. After his return, she shuns Enrique again, in spite of her feelings, out of respect for her marriage vows. Later, when she learns what is to be her final destiny in the cruel note left for her by Gutierre, that she has only two hours remaining to live and that she would do best to work on saving her soul, she quite understandably laments and panics. However, the next time we see her, in the death scene, she has done the only thing she can, which is to calmly accept her fate. She is found lying in her bed, surrounded by candles, with a cross hanging over her head, silently awaiting her death. We learn later from Ludovico, however, that as she was bleeding to death, she continued to insist that she was innocent and, therefore, that God did not condone this murder (III.2688–90).

If we remember Aristotle's description of the tragic hero, Mencía corresponds most directly. The most important trait of the tragic hero is that she be one that elicits fear and pity in the spectator. In order to feel fear, according to Aristotle, we must feel the character is like us. In comparison with Gutierre and Pedro, Mencía is undoubtedly the most sympathetic character. She wrestles with the conflicting desires of love and honor, and tries to do right. She has little power, but she endeavors to use what power she has to prevent catastrophe and live a good life. Even more so, Mencía is clearly the character that evokes the most pity. As we saw earlier, by Aristotle's definition, the spectator does not have to consider the character to be entirely innocent, but we must feel that she deserved better. This is certainly true in the case of Mencía. Not only will most spectators feel she deserved better, many characters in the play believe so as well, such as Pedro, Coquín, Jacinta, and Ludovico. It is for this reason, then, that *The Surgeon of His Honor* can be said to contain an Aristotelian tragedy within its hybrid plot, and its tragic hero is undeniably Mencía.

MacCurdy notes that in *The Surgeon of His Honor*, there is a "linking of dramatic causality with some degree of moral guilt in all the major characters of the play" (6). Calderón's intertwining of three dramatic plots, all of which include the characters' mistakes and eventual downfall, do implicate all characters in Mencía's tragic fate. Furthermore, society itself seems to be at fault, for adhering to an honor code that is dictated not by prudence but rather irrational emotions such as jealousy. It is for this reason that attempts at interpreting this play lead to conflicting conclusions. The spectator is led down the traditional path of tragic emotions as witness to Mencía's tragic fate, while morally shocked at the happy ending awarded to the murderous Gutierre, and at the same time infused with doubt and confusion by the contradictory actions of the supposed supreme justice of the land, King Pedro. Nevertheless, we must not conclude that Calderón simply failed to convey a clear message. As Stroud notes, the plurality of "truths" in this drama allows for a play that is "both thematically and dramatically more interesting, more ironic, more unstable" (21). In other words, the spectators will not get off so easy. They are instead forced to decide for themselves whether the values of their society, which dictate the actions of this play, are values worth maintaining.

Notes

1. In a recent and interesting study, "Mencía (in)visible. Tragedia y violencia doméstica en *El médico de su honra*" ["Mencía (In)visible. Tragedy and Domestic Violence in *The Surgeon of His Honor*"], María Carrión also notes the subjugated role that most of the criticism has given Mencía to her husband, Gutierre. She affirms that Mencía plays a critical role in the unfolding of the tragedy of *The Surgeon of His Honor*, such as in helping to bring about the error and the catharsis of the tragedy. She agrees with Parker that multiple characters in this play contribute to the tragic error. This reading is certainly compatible with my view that there are multiple layers of tragedy in this play; however, her study does not consider Mencía as a tragic hero in her own right.
2. "[S]uch critics could say that many of the tragedies of 'the most tragic of the poets' [*sc.* Euripides] were not really tragedies at all because they were not truly tragic. By the same token, many of Aeschylus' and Sophocles' tragedies would suffer the same fate—at the hands of critics who think they know better what is tragic or a tragedy than did Aeschylus, Sophocles, Euripides, and Aristotle" (365).
3. First, Plato claims in the *Timaeus* that tragedy lies about the world. Plato holds that the world is not a tragic place, but rather, that it is governed by a rational and good intellect. Second, in the *Republic* II and III, Plato argues that poetry in general should be heavily censored for children because poets are often wrong about morality and the world. As a result, they tell lies about morality and about the nature of the Gods, which are good according to Plato. Third, in both the *Ion* and in the *Republic* X, Plato attempts to prove that poets do not need any knowledge of their subject matter

in order to achieve a brilliant mimesis of it. From this comes Plato's famous suggestion that poets are either divinely inspired (a suggestion that Plato himself probably did not take too seriously) or simply mad. Fourth, in the *Republic* X, Plato explains why he bans tragedy from his ideal state altogether. He claims that tragedy damages the character of a healthy, educated adult by eliciting emotions that conflict with his or her reason. Finally, in support of this previous claim, in the *Republic* X, Plato argues that the emotional experience we have in the theater exercises and strengthens the emotional points of view that are in conflict with our reason. As a result, we have to struggle with these emotions more in our daily lives. For example, a healthy rational person, in his or her daily life, may suppress the urge to cry in situations that he or she does not deem appropriate for crying. In the theater, this person may find an opportunity to release that pent-up desire to cry. Plato, however, believes that this exercise will only increase the desire to cry in daily life, as opposed to the 'purging' of this desire suggested by Aristotle. I have John Heil to thank for directing me to passages of both Plato and Aristotle that have been pertinent to my discussion here.

4. "Since the construction of the finest tragedy should not be simple but complex, and moreover it should represent terrifying and pitiable events (for this is particular to representation of this sort), first, clearly, it should not show (i) decent men undergoing a change from good fortune to misfortune; for this is neither terrifying nor pitiable, but shocking. Nor [should it show] (ii) wicked men [passing] from misfortune to good fortune. This is most untragic of all, for it has nothing of what it should; for it is neither morally satisfying nor pitiable nor terrifying. Nor, again, [should it show] (iii) a thoroughly villainous person falling from good fortune to misfortune: such a structure can contain moral satisfaction, but not pity or terror, for the former is felt for a person undeserving of his misfortune, and the latter for a person like [ourselves]" (*Poetics* XIII, 1452b32–1453a5).

5. For an excellent explanation of how Aristotle most likely understood this term, see Lear's fine article.

6. One difficulty in definitively classifying any given work as a tragedy lies in the subjective nature of its definition. Not only does the level to which a play is deemed tragic depend upon the extent to which it evokes fear and pity in the spectator, we see that equally crucial is the extent to which the spectator identifies with and admires the tragic hero. It is unavoidable that spectators will have different emotional responses to the action represented on the stage. This is true among a group of spectators witnessing the same performance, and even more so across the boundaries of time and culture, where values and sensibilities inevitably change. Still, *most* spectators agree that *Oedipus Tyrannus* and even *Hamlet* should be considered tragedies. The critic can therefore draw upon what unifies human values across the expanse of different time periods and cultures, and discuss what can *reasonably* be considered admirable, fearful, and pitiable to *most* people.

Works Cited

Aristotle. *Poetics*. Trans. Richard Janko. Indianapolis, IN: Hackett, 1987. Print.

Calderón de la Barca, Pedro. *El médico de su honra. Association for Hispanic Classical Theater.* Ed. Matthew Stroud and Laura Vidler. Web. 14 Dec. 2014. <http://comedias.org>.

Carrión, María. "Mencía (in)visible. Tragedia y violencia doméstica en *El médico de su honra*." *Hacia la tragedia áurea: Lecturas para un nuevo milenio*. Ed. Frederick A. de Armas, Luciano García Lorenzo, Enrique García Santo-Tomás. Madrid and Frankfurt: Iberoamericana and Vervuert; 2008. 429–48. Print.

Fox, Dian. "*El médico de su honra*: Political Considerations." *Hispania* 65.1 (1982): 28–38. Print.

Gordon, M. "Calderón as Tragedian: The Case of *Las tres justicias en una*." *The Modern Language Review* 81.2 (1986): 337–48. Print.

Kaufmann, Walter. *Tragedy and Philosophy*. New York: Anchor Books, 1969. Print.

Lear, Jonathan. "Katharsis." *Essays on Aristotle's Poetics*. Ed. Amélie Oksenberg Rorty. Princeton: Princeton UP, 1992. 315–40. Print.

MacCurdy, Raymond R. "The 'Problem' of Spanish Golden Age Tragedy: A Review and Reconsideration." *South Atlantic Bulletin* 38.1 (1973): 3–15. Print.

Moir, Duncan. "The Classical Tradition in Spanish Dramatic Theory and Practice in the Seventeenth Century." *Classical Drama and Its Influence. Essays Presented to H. D. F. Kitto*. Ed. M. J. Anderson. London: Methuen, 1965. 193–228. Print.

Nietzsche, Friedrich. *The Birth of Tragedy* and *The Case of Wagner*. Trans. Walter Kaufmann. New York: Random House, 1967. Print.

Parker, Alexander A. "Towards a Definition of Calderonian Tragedy." *Bulletin of Hispanic Studies* 39 (1962): 222–37. Print.

Plato. *Complete Works*. Ed. John M. Cooper and D. S. Hutchinson. Indianapolis, IN and Cambridge: Hackett, 1997. Print.

Sánchez Sánchez, Juan Pedro. "El personaje del rey Pedro I en las dos versiones de *El médico de su honra*." *Biblioteca Digital de la Universidad de Alcalá de Henares*. Web. 14 Dec. 2014. <http://hdl.handle.net/10017/4524>.

Steiner, George. *The Death of Tragedy*. New York: Alfred A. Knopf, 1961. Print.

Stroud, Matthew. *Fatal Union: A Pluralistic Approach to the Wife-Murder Comedias*. Lewisburg, PA: Bucknell UP, 1990. Print.

ter Horst, Robert. "From Comedy to Tragedy: Calderón and the New Tragedy." Spec. Hispanic issue of *Modern Language Notes* 92.2 (1977): 181–201. Print.

Thiher, Roberta. "The Final Ambiguity of *El médico de su honra*." *Studies in Philology* 67 (1970): 237–44. Print.

Trubiano, Mario F. "*El médico de su honra* y el médico de su deshonra: Tragedia y anti-tragedia." *Discurso: Revista de Estudios Iberoamericanos* 7.2 (1990): 431–37. Print.

White, Stephen. "Aristotle's Favorite Tragedies." *Essays on Aristotle's Poetics*. Ed. Amélie Oksenberg Rorty. Princeton: Princeton UP, 1992. 221–40. Print.

We Too Suffer: Calderón's Honor Husbands

EZRA ENGLING
Eastern Kentucky University

Thou dost weep like a woman for what thou couldst not defend as a man.
(Attributed to Aisha, mother of Abdallah Muhammad XII [Boabdil], on the surrender of Granada, 1491)

One of the main features of Aristotelian tragedy is that a tragic human flaw leads to the downfall of an otherwise happy and perfect person. There are many variations on this formula, and in Early Modern Spanish drama one variety stands out, in particular, due to a socio-literary convention known as the honor code. According to this code, a gentleman's honor was his most valuable social and moral attribute, and the women of the family were the reluctant repositories of this principle. The wife was particularly vulnerable, inhabiting a space where "a hyper-sensitivity to conjugal infidelity frequently led to unjustified homicide" (Wardropper viii). In two Calderonian wife-murder plays, *El médico de su honra* [*The Surgeon of His Honor*] and *El pintor de su deshonra* [*The Painter of His Dishonor*], the women are murdered and the men live on unhappily ever after. Without justifying the husbands' horrific actions, or dismissing the wives' brutal deaths, this study will consider Calderón's investment in the suffering of the two tragic heroes.

A. Irvine Watson describes the personality of the tragic hero, according to the Aristotelian and Neo-Aristotelian theories of tragedy, thus:

> He should be a person of middling virtue ... who is to some degree responsible for his own downfall, in order that the audience's sense of justice ... may not be outraged. (209)

This description, though applied to *El pintor de su deshonra*, works just as effectively for *El médico de su honra*. The two husbands bear the burden of the titles that clearly designate the Physician and the Painter as the stars of the respective shows. These men are connected by murder, they emerge as the tragic heroes, and they engage our sympathies. According to Matthew Stroud, "an interesting murder has always provided good dramatic plot material" (13). These two plays present not only interesting murders, but also even more intriguing aftermaths that result from the arranged marriages of two noblewomen to jealous men whom they do not love. Stroud continues, displaying the palette of possibilities native to dysfunctional unions:

> ... it is hard to find more extreme examples of emotional and social conflict than those in which the husband—sometimes for love, sometimes for hate, sometimes for jealousy, sometimes in spite of himself—kills his wife, who may or may not be guilty of any particular offense. (13)

Calderón gives graphic attention to the horrendous deaths of these innocent, if circumstantially guilty, women, but he also highlights the men's vulnerabilities that drive them to murder.

While discussions of these plays usually examine both sets of spouses, the women lay claim to our sympathies, and essentially steal the show. The terms "uxoricide," "wife-murder" or "wife murderer" appear in almost all studies of the genre, and this perspective sometimes overlooks the fact that the plays are about *El médico* and *El pintor*. When studies do focus on the husbands, the characters are usually regarded as privileged, melancholic, unstable and blood-thirsty men, selfishly defending the *status quo*.[1] As P. N. Dunn explains, "Honour is a religion of perfection, but since humanity is not perfect, men of honour may find that they have to avenge themselves on what they love most" (35). In the spirit of this concession, Gutierre (*El médico*) and Juan Roca (*El pintor*) are seen as chafing uncomfortably between the cloak and dagger. They are as subject to the honor code as are their wives; they, too, are victims of their circumstances.

Mencía comes into her marriage to Gutierre with a past that includes no less an admirer than the King's brother, Enrique. When fate leads him to her door, the Prince quickly recovers from his surprise that she has married Gutierre, and tries to resume their relationship. Trapped between love and duty, Mencía tries to protect her honor:

> Quien oyere a vuestra Alteza
> quejas, agravios, desprecios,
> podrá formar de mi honor
> presunciones y conceptos,
> indignos dél ... (I.277–81, 26–27)[2]

[Anyone, thus, to hear your Highness raging / accusing me, and cursing this way, / would form opinions and suspicions of / my honour, quite unworthy of it (10).[3]]

As her anxiety increases, she engages in a series of imprudent and compromising actions that culminate in her destruction. Unlike Mencía, Serafina symbolizes perfection and constancy, her beauty and demeanor placing her among the highest order of angels: the seraphim. When her fiancé, Álvaro, goes to sea and is presumed drowned, her father marries her off to her older cousin, Juan Roca. Álvaro resurfaces and tries to stake his original claim, but he is brutally rebuffed:

don Álvaro, yo te amé
cuando imaginé ser tuya,
y pasando mi esperanza
desde perdida a difunta,
me casé: ahora soy quien soy. (I.1017–21, 156)

[Don Álvaro, 'tis true I loved you once. / But when all hope of being yours / vanished with your reported death / I wed another: now I am what I am!][4]

He later abducts Serafina while she is unconscious. Roca pursues, discovers the couple in what appears to be a loving embrace, and wreaks a terrible vengeance.

The women pay the ultimate price for their husbands' extreme responses to dishonor, but the men too pay a price. Apparently, there was a historical precedent for this. Stroud reveals that "those cases that were adjudicated, and that indicated the husbands' punishments, noted that some penalty was always exacted from the husband" (14). Calderón was obviously aware of this, but his dramatic husbands escape legal punishment via royal intervention. Most scholars agree that Calderón's audience would have been shocked by the savagery displayed by the husbands. With reference to Gutierre, Everett Hesse's psychological study of the character is useful:

> There is no record to indicate the reaction of Calderón's audience, the majority of whom were *caballeros* witnessing what could happen under the honor code. They could plainly see the cruelty and injustice in a world of men, and perhaps saw their own guilt dramatized in the events on stage. (83)

John Bryans asserts that "Gutierre's extremely rigorous application of the laws of honour is far from being accepted as the norm" (285). We are not sure, however, what that norm was. Divorce was not an option, since this would have further publicized the dishonor of both husband and wife. Gutierre's response is calculated while Roca's is impulsive, but royal figureheads sanction

the actions of both noblemen. Teresa Scott Soufas perceives Roca's presentation as unfavorable, revealing "Calderón's condemnation of the melancholy
temperament through portrayal of a character who degenerates into instability and criminality" (198). Still, any consideration of the husbands exclusively
as jealous tyrants oversimplifies the complex relationship between character
and situation in the two plays.

Both men rail against societal expectations and the impossible demands
of the honor code, but are unable to challenge a system so rooted in tradition and their own identities. Gutierre can be calculating and emotional in
the same breath. He asks "¿Qué injusta ley condena / que muera el inocente
y que padezca?" (II.641–42, 74) [What unjust decree / is this whereby the
innocent / are doomed to suffer death! (45–46)]. This led Don Cruickshank
to suggest that, "hay una ironía macabra en esta pregunta: don Gutierre pade-
cerá, pero será la inocente Mencía la que muera" (37) [This question embodies a macabre irony: Don Gutierre will suffer, but the innocent Mencía will be
the one who dies]. Perhaps the innocent party in this formula is neither Gutierre nor Mencía, but Gutierre's honor. In refusing to be explicit, Calderón
allows innocence and suffering to be attributed to both husband and wife.
When the nobleman creeps up on his wife in the dark, and she addresses him
as "Your Highness," Gutierre is so shattered that he takes refuge in the persona of a surgeon procuring a cure for his wounded honor.

Nevertheless, he vacillates once more, seeking assistance from King Pedro,
the fountainhead of honor, and showing him the dagger that Prince Enrique
had dropped while fleeing the house. The King brusquely advises the nobleman to follow the rules, while helping his brother to escape from justice at
the same time. These royal actions in effect nullify any honorable content that
the code may have had, and render Gutierre's diseased honor insidious and
inaccessible. King Pedro also complicates an already thorny situation by having promised to restore honor to Gutierre's erstwhile lover. As John Bryans,
citing Alexander Parker, explains, "King Pedro by making his rash promise to
Leonor … unwittingly established an interest in the only means by which this
would be accomplished—by Mencía's death" (287).

Cruickshank is correct that Gutierre's honor, not his wife, is the disease,
therefore "Gutierre debería sangrar al honor y no a doña Mencía" (23) [Guti-
erre should bleed honor, not Mencía]. Since honor is much too abstract and
unattainable, Mencía is the victim by default. Yet, after the gruesome murder
by blood-letting, Gutierre remains unhappy and compromised. Perhaps the
murder of his wife made sense to him, because he regarded her as the origin of
the malady, or the tangible part of his honor that had been infected. Another
way of explaining his predicament might be to consider that he saves his honor

but loses his wife and his mind. In either case, he does not feel cured, is soon abandoned by his sense of honor, and then by the hypocritical King. Realizing now that his 'dis-ease' is terminal, the nobleman wishes for a quick death:

¡Hoy me he de desesperar,
cielo cruel, si no baja
un rayo de esas esferas
y en cenizas me desata! (III.766–69, 114)

[Today I shall despair, / you angry heavens / unless you loose on me a bolt of thunder / to strike me into ashes! (79)]

When Mencía's lifeless body is revealed on stage, the monarch is as shocked as everyone else and, moreover, embarrassed. Refusing to accept any responsibility for the bloody revenge, he attempts to make the problem disappear:

Cubrid ese horror que asombra,
ese prodigio que espanta,
espectáculo que admira,
símbolo de la disgracia. (III.828–31, 116)

[Now cover up this horror-striking sight / this prodigy of sorrow and affright, / this spectacle of wonder and despair, / this symbol of misfortune (80)]

Then, in practically the next breath, Pedro condemns Gutierre to further grief by ordering the nobleman to give his bloody hand in marriage to his jilted love, Leonor. This indecent haste to reconcile the former lovers is the King's way of facilitating a happy ending. If happiness is the restoration of honor to Gutierre and Leonor, then the royal intent is achieved: thus too, one of the tenets of Aristotelian comedy. However, Calderón is interested in the tragic dimensions of the reunion; the unvarnished resignation exhibited by the former lovers hardly betokens felicitous domesticity.

In *El pintor de su deshonra*, Juan Roca, has no such former loves in his life. In fact, we are at pains to locate any involvement with women before he marries Serafina. Like Gutierre, his honor becomes compromised through the dishonorable intervention of another. When Serafina is abducted, he rages helplessly about his brusque change in fortunes:

una desdicha, una rabia
una afrenta, una deshonra
tan grande, ¡ay de mí! tan rara,
que no me atrevo a decirla
hasta después de vengarla. (II.1001–06, 196)

[Who can fathom this misfortune, / this outrage, this treachery, this dishonor / so great that I dare not name it / until I am avenged!]

Since the spilling of blood is a sanctioned ritual in the restoration of honor, Roca pursues the couple and kills them both. Soufas, who sees Roca as little more than a man suffering from melancholy states that, "for Juan Roca this incident marks a serious change—from the innate melancholy condition to the unhealthy disease" (200). Calderón, however, presents the hero from a very human perspective. Although the painter has acted carelessly in thrusting his wife into the arms of a stranger in order to rescue victims of the fire, anyone can empathize with him, melancholic or not. We also share his outrage that another could perpetrate such a heinous act upon a gentleman, moreover, one involved in a humanitarian act at the time of the incident.

> ¡Valgame, Dios!, ¡que de cosas
> debe en el mundo de haber
> faciles de suceder
> y de creer dificultosas! (III.477–80, 214)

> [Oh, my stars! What a world / when dishonorable acts / transpire forth / with such facility!]

In this soliloquy, Roca is no longer the pompous aristocrat of the first two acts of the drama. He feels betrayed and searches in vain for an explanation, demanding a response from honor, prefaced with an oath: "¡Mal haya el primero amén / que hizo ley tan rigurosa!" (III.487–88, 214) [Cursed be the origin and commencement / of such an inflexible edict!]. Moreover, as in the case of Gutierre, the wife's death does not bring the anticipated satisfaction and relief, and the husband must take responsibility for an outcome to a situation that he unwittingly created.

> Un cuadro es
> que ha dibujado con sangre
> El pintor de su deshonra.
> Don Juan Roca soy. (III.1005–09, 230)

> [It is a picture / inked in blood by / the painter of his own dishonor / Don Juan Roca am I.]

Juan Roca, too, becomes the unwilling architect of his dishonor while trying to protect a fragile honor and sense of self.

Until now, we have seen the husbands only at moments of heightened emotions and vulnerability immediately before and after the demands of honor have been satisfied. In order to appreciate the two noblemen further as victims in their own right, an examination of their stories before the crises is useful. Stroud believes that "these husbands separate jealousy from reason inversely by demonstrating serenity to the rest of society while inwardly struggling with irrational emotions" (137). There are no details of Gutierre's love life before his engagement to Leonor. We do know that while visiting her one night, he bumps into an unidentified man leaving her home. This turns out to be Don Arias, who was in fact visiting another woman in the house. Gutierre does not have this information, so despite Leonor's explanations and entreaties, he terminates the engagement: "Fue bastante esta aprensión / a no casarme ..." (I.926–27, 50) [Nevertheless it was sufficient reason / Not to be married to her ... (26)]. But being virtually wedded to the dictates of the honor code, he requires a wife to complete the picture of the respectable gentleman of his day. So, already conditioned to the idea that woman is fickle, he marries Mencía.

Gutierre speaks of her in terms of an "... esposa / tan honesta, casta y firme" (III.71–72, 89) [... my wife is / constant, chaste and firm (59)], and "la mujer que yo he querido / más en mi vida ..." (III. 424–25, 103) [the wife I loved / above all other women in my life (69)]. Yet, he and Mencía seem to love each other only when they are apart. When he is jailed for fighting with Arias in the royal presence, she orders her servants:

... Que traigas luces,
y venid todas conmigo
a divertir pesadumbres
de la ausencia de Gutierre. (II.34–35, 54)

[... Bring lights / and let us distract ourselves / from the desolation / of Gutierre's absence.]

Meanwhile, he receives a brief reprieve from jail to assure his wife of his safety, and returns home only to bump into another unidentified man leaving their home. Mencía's attempt to cover up Enrique's brazen visit fails, because he has dropped his dagger while escaping. Frances Exum suggests that this incident perhaps makes Enrique "the instrument of divine punishment for Gutierre's earlier abandonment of Leonor, on the mere suspicion of inconstancy" (62). It should be remembered, however, that Gutierre's discarding of Leonor was the response unequivocally dictated by the honor code.

Soufas believes that "though initially unaware of Enrique's past interest in his wife, Gutierre ruminates and broods and eventually builds an imaginary case of dishonor against the two based on unprovable evidence" (191). Yet, his case is hardly imaginary, and the evidence, though circumstantial, is admissible. He is not psychotic when he notices a change in the tension between his wife and the Prince, as well as other changes in her behavior. Later comes the very tangible royal dagger left at the scene. Mencía's recognition of this evidence initially throws her into hysterics; still later, she writes an incomplete letter to Prince Enrique, begging him not to leave town on her account. These crucial bits of information strongly suggest to Gutierre a guilty verdict. He does not enjoy the advantages of total disclosure and witness available to the reader or audience. Gutierre (and later, Roca) can act only on what he sees, and knows.

Since honor requires neither research nor explanation, we wonder at his subsequent vacillation. Is Gutierre obsessive, vengeful, morbidly fascinated, or terrified of what the revelation would mean for his social standing? Is it possible that he truly loves Mencía, and attempts to delay committing the dreaded deed dictated by the honor code? Whatever the reason may be, only when he surprises Mencía in the act of composing the aforementioned letter does he finally determine to take action. The letter has confirmed his suspicions, and his jealousy spirals out of control, possibly yielding to imaginary scenarios about the Prince's accident at his door, multiple nocturnal royal visits to his house, his own inadequate lovemaking and Mencía's royal aspirations. So, Gutierre signs Mencía's death warrant on the reverse side of what he regards as the final piece of evidence of her guilt:

> El amor te adora, el honor te aborrece; y así el uno te mata y el otro te avisa. Dos horas tienes de vida; cristiana eres, salva el alma, que la vida es imposible. (III, 103)

> [*Though love adores you, honor must abhor you. Though honor slays you, love would give you warning and counsel. You have two more hours of life. You are a Christian: save your soul, since, now it is impossible to save your life.* (69–70)]

This obsession with the royal penetration of the nobleman's inner sanctum is also mirrored when the Prince's dagger becomes the instrument delivering the cure. Curiously, although Gutierre fancies himself the doctor of his honor, he cannot bring himself to perform the surgery. Instead, he hires the *sangrador* [blood-letter] Ludovico, whom J. Andrew Brown describes as "the only real medical practitioner in the play" (24). Unfortunately, as Ludovico becomes part of the revenge intrigue, he emerges as more hired assassin than blood-letter. Gutierre's parting words to his wife were "que la vida es imposible" (III, 103) [now it is impossible to save your life]. The irony, however, is that life is to become really *imposible* for him. In marrying Leonor after Mencía's death, he is condemned not only to reunite with a woman he had discarded, but also to suffer what Melveena McKendrick describes as "the eternal suspicions of the pathologically jealous" (141). For, to be a man of his time is to be permanently subject to jealousy.

The difficulty is that Gutierre trusts nobody, and has no real confidant or male friends. He cannot show himself to be in love with his wife, and expressing this love, or discussing his insecurities with other men, or worse,

Mencía herself, would destroy his concept of manhood. As Michaela Heigl explains, "passion, although condemned in either sex, was especially pernicious for men, because it incurred the risk of effeminacy" (335). In this light, his response to being dishonored is a vital, if extreme, example of masculine maintenance and affirmation. Cruickshank captures our sometimes-conflicted response to this complex character:

> Don Gutierre nos infunde terror, pero tenemos que ahondar en nuestros corazones para encontrar alguna compasión hacia él. Debemos recordar, sin embargo, que él es también una víctima: una víctima de lo que él mismo cree que la sociedad exige de un caballero. (39)

> [Don Gutierre is terrifying to us, and we have to reach deeply into our hearts to find any sympathy for him. Nevertheless, let us remember that he too is a victim: a victim of what he believes society demands of a gentleman.]

Juan Roca is equally trapped by societal expectations. His circumstances are not as complex as Gutierre's, and he is more impetuous, extroverted, and theatrical. A typical Renaissance scholar-artist, he has spent all of his life in the pursuit of art and literature. Frederick de Armas finds that "Juan Roca shares with Don Quijote an obsession with reading, which leads both characters deeper and deeper into a melancholic imbalance" (865). Nonetheless, his position may be simpler, or more complicated, than that. At the beginning of the play, he explains:

> … aunque siempre fui
> poco inclinado al amor,
> de mis deudos persuadido,
> de mis amigos forzado
> traté de tomar estado. (I.19–23, 121–22)

> [… Then, little / disposed to love, / I was by relatives and / friends finally persuaded / to enter the married state.]

His remarkable lack of enthusiasm for companionship apparently changed, however, when the question of an heir for his considerable fortune arose.

Roca's decision to wed may also have been inspired in a desire to silence wagging tongues about his sexuality. In his search for a wife, he hardly casts a wide net, deciding to marry his cousin. Even more telling is that it is the artist in him who falls in love with the portrait of Serafina; not the man with the woman. He does not see a female person, because she is an object to be admired, not touched. Perhaps, like Carrizales' child-bride Leonora, Serafina is destined to fulfill the combined roles of adopted child and heiress.[5] For, if he means to father an heir, how exactly is this is to be managed? First, there is his more advanced age, underscored in the *gracioso* Juanete's story about the couple picnicking on warm wine and cold chicken, inserting the chicken into the container of wine in order to "hacer que el vino enfríe el vino / o el vino al pollo caliente" (I.227–28, 129) [Making the wine heat the chicken, / while the chicken cools the wine.] The servant's obvious jibe at mismatched spouses generally, and Roca's impotence specifically, is lost on the gathering, and on Roca himself.

In the painting scene in Act II of *El pintor*, Roca's flaccid paintbrush proves unequal to the task of capturing his wife's perfect beauty:

> y así cuando su destreza
> forma una rara belleza
> de perfección singular,
> no es facil de retratar. (II.22–26, 161)

> [Thus when mere human artists / countenance an object / of divine perfection / replication thereof is impossible.]

Or, as de Armas puts it, when the *gracioso* tells the story about a deaf man who presumes that others are only mouthing words, "Juanete's purpose is to make Juan Roca realize that his artistic failure is not due to Serafina's ideal character but to Juan Roca's lack of knowledge about his wife" (866). We should probably not be surprised that pistols later replace paintbrushes. In his deepest recesses, Roca knows that he is no Don Juan, but he does try to live up to the rock-hard properties of his name. The three most important and compensatory acts in his life conform to those of the swashbuckling, macho hero that he is not: his very public marriage to an earthly angel; the daring rescue during the fire at sea; and the murders he commits at the end of the drama. These actions are also rooted in the honor code, but as we applaud his apparent generosity in abandoning Serafina to save others, we also recognize his passive-aggressive control of an erstwhile trophy wife.

Nor is Roca a very clever man. During the rescue at sea, he entrusts the unconscious body of his wife to a stranger, Don Álvaro, as it happens. The very fact that he could so easily disregard her when she is most vulnerable highlights our suspicion that there is no emotional connection between the couple. Thus, when Serafina, his most valuable piece of art is appropriated, he pursues and locates his wife and her abductor, secretly observing them through a grilled door. As a result of the "guilt" that Serafina feels, and knowing what her fate is likely to be, she awakens from a hallucination of her death. Álvaro rushes to comfort her, and in a state between dream and wakefulness, she seals her doom with the admission that his embrace was never more comforting. Roca then enters the room and shoots his wife and her former fiancé.

Like Gutierre, Roca does not have all of the information, but honor could not care less. And once the expiating deed is achieved, the painter collapses from anger and frustration. Again, inept royalty, in the person of the Prince, intervenes to pour the proverbial oil on troubled waters. His initial solution is to help Roca escape but when the parents of Álvaro and Serafina refuse to fault a man for defending his honor, Roca's resolve is to remove himself from their company. The Prince, determined to celebrate what he regards as a triumph of honor, swiftly announces Roca's marriage to Porcia, the Prince's own former fiancée. Like the King in *El médico,* the Prince hopes to extract (or exact) a happy ending from the tragedy. However, a happy ending was never Calderón's intention. If readers and audience leave *El médico* with the disturbing image of the groom's bloodied hands united with Leonor's, they leave *El pintor* with the perception that the Juan-Porcia union can only lead to further unhappiness, boredom, and even tragedy. While Roca is deadly silent, Porcia expresses her happiness, but Juanete, the *gracioso,* quickly underscores the dramatist's position: "Porque en boda y muerte acabe / EL PINTOR DE SU DESHONRA" (III.3137-28, 231) [And so, THE PAINTER OF DISHONOR / ends in blood and marriage].

Stroud has remarked, "There is no one truth, but many truths" (145). This assertion is a worthwhile caveat when considering questions of guilt, innocence and punishment in these dramas. If the husbands, Gutierre and Roca, seem to get away with murder, they live to regret not only their deeds, but also their ever having been born. The overt expression of agony comes only at the climax of the dramas when the foundations of their honor-constructed worlds collapse. At the end of the plays, Gutierre recognizes the tragic irony of his second marriage, and Roca, unable to bear even his own company, seems to be contemplating suicide. If we acknowledge that they have been bravely holding in the pain of being men, from the beginning of the drama, they deserve a measure of sympathy. This is in accordance with the final ingredient of the Neo-Aristotelian three-point recipe for the making of a tragic hero, as summarized by Irvine:

> He should make some mistake which contributes to his downfall, but if the mistake takes the form of a mortal error, it must be involuntary so that the spectator may sympathize with him in his subsequent misfortune and thus feel pity for him. (212)

Calderón was aware that the "many truths" formula was at the heart of the great tragedies, and he engineers our responses to complex characters and situations. The perhaps ambiguously named "poeta de honor"—he presents the honor code positively in such plays as *El alcalde de Zalamea* [*The Mayor of Zalamea*]—reveled in the dramatic possibilities and multiple perspectives occasioned by the honor theme. In so doing, Calderón displays the characters' humanity down to the bone, while engaging the audience's capacity for empathy and learning. For, at the end of these companion dramas, the "tragic flaw" is not so much the murderous potential of the husbands, or the fact that the women are trapped in untenable situations, as it is the unrealistic expectations of a rarified honor code. We can agree that wives and husbands both suffer, but perhaps the scars of the husbands are not as immediately obvious because, as men of their time, they suffered in silence, with limited options to do otherwise.

Notes

1. I too followed this trend for some time, even presenting the wives, Mencía (*El médico*) and Serafina (*El pintor*), as starring in a fairytale turned nightmare, with the husbands cast in the role of dark Princes. "Kiss the Girls and Make Them Die: The 'Grimm' Lives of Mencía and Serafina." AHCT Spanish Golden Age Theater Symposium, El Paso, TX, March 6–8, 2003. Unpublished.
2. Citations for both plays are from Ángel Valbuena Briones's edition.
3. All translated quotes from *El médico* are those of Roy Campbell.
4. In translating the quotes from *El pintor* I consulted Fitzgerald's translation, *The Painter of His Own Dishonor*. While Fitzgerald provides some brilliant equivalents, I found other verses infelicitous, with whole fragments of the play excised. The translations, here, are a hybrid of his choices and mine.
5. In Miguel de Cervantes's exemplary novel "El celoso extremeño" ["The Jealous Extremaduran"] the impotent octogenarian Carrizales marries teenager Leonora, intending to produce an heir.

Works Cited

Armas, Frederick A. de. "The Soundless Dance of the Passions: Boscán and Calderón's *El pintor de su deshonra*." *Modern Language Review* 87.4 (1992): 858–67. Print.

Brown, J. Andrew. "The Mark of the Doctor in Calderón's *El médico de su honra*." *A Society on Stage: Essays on Spanish Golden Age Drama*. Ed. Edward H. Friedman, H. J. Manzari, and Donald D. Miller. New Orleans: UP of the South, 1998. 21–29. Print.

Bryans, John. "System and Structure in Calderón's *El médico de su honra*." *Homenaje a Pedro Calderón de la Barca*. *Revista Canadiense de Estudios Hispánicos* 5.3 (1981): 271–91. Print.

Calderón de la Barca, Pedro. *El médico de su honra*. Ed. Don Cruickshank. Madrid: Castalia, 1987. Print.

———. *Dramas de honor, II: El médico de su honra y El pintor de su deshonra*. Ed. Ángel Valbuena Briones. Madrid: Espasa-Calpe, 1970. Print.

————. *The Painter of His Own Dishonor.* Trans. Edward Fitzgerald. *Eight Dramas of Calderón.* London: McMillan, 1921. 3–79. Print.

————. *The Surgeon of his Honor.* Trans. Roy Campbell. Westport: Greenwood P, 1978. Print.

Cervantes Saavedra, Miguel de. "El celoso extremeño." *Novelas ejemplares,* II. Ed. Harry Sieber. Madrid: Cátedra, 1986. 99–135. Print.

Cruickshank, Don. Introducción. *El médico de su honra.* Madrid: Castalia, 1987. 7–58. Print.

Dunn, P. N. "Honour and the Christian Background in Calderón." *Critical Essays on the Theatre of Calderón.* Ed. Bruce Wardropper. New York: New York UP, 1965. 24–60. Print.

Friedman, Edward H., H. J. Manzari, and Donald D. Miller, eds. *A Society on Stage: Essays on Spanish Golden Age Drama.* New Orleans: UP of the South, 1998. Print.

Heigl, Michaela J. "Erotic Paranoia and Wife Murder in Calderonian Drama." *Hispanic Review* 70.3 (2002): 333–53. Print.

Hesse, Everett*: New Perspectives on Comedia Criticism.* Potomac, MD: J. Porrúa Turanzas, 1980. Print.

McKendrick, Melveena**.** "Calderón and the Politics of Honour." *Bulletin of Hispanic Studies* 80 (1993): 135–46. Print.

Parker, A. A. "*El médico de su honra* as Tragedy." *Hispanófila especial* 2 (1975): 3–23. Print.

Soufas, Teresa Scott. "Calderón's Melancholy Wife-Murderers." *Hispanic Review* 52.2 (1984): 181–203. Print.

Stroud, Matthew D. *Fatal Union: A Pluralistic Approach to the Spanish Wife-Murder Comedias.* Lewisburg, PA: Bucknell UP; London: Associated UPs, 1990. Print.

Watson, A. Irvine. "*El pintor de su deshonra* and the Neo-Aristotelian Theory of Tragedy." *Critical Essays on the Theatre of Calderón.* Ed. Bruce Wardropper. New York: New York UP, 1965. 203–23. Print.

Wardropper, Bruce, ed. *Critical Essays on the Theatre of Calderón.* New York: New York UP, 1965. Print.

————. Preface. *Critical Essays on the Theatre of Calderón.* New York: New York UP, 1965. vii–xiii. Print.

El médico de su honra: *A Crisis of Interpretation*

WILLIAM R. BLUE
The Pennsylvania State University

Like a car wreck we can see coming right in front of us, *El médico de su honra* [*The Surgeon of His Honor*] both fascinates and repels. Despite our racing pulse, despite our desperation, we cannot turn away; we fight to hold back our shouts of "No!" or "Talk to each other!" or "You don't understand!" We sense doom from the start. A man is thrown from his horse and, injured or possibly near death, carried to a nearby house as his own brother, his flesh and blood, rides away leaving him behind. The play ends with a bloody murder, a forced marriage, and the threat of another murder to come. In between the portentous beginning and the ominous ending, there is scarcely a moment when we can relax and catch our breath. In addition, there is a royal family feud that also promises future violence as one half-brother will kill the other and provoke a change in dynasty in Spain.

Writing about this and other wife-murder plays, Matthew Stroud observes that these dramas "challenge the reader on a number of levels ... by offering some morally repugnant or intensely ambiguous scenarios and by wrapping the entire edifice in a thick layer of historical and mythological reference, dense and often impenetrable poetry, an epistemological haze that frequently prevents us from knowing exactly who to blame for the tragedy."[1] In this brief essay, I want to look again at the haze and think about how, in this play, it is created and what it does to the audience and to the characters. Creating haze is what good theater does; it invites us to watch the characters feel their way along trying to figure out where they are going and why, as we engage with their perceptions and trials and contrasting what we see with what they think they see and measuring how they respond to the situations they find themselves in. James A Knapp, writing about *The Winter's Tale*, avows that "[A]rt possesses the ability to stage the encounter with obscurity; and drama in particular emphasizes the double nature of that encounter: always (and forever) allowing the moment of confusion (or wonder) and the interpretive resolution to co-exist in an impossible recurrence ... art places us in an encounter with obscurity ..." (267).

Language, communication, its success and failure is front and center—along with the visual—in Calderón's play. There are, as Stroud signals, mythological and classical references: Erebus, Acteon, Diana, Lucretia, Portia; references to folktale or folklore: the heron and the falcon (II.85–115, 531), to the Bible, as in the grotesque re-enactment of the Passover scene; and of course to history with King Pedro and Enrique. In addition, polar oppositions undergird much of the play and emphasize how the characters see and configure their world, themselves, each other, and their circumstances: honor/dishonor, love/jealousy, truth/lie, prudent/imprudent, superior/inferior. Rather than clarity, often such apparent opposites lead to statements of confusion. A few examples jump out: "¡Vivo callando, pues callando muero!" (I.154, 504) [I live holding my tongue, since holding my tongue I die!], "... pues ¿soy para dama más / lo que para esposa menos?" (I.305–36, 509) [... Am I worth more as a mistress / but less as a wife?], "¿Quién vio triste la alegría? / ¿Quién vio alegre la tristeza?" (I.333–34, 509) [Who has seen happiness sadly? / Who has seen sadness happily?]. Into that category as well fall Coquín's (often bad) puns. Congratulating Enrique on his terrible fall, Coquín says this is really a day he should celebrate:

> ENRIQUE.   ... ¿Mi día?
> COQUÍN.   Es cosa sabida.
> ENRIQUE.   Su día llama uno aquel
>   que es a su gusto fiel;
>   si lo fue a la pena mía,
>   ¿cómo puede ser mi día?
> COQUÍN.   Cayendo, señor en él. (I.397–404, 511).
>   [E: ... My day? / C: Certainly. / E: One's day is / the day one likes / so if mine caused me pain, / how can it be my day? / C: By falling just now, Sir.]

Certain words repeat throughout the play and gain multiple meanings—*sangre* [blood] (23 times) being primary and running the gamut from literal blood to blood ties, to blood lines while acquiring secondary connotations of pedigree, temperament, guilt, innocence, sickness, and honor. The iteration of *morir* [to die] (14 times) and *muerte* [death] (30 times)—"... pienso / que no fue sino venganza / de mi muerte, pues es cierto / que muero, y que no hay milagros / que se examinen muriendo" (I.274–76, 506) [... I believe / that it was revenge / for my death because it is certain / that I am dying and that there is no point in telling miracles / when you're dying]—thickens the threatening atmosphere from first to last scene as does the constantly repeated *silencio* [silence] and *noche* [night]: "En el mudo silencio / de la noche, que adoro y reverencio" (II.841–42, 552) [in the mute silence / of night that I adore and revere].

Characters intentionally use double-edged language to talk through one character to another who is also there or to speak their private thoughts to themselves. Enrique's story about a friend who traitorously gave a woman he loved to another man, a story he tells standing right in front of Gutierre but speaking "metaphorically" to Mencía, is a case in point: "en cualquier parte que estoy, / estoy mirando mis celos, / tan presentes mis desvelos / están delante de mí / que aquí los miro" (I.397–401, 511) [No matter where I am / I'm always looking at my jealousy; / my troubles are so present to me / that I am seeing them right here]. Or we could point to Gutierre's extended metaphor on the west wind and the candle. After scaling the wall around his garden at night; after hearing Mencía mistake him for Enrique; after deciding, in effect, that he will visit vengeance on her, she hears a noise and tells "Enrique" to *once again* hide. She says to Jacinta that the wind blew out the candle as she slept and that she should bring more. Gutierre overhears and says to himself: "Yes, but lighted by my burning fire" (II.948–49, 555). To avoid discovery, he announces himself and enters asking Mencía what she has been doing. Enjoying the evening in the garden, she states, but "me dejó el aire a oscuras" (II.972, 556) [the breeze left me in the dark]. Gutierre picks up the phrase:

No me espanto, mi bien;
que el aire que mató la luz, tan frío
corre, que es un aliento
respirado del céfiro violento,
y que no solo advierte
muerte a las luces, a la vida muerte,
y pudieras dormida
a sus soplos perder también la vida. (II.973–80, 536)

[I am not surprised, my love; / the breeze that snuffed out that light, so coldly / blew because it was a breath / from fierce Zephyrus / and that not only announces / death for lights, but for lives too. / And even though asleep / you too could lose your life to gusts.]

On the surface, it was that cold wind that blew out the candle, but also that same wind could give people (you) a cold that could cause their death. But the wind as *aliento respirado* or words spoken or gossip could also cause her death. And moreover Gutierre says it's not just any wind but a *céfiro violento* [violent zephyr] which adds yet another level. Zephyrus, one of the four winds, God of the west wind, was a rival of Apollon for the love of Hyakinthos. When he saw the two of them playing with a discus in a meadow, in a jealous rage he struck the discus with a gust of wind, sending it off course and hitting Hyakinthos in the head, causing sudden death ("Zephyrus" 1). Apollon was another name for Apollo, and Zephyrus could never have attacked him (as Gutierre could never attack Enrique). It is no wonder then that Mencía responds, "… Entenderte pretendo, / y aunque más lo procuro, no te entiendo" (II.981–82, 556) [… I'm trying to understand you / but no matter how hard I try, I don't understand you].

Gutierre, in the course of the play, learns the value of double speak, the kind Enrique used in the first act to talk about his loss. In the middle of Act II, Gutierre lets Enrique know that he knows that the Prince came to his house at night and that if it were to happen again, Gutierre might not be able to make out who the man was in the dark and thus attack "mistakenly" the untouchable Prince:

> Tanto enojaros temiera
> el alma cuerda y prudente,
> que a miraros solamente
> tal vez no me atreviera;
> y si en ocasión me viera
> de probar vuestros aceros
> cuando yo sin conoceros
> a tal extremo llegara,
> que se muriera estimara
> la luz del sol por no veros. (II.545–54, 545)

[A wise and prudent soul / would fear angering you; / perhaps I shouldn't even dare / to look at you / but if perchance I were to see myself in a situation / where I would test your sword / without knowing it was yours / it would be better / for the sun to die / so that I shouldn't see you.]

Such language, intended to reveal and hide at the same time, helps create the haze.

There is an echoic quality to the speeches, scenes and events in the play that should give the audience a sense of knowing what to expect next and should also help characters navigate through the fog, but it doesn't always do so. The play begins, as noted, with a near death, with Enrique "tropezando … / en los brazos de la muerte" (I.30–31, 501) [stumbling … / into death's arms], and ends with a bloody tableau scene, that of Mencía's death. Before the play begins, Gutierre had discovered a man in Leonor's house and broke off his engagement. He discovers a man in his and Mencía's house and ends up having her killed. The King interviews Leonor about Gutierre, has her hide as he interviews Gutierre and the scene ends in drawn swords. Later, Pedro interviews Gutierre about Mencía and Enrique, has Gutierre hide as he interviews Enrique and the scene ends with the King wounded and Gutierre going off to kill his wife. Leonor loses her future husband and her honor; Gutierre abandons Leonor and marries Mencía, has her killed and then must marry Leonor. No one seems to learn from his or her experiences and the effect on the audience is to see the characters stumble toward tragedy.

But let me back up and look at what Gutierre does think he has learned from his experience with Leonor. First he went through all the appropriate steps—discovering her, approaching her, being rejected by her, persevering, spending evenings beneath her balcony, finally speaking to her and then proposing and being admitted to her house. Leonor too went from surprise to disdain to *obligada* [obligation] and "De obligada pasé a agradecida, / luego de agradecida a apasionada" (I.637–38, 518) [From beholden I grew to appreciative / and then from appreciative to passionate]. But only after he proposed did she allow him to enter her house, always however, "el honor fue reservado" (I.658, 518) [but my honor was always preserved]. Gutierre says he planned to marry her but after seeing a man in her house one night, he walked away despite her claims of innocence. She brought suit against him but "el más riguroso juez / no halló causa contra mí" (I.862–63, 525) [but the most rigorous judge / could not find cause against me]. It is only during the interview with Pedro that he discovers that Arias was the man in Leonor's house and that he was there not to see Leonor but to court another woman who was visiting her. Arias hid when Gutierre came in because Leonor asked him to, but fled when discovered. Now he challenges Gutierre, swords are drawn in the presence of the King; thus both are sent to jail.

When Gutierre finds himself in a similar situation—Mencía tells him she saw a man in their rooms—he rushes in, finds no one, but he does find a dagger. When Mencía reacts so inexplicably, so exaggeratedly upon seeing the dagger, Gutierre does not act precipitously; rather he decides to meditate on what he has seen. But first, he admits, he doesn't quite know what he has seen and wonders if he can figure it out. "¡Ay, Dios!" he exclaims, "¡quién supiera / reducir solo a un discurso, / medir con sola una idea / tantos géneros de agravios / tantos linajes de penas!" (II.566–70, 545) [Oh, God! Who could imagine / a way to reduce to one speech, / to measure with one thought / so many kinds of offenses, / so many lines of misery!]. He decides on a rational investigation. He notes all the evidence of Mencía's innocence: she opened the door when Gutierre arrived; she was calm; she told him she saw a man; yes, the candle went out but that could have been due to a gust of wind; he then states, yes, he found a dagger but it could belong to someone in his household; moreover, one of the maids could have let the man in. That's it, he concludes, "Mencía es quien es / y soy quien soy. / No hay quien pueda / borrar de tanto splendor / la hermosura y la pureza" (II.629–33, 547) [Mencía is who she is / and I am who I am. / No one can rub out the beauty / and purity of such brightness].

Unfortunately, he doesn't stop there. A dark cloud can smudge the sun, he finds, even block it out. Despite that gnawing doubt, or perhaps because of it, he will now observe like a physician taking a watchful waiting approach to the patient. Moreover, he will prescribe preventive medicines: "... finezas, / agrados, gustos, amores, / lisonjas ..." (II.658–60, 547) [... affection, / friendship, pleasure, love, / praise ...] to combat the possible infection brought about by "sentimientos, disgustos, / celos ..." (II.663–64, 547) [regrets, sorrows, / jealousies ..."]. Based on his past precipitous behavior, this time he will act cautiously; he will *apurar, saber, examinar* [investigate, learn, examine].

And all goes well until, that night when Mencía mistakes him for Enrique, at which point suspicion becomes full blown jealousy. In his interview with the King, when he asks Gutierre what he saw, Gutierre declares, "Nada: que hombres como yo / no ven; basta que imaginen, / que sospechen, que prevengan, / que recelen ..." (III.79–82, 560) [Nothing, because men like me / don't need to see; it's enough for them to imagine, / to suspect, to antici-pate, / to fear ...]. But he **has** seen and, like Othello with the handkerchief, believes he has "ocular proof." He has seen that the design on Enrique's sword matches that on the dagger. In addition, he has aural proof when Mencía addressed him as "... tu Alteza" (II.911, 554) [... Your Highness]. And he will find two more proofs, each feeding off the same suspicions.

After hearing Gutierre's complaints, the King listens to Enrique's defense during his cross-examination. But the statements quickly get out of control and, with Gutierre hidden and listening, Pedro tries desperately to shut Enrique up. But he cannot and Enrique insists, "Pues yo, señor, he de hablar; / en fin, doncella la quise. / ¿Quién, decid, agravió a quién? / ¿Yo a un vasallo ...? / que antes que fue su esposa / fue ..." (III.187–92, 563) [Well, Sire, I must speak. / In sum, I loved her when she was a maiden. / So, who has offended whom? / I offended a vassal ... ? / But before she was his wife, / she was ...] at which point Pedro shouts "callad, callad ..." (III.182, 563) [Enough! ...]. But the damage is done because Gutierre believes he knows what goes in the blank. And then he finds Mencía writing a letter to Enrique.

That's why the audience wants to shout "Stop, you don't really understand!" We agree with Coquín who, too late, rushes to the King and says Gutierre is about to do something terrible because "… Mal informado / por aparentes recelos, / llegó a tener viles celos" (III.690–92, 578) [… Ill informed / because based on apparent suspicions, / he became vilely jealous]. But Coquín has mistaken the effect for the cause. It was jealousy that produced the bad information. Jealousy is a crisis of interpretation, as Terry Eagleton has observed, it "rigs out the evidence against which it tests its hypothesis" (65). Gutierre, based on his prior experience with Leonor procedes cautiously this time but the die has been cast. The jealous trait already exists, as he tells Pedro, "hombres como yo no ven; / basta que imaginen" (III.78–79, 560) [men like me don't need to see / it's enough for them to imagine].

Matthew Stroud, and others, have stated that Gutierre suffers from an epistemological obsession, and argues that the wife-murder plays:

> … have at their core an epistemological question … Because deception is always a possibility, one must test the validity of presentations and judge the results of testing. Judgment is central to the correct perception of reality because it brings together all the components of the cognitive process: human *logos* decides whether to accept a presentation as true or false based on what the senses perceived and on the results of testing the validity of that presentation as compared to one's prior knowledge of reality. (*Fatal* 116–17)

The problem is that perception itself "is a text, requiring interpretation before it means anything at all. And since interpretation is both partial and interminable, seeing [or hearing] the 'facts' is more likely to complicate the issue than resolve it" (Eagleton 65–66). Here the problem is that jealousy predetermines the outcome of whatever Gutierre discovers. He "knows" that Leonor was guilty of bad faith; he "knows" that Mencía had been Enrique's lover; he "knows" she begged him to stay.

But that doesn't mean that Gutierre was hallucinating, for what do we know of Mencía's motives? She had indeed loved Enrique, "tuve amor" she says "y tengo honor" (I.573, 516) [I had love and I have honor]. And yet in front of her husband, she counsels Enrique to listen to the woman who left him, "oídla vos, que yo sé / que ella se disculpará" (I.423–44, 512) [listen to her, because I know / that she can explain what happened]. And when he does come to hear from her, she says, I didn't mean it the way you took it.

Gutierre hears what he hears; Mencía says what she says; Enrique hears what he hears; and the audience must contemplate through the haze the intentions and consequences of what the characters say, hear, and mean.

Indeterminacy will not suffice. In the King's final question and answer with Gutierre the latter posits a number of situations: if he finds a man in his home again?; if he finds a dagger behind his bed?; if he sees a man prowling around his house at night? The King responds: don't believe your suspicions; assume there are maids who can be bribed; complain to me; trust your wife. And, counters Gutierre, if I find her writing a letter asking the man to stay? The King replies, then "... Sangrarla" (III.882, 583) [... Bleed her].

Gutierre decides, the King decides, Arias decides, Enrique decides, Leonor decides ... and so do we even if the play doesn't. The play foregrounds what it means to make an interpretive choice, even if the haze doesn't let us see clearly. The characters interpret and finally so do we, but, hopefully, with the full understanding that our interpretation may well be flawed.

Upon reflection, it seems to me that Calderón and other Golden Age dramatists were quite precocious in their understanding of emotions, in this case jealousy. In an article in *Psychology Today* entitled "Jealousy: Love's Destroyer," Hara Estroff Marano makes the following observations based on a detailed study. Feelings of jealousy burn:

> with such intensity ... obliterating rational thought ... setting off behaviors that create a self-fulfilling prophecy ... [It is] the most destructive of passions ... As a complex emotion, it involves, at a minimum, such distressing feelings as fear, abandonment, loss, sorrow, anger, betrayal, envy, and humiliation ... Jealousy is not just the main motivation for spouse battering. Sexual jealousy is the leading cause of spousal murder worldwide ... When we are jealous, we are in fact in the grip of an identity crisis ... Jealousy lands with brutal force, lending itself far too readily to obsession and delusion. It makes you think the same thing over and over ... Emotions have an illusion of certainty, and jealousy makes you certain of your perception of the world.

And, finally, the study reaches the interesting conclusion that:

> Neuroimaging is only at the earliest stages of investigation of jealousy. In a 2006 study, reported in *Neuroimage*, Takahashi found some significant sex differences in the neural response to statements depicting sexual and emotional fidelity. In men, jealousy activates the amygdala and hypothalamus, regions rich in testosterone receptors and involved in sexual and aggressive behavior. In women, by contrast, especially in response to thoughts of emotional infidelity, activation was greater in the posterior superior temporal sulcus, a region implicated in detection of intention, deception, and trustworthiness as well as violation of social norms.

Calderón seems to have known all that, as did Shakespeare, Tirso, and others. Perhaps now, over three hundred years later, we are just catching up to them.

Note

1. "Wife-Murder Plays" ms. I would like to thank Prof. Stroud for letting me see this manuscript in advance of its publication.

Works Cited

Calderón de la Barca, Pedro. *El médico de su honra. Teatro del siglo de oro.* Ed. Bruce W. Wardropper. New York: Scribner's Sons, 1970. 497–609. Print.

Eagleton, Terry. *William Shakespeare.* Oxford: Basil Blackwell, 1986. Print.

Knapp, James A. "Visual and Ethical Truth in *The Winter's Tale.*" *Shakespeare Quarterly* 55.3 (2004): 253–78. Print.

Marano, Hara Estroff. "Jealousy: Love's Destroyer." *Psychology Today.* Web. 10 Nov. 2013. <www.psychologytoday.com/articles/200906/jealousy-loves-destroyer>.

Stroud, Matthew D. *Fatal Union: A Pluralistic Approach to the Spanish Wife-Murder Comedias.* Lewisburg, PA: Bucknell UP, 1990. Print.

———. "The Wife-Murder Plays." *A Companion to Early Modern Hispanic Theater.* Ed. Hilaire Kallendorf. Leiden, Neth., and Boston: Brill, 2014. 91–103. Print.

"Zephyrus: Greek God of the West Wind. Theoi Greek Mythology." Web. 10 Nov. 2013. <www.theol.com/Titan/Anemos/Zephyrus.html>.

Incest, Natural Law and Social Order *in* El castigo sin venganza

Manuel Delgado
Bucknell University

Everett Hesse has rightly argued that "Lope's *El castigo sin venganza* [*Punishment Without Revenge*] is a powerful drama about the perversion of love, not only in the sexual sense but also in the broader connotation of human relationships" (430). Although this "perversion of love" has been extensively studied by a number of critics, in the present study I intend to analyze this important component of the play under the rubric of the incest and the adultery motifs. I will also analyze their causes, circumstances and tragic results through the lenses of Medieval and Renaissance ideas on Natural Law and related concepts, such as the positive and divine laws, as well as the cardinal, intellectual and political virtues of prudence and justice.

After reading or viewing this tragedy, we can assume that one of the first responses of the reader-spectator is to judge what is right or wrong with the actions of the characters. Indeed, many of the actions of the characters are judged or condemned by the characters themselves. One of the most remarkable examples occurs when the disguised Duke of Ferrara and his servants wander around the streets of Ferrara at night in search of women who are willing to acquiesce to the Duke's sexual desires. Without realizing that the Duke is listening, the prostitute Cintia, one of the approached women, criticizes the wrongdoings and vices of the Duke, both on the personal level and in his role as head of the state of Ferrara. According to her, the Duke has spent his youth unworthily, with "... viciosa libertad" (I.100, 128) [... vicious freedom]. He has not married until that night "por vivir más a su gusto" (I.200, 138) [for living more to his liking], without caring for the injustice he has done to the people of Ferrara because he has not given them a legitimate heir. Indeed not only Cintia, but also Federico, Lucrecia and Batín are convinced that the Duke is a dissolute man. At the end of the play, the Duke himself admits that the incest and adultery carried out by Federico and Casandra are the result of his own past licentious lifestyle, "el vicioso proceder / de las mocedades mías / trajo el castigo ..." (III.2016–18, 252) [the vicious behavior / of my youth / brought me the punishment ...].

From the previous examples we can conclude that these characters, a cross-section of the society of Ferrara, have a clear idea of what is morally— and politically—right or wrong, not only with the actions of the Duke, but in everyday life. I would argue here that their moral judgments and condemnation of the Duke's behavior are based on a norm, on a rule or law that, according to them, should be obeyed by the Duke. I would also argue that this implied rule or norm is none other than Natural Law. Although there are many definitions of—and disagreements about—the term "Natural Law," because of the numerous schools of philosophy, history, theology and law, I believe that the most appropriate for understanding Lope's *El castigo sin venganza* is the one given by Thomas Aquinas and the Neo-Scholastics of the University of Salamanca. As *The Catholic Encyclopedia* points out in the case of Thomas Aquinas,

> Natural law is nothing else than the rational creature's participation in the eternal law. The eternal law is God's wisdom, inasmuch as it is the directive norm of all movement and action ... There is, then, a double reason for calling this law of conduct natural: first, because it is set up concretely in our very nature itself, and second, because it is manifested to us by the purely natural medium of reason. In both respects it is distinguished from the Divine positive law, which contains precepts not arising from the nature of things as God has constituted them by the creative act, but from the arbitrary will of God. We learn this law not through the unaided operation of reason, but through the light of supernatural revelation.

In my opinion, Aquinas' and the Neo- Scholastics' ideas on natural, positive, and divine laws are quintessential to the understanding of the actions of the Duke of Ferrara, not only as the father-figure of Federico or as the husband of Casandra, but as the head of the state of Ferrara. As I will try to demonstrate, in *El castigo sin venganza* natural and divine laws are transgressed, first by the actions of the Duke, and ultimately by the positive law he dictates in his act of "justice" (=punishment) against Federico and Casandra. As Richard A. McCabe has observed in the case of the English theater (5), I must emphasize that although incest—and adultery—can be a blatant infraction of Natural Law, in *El castigo sin venganza* however, it becomes a powerful symbol/ sign of domestic, social and political corruption. And, as Herbert Maisch has explained in his sociological and psychopathological study of incest (145), the incest and adultery involving Federico and Casandra must be considered as an effect or symptom of the moral disorder introduced by the Duke of Ferrara in his house and state, never as the first cause.

Having in mind Aquinas' definition, we can conclude with Larry Arnhart that ethics are rooted in biology. According to Arnhart, "Morality, at the deepest level, depends on gut feelings that some things are right and others are wrong. The precise content of these feelings depends on what human beings learn through social experience" (27). These "gut feelings," common sense or Natural Law that establish as an error that an old man marries a young woman is what impels Lucrecia to tell Casandra that it would have been better for her to marry Federico instead of the Duke. In this way, Lucrecia argues, the future grandson of the Duke, in other words, the would-be son of Federico and Casandra, could become one day the legitimate heir of the dukedom of Ferrara, a fact that would consequently secure and consolidate the state. In a similar way, Batín, who does not mention the good of the state, also believes that the young Federico, instead of his father, should marry "esta clavellina fresca, / esta naranja en azahar, / ... / esta Venus, Elena" (I.639–43, 160). [this fresh carnation, / this orange blossom, / ... / this Venus, this Helena] that, according to him, is the young Casandra.

As it is well known, the disparity of age between the old husband and his young wife was also treated by Cervantes in *El celoso extremeño* [*The Jealous Extremaduran*] and *El viejo celoso* [*The Jealous Old Man*], and by Calderón in *Las tres justicias en una* [*The Three Justices in One*]. Without a doubt, this disparity of age helps the audience to understand the injustice done to the young woman and condemn the old man. As Eduardo Urbina has explained with regard to Carrizales of *El celoso extremeño*, the Duke of Ferrara and the father of Casandra contravene the laws of nature when they impose an insane and forced marriage on her. To support his argument, Urbina quotes Américo Castro who, based on Leo the Hebrew's and Erasmus's philosophy, concluded that "Ni un solo momento olvida Cervantes ese dogma del amor libremente correspondido; sus mujeres están protegidas por los más violentos rayos de su pluma contra quienes se empeñan en forzarles la voluntad" (Castro 131) [Not even for a moment does Cervantes forget the dogma of love freely corresponded; his women are protected by his most violent attacks against those who insist on forcing their will].

If I have mentioned the cases of incest in the works of Cervantes and Calderón, it is because they can shed significant light on the unnatural marriage between the old Duke and the young Casandra, as well as on the tragic consequences of such marriage. The results of this marriage, which Casandra both foresees and fears on the way from Mantua to Ferrara, are clearly exposed in her complaint to Federico. According to Casandra, the only reason the Duke married her was that he felt obliged by his vassals to abide by the rules of Ferrara. After their marriage, the Duke has only spent one night with Casandra, who, on the other hand, accuses her imposed husband of breaking the vows of the "... matrimonio santo" (II.1367, 195) [... holy matrimony] and of having sexual encounters with "... mujercillas viles" (II.1368, 195) [... vile prostitutes]. In sum, Casandra concludes, the Duke has not only not changed his past moral behavior, but has also dishonored himself, his house and his illustrious and virtuous ancestors. The Duke is not only a tyrant for Casandra when he makes her a slave in his *palacio de Argel* (II.1383, 196) [Algiers palace] but has also demonstrated that he will not give a legitimate heir to the state of Ferrara because of his reprehensible sexual behavior.

One of the most pernicious results of the corruption of the Duke is the moral chaos of Ferrara and the way truth is treated in its Court. Not only the Duke disguises himself at night to carry out his sexual appetites, but also Federico, who has closely seen and experienced the *modus operandi* of his father. Federico recommends to Casandra that she pretend to be happy with the Duke, so they can keep hidden their love affair, "Pues vete, señora mía, / y pues tienes discreción, / finge gusto, pues es justo, / con el duque ..." (III.2770–73, 263) [Thus leave, my Lady, / and since you are discrete, / pretend that you are comfortable with the Duke, / because it is fair ...]. Amid his incestuous relation with Casandra Federico also decides to pretend that he loves Aurora and that he plans to marry her: "Quiero fingir desde agora / que sirvo y que quiero a Aurora" (III.2270–71, 241) [From now on, I want to pretend / that I serve and love Aurora].

Indeed, within the Court of Ferrara, disguising, pretending and lying usually occur, and many of the characters know that the others are lying to them or that they are pretending. Even Batín tells Federico at the beginning of the play to pretend, because, according to him, discrete and clever men pretend to be happy and confident in adverse circumstances:

> Señor, los hombres cuerdos y discretos
> Cuando se ven sujetos
> a males sin remedio
> poniendo a la paciencia de por miedo
> fingen contento, gusto y confianza. (I.313–17, 144)

> [Sir, discreet men, / when they see themselves subject / to harms with no solution / resort to patience / and pretend to be happy, to enjoy, and to be confident.]

But the wise and cunning servant Batín, who perfectly knows Federico's and Casandra's hearts, also describes the Duke as "santo fingido" [fake saint]

(III.2801, 265), a description that is closely related to the scene where Batín himself ironically tells the Duke that the latter can found a *Camaldula* after his return from a war in which he helped the Pope. As Pancracio Celdrán has explained, the term Camaldula was associated with simulation and hypocrisy at the end of the 16th century, and even Tirso de Molina used it with this connotation (50).

Well considered, the guile, lying and hypocrisy of the Duke correspond to Machiavelli's advice that a Prince should conduct himself as a fox. According to Machiavelli, the Prince should be a master of deception,

> But it is essential to know how to conceal how crafty one is, to know how to be a clever counterfeit and hypocrite. You will find people are so simple-minded and so preoccupied with immediate concerns, that if you set out to deceive them, you will always find plenty of them who will let themselves be deceived. Among the numerous recent cases one could mention, there is one of particular interest. Alexander VI had only one purpose, only one thought, which was to take people in, and he always found people who were willing victims. There never has been anyone who was more convincing when he swore an oath, nor has there been any-body who has ever formulated more eloquent oaths and has at the same time been quicker to break them. Nevertheless, he was able to find gulls one after another, whenever he wanted them, for he was a master of this particular skill. (54–55)

As we are seeing, the Duke of Ferrara uses this technique from the beginning to the end of the play. The Duke not only lies and deceives, but also violates Natural Law. As Maurizio Viroli has pointed out with regard to Machiavelli, the latter's political thinking is,

> …very distant from and even opposite to Natural Law doctrines … Niccolò Machiavelli never used the term "Natural Law" and never discussed the subject. His silence is quite eloquent, if we consider that the concept amply circulated in the political and intellectual context of his time.

In my opinion, the "justice" or cruel punishment applied by the Duke to the incest and adultery of Federico and Casandra can be better understood in light of Machiavelli's distancing and (intentional?) oblivion from Natural Law, and his insistence, on the contrary, on civil or positive laws as more appropriate for the reason of state. As we have seen, the Duke's actions have persistently contravened the principles of Natural Law, a fact that must serve as a frame of reference for the interpretation of his final act of justice as a positive law that is also opposed to such principles. Nonetheless, the fact that the Duke invokes Heaven or God to support his decision to kill Federico and Casandra has led some critics to believe that as a ruler of a positive law—the last and only positive law he delivers—he is abiding by the dictates of the supreme or divine laws and that he is a converted man,

Este ha de ser un castigo
vuestro no más, porque valga
para que perdone el cielo
el rigor por la templanza. (III.2842–45, 267–68)

[This punishment must be / only yours, / so Heaven forgives the rigor /
instead of the temperance.]

Geraldine Nichols, for example, has taken her belief in the sincere conversion
of the Duke to an extreme when she declares "that it is 'crucial' to accept at
face value the Duke's conversion in Act III and to reject the views of those
critics who have found the conversion unbelievable" (qtd. in Thompson
225). Although I respect the arguments of those critics who believe otherwise, I must insist on the mendacious and fallacious nature of the Duke's
arguments, whose true reasons are covered with the same disguise that his
nocturnal sexual encounters at the beginning of the play. After a close reading of this scene, I conclude that the first impulse that leads the Duke in his
determination to kill his son and wife is simply because his honor has been
offended. Indeed the ire that at first invades his heart makes him to want to
kill Federico, not only once but as many times as he would be able to bring
him up. In my view, instead of a desire for justice, the Duke's words reveal a
strong urge for vindictiveness.

Pero si me has ofendido,
¡oh, si el cielo me otorgara,
que, después que te matara,
de nuevo a hacerte volviera,
pues tantas muertes te diera,
cuantas veces te engendrara! (III.2526–31, 253)

[But if you have offended me, / oh, if only Heaven would grant me / that after I
killed you, / I could breed you again, / because I would kill you as many times /
as I was able to breed you!]

In my view, instead of a desire for justice this passage shows an irresistible urge
for vindictiveness. Consequently, I do not agree with Karl Vossler's interpretation that the Duke's action is a "punishment inflicted without vindictiveness, whose cruelty is lovingly and piously intended" (qtd. in Dixon, Parker
158). On the other hand, and in a theological sense, the Duke is taking the
name of God in vain. Before sending the adulterers to God's court, "En el
tribunal de Dios, / traidor, te dirán la causa" (III.2998–99, 275) [In God's
court, / oh traitor, you will be told the reason], the Duke creates his own
allegorical or imaginary court in which he is the victim, the witness and the
judge, a judge that in the legal terms arranged by the Duke has to deal with

"honra, sentencia y castigo" (III.2747, 262) [honor, sentencing, and punishment]. At the same time, and as a judge, a witness and a victim, the Duke establishes his own conditions on how to proceed: the trial, the sentence and the punishment have to be hidden from the people of Ferrara to safeguard the honor of the judge, the witness and the victim. To put it in Antonio Carreño's words, "El duque que sale enmascarado en el primer cuadro ... es el mismo que enmascara ante el espectador el final de la tragedia y sus propios hechos" (59) [The Duke who is disguised in the first scene ... is the same Duke that disguises the end of the tragedy and his own deeds before the audience].

This scene provides an excellent example of metatheater. Among the six traits given by Dixon to identify metatheater in a play, I believe that the sixth perfectly corresponds to the monologue represented by the Duke:

> Una sexta, más amplia y más sutil: el tema de la percepción ..., pues creamos y creemos en ficciones propias e intentamos imponerlas a nuestros vecinos ...; metafóricamente, hacemos papeles más o menos falsos, inventados por nosotros o por otros, que por fin tendremos que abandonar cuando se acabe nuestra representación en el teatro que es el mundo. (qtd. in Serés 87)

> [The sixth, broader and more subtle; the theme of perception ... because we create and believe in our own fictions and try to impose them on our neighbors ...; metaphorically, we perform more or less false roles, invented by ourselves, or by others, that finally we must abandon when our staging in the theater of this world is over.]

For my part, I must point out that in the metatheatrical, illusory court staged by the Duke, the presiding judge is not God, nor the love that a father should have for his own son, but honor. An honor that ironically presides the so called "court of reason" by the Duke, at the same time that delivers the death sentence verdict:

> Perdona, amor; no deshagas
> el derecho del castigo,
> cuando el honor, en la sala
> de la razón presidiendo,
> quiere sentenciar la causa. (III.2897–901, 270)

> [Forgive me, love, do not undo / the right to punishment, / when honor, / presiding in the court of reason, / wants to sentence the case.]

Critics who believe in the "pious" and good intentions of the Duke frequently forget that in this "court of reason," in this self-staged or self-referred allegory, the name of God and Heaven are replaced by the examples of pagans like Artaxerxes, Darius, Torquatus (Manlius) and Brutus (III.2892–94, 270), all of whom were known for killing their brothers and sons to keep their

position and power. As Brian Harding argues, "The killing of his son by Manlius Torquatus is later cited by Machiavelli as an example of how one person's
virtue can restore order and discipline in the people. Machiavellian *virtù*,
then, includes a judicious use of cruelty and force" (51). Indeed, Titus Manlius Torquatus's example, told by Titus Livius in his *History of Rome*, and the
use of this example by Machiavelli may have played an important role in this
scene of *El castigo sin venganza*. According to Livy's story, when Titus Manlius Torquatus ordered the death of his son Titus Manlius, all the soldiers:

> became motionless, more through fear than discipline, astounded by so cruel an
> order, each looking on the axe as if drawn against himself. Therefore when they
> stood in profound silence, suddenly, when the blood spouted from his severed
> neck, their minds recovering, as it were, from a state of stupefaction, then their
> voices arose together in free expressions of complaint; so that they spared neither
> lamentations nor execrations: and the body of the youth, being covered with his
> spoils, was burned on a pile erected outside the rampart, with all the military zeal
> with which any funeral could be celebrated: and Manlian orders were considered
> with horror, not only for the present, but of the most austere severity for future
> times. (512–13)

It is worth noting that these "Manlian orders," also known as "Manlian
discipline," may have come to Lope's mind when he wrote the final scenes
of *El castigo sin venganza*. As the *Bibliotheca Classica* says of these orders,
"From the rigour of Torcuatus, all edicts, and actions of severity and justice
have been called *Manliana edicta*" (495). We need to wonder if Lope had
in mind that "though Torquatus was honoured with a triumph,"—just like
the Duke of Ferrara was—"and commended by the senate for his services,
yet the Roman youth showed their disapprobation of the consul's severity"
(*Bibliotheca* 495). After all, one of the main issues of *El castigo sin venganza*
is the cruelty and the rigor employed by the Duke to punish his son and wife.
In my opinion, the Duke carries out this act of cruelty in cold blood at the
same time that he disguises his true motives, as, for example, when he tells
Federico that the veiled Casandra is a nobleman from Ferrara who has con-
spired against him, and when he tries to convince everybody in his palace that
Federico has killed Casandra because, according to the Duke, she told the
former that she was bearing a child who would be one day the heir of Ferrara.

With regard to the punishment inflicted on Federico and Casandra, I
must say that, strictly speaking, the Duke's action is not an act of justice,
because it is not accompanied by the virtue of prudence, a cardinal virtue
that according to Aristotle and Thomas Aquinas must guide all moral virtues,
among them, the virtue of justice. Taking into account Aquinas' ideas on
prudence and the vices that, according to him, oppose this virtue, the alleged

act of justice of the Duke is only an act or *prudentia carnis*, in other words, an act of cunning, deception and duplicity (*Summa Theologica* 2a2ae, 49). As it is well known, all of these vices were unanimously condemned in many political and literary works of 17th-century Spain.

To conclude, I would like to add that the justice (=punishment) carried out by the Duke of Ferrara also lacks the charity recommended by St. Thomas and Aristotle. This fact is obvious when in the illusory trial performed by the Duke, the latter puts aside love (=charity) in favor of his honor's impulses. In this way, when the Duke orders to kill Federico and Casandra he is perpetuating the moral and political chaos that he started with his sexual behavior, with his self-regarding and with his continuous deceiving.

Works Cited

Arnhart, Larry. "Thomistic Natural Law as Darwinian Natural Right." *Natural Law and Modern Moral Philosophy*. Ed. Ellen Frankel Paul, Fred D. Miller, Jr., and Jeffrey Paul. Vol. 18. Cambridge, UK: Press Syndicate of the U of Cambridge, 2001. 1–33. Print.

Aquinas, Thomas, Saint. *Summa Theologica*. New York: McGraw-Hill, 1964. Print.

Bibliotheca Classica: Or A Classical Manual: Being a Mythological, Historical, and Geographical Commentary on Pope's Homer and Dryden's Aeneid of Virgil. London: John Murray, 1833. Print.

Carreño, Antonio. Introduction. *El castigo sin venganza*. By Lope de Vega. Madrid: Cátedra, 2012. 15–93. Print.

Castro, Américo. *El pensamiento de Cervantes*. Barcelona-Madrid: Noguer, 1973. Print.

Catholic Encyclopedia, The. Web. 11 June 2014. <http://www.newadvent.org.cathen/09076a.htm>.

Celdrán Gomáriz, Pancracio. *Inventario general de insultos*. Madrid: Ediciones del Prado, 1995. Print.

Dixon, Victor, and Alexander A. Parker. "*El castigo sin venganza*: Two Lines, Two Interpretations." *Modern Language Notes* 85.2 (1970): 157–66. Print.

Harding, Brian. "Machiavelli's Politics and Critical Theory of Technology." *Argumentos de Razón Técnica* 12 (2009): 37–57. Print.

Hesse, Everett W. "The Perversion of Love in Lope de Vega's *El castigo sin venganza*." *Hispania* 60.3 (1977): 430–35. Print.

Livius, Titus. *The History of Rome*. Trans. Canon Roberts. Ed. Ernest Rhys. Vol. 2. London: J. M. Dent & Sons, Ltd., 1905. Web. 11 June 2014. <http://mcadmas.posc.mu.edu/txt/ah/livy/Livy08.html>.

Machiavelli, Nicolo. *The Prince*. Trans W. K. Marriott. Web. 11 June 2014. <http://www.gutenberg.org/files/1232/1232-h/1232-h.htm#link2HCH0017>.

Maisch, Herbert. *Incest*. Trans. Colin Bearne. New York: Stein and Day, 1972. Print.

McCabe, Richard. *Incest, Drama and Nature's Law: 1550–1700*. Cambridge, UK: Cambridge UP, 1993. Print.

Serés, Guillermo, "Consideraciones metateatrales en algunas comedias de Lope de Vega." *Revista sobre teatro aúreo* 5 (2011): 87–117. Print.

Urbina, Eduardo. "Incesto en *El celoso extremeño* de Cervantes y en *L'École de Femmes* de Molière." *Homenaje al profesor Antonio Vilanova*. Barcelona: Departamento de Filología Española, 1989. 709–21. Print.

Thompson, Currie K. "Unstable Irony in Lope de Vega's *El castigo sin venganza*." *Studies in Philology* 78.3 (1981): 224–40. Print.

Vega Carpio, Lope de. *El castigo sin venganza*. Ed. Antonio Carreño. Madrid: Cátedra, 2012. Print.

Viroli, Maurizio. "Machiavelli, Guicciardini and Reason of State." *Natural Law, Natural Rights, and American Constitutionalism: Critics of the Natural Law Tradition*. Web. 13 June 2014. <http://www.nlnrac.org/critics/machiavelli>.

Duelling (Dis)Honour in Mira de Amescua's La adúltera virtuosa

GWYN E. CAMPBELL
Washington and Lee University

The limited critical attention given to *La adúltera virtuosa* [*The Virtuous Adulteress*], penned in 1603,[1] I posit, largely dismisses Mira's *comedia* as the product of a yet-developing dramatist. The play's "uneven" (Castañeda 86) rhythm and the juxtaposition of scenes "torpemente imbricadas" (García Godoy, "Lógica" 238) [clumsily interwoven] in the Naples Court, surrounding countryside and at sea, are perhaps anticipated in Don Felipe's furious travels across much of Europe during the play's pre-text. The action, furthermore, centers on spectacular "duelos fictos" (Chauchadis 90) [sham duels] that merely precipitate a series of events without resolution for the protagonist at play's end (García Godoy, "Lógica" 248), although they provide a "colofón espectacular, muy del gusto barroco" (García Godoy, "Lógica" 248) [a spectacular climax, very much conforming to Baroque tastes] for the public. Certainly, a semblance of chaos might permeate any work that incorporates dual plots (revenge, adultery), meditated disguises and deceit, multifarious misunderstandings, a central love quadrangle together with a supposed love triangle, not to mention the leitmotif of the biblical Susanna, artfully split between two virtuous noblewomen. As Moir has well argued with respect to Mira's tumultuous dramatic intrigues in general, any "incoherence in action may also be an invitation to seek underlying coherence of theme" (83). The allegedly anarchic argument, I believe, encompasses a moralizing precept about honour itself. In this labyrinthine Babylon about chivalry, the Court, and corruption stands the feeble King—ever accompanied by his Court favourites—whose unbridled lust and clandestine plans for reprisal and revenge, even nefarious *desafíos* [rivalrous challenges], stand in stark counterpoint to the solemn rule of the *duelo* [formal duel].[2]

Set in the Kingdom of Naples, ostensibly in the late 15th century based on a conflation of historical references,³ the primary plot of *La adúltera virtuosa* centers on a typical dramatic recourse: vengeance. In the *comedia*'s pretext, the dually aggrieved Felipe, Count of Ampudia, is engaged to Doña Juana in a political marriage, albeit a love match, contrived to bring peace to rivaling Barcelona and Aragón. His absence, however, allows the wily Milanese nobleman, Francisco Esforcia, to bribe both Juana's father and the Count of Barcelona, so that his own son, Mauricio, might marry Doña Juana. When Felipe and his brother separately merge on Zaragoza, a Babylon-like Court (I.406, 32) of confusion and swarming courtiers, Mauricio's men fatally stab Carlos in the back. Felipe's chivalric mission from *La adúltera*'s outset then, is first to avenge his brother's tragic end through Mauricio's death, before (re)claiming Juana as his "... amada esposa" (I.488, 33) [... beloved wife].

To preserve his honour, the deceived *galán* requires a public duel in a list authorized by a monarch. Felipe has frenetically traversed France, Germany and the Duchy of Savoy, in search of this formal recognition. In the guise of a sailor aboard Marquis Astolfo's ship, he finally travels to Naples to plead his cause for a secure field of duel there. This central duel, postponed on several occasions for significant reason, on the one hand does maintain the dramatic tension of *La adúltera*, while, historically, it responds to two chivalric ideals: "el deseo de hacer alarde de su heroismo en la demostración de las armas y la *desconfianza frente a toda clase de justicia en que intervenga la justicia procesal*" (Chauchadis 80; emphasis added) [the wish to display heroism in the show of armed skill and *mistrust of any procedural justice*], be that justice even a monarch's ultimate proclamation.

The Count of Ampudia's revenge must, however, weave to the forefront as necessitated by the developments in the second plot line, with which *La adúltera* commences and which largely dominates the first act. In Naples, King Alonso, both married himself, as well as the *padrino* (I.12, 20) [sponsor] of the nuptials between Mauricio and Doña Juana, falls captive to the Aragonese noblewoman's beauty in what is now the central amorous axis of Juana and three *galanes*, that further intertwines the two plots. Captivated by Juana's beauty, Alonso not only recognizes his own dual person, he even goes so far as to declare his interest—"Pero soy rey y hombre soy / y enamorarme es posible" (I.72–73, 21) [But I am King and a man / and falling in love is possible]—to the awaiting bride and groom. Ironically, as Don Mauricio notes, he and his betrothed are the prisoners, awaiting the King's arrival in their palace to escort them to the church. Moreover, the very "primacy" of this secondary plot underscores the power of a capricious monarchy, already evidenced in his bold speech.

Too, the King's further delay in blessing the impending nuptials accents the play's strong undercurrent of the politics of the Court. Never present on stage without his two favourites, the anonymous *conde* and *barón* who act as secretaries, sounding boards and spies, Alonso instructs the Count to feign proffering him a letter from the Queen. The deception allows the King to send Juana and Mauricio ahead to the church while he airs his quickly mounting passion to his two minions. Alonso acknowledges that as a sovereign he is above mere love: "… que enamorarse un rey / es bajeza conocida" (I.147–48, 24) [… a King falling in love / is recognized as a base act]. The obsequious Baron bolsters a King's lecherous domain that knows "no shame" (I.146, 24). Alonso is, nonetheless, fearful even to confer with Juana's lady-in-waiting, Doña Inés, until the Count cynically retorts that no *dama* can resist a King in love and that women fall prey to gifts: "Eva tomó la manzana / porque supiese tomar" (I.179–80, 25) [Eve took the apple / because she knew how to take]. Alonso undertakes idle banter about Juana's favourite past times—the hunt[4]—with Inés, before he finally can attempt to bribe the lady-in-waiting with a suitably arranged marriage, if she will but take a message to her mistress. A loyal Inés violently rejects the King's offer, and the two noble lackeys must clearly be what Inés describes as "actor[es] de tan torpe hazaña" (I.253, 27) [actor(s) of such vile deeds] who can serve as *tercero* [the go-between] instead. Undaunted, the Baron advises the King to write to Juana, while the Count, who will be the messenger, furthers his misogynistic criticism: even if Juana becomes irate, "es pedir que otro le des, / que ésta entre las damas es / una lición muy usada" (I.676–8, 39–40) [she is asking you to write again; / among ladies this is / a well-known strategy]. Even Felipe, who has now learned from the largely uncomical *gracioso*, Frisón, that Juana has just wed Mauricio, disparages the woman he claims to love. Juana's father may well have insisted upon the marriage, but she possessed the free will to resist: "¡Malaya el hombre que en mujeres fía!" (I.570, 36) [Pity the man who trusts a woman!].

It is on a sinister note, despite a fleeting comical lexical misunderstanding, that the opening act moves to its conclusion. As Alonso commands the Count to send for a *camarero* [servant], the Baron announces that Juana is returning to the palace to pay her respects to the Queen. The smitten King, believing that the Baron has just announced Juana's arrival, nonchalantly rewards him with five fine mounts in exchange for the fortuitous information. Alonso sends the Baron out to greet Doña Juana and the Count puzzles out loud about why a nobleman should receive a servant. The King, of course, immediately realizes the mistake caused by his ardour. Furthermore, he makes clear to the Count his aversion to hearing the truth when it does not suit—"No todas las veces, Conde, / se ha de decir la verdad" (I.617–18. 37) [One should not speak the truth / all the time, Count]—such as the news that Juana and Mauricio will immediately leave for Milán. In order to placate his monarch, the Count suggests nothing less than cold-blooded murder. Like the Biblical David who "... hizo con Urías / lo mismo que Bersabé" (I.643–4, 38) [... did with Uriah / and Bathsheba], Alonso must permanently dispose of Mauricio if he hopes to enjoy Juana. Momentarily weighing up homicide, in addition to what he himself recognizes as adultery (I.641, 38), the King likens himself to the biblical David who rued his defeat at Guilboa as the divine sentence for his lustful conquering of Bathsheba. The Count advises him to cry after he has enjoyed his own heinous conquest. Alonso thus quickly rationalizes that the King must "live" metaphorically, while another must die in reality.

The arrival of Queen Catalina, clearly suspicious of the Count and Baron's influence over her husband, prevents further plotting between the monarch and his henchmen, although not before Alonso quickly invents the subterfuge that an Ottoman force assembles in Famagusta.[5] With this nefarious ruse in place, Alonso commands General Astolfo, who has arrived in the palace with Felipe, to strike down the Duke of Milan in battle. The Queen's pious mission stands in stark counterpoint. She has received a missive—to finish the roof of a local convent—which she shares with the King, who charges the Count with overseeing the charitable act. In response to the Duke and Duchess of Milan's request for an audience, Alonso commands, ineffectually, that Juana enter alone, further proof for the Queen of her husband's lust, as much as Catalina intuitively recognizes Juana's virtue. As the artful Baron contrives a pretext to give Alonso's love letter to Juana—a poor Spanish widow in Naples, he lies, seeks to serve the Duchess—he passes the missive to the Queen, to hand on to the Duchess. Queen Catalina implores Juana to agree to all that the note requests. As Juana reads the letter handed to her by the Queen, the Baron notes with surprise the pleasure on Juana's face. For his part, Alonso interprets Juana's reaction as her ready acquiescence to her husband's death. The King therefore anoints Mauricio "príncipe del mar ..." (I.860, 44) [Prince of the Sea ...] and orders his immediate sally with Astolfo. In the meantime, Felipe leaves the audience when he spots Mauricio, because he is unable to kill him on the spot. Astolfo does, however, secure the King's sanction of Felipe's duel once the victory against the supposed Ottoman invasion is secured.

Alone on stage after sending the Baron for her confessor, Queen Catalina pauses to re-read the humble request of the local nuns. We now understand Juana's apparent submission to Alonso's amorous demands: the Queen unwittingly handed the Duchess of Milan the request to complete the convent roof. Instead of that petition, Catalina is actually reading her husband's amorous letter to the Duchess. Incensed that her husband would disrepute an honest woman and deceive a noble husband, the Queen directs her ire at the now-returned Baron and absent Count. The letter she holds is proof of their sycophantic nature and their sins (I.984, 48). Under the penalty of death, the departing Queen orders the *barón* from the palace immediately. The Count returns in time to quickly allay the Baron's concerns with his observation that only the King rules in the palace. The Count's belief that Alonso is "... mi gallo" (I.1019, 49) [... my rooster] reverberates in Act I's closing line.

Act II opens aboard Astolfo's galley, as the General reads aloud the King's written decree to kill Mauricio for unspecified reasons of state. For Astolfo, whose reward will be title of Prince of the Sea upon Mauricio's demise, the secret royal edict is all the authority that Felipe needs to fulfill his single purpose. The Count of Ampudia, however, takes a higher moral ground. As much as he must avenge his brother's death, as much as it is the King's decree, he will not stray from his unwritten code of honour. For Felipe, the King's command takes on the unchivalrous taint of "venganza con afrenta / darle muerte con traición" (II.1054–55, 51) [vengeance with added insult / to kill him in a treacherous manner]. The Count, however, will dissimulate his duty. Unbeknownst to Astolfo, a masked Felipe calls the Duke aside that night, announces himself only as Mauricio's worst enemy, yet saves his life instead. After Felipe shows his foe the King's written edict, in a repartee tellingly dominated by the imagery of masks, Mauricio declares that he now understands the two faces of the King of Naples. Felipe advises the Duke to flee to Sicily or Milan with the promise that he will reunite him, there, with his wife. Felipe will further his own necessary deception with the bloodied body of Frisón, dressed in the Duke's finery, as all the proof that Astolfo might require.

As Mauricio's men run off in search of the assassin, angry that Astolfo does not search out the "traidores en palacio ..." (II.1392, 61) [traitors in the palace ...], back in the palace at Naples the King seeks out his Susanna in her quarters, confident that the Duchess is now a widow, although he makes certain to inquire after Mauricio. Anxious not to be in a defensive position, Juana initially refuses the King's command to take a seat. For Alonso the "[c]alor ..." (II.1438, 62) [heat ...] he mentions alludes to his desire, while an apparently innocent Juana initially requests a glass of water for him. Juana's ire is flamed when she finally understands his metonymical "... fuego" (II.1465, 63) [... fire] of desire. She adamantly declares she has received no written missive from Alonso, certain that the Count or Baron has deceived him, as much as the Duchess is loath to believe that a nobleman might commit such deception and treason. Juana's abrupt departure, in turn, angers the monarch, who is finally mollified by the Count's explanation of the lady's initial coyness. Evidently wary themselves of the constant voyeurism at Court, the Count and Baron are eager to leave the Duke's residence so as to avoid suspicion.

The Duchess of Milan has finally understood Inés's words of caution about Alonso. When she hears from her husband's aide of Mauricio's death—"que era por orden del Rey / esta tragedia y desgracia" (II.1586–87, 66) [this tragedy and disgrace / were on the orders of the King] as rumour has it—Juana primarily calls out to God to avenge her husband's murder, if God can so act against a monarch, as much as King Alonso best resembles a Roman tyrant. Carlos urges the Duchess to disguise herself and leave for her father-in-law's palace in Milan forthwith.

The news of the Duke's death and the deception about the Ottoman invasion has reached the Queen. Catalina summons the Count and Baron before her, aware that they—not the King, it is noted—have plied the Duchess with gifts and threats. Certain that her wish is her husband's command, the Queen exiles the pair from Naples under the penalty of death. The Count insists that any advice they offer the King is for his good and, moreover, that Alonso's will outweighs their counsel. As further proof of the King's ignominy, a braggadocian Frisón arrives and requests his reward for killing Mauricio by the King's command. Catalina now contemplates taking the Count and Baron into custody to await their execution. Aware that no solider dare seize them, nevertheless, the *privados* [Court favourites] grasp at proverbial straws with their hands on their swords. The calumniators declare their intention to inform the King of his wife's adultery.[6] Therein, these two "witnesses" transpose the Susanna motif to Queen Catalina, because it is a charge that Alonso overhears.[7]

The Queen demands that Alonso either punish the calumniators as monarch or avenge the affront as an aggrieved husband. The Count and Baron apologize for their defamation, certain that their humility will prevail, but Alonso orders them executed instead. As a result, under the imminent threat of death, the two noblemen opt to confess the "truth": "ella comete, señor, / adulterio con un hombre" (II.1769–70, 71) [she (the Queen) was committing, Sir, / adultery with a man], so they drew their weapons and cried, "Adulteress!," they tell the King. Alonso believes his advisors, implicitly reminded of God's punishment of King David. As Act II ends, King Alonso insists that the Count and Baron—who were prepared to kill the Queen for their own purposes—catch the Queen in the act. The Count's awareness of the best location to watch her suggests that he is no stranger to the role of spy.

Act III begins with royal servants carrying the murderer Frisón into the countryside, to execute him there in secrecy. The royal servants tell the peasants whose path they cross that it is at the command of "… su alteza …" (III.1853, 74) [… His/Her Highness …]; interestingly, these rustic characters wish to have the servants clarify whether the King or Queen gave the command. Saved by Duke Mauricio, who has been hiding out in the area, Frisón rues the central trait of "[l]os habladores …" (III.1916, 77) [gossips …] such as he: they lie. The scene immediately jumps to the palace, where the lying Count and Baron await the King so as to spy on the Queen. Accompanied by Felipe, who has been admitted to Alonso's inner circle as the elite French nobleman who took Mauricio's life, the King now laments his order to kill the Duke. Felipe's ironic observation reflects his actual actions: he would have spared the Duke's life, although letting it be known that Mauricio was dead, the Count of Ampudia tells the monarch.

As the group observes, a man enters followed by the Queen. Felipe wisely counsels the monarch not to rush to a hasty decision. But when Catalina and her "paramour" hug, the Queen also explains her sincere regret that the King's behavior forces them apart and gifts her companion with a ring. In an aside, the Count thanks God for putting the propitious earlier accusation against the Queen in his mouth. The "truth" evident, Felipe advises the distraught King to kill the Queen's lover in secret and to poison or strangle the adulteress the following day. Alonso heeds Felipe's advice, and the Count of Ampudia, charged with the lover's execution, seizes and carries off Queen Catalina's *galán*.

Alonso, however, sees no reason to postpone his wife's demise. He sends the gleeful Count to the Queen's private quarters, with a basket of items that allows her to choose the manner of her death: a dagger, poison, or a rope. An outraged Queen calls for the guard, the King, the Kingdom and the Universe, because she is innocent. Indignant, Catalina rejects a secret death, as the dominant chivalric honour code would demand, choosing instead to die, "… en fuego y por sentencia / cumpliendo el romano fuero" (III.2170–71, 84) [… burned at the stake by sentence / in accord with old Roman law], if found guilty. The Baron and Count voice no objection, since they will attest to her treason; the Queen will have but three hours to prove her innocence in the appointed list.

In the countryside, Felipe is at the point of executing the Queen's lover when he realizes that his prisoner is none other than his erstwhile beloved, Doña Juana, dressed in male attire to flee the Court. Felipe again combats conflicting interests: the King's death sentence on the "man" and his own desire to kill Juana, the woman who betrayed him. Perhaps accepting Juana's explanation that Felipe did not get to her side in time to prevent her marriage, the noble *galán* again will feign for a second time that he has carried out the death sentence commanded by the King. Felipe thus leaves Juana in the same woods where, as it happens, Mauricio hides out. When Mauricio learns from Juana's frantic servant that Felipe has just killed his wife, the two foes meet. Duke Mauricio challenges Felipe to a duel—the Count of Ampudia's general goal since the play's start.

Once again, Felipe's much anticipated vengeance is postponed: they are not on a royally sanctioned field of honour and, more importantly, a more pressing need has arisen. From the arriving Frisón, Felipe and Mauricio learn of the spectacular stockade that Alonso has arranged for his adulterous wife. Mauricio chooses to leave immediately in order to take up the innocent Queen's cause; Felipe's response is more cryptic: "... en venganzas no me meto" (III.2392, 91) [... I don't get involved in revenge].

At the Queen's trial, Alonso presides; Catalina's head is covered with a blanket, and her seat is held up high for all to see the accused adulteress. To the blare of trumpets, the Baron and the Count enter, declare her adultery and await, expecting no knight to come to her aid. Drums, however, announce the arrival of the Duke of Milan, still in disguise, who charges the *privados* with calumny and proclaims Queen Catalina's innocence. A similar musical score next heralds the entrance of Frisón, and a disguised Doña Juana and Felipe. The Count of Ampudia asks for a place on the list to do battle because, he states, the innocent Queen but embraced a woman on the night in question. Immediately, the Count and Baron recognize that their lies will not prevail. The disgraced Count and Baron declare their guilt and Alonso orders their immediate death by strangulation, their bodies then thrown onto the bonfire that awaited his Queen.

Only in the closing verses of *La adúltera* do we finally return to the central argument and closure of the primary plot. Felipe reveals his identity and requests a sanctioned field in which to duel Mauricio and avenge the death of his brother, although the stupefied King has long presumed the Duke to be dead. Mauricio accepts the challenge in order to satisfy the death of his wife, he believes, at Felipe's hands. Before the Duke and Felipe can face off, Mauricio learns from a repentant King that Juana died at his command, because he thought her a man. Mauricio relents, asks Felipe for his pardon, and gallantly offers up his life to satisfy the Count of Ampudia. The contrite King quickly resorts to favours again: his sister's hand in marriage to Mauricio, although the Duke declines, the late Count's holdings to the Duke, and the Baron's estate to the *infanta*[8] [royal daughter].

Far surpassing the King in generosity, Felipe pardons Duke Mauricio, finally reveals that Doña Juana is alive and present, and blesses Juana's (re)union with his former foe. While Juana's faithful servant is rewarded with Inés's hand in marriage, and a whining Frisón will receive 2000 ducats a year for his service, no further *tangible* reward awaits Felipe, who merely offers the play's closing lines. But this lack of monetary recompense stands, I believe, as the heart of the *dénouement* in its "stress on the importance of right conduct, *obrar* bien, through good and ill fortune alike" (M. Wilson 27). Although Felipe neither avenges his brother's death with Mauricio's blood nor reclaims his lady fair—an inept conclusion of the primary plot, some claim—I would argue that the resolution transcends to a higher plane. Throughout the play, Felipe's actions have, ultimately, responded to a true code of honour that defies *desafíos, duelos*, and arguably compromised chivalric comportment. It would seem, in *La adúltera virtuosa*'s resolution, that the extant code of conduct might, in fact, not be black and white at all. But more importantly, Mira de Amescua's heroic Don Felipe shows us that what it means to be truly honourable, indeed, is patently clear-cut.

Notes

1. Vern Williamsen's admirable chronology of Mira's works suggests a date of composition prior to 1604, based on the play's predominant *quintilla* [five-line stanza] and the absent *décima* [ten-line stanza]. More recently, García Godoy argues that the setting and certain lexical usages (e.g. *Adúltera* 18n1) suggest a date of composition that better coincides with Mira's six-year residency in Naples (1610–1616) while in the service of the Count of Lemos. Too, the thematic undercurrent of the vicissitudes of political favour more aligns this work with Mira's two later (1618–24) *comedias* about the *privado*, Álvaro de Luna. In point of fact, the title of *La adúltera*'s protagonist, *Conde de Ampudia* [Count of Ampudia], was created by Phillip III in the waning days of 1602 for his own Court favourite, the Duke of Lerma. Choosing to concur with Williamsen's study, 1603 must stand as the date of *La adúltera*, a forerunner in many ways, then, of Mira's later *privado* plays.
2. In his study of the treatises on duels in Early Modern Spain, Chauchadis notes that *desafío* tends to signify a "duelo privado o secreto" [private or secret duel], particularly in vogue after the 1480 prohibition against "los llamamientos por carteles" (79) [publically posted challenges]; *duelo* routinely signifies a more solemn and codified duel in "campo cerrado" [a secure sanctioned list]. These duels were banned in Spain in 1522, and were greatly restricted elsewhere by the Tridentine Council in 1563 (79). Calderón's *El postrer duelo de España* [*The Last Duel in Spain*] criticizes the extremes to which noblemen go to "conservar la honra que estiman por encima del amor, la amistad y la franqueza" (Chang-Rodríguez and Martin 451) [to preserve the honour they esteem above love, friendship and honesty].
3. In Mira's play, Juana de Aragón, the central *dama* of the first plot is both: the daughter of the Duke of Ribagorza, although the historical Juan de Aragón (1457–1527)

was but Count of said municipality and a Viceroy of Naples; and the daughter-in-law of Franciso Esforcia (I.348, 30), Duke of Milan (1401–1466). Two Alfonsos—Mira's once-named King is Alonso—ruled in Naples: Alfonso the Magnanimous (1442–1458) and Alfonso II (1494–1495), who abdicated in the face of the Angevin pretensions of Charles VIII.

4. Juana is likened to the virgin Goddess of the hunt, Diana. This is the first of the allusions to three notable women, who are the object of a lustful eye. The subsequently mentioned Bathsheba (2 Sam.) and the implicit motif of the virtuous Susanna (Sus.), accused of adultery by two lecherous Elders, complete this triad.

5. The Turkish port of Famagusta, used as a base for attacks along the Mediterranean coastline, did not fall to the Ottomans until 1571.

6. In his seminal study of wife-murder plays, Stroud articulates the "devastating effect of calumny" (42) in the *romance* [ballad] source texts of those plays, noting that in "Neo-Senecan drama [it combined the traditions of] a husband and *tyrant* who is too quick to believe the worst about his wife, a calmuniator, and actions predetermined by guilt" (44). *La adúltera*, of course, avoids the tragedy of uxoricide, thus the calumny further underscores the theme of corruption at Court. See Tyler for details on false accusations in Mira's plays.

7. Smith points out that "Susanna's condemnation by two Elders was in accord with the strictest precepts of Mosaic law, which required the testimony of *two or more* witnesses in order to condemn the accused to death (Deut.17:6; 20:15)" (6; emphasis added). This may well explain Mira's recourse to two *privados* in the play, to further underscore *La adúltera*'s intertextuality.

8. In this first reference to the royal child, Mira again reflects the trial of Susanna. Susanna's husband, Joachim, is absent during the proceedings. Only at the conclusion of the apocryphal books, as Levine notes, is the virtuous Jewess "reincorporat[ed ...] into her family [... but] because she has been treated like the suspected adulteress, her life will always be suspect" (187). It is hard to imagine, given the actions of Alonso and the splitting of Susanna in two, that any recrimination will follow Queen Catalina in *La adúltera*'s postscript.

Works Cited

Calderón de la Barca, Pedro. *El postrer duelo de España*. Ed. Guy Rossetti. London: Tamesis, 1977. Print.

Castañeda, James. *Mira de Amescua*. Boston: Twayne, 1977. Print.

Chang-Rodríguez, Raquel, and Eleanor J. Martin. "Amor y honor en una olvidada obra de Calderón: *El postrer duelo de España*." *Modern Language Notes* 95.2 (1980): 446–52. Print.

Chauchadis, Claudio. "Libro y leyes del duelo en el Siglo de Oro." *Criticón* 39 (1987): 77–113. Print.

García Godoy, (María Teresa) Mayte. Introduction. *La adúltera virtuosa*. By Antonio Mira de Amescua. *Antonio Mira de Amescua: Teatro Completo*. Ed. Agustín de la Granja. Vol. 1. Granada: U de Granada-Diputación de Granada, 2001. 1–17. Print.

———."La lógica de las apariencias: duelo ficto en *La adúltera virtuosa*." *Revista del Instituto de Lengua y Cultura Españolas* 1 (1991): 237–48. Print.

Levine, Amy-Jill. "'Hemmed in on Every Side': Jews and Women in the Book of Susanna." *Reading from this Place*. Vol. 1: *Social Locations and Biblical Interpretation in the United States*. Ed. Fernando F. Segovia and Mary Ann Tolbert. Minneapolis, MN: Fortress, 1995. 175–90. Print.

Mira de Amescua, Antonio de. *La adúltera virtuosa. Antonio Mira de Amescua: Teatro Completo*. Ed. Agustín de la Granja. Vol. 1. Granada: U de Granada-Diputación de Granada, 2001. 19–96. Print.

Smith, Kathryn A. "Inventing Marital Chastity: The Iconography of Susanna and the Elders in Early Christian Art." *Oxford Art Journal* 16.1 (1993): 3–24. Print.

Stroud, Matthew D. *Fatal Union: A Pluralistic Approach to the Spanish Wife-Murder Comedias*. London, Toronto: Associated UP; Lewisburg, PA: Bucknell UP, 1990. Print.

Tyler, Richard W. "La acusación falsa de la mujer en el teatro de Mira de Amescua." *Actas de la Asociación Internacional de Hispanistas* (1971). Ed. Maxime Chevalier, François Lopez, Joseph Perez, and Noël Salomon. Bordeaux: PU de Bordeaux, 1977. 853–57. Print.

Williamsen, Vern G. "The Versification of Antonio Mira de Amescua's *Comedias* and of Some *Comedias* Attributed to Him." *Studies in Honor of Ruth Lee Kennedy*. Ed. Vern G. Williamsen and A. F. Michael Atlee. Chapel Hill, NC: Estudios de Hispanófila 46 (1977). 151–67. Print.

Wilson, Edward M., and Duncan Moir. *A Literary History of Spain: The Golden Age of Drama, 1492–1700*. London & New York: Benn and Barnes & Noble, 1971. Print.

Wilson, Margaret. "*La próspera fortuna de don Álvaro de Luna*: An Outstanding Work by Mira de Amescua." *Bulletin of Hispanic Studies* 33 (1956): 25–36. Print.

Act Two

Reflections and Refractions: Cognitive Play(s) in the Mirror

Ovid, Gender, and the Potential for Tragedy in Don Gil de las calzas verdes

CHRISTOPHER WEIMER
Oklahoma State University, Stillwater

Ovid's *Metamorphoses* may well be the classical palimpsest most persistently visible to students of Early Modern Spanish theater. Not only are textual references to its myths a constant, the *comedia* as a genre would scarcely exist without a plethora of characters that conceal, reveal, discover, and recover their own true identities and those of others. The *Metamorphoses* likewise overflows with tales of identities lost and (re)gained, discarded and stolen, embraced and imposed; the categories which constitute identity repeatedly prove fluid and porous rather than fixed. Still more significantly, sexual desire serves as a frequent catalyst throughout Ovid's encyclopedic catalogue of changes. Sexuality and even gender are unstable and often exert a destabilizing force. Similarly, Matthew Stroud notes regarding Early Modern Spanish theater with its innumerable erotic intrigues and masquerades, "The *comedia* raises the fears of sexual fluidity, of transgression, of perversion, of women usurping the power of men, of the traps of sexual expectation, of desire out of control" (*Plot* 83).

Tirso de Molina's *Don Gil de las calzas verdes* [*Don Gil of the Green Breeches*] (1615) exemplifies these aspects of Ovid's poetics,[1] thanks to the many inventions and transformations of identity, including extravagant confusions of gender and its cultural norms, to which Tirso's characters resort in their struggles to achieve their amorous and monetary ends: by the play's end, no fewer than four of the characters, two men and two women, will have disguised themselves as the entirely imaginary Don Gil. Few of the playwright's heroines could be considered more Ovidian than the protagonist

Doña Juana, who remains memorable not only for her unrelenting determination and limitless ingenuity, but also for what Stroud has described as
her "enormous fluidity of identity and sexuality" (*Play* 167). Juana's onstage
gender oscillates between male and female: she makes her first entrance in
the play in masculine garb, posing as Don Gil in order to usurp that same
fabricated identity from her inconstant lover Martín, who adopted it when he
abandoned Juana at his father's insistence in order to court the wealthier Inés.
While impersonating Don Gil, Juana herself will ardently woo Inés as well as
the latter's cousin Clara, both of whom, attracted to "Gil's" remarked-upon
androgyny, will fall in love with the cross-dressed heroine. Juana will also create a new female alter ego, Elvira, to whom she will attribute her masculine
imposture. Throughout these complications, Tirso inserts into his characters'
dialogue specific classical references to figures associated in the *Metamorphoses*
with androgyny and gender instability. Using those allusions as touchstones,
this study will foreground some of *Don Gil*'s intertextualities with the *Metamorphoses* to examine how Tirso reinscribed specific episodes from that poem,
and for what possible effect.[2]

Tirso introduces the first such reference quite early in the action, before
even one hundred lines of the play have been recited. In this passage, Juana
recounts her fateful initial encounter with Martín in Valladolid: "… porque
junto a la Vitoria / un Adonis bello vi, / que a mil Venus daba amores, / y
a mil Martes celos mil" (I.73–76, 99) […for by the church of La Vitoria /
I saw a handsome Adonis / bewitching a thousand Venuses / and provoking a thousand jealousies in a thousand Mars].[3] Adonis, of course, served
countless Early Modern writers as a commonplace to denote men's beauty,
and Juana expands the allusion to the *Metamorphoses* by including Mars
and Venus in her hyperbolic account of Martín's alleged impact on unwary
passers-by both male and female.[4] It is important to note that the classical
tradition Juana invokes attributed the adolescent Adonis's beauty in large
part to the androgyny resulting from his youth. The Venus and Adonis story
(IV.110–16, X.519–739, 347–56)[5] offers an instance of what Jonathan Bate
terms "the girlish-boy motif" in the *Metamorphoses*: "Adonis is one of Ovid's
many beautiful young men on the threshold of sexual maturity" (60). In
17th-century Spain, Lope similarly referred to Adonis as a *mancebo* [youth]
in his poem "La rosa blanca" ["The White Rose"] (Cebrián 206), and Tirso
would later use the same noun in his "Fábula de Mirra, Adonis y Venus"
["Fable of Myrrha, Adonis and Venus"], included in *Deleitar aprovechando*
[*Edifying Amusements*] (33).[6] Adonis's immaturity of course proves fatal: he
imprudently ignores Venus's warning, then his strength and javelin fail him
against the boar he rashly provokes, demonstrating in the most brutal, final

way that "he is not ready for manhood" (Salzman-Mitchell 202). Throughout nearly all of *Don Gil*, Adonis's counterpart Martín's behavior remains
that of a self-centered, heedless adolescent. Halkhoree notes that he "has no
real understanding of the nature of love and its responsibilities," a deficiency
he shares with Ovid's Adonis, and goes so far as to call him "a pathetic,
passive, spineless and immature creature" for his acquiescence to his merce-
nary father's matrimonial schemes (46). Martín's evasive response to Don
Juan's challenge in Act II, offering a "string of casuistical arguments instead
of drawing his own sword" (Sullivan 91), further distances him from the
expectations of mature masculinity in that milieu. In sum, though Martín
might sport enough adolescent beard growth to justify the hyperbole-prone
Inés's petulant and disparaging comparisons of his chin to Juana-dressed-as-
Gil's hairless one (I.979, 134; II.1206, 143), Juana's Adonis, like Venus's
callow beloved, falls significantly short of manhood. Moreover, Martín comes
dangerously close to paying a price similar to Adonis's: facing execution for
his alleged murder of Juana as well as other characters' demands for revenge,
he himself concedes after Juana reveals herself and rescues him, "La muerte
tuve tragada" (III.3226, 216) [I was as good as dead].

Martín's youthful androgyny corresponds to and is foregrounded by the
crossed-dressed Juana's own, a gender instability which is further reinforced
by their Ovidian role reversal in Tirso's comedy: Martín spends most of *Don
Gil* pursued by the determined and frequently cross-dressed Juana, just as
Adonis is the object of an enamored Venus's fascination. The *comedia*'s parallel between the two youths thus immediately suggests a corresponding parallel
between the goddess and the mortal woman who respectively love them without sufficient reciprocation. Bate emphasizes the Ovidian narrative's place-
ment within Book X of the *Metamorphoses*, Orpheus's account of transgressive
passions which "teems with aggressive female wooers" (54); in this book of
the epic, Bate observes, sexual desire is especially often "bound up ... with a
dissolution of the conventional barriers of gender, for in these stories women
take the active role usually given to men and young men always look like
girls" (60). Though Adonis does not reject Venus's advances, the Olympian
deity is the one besotted with her paramour's beauty to the point of obsession. It is Venus who forsakes her own unique divine identity and customs—
"Transformed by love, she goes about dressed like Diana and hunts animals"
(Newman 252n2)—and it is Venus who tries to control Adonis by forbidding
him to pursue wild beasts. The interpolated narrative she recounts to explain
her fear of such creatures, that of Hippomenes and Atalanta's metamorphosis
into lions after failing to properly honor her, is an attempt to assert domi-
nance in the form of a veiled threat: "it's not really a tale warning against wild

animals, it is Venus saying 'don't rile me,' 'do as I say, I'm a powerful woman' …
She tells the story to demonstrate her power" (Bate 57).[7] Similarly, as in
many of Tirso's *comedias*, the protagonist of *Don Gil de las calzas verdes* is
its heroine, not its *galán* [young nobleman]. It is Juana who initially falls
in love with Martín's beauty and is led astray by her excessive passion; like
Venus, she is "vanquished by an inferior man" (Salzman-Mitchell 202), and
she likewise becomes a huntress. Unlike Venus, though, Juana succeeds in
imposing her will on her wayward lover. By dint of both ingenuity and luck,
she brings Martín to heel and effects at least some degree of maturation, as
demonstrated by his final public surrender to Juana and apology to her father
(III.3221–30, 216).

New Ovidian references occur in *Don Gil* when Inés praises Juana's
beauty in her guise as Elvira: "… mereces / por ti sola enamorar / a un
Adonis, a un Narciso, / y al sol que tus ojos viere" (II.1266–69, 146) [… you
yourself deserve / to capture the love of an Adonis, of a Narcissus, / and of
the sun which beholds your eyes]. Whether intentionally or not on Inés's
part, these classical models promise little happiness for Juana. We have already
seen that Venus will only permanently possess Adonis in death, when she
creates flowers from his spilt blood to memorialize him. Beguiling the sun, in
turn, meant one thing in the *Metamorphoses*: an encounter with Apollo, which
never boded well for the recipients, male or female, of the sun god's amorous
attentions. In this context, perhaps the most pertinent of these metamorphic
episodes, though it does not involve gender instability, is that of Leucothoe,
with a passion for whom Venus afflicted Apollo as revenge for his exposure
of her adultery with Mars. When Leucothoe's father learns that his daughter
failed to resist Apollo's ardor, he follows honor's relentless demands and buries
her alive; like Venus in the Adonis episode, Apollo does not return in time to
rescue her and can only transform her remains into a frankincense plant, creating an additional parallel with Adonis (III.190–96, IV.190–255, 116–19).
This murder recalls the lie that Juana instructs Quintana to tell Martín: that,
pregnant and helpless, she has left home to take refuge in a convent, "… y
que si sabe / mi padre de mi preñez, / malograré su vejez, / o me ha de dar
muerte grave" (II.1160–63, 141–42) [… and if / my father learns about my
pregnancy, / I will ruin his old age / or he will surely kill me]. Tirso's plucky
heroine invents an imaginary "Doña Juana *in absentia*" (Donahue 177), a
miserable alter ego who fears sharing Leucothoe's fate.

The inclusion of Narcissus—a third mortal doomed to horticultural
immortality—in Inés's triad of ambiguous compliments is perhaps most
intriguing. Inés's declaration that Juana-as-Elvira deserves to win the love
of an Adonis or a Narcissus links Martín, whose love Juana must regain if

she hopes to avoid ending her days in a real convent, to both mythological figures. Narcissus is another of Ovid's alluring young men (the text specifies that he is only sixteen), like Adonis more interested in hunting than love. His indifference to the passion his beauty ignites in others receives its reward when he famously encounters and is destroyed by his own reflection (III.148–69, III.339–510, 90–97). The same might be said somewhat more figuratively of Tirso's Martín, whose attempt to escape his obligation to Juana by adopting the identity of Don Gil is thwarted when Juana usurps that guise, seizing control of it to trap him. Martín-as-Gil unexpectedly confronts the machinations of Juana-as-Gil (not to mention the confusion caused by two other Giles before the end of the *comedia*), ultimately causing this false persona to disintegrate much as Narcissus dissipated into nothingness. Martín's pursuit of a financially advantageous marriage with Inés also recalls the common Medieval and Early Modern interpretation of Narcissus's fatal self-absorption: "the folly of trusting in riches, beauty, and the things of this world" (Kahn 353). Moreover, Juana's love for Martín and her appropriation of his imposture link her to the only one of Narcissus's admirers whom Ovid names: Echo. Though Echo is not the primary focus of Ovid's narrative, in the 16th and 17th centuries many poetic treatments of the myth made her their protagonist, focusing more on her unrequited love and transformation than on Narcissus himself (Vinge 196–206); Tirso's *comedia* adheres to this shift in emphasis. Juana, however, has no desire to share Echo's misfortunes in the *Metamorphoses*, which again recall Juana's invented but fearsomely plausible refuge within convent walls: after Narcissus flees from Echo's embrace, "scorned and spurned, she hides within the woods; / there she, among the trees, conceals her face, / her shame; since then she lives in lonely caves" (III.152, III.393–94, 93). Ovid's Echo, Barkan notes, is "trapped in imitation and reflection" (48), her attempts to woo Narcissus restricted by Juno's curse to repetitions of the boy's words. Juana's assumption of Martín's disguise and her preemptive courtship of his intended bride Inés are similarly mimetic, but Tirso gives her additional capacities not limited to imitation alone. Rather than simply following and echoing Martín, as Ovid's nymph is forced to do with Narcissus, Juana is able to ensnare Martín in webs of her own devising. Overcoming his resistance, she saves herself from Echo's hopeless corporeal dissolution into nothing more than "an empty voice with no self-agency" (Salzman-Mitchell 37)—a fate which might serve as a plausible analogue to the chaste confinement and repetitious, mechanistic prayer of convent life to which a dishonored Juana might have been condemned were she less resourceful and more bound by social conventions, particularly those which policed gender differences (Donahue 177).

Finally, Echo is not the only nymph in the *Metamorphoses* who lurks by a pastoral pool, burning for an unreceptive youth: Salmacis is likewise, but far less passively, enthralled with the beauty of Hermaphroditus, the son of Mercury and Venus. She ultimately dives into the water as he bathes naked there, clutches him in an unbreakable embrace, and begs the gods that they might never be separated. The boon is granted: their two bodies merge into one. Salmacis and Hermaphroditus become the first hermaphrodite, lending the latter's already androgynous name to their successors (III.198–204, IV.285–388, 120–24). The parallels between this tale and those of Echo and Narcissus and of Venus and Adonis have been noted for centuries. When adapting Ovid's account of the latter, to give the most prominent example, Shakespeare borrowed multiple elements from the other two myths for his "Venus and Adonis" poem: "Besides (1) the story of Venus and Adonis, he found (2) the story of Narcissus, and (3) the story of Salmacis and Hermaphroditus. The common denominator in all three is the irresistibly beautiful youth wooed by the over-ardent female" (Baldwin 84).[8] Tirso de Molina similarly recognized and utilized this cluster of Ovidian associations in *Don Gil* only two decades later; in addition to invoking Adonis and Narcissus, the text of *Don Gil* alludes to Hermaphroditus not once but twice. In both instances, Juana's uneasy servant Caramanchel speaks of his bewildering "amo hermafrodita" [hermaphrodite master] (I.724, 124; III.2707, 198).

Ovid's narrative relies upon and develops the gender ambiguities likewise inherent in the Venus and Adonis and the Echo and Narcissus episodes: "Hermaphroditus's very name, which Ovid properly etymologizes as coming from his parents Hermes and Aphrodite, suggests another confusion: he is both sexes in one. And Salmacis's relentless pursuit of him, in the face of his very maidenly shame, again makes mirror images of the sexual roles" (Barkan 57). Hermaphroditus is perhaps Ovid's most extreme example of boyish androgyny: at fifteen he is one year younger than Narcissus, with a divinely favored face prone to modest blushes and a slender body compared by the poet to white lilies and ivory (III.202, IV.352–55, 123). Like Juana when she first beheld Martín, Salmacis becomes entranced with the youth, only to have her own beauty, again like Juana's, prove insufficient to prevent her beloved's rejection. After having so often refused her naiad sisters' invitations to join them in Diana's chase, preferring more conventionally feminine pastimes, Salmacis responds to Hermaphroditus's rebuff by finally becoming a huntress herself. Feigning obedience to his demand that she depart, she lurks in the foliage near her pool and stalks the boy until the opportunity presents itself for her to capture him, much as Juana disguises herself as Don Gil to pursue Martín and enmesh him with her stratagems. If Venus, Echo, and Salmacis in the three Ovidian myths share with Juana the transgressive role of female pursuer, success in that pursuit is Salmacis's unique parallel with Tirso's heroine: death eternally separates Venus and Echo from Adonis and Narcissus, but Salmacis does achieve perpetual intimacy, albeit in an unsettling fashion, with her unwilling beloved. Like the trapped Martín, Hermaphroditus cannot elude the determined Salmacis's grasp once she springs forth from her concealment and seizes him: "'However hard / you try, you won't escape, you wayward one! / O Gods, do grant my plea: may no day dawn / that sunders him from me, or me from him'" (III.204, IV.370–72, 124). In the *comedia*'s final scene, the victorious Juana might well echo Salmacis's triumphant "I win—now he is mine!" (III.202, IV.356, 123).

Juana's realization of a permanent (re)union with Martín thus evokes Ovid's account of the corporeal fusion which created the hermaphrodite: "Her plea is heard; the Gods consent; they merge / the twining bodies; and the two become / one body with a single face and form" (III.204, IV.373–75, 124). Tirso's spectators with a Neoplatonic bent might also have recalled Plato's sundered hermaphrodites from the *Symposium* in this context, while the Judeo-Christian scriptural trope of man and wife becoming "one flesh" (Genesis 2:24; Mark 10:8; Ephesians 5:31) would have been most immediate for many audience members.[9] Indeed, this outcome in the *comedia* is foreshadowed by the erstwhile couple's respective disguises as the imaginary Don Gil. This constructed and contested figure, whose unmoored identity is assumed and fashioned at various points in the plot by two male and two female characters, is the *comedia*'s true hermaphrodite; significantly, Tirso's dialogue alludes to the Ovidian myth for the first time when the *gracioso* Caramanchel mistakes the cross-dressed Juana for a presumptuous pageboy and, as noted above, coins the epithet "amo hermafrodita" for the new employer he knows only as Don Gil (I.724, 124). Juana and Martín spend much of the play sharing this name as they struggle for control of it, in the process predictively blurring the lines between their individual identities. When Juana appropriates Martín's disguise as Don Gil, she figuratively "becomes" Martín by seizing control of and becoming Gil, evoking how Salmacis became one with Hermaphroditus. Prefiguring the marriage she seeks, Juana's imposture converges with Martín's to unite her with him in the invented person of the *comedia*'s title character, the hermaphroditic Don Gil.

Martín, it should be noted, ultimately surrenders to matrimonial metamorphosis far more willingly than does Hermaphroditus. The latter struggles against Salmacis's grip as she kisses and fondles him: "But he, / who does indeed descend from Atlas' line, / won't yield; what she desires he still denies" (III.204, IV.368–69, 124). His corporeal amalgamation with the mad nymph occurs violently and against his will, a wish possibly granted to her as revenge against his parents for the dalliance which produced him (Robinson 222–23), and immediately afterwards he prays to his parents that the waters of Salmacis's pool will similarly emasculate all other men who touch or enter them (III.204, IV.383–86, 204). His initial aversion to Salmacis deepens into hatred; he never loves her. The embattled Martín, however, ultimately regards Juana as his savior and thankfully accepts her hand in both the literal and figurative senses of the phrase, making public his prior promise of marriage: "… Confuso / te la beso, prenda cara, / y agradecido de ver / que cesaron por tu causa / todas mis persecuciones" (III.3221–25, 216) [I kiss your hand / in confusion, dear one, / grateful to see / that all my persecutions / ceased because of you]. "Manhood is what Hermaphroditus loses to Salmacis," Silberman observes of Ovid's narrative (646), but Martín's public act of commitment to Juana signals the beginning of his maturation from boy to man. The two women display a similar contrast. Though Salmacis does achieve her goal, it appears a hollow victory won at the cost of her very identity. As Robinson notes, Ovid "seems to present the result of the metamorphosis not as a seamless combination of Hermaphroditus and Salmacis … but rather as just Hermaphroditus alone, angry at the loss of his masculinity; Salmacis has been removed from the text" (220). Juana, on the other hand, is not rendered invisible, mute, or even submissive by her long-sought public betrothal to the contrite, relieved Martín. Instead she remains the play's dominant figure, engaging in exasperated comic banter with Caramanchel and joining the *gracioso* to announce the *comedia*'s title in its closing lines (III.3250–73, 217–18).

When considering Tirso's reinscriptions of Ovid's gender instabilities in *Don Gil*, what is perhaps most immediately striking is the comparative darkness of the episodes from the *Metamorphoses* which he chooses for his comedy; none of the three principal narratives (nor that of Leucothoe) can be said to end happily for the mismatched couples. The episodes are instead accounts of erotic passion's capacity for visiting havoc and destruction on both lover and beloved; the reversal of traditional gender roles in all three is, rather than celebratory, symptomatic of the chaos Ovid portrays. Tirso, of course, instead creates a happy ending for Juana and Martín, ultimately containing the transgressive forces of Ovidian disorder. To do so he reworks Ovid's narratives: the seduced and jilted Juana now has a justification beyond that of intense attraction for her pursuit of Martín during the *comedia*, while the latter's evasive tactics become more self-interested, hence less justifiable, even as much of the blame is conveniently shifted to his father's greed. As a result, Juana's desperate assumption of masculine agency need not doom her love for Martín to the frustration of Venus's, Echo's, and Salmacis's passions, while Martín likewise escapes the unenviable fates of his mythological counterparts. The potential for an outcome more similar to those inscribed by Ovid remains intrinsic to the *comedia*, however: "there seems to be only a thin line that separates comedy from tragedy; if Juana … had been unable to win back Martín, her life might well have ended tragically" (Hesse 144). It is this danger which propels and lends dramatic urgency to Tirso's gender-bending comic intrigues, a threat which the playwright repeatedly underscores with his Ovidian allusions and intertextualities.

Notes

1. See Weimer, "Tirso's Counter-Ovidian Self-Fashioning" for additional discussion of Ovid's importance in Fray Gabriel Téllez's literary career.
2. Beyond editors' footnotes, previous critical commentary on *Don Gil* has paid relatively little attention to its mythological references or, especially, to those references' literary contexts. Roux's essays are an exception, but her focus is the play's possible structural debts to ancient Greek ritual and religion. Minter's footnotes to his bilingual edition of *Don Gil* (1991) identify the presence of Aphrodite/Venus mythology in the play (248, 262–63, 273), though he does not develop the argument or locate those myths within specific classical texts.
3. All citations from *Don Gil* will refer by verse number to García Santo-Tomás's 2009 Cátedra edition. All translations are mine.
4. Close readers of the *Metamorphoses* might recall that Ovid does not explicitly attribute Adonis's death to Mars, but in Tirso's era this was already a common interpretation of the text. Natale Conti, for example, writes in his *Mythologies*, "Out of jealousy, Mars had Adonis gored to death by a boar, as Ovid says in Book 10" (226).
5. All citations from the *Metamorphoses* will refer to the Book, page, Volume and verses of Loeb's Latin *Ovid*, followed by the page number of Mandelbaum's translation.
6. See Weimer, "The Poetry of Metamorphosis and the Prose of Sainthood" on Tirso's reworking of Ovid in this poem.
7. Salzman-Mitchell offers a similar argument (202).
8. See Baldwin (1–93), Bate (48–65), and Kahn.
9. See Robinson (221–22) for more on this aspect of Ovid's narrative, including additional classical sources. See also Nugent and Salzman-Mitchell (32–35, 160–63). Bate (61–65), Greenblatt (66–93), Long, Restrepo-Gautier, and Silberman consider the significance of the hermaphrodite in Medieval and Early Modern texts.

Works Cited

Baldwin, T. W. *On the Literary Genetics of Shakespere's Poems and Sonnets.* Urbana: U of Illinois P, 1950. Print.
Barkan, Leonard. *The Gods Made Flesh: Metamorphosis and the Pursuit of Paganism.* New Haven, CT: Yale UP, 1986. Print.

Bate, Jonathan. *Shakespeare and Ovid*. Oxford: Clarendon, 1993. Print.

Cebrián, José. *El mito de Adonis en la poesía de la edad de oro (El* Adonis *de Juan de la Cueva en su contexto)*. Barcelona: Promociones y Publicaciones Universtarias, 1988. Print.

Conti, Natale. *Natale Conti's* Mythologies: *A Select Translation*. Ed. and trans. Anthony DiMatteo. New York: Garland, 1994. Print.

Donahue, Darcy. "The Androgynous Double and its Parodic Function in *Don Gil de las calzas verdes.*" *Tirso de Molina: Vida y obra*. Ed. Josep M. *Solà-Solé* and Luis Vázquez Fernández. Madrid: Revista *Estudios*, 1987. 175–82. Print.

Greenblatt, Stephen. *Shakespearean Negotiations*. Berkeley: U of California P, 1988. Print.

Halkorhee, P. R. K. *Social and Literary Satire in the Comedies of Tirso de Molina*. Ed. José M. Ruano de la Haza and Henry W. Sullivan. Ottawa: Dovehouse, 1989. Print.

Hesse, Everett W. *The Comedia and Points of View*. Potomac, MD: Scripta Humanistica, 1984. Print.

Kahn, Coppélia. "Self and Eros in *Venus and Adonis.*" *The Centennial Review* 20 (1976): 351–71. Print.

Long, Kathleen P. *Hermaphrodites in Early Modern Europe*. Aldershot, UK: Ashgate, 2006. Print.

Molina, Tirso de (Gabriel Téllez). *Deleitar aprovechando*. Ed. Pilar Palomo. Madrid: Turner, 1994. Print.

———. *Don Gil de las calzas verdes*. Ed. Enrique García Santo-Tomás. Madrid: Cátedra, 2009. Print.

———. *Don Gil of the Green Breeches*. Ed. and trans. Gordon Minter. Warminster, UK: Aris & Phillips, 1991. Print.

Nugent, Georgia. "This Sex Which Is Not One: De-Constructing Ovid's Hermaphrodite." *Differences* 2.1 (1990): 160–85. Print.

Ovid. *Ovid in Six Volumes*. Loeb Classical Library. Rev. G. P. Goold. 3rd ed. 6 vols. Cambridge, MA: Harvard UP, 1977–89. Print.

———. *The Metamorphoses of Ovid: A New Verse Translation by Alan Mandelbaum*. Trans. Alan Mandelbaum. San Diego: Harcourt Brace, 1993. Print.

Restrepo-Gautier, Pablo. "Ovid's 'Hermaphroditus' and Intersexuality in Early Modern Spain." *Ovid in the Age of Cervantes*. Ed. Frederick A. de Armas. Toronto: Toronto UP, 2010. 191–200. Print.

Robinson, M. "Salmacis and Hermaphroditus: When Two Become One: (Ovid, *Met.* 4.385–388)." *The Classical Quarterly* New Series 49.1 (1999): 212–23. Print.

Roux, Lucette-Élyane. "L'actualisation des rites antiques de déguisement intersexuel prénuptial dans *Don Gil de las calzas verdes*, de Tirso de Molina." *Thalie: mélanges interdisciplinaires sur la comédie*. Ed. Paulette Ghiron-Bistagne. *Cahiers du Groupe Interdisciplinaire du Théâtre Antique (GITA)* 5 (1989): 61–85. Print.

———. "Le *Don Gil* de Tirso de Molina ou le daimon des amour dionysiaques: une resurgence de la bacchanale dans le théâtre du Siècle d'Or." *Cahiers d'études romanes* 17 (1993): 139–77. Print.

Salzman-Mitchell, Patricia B. *A Web of Fantasies: Gaze, Image, and Gender in Ovid's Metamorphoses.* Columbus: Ohio State UP, 2005. Print.

Silberman, Lauren. "Mythographic Transformations of Ovid's Hermaphrodite." *The Sixteenth Century Journal* 19.1 (1988): 643–52. Print.

Stroud, Matthew D. *The Play in the Mirror: Lacanian Perspectives on Spanish Baroque Theater.* Lewisburg, PA: Bucknell UP, 1996. Print.

———. *Plot Twists and Critical Turns: Queer Approaches to Early Modern Spanish Theater.* Lewisburg, PA: Bucknell UP, 2007. Print.

Sullivan, Henry W. "Love, Matrimony and Desire in the Theatre of Tirso de Molina." *Bulletin of the Comediantes* 37.1 (1985): 83–99. Print.

Vinge, Louise. *The Narcissus Theme in Western European Literature up to the Early 19th Century.* Lund, Swed.: Gleerups, 1967. Print.

Weimer, Christopher B. "The Poetry of Metamorphosis and the Prose of Sainthood: Interpolated Verse Narrative in Tirso de Molina's *Deleitar aprovechando.*" *Calíope* 6.1–2 (2000): 167–78. Print.

———. "Tirso's Counter-Ovidian Self-Fashioning: *Deleitar aprovechando* and the Daughters of Minyas." *Ovid in the Age of Cervantes.* Ed. Frederick A. de Armas. Toronto: Toronto UP, 2010. 244–61. Print.

The *Queen's Dreams: Lope's* *Representation of Queen Isabel I* *in* El mejor mozo de España *and* El niño inocente de La Guardia

BARBARA F. WEISSBERGER
University of Minnesota, *Emerita*

Lope was clearly fascinated by the founding mother of the Spanish nation. In fourteen of his plays she is at least mentioned; in six of them she plays a major role.[1] Until recently, however, only *Fuenteovejuna* has received extensive critical attention. In this essay I deal with a very effective dramatic element in two of the lesser-studied plays, *El niño inocente de La Guardia* [*The Innocent Child of La Guardia*] (written between 1594 and 1597)[2] and *El mejor mozo de España* [*The Best Boy in Spain*] (1611). Early in Act I, Scene One in each play, Isabel falls asleep and dreams. The Queen's dreams materialize on stage, and in them a powerful allegorical or historical figure exhorts Isabel to unify and purify her kingdom by eliminating its religious and ethnic minorities. These staged dreams provide a window into the powerful ruler's unconscious, as imagined by Lope, and empower her to act.

Dreamers and visionaries were ubiquitous in Lope's Spain. So much so that priests were instructed to inquire about dreams in the confessional and to be able to discern which dreams were divinely inspired and which were inspired by the Devil. Richard Kagan estimates that in the 16th century there were some ten thousand oneiromancers in Spain, most of them women (37). A crescendo of visionary activity in Madrid occurred in the years 1587–1590, the years leading up to and following the defeat of the Armada. The best-documented case is that of the charismatic laywoman Lucrecia de León (b. 1567), who became something of a celebrity in Madrid. Just a few years before Lope wrote the first of the two plays I deal with in this essay, León dictated four hundred of her often prophetic dreams to two theologians (Kagan 37).[3] In 1590 her career was cut short when she was arrested by the Inquisition. Five years later she was sentenced to one hundred lashes and exile for life from Madrid for the blasphemous and heretical propositions contained in her dreams as well as statements injurious to the honor of King Philip II (Kagan 1). As Peter Holland observes, in Spain, "dreams become an important locus for the battle between the community and systems of authority to an extent unknown in say, England in the period" (140). In the specific literary case that interests me, dreams also became a locus for the transgression or negotiation of gender norms and roles at the highest level of society.

Only María Y. Caba has analyzed Isabel's dreams in any detail.[4] She maintains that they confirm Lope's traditional view of proper gender roles and behavior for women, namely, passivity and submission to husbands and other patriarchal authority figures. In the case of Isabel, whose crucial role in Spain's foundational narrative Lope extolled time and again, transgression of the rules of feminine behavior were required in order for her to defend her claim to the throne of Castile and to accomplish the religious unification of the kingdom by expelling the Jews and conquering Muslim Granada. For Caba, the role of the dreams in Lope's plays is to authorize those gender transgressions externally, relieving Isabel of responsibility for them and in the process reinforcing her passive femininity (e.g., 43). There are two related problems with this interpretation. First, it separates the dream from the dreamer instead of considering the dream as an important element in Lope's characterization of Isabel. Second, in treating the dream as external to Isabel, Caba elides Lope's obvious fascination with the Queen's interiority, what we post-Freudians would call her unconscious.

I propose that if we consider these dreams from the perspective of psychoanalytic theory, specifically feminist psychoanalytic theory, quite a different picture emerges. Psychoanalytic critics like L. O. Aranye Fradenburg, Steven Kruger, and Peter Brown have been instrumental in dismantling the notion that subjectivity and interiority are exclusive to modernity, identifying the exploration of subjectivity in Chaucer, Milton, and Shakespeare, among other Medieval and Early Modern writers. In particular, they have analyzed the space of the dream as "unquestionably that of an interiority that can only be called subjective" (Brown 3). For their part, feminist psychoanalytic critics of the Early Modern period have used revisions of Freudian and Lacanian theories of desire and gender to present literary dreams as "alternative realities" (McCluskie 149). As Teresa De Lauretis states, "it is important to understand the unconscious as a point of resistance and to take into account its specific ability to exceed the mechanisms of social determination" (125). That this applies to gender roles for women, and paradigmatically for Queens ruling in their own right, like Isabel of Castile is clear.

Looked at from this perspective, Isabel's dreams give her access to a space of resistance to the domestication and subjection that Caba and other critics believe Lope seeks to impose.[5] Although in the case of *Mejor mozo*, the resistance is foreclosed by the weight of patriarchal authority almost as soon as Isabel awakens; in *Niño inocente* the dream empowers Isabel to prevail over both Fernando and the Inquisition. In undertaking an analysis of Isabel's unconscious, my indebtedness to Matthew Stroud should be clear. His use of psychoanalytic theory in *The Play in the Mirror: Lacanian Perspectives on Spanish Baroque Theater* was groundbreaking. His more recent book, *Plot Twists and Critical Turns: Queer Approaches to Early Modern Spanish Theater*, accomplishes something equally significant with queer theory. In that book's brilliant analysis of sexuality in Vélez de Guevara's *La serrana de la Vera* [*The Mountain Woman of La Vera*] (Chapter Six), Isabel appears briefly, but strikingly, as the object of the protagonist Gila's desire: "Ha muchos días que estoy / enamorada ..." (qtd. in *Plot Twists* 134) [For many days I have been / in love ...]. More surprisingly, Isabel reciprocates the *serrana*'s lesbian desire: "... Enamora / verla tan valiente y bella" (qtd. in *Plot Twists* 134) [... It makes me fall in love / seeing her so brave and beautiful]. Although love in the two plays I will deal with here is strictly heterosexual, I hope to show that Isabel's dreams in those works are also queer, to the extent that they empower her to resist the traditional marriage plot.

A brief summary of the plays is in order before proceeding. *El mejor mozo de España* deals with events leading up to then Princess Isabel's marriage to Fernando in 1469. Various obstacles face Isabel, primarily the desire of her half-brother King Enrique IV to control her circulation in the European royal marriage market so as to turn it to his own political advantage. The play represents Isabel as a beleaguered but strong-willed adolescent who, after the unexpected death of her brother Alfonso, becomes the contested heir to the Castilian throne, opposing the claims of Enrique's daughter Juana de Castilla, presumed by some to be illegitimate. The process of selecting a suitable husband is protracted and largely carried out behind Enrique's back. Isabel and her advisers consider and reject several suitors, finally deciding on Fernando, heir to the throne of Aragon. The latter travels to Castile disguised as a *mozo* or stable hand to meet his future bride.

El niño inocente de La Guardia, although written over a decade earlier, deals with a later moment in Isabel's life. It is set in 1479, ten years after her marriage, and five years after she has secured her crown by winning the civil war against her rival Juana. It is also the year after she and Fernando obtained the Papal Bull establishing the Inquisition in Spain. *Niño inocente* portrays a monarch at the peak of her power. The main focus of the play is the presumed child martyr known as El Santo Niño de La Guardia. He is the protagonist in Spain's most elaborate version of the anti-Semitic ritual murder and blood libel myths that circulated throughout Europe in the Middle Ages and beyond. The heinous crime Lope dramatizes allegedly took place around 1489. A group of Jews and *conversos* [Jews converted to Christianity] were said to have abducted a Christian boy from Toledo and proceeded to torture and crucify him in imitation of Christ's Passion. The ultimate goal of the mock-deicide was to use the child's heart in a magic potion that would destroy the Inquisition and Christendom in general. After their arrest and long interrogation by the Inquisition, eight of the accused were burned at the stake in 1491, only a few months before Isabel and Fernando signed the edict expelling Spain's non-converted Jews. Modern historians agree that the fabricated case was highly influential in their decision to take such a drastic step (Kamen 68).

The opening lines of *El mejor mozo de España* seem to support the notion that the character of Isabel is stereotypically feminine. The Princess asks her lady-in-waiting for her distaff and spindle in order to continue spinning threads for a cloth she is fashioning for the Holy Sepulcher in Jerusalem. Interestingly, the other characters on stage, her lady-in-waiting Juana and the page Rodrigo, express surprise at her domestic activity, but the Princess insists on its rightness: "Tres cosas parecen bien: / el religioso rezando, / el gallardo caballero / ejercitando el acero, / y la dama honesta hilando" (I.36–40, 4) [Three actions appear good and true; / The first, a pious monk at prayer; / the second is a gallant knight / with sword in hand, ready to fight; / and women spinning clothes to wear.][6] In this clear reference to the traditional orders of Medieval society—the *oratores*, *bellatores*, and *laboratores* [those who pray, those who fight, those who labor]—Isabel humbly substitutes herself for the latter, underscoring the value of domestic labor and chastity in women.

The page Rodrigo objects to her self-characterization, comparing her with one of the three Parcae, or Fates, specifically the one who "… antiguamente / con una rueca pintaban." (I.41–42, 4) [The ancients used to depict / holding a distaff and a skein]. That is to say, he conflates the Princess with the powerful Clotho, who spun the thread of life, later to be measured off by Lachesis and finally cut by Atropos. Rodrigo states that, like her mythological counterpart Clotho, Isabel with her distaff: "podéis hilar las vidas / que tenéis suspensas" (I.47–48, 4) [can spin to your design / the lives that come under your spell]. The page goes on to sing for his Queen the famous ballad of the last Visigothic King Rodrigo, whose rape of La Cava, legend had it, led to the 711 invasion of Hispania by the North African Muslims. At this point, Isabel's servants—along with the audience, of course—know more about Isabel's destiny than she herself does: in what is considered the major accomplishment of her reign she will defeat the Muslims of Granada in 1492, symbolically undoing the damage done by Rodrigo.

Listening to the *romance* of Rodrigo, Isabel falls into a fitful sleep. She calls out that because of Rodrigo "quedó el español valor / al africano postrado" (I.99–100, 8) [our Spanish valor came / to lie beneath the conqueror], but simultaneously disavows any responsibility for righting his wrong: "Yo soy mujer; no me toca / la Guerra ..." (I.105–06, 8) [I'm a woman. It's not for me / to go to war ...]. Immediately following this re-affirmation of her femininity comes the stage direction announcing the materialization of her dream: "Tocan cajas y descubren a España vestida de luto en el suelo, y un Moro por un lado a caballo, y un Hebreo por el otro teniéndola entre los pies" (8) [A drum roll is heard. Spain is revealed dressed in mourning clothes, lying on the ground, with a Moor on horseback on one side and a Jew on the other, holding her between their feet]. The allegorical female España solemnly addresses Isabel: "Si a lástima te provoca / el ver mi luto y tristeza / ... / trueca la rueca en espada; / que no eres de las mujeres que han de hilar, mas pelear" (I.108–18, 8–9) [If you feel pity when you see / my sadness and mourning dress / ... / it's time to trade your distaff for a sword. / You're not the sort of woman who sits and spins. You must rise and fight]. Providence has reserved this task for her alone: "... Y quien librar / puede mi cuello, tú eres, / del moro y del fiero hebreo / ... / que guarda el cielo esta hazaña / a tu valor y deseo" (I.119–24, 10) [... And the one / to free me will be you. / You're the one to expel / the Muslims and the Jews from Spain; / for the Heavens have made it plain / that this task is yours, Isabel].

The vision disappears and Isabel awakens. After a moment of doubt she acknowledges that freeing Spain from oppression "sueños son de mi deseo" (I.43, 10) [My dreams reflect my hopes, I'm sure]. Doing her own dreamwork, Isabel here confirms Freud's dictum that all dreams, including those that cause anxiety, are "a disguised fulfillment of a suppressed or repressed wish" (ctd. in Wright 17). The dream also displays the two basic operations of Freudian dream analysis: displacement and condensation (Wright 19). The page Rodrigo earlier sang of his defeated historical namesake riding horseback across the fields pursued by the Moorish King Muza. Within the dream itself the female España is being trampled by a Moor on horseback as well as by a Jew. Similarly, when España orders Isabel to exchange her distaff for a sword, so as to free España from her enemies, she condenses the *rueca* of the play's opening lines and the previously-mentioned *espada* of the gallant knight invoked by the Princess. The displacement of the feminine distaff by the masculine sword is repeated when the Marquis of Villena enters to announce that Alfonso, Isabel's brother and heir to the Castilian throne, has died, making Isabel the crown Princess. His words reinforce España's earlier call to virile action: "Dejad, Isabel, de hilar; / dejad la rueca, señora, / que ya es menester la espada" (I.73–74, 12) [Let what you've spun 'til now suffice. / Lady, put your spindle aside. / It's time now to take up the sword].

But if the oneiric España revealed the Princess's unconscious desire to defeat her enemies herself, Villena and her other male advisers almost immediately thwart that desire. The Marquis concludes his speech by insisting that she must give her supporters permission to find her a husband. Even the Biblical judge Deborah, another nobleman reminds her, eventually had to enlist the help of the warrior Barak. When Isabel resists letting go of the sword prophetically assigned her, he warns her that if she does not find a husband to defend her rights, Enrique might deprive her of the crown that is legitimately hers, giving it to his daughter Juana instead. Isabel insists that she will not let that happen. From the skeins she has spun that year she will make ropes "… para atar / las manos a los traidores, / que a legítimos señores / pretenden desheredar" (I.253–56, 16) [… to tie the hands / of all those traitors who defy / the force of law and would deny / the true inheritors of their land].

This complicated condensation/displacement of the distaff/sword culminates in a startling image. Not content with using her rope to tie the traitors' hands, she warns that "… de las manos atadas / se las subiré a los cuellos, / y si hay pocas, mis cabellos / les servirán de lazadas" (I.257–60, 18) [And when I've tied their hands, I'll bring / the ropes up to their necks; and when / I run out of rope to use, then / my hair their treasonous necks will wring]. Here we could say that Isabel becomes the mythological Medusa. Freud read Medusa's decapitated head as a feared sign of castration arising from the male child's sight of his mother's genitals (ctd. in Garber and Vickers 4). In his interpretation, the multiple snakes that form Medusa's hair and their power to turn the one who dares look at her to stone are compensatory symbols for the child's fear. But as Marjorie Garber and Nancy Vickers point out (3), some etymologies derive the word Medusa from the Greek for ruler or Queen, and she has long been associated with female rulers. Also, according to myth, Perseus gave the Medusa's head he had severed to Athena, who wore it in the center of her aegis and used its atropopaic power to subdue her foes (2). The Isabelline Medusa that Lope evokes threatens to do precisely that. In *El niño inocente de La Guardia* the royal threat comes closer to realization.

Isabel's dream in Act I, Scene One of *Niño inocente* is more complicated than its counterpart in *Mejor mozo*, and the space of resistance it opens up less transparent but more enduring. Unlike the earlier dream, it is a man who appears to exhort Isabel, not a woman. As we shall see, however, powerful female figures, namely mothers, figure prominently in this dream. As the play opens, Don Íñigo de Mendoza enters to announce that Fernando is discussing with Tomás de Torquemada, the first Grand Inquisitor, "… la extirpación / de los herejes, que son / basiliscos de su pie" (I.8–10, 51) [… the extirpation / of heretics, who are / basilisks at his feet].[7] Isabel then assigns the destruction of the basilisk, symbolic of evil, to the Inquisition itself, foretelling that it will crush "el áspide que mora / en nuestros reinos …" (I.14–15, 51) [the asp that dwells / in our kingdoms …]. The comparison of the Judaizing *conversos* to the poisonous basilisk and the asp will be developed later in the scene.

After Don Íñigo exits, Isabel asks for her Book of Hours, demonstrating her piety, another feminine aspect of her hagiographical construction. But no sooner does the Queen open the Book than sleep overtakes her. As she succumbs, she laments the burdens of ruling a kingdom: "Oh, reinar, cuidado eterno, / y más en una mujer!" (I.74–75, 53) [Oh, governing, constant anxiety, / and more so in a woman!]. But Fernando has asked for her help and she must comply. In other words, paradoxically she shares in the governance of the land out of obedience to her husband. The dream she is about to have will alter her perspective on that relationship.

At this point the stage directions announce the appearance of the dream's protagonist: "Tocan chirimías, y córrese una Cortina, y véase Santo Domingo con su ramo de azucenas y insignias, que es un perro con un hacha" (53) [Shawms are played; a curtain is drawn, and we see Saint Dominic with his spray of lilies and his emblems, a dog with a lighted torch]. The founder of the Dominican order (1170–1221), at times called Saint Dominic de Guzmán, explains the meaning of the symbols commonly associated with him. First, however, he makes an important connection with the woman who is dreaming of him:

> Yo soy Domingo, no sólo
> De tu misma tierra y patria,
> Pero de tu sangre misma,
> Y ascendencia de tu casa.
> Soy Guzmán, de quien
> Enrique la tomó, dándote tanta,
> Que eres por padre Castilla,
> Y eres por madre Guzmana (I.90–97, 53)

[I am Dominic, not only / from your same land and nation, / but also from your same blood, / and lineage. / I am Guzmán, from whom / Enrique inherited it, giving you so much / That on your father's side you are of the house of Castile, / and on your mother's you are a Guzman].

The Guzmán mentioned by Domingo was Leonor de Guzmán (1310–1351), the mistress of King Alfonso XI (1311–1350). Among their many children was Enrique II de Castilla (1369–1379). After having his half-brother King Pedro I (1350–1369) assassinated, Enrique rose to the throne and founded the Trastámaran dynasty that culminated in Isabel and her daughter Juana. Converting their shared lineage into a matronymic, "Guzmana," St. Dominic underscores Isabel's maternal line, making it equal to the paternal. Blood relatives Domingo and Isabel thereby become as important a couple for Spain's desired future as a purely Christian nation as Fernando and Isabel will be.

In a lengthy monologue, Domingo recalls his arduous work in eliminating heretical sects in Spain, Italy, and France and identifies the dog with its torch as the symbol of his evangelical zeal. The dog's barks symbolize his future sermons and counsel against heresy; the torch is the fire with which he burned members of various heretical sects. Most interesting for my purposes, however, is his mention of the fact that the dog and torch first appeared in a dream to his pregnant mother, prophesying the saintly vocation of her future son. He also identifies himself as the first official Inquisitor and praises Isabel and Fernando for reinstituting the Inquisition in Spain. But his praise abruptly turns into admonishment when he insists that the Inquisition cannot discern "lo que ocultan los pechos" (I.66, 55) [what hearts hide]. For this reason Isabel must expel the Jews from Spain forever by royal edict. Thus the dream of Domingo's mother predicting her future son's saintly work is embedded within and reinforces Isabel's dream of Domingo, predicting her own future work to purge Spain of its religious others. The prominent matriarchal imagery in both provides the insight and impetus for Isabel to carry out her subsequent manly action.

As Isabel awakens, Fernando enters to announce that following Papal confirmation the Inquisition is now fully operational. Accordingly, he has appointed three Inquisitors, the very ones who will conduct the trial of the La Guardia conspirators whose crime is the main focus of the rest of the play. The newly empowered Isabel immediately echoes Santo Domingo's earlier exhortation, urging Fernando to sign the edict of expulsion. She repeats her own initial comparison of the *conversos* with basilisks and asps: "mientras no ... le cortéis / a esta sierpe el cuello impío / no habéis de tener sosiego" (I.215–18, 57) [as long as ... you don't cut off / this serpent's impious neck / you will have no peace]. Fernando at first resists his wife's initiative by appropriating the phallic snake imagery and comparing himself to Hercules, whose second labor was the slaying of the many-headed Lernaean Hydra: "Yo saqué ... / la espada con que este día / corto el cuello a la herejía. / Quien ha de poner el fuego / es la santa Inquisición" (I.234–38, 57) [I unsheathed ... / the sword with which this day / I cut off heresy's neck. The one who is to set the fire / is the Holy Office of the Inquisition]. Isabel agrees, somewhat dismissively, that the world will indeed call Fernando a modern Hercules for his Inquisitional labors, but she also insists "... desterrar deseo / este enemigo inhumano" (I.244–45, 57) [... I wish to exile / this inhuman enemy].

I suggest that Isabel is able to express her desire to expel the Jews so forcefully because of the space of resistance created in the dream of her maternal bloodline. This accords with the feminist critique of the primary role assigned to the father by both Freud and Lacan. In her influential *The Daughter's Seduction*, Jane Gallop singles out Julia Kristeva for her subversion of the Freudian model whereby the father dominates the son via the threat of castration, a model which makes both the mother and the daughter secondary actors in the family romance. Kristeva's most powerful subversion of this dynamic is, in Gallop's words: "to expose the phallus of the phallic mother. Not merely to theorize the phallic mother, but to *theatricalize* her as spectacle, to open the curtain ..." (118; my emphasis). This insight clearly applies to the oneiric Isabel of *Mejor mozo* and, even more so, of *Niño inocente*. Lope's theatricalization of the phallic mother of the Spanish nation demonstrates not his need to subject her to traditional gender roles, but rather his desire to understand the psychic sources of her power.

But whereas in *Mejor mozo* Isabel finally surrenders her desire and the action necessary to fulfill it when she accedes to her advisers' insistence that she pass the sword to a husband, in *Niño inocente* she retains the empowerment provided by the dream long enough to convince Fernando to expel the Jews, calling them basilisks once again and exclaiming "¡Si os contase lo que vi / en sueños! ..." (I.271–72, 58) [If I told you what I saw / in dreams! ...]. But she keeps the content of her dream to herself, underscoring the sense of self it has promoted.

In conclusion, it may well be that Lope's interest in Isabel's dreams was sparked by the disruptive power of his contemporary Lucrecia de León and her sister oneiromancers. It is certainly noteworthy that Lucrecia at times "se soñaba reyna" [dreamed she was a Queen] and in one dream predicted that "por pecados que el Rey nuestro señor había cometido ... los moriscos y herejes habían de destruir España" (Fernández Luzón 12) [due to sins committed by the King our lord ... the *moriscos* (Moslems converted to Christianity) and heretics would destroy Spain]. The dreaming Isabel of *Niño inocente* may

also speak of (or to?) Philip II, a male monarch who has failed to live up to
the power and accomplishments of his great-grandmother.

Notes

1. See the complete list provided by Caba, p. 29n1. Ostlund analyzes five history plays
   that feature the Catholic Monarchs, *El mejor mozo de España, Fuenteovejuna, El
   cerco de Santa Fe* [*The Siege of Santa Fe*], *El nuevo mundo descubierto por Cristóbal
   Colón* [*The New World Discovered by Christopher Columbus*], and *Las cuentas del Gran
   Capitán* [*Accounts of the Great Captain*]. Caba's book is a survey of Golden Age
   theater's representation of Isabel. Her chapter on Lope focuses on the two plays that
   concern me here.
2. *Niño inocente* has been traditionally dated as c. 1604. Cañigral Cortés has convincingly argued for the earlier date of composition.
3. Kagan provides an excellent overview of León's life and career.
4. For a wide-ranging survey of the role of dreams in the *comedia*, see Voros and Sáez.
5. See Ostlund and, for *Niño inocente*, Brooke.
6. All English translations of *Mejor mozo* are taken from Gitlitz's bilingual facing-page
   edition.
7. English translations from *Niño inocente* are my own. As Farrell observes (143), basilisks symbolized evil and were often portrayed in post-Tridentine art as trodden
   underfoot by the Virgin Mary.

Works Cited

Brooke, Alice. "'El mejor mozo'?: The Representation of the Future Catholic Monarchs
   in Lope de Vega's *El mejor mozo de España*." *Bulletin of the Comediantes* 63.2 (2011):
   15–26. Print.

Brown, Peter, ed. *Reading Dreams: The Interpretation of Dreams from Chaucer to Shakespeare*. Oxford: Oxford UP, 1999. Print.

Caba, María Y. *Isabel la Católica en la producción teatral española del siglo XVII*.
   Woodbridge, UK: Tamesis, 2008. Print.

Cañigral Cortés, Luis. "*El niño inocente de La Guardia* de Lope de Vega: Análisis de sus
   fuentes." *Revista de Literatura* 56.112 (1994): 349–70. Print.

De Lauretis, Teresa. "Eccentric Subjects: Feminist Theory and Historical Consciousness."
   Feminist Studies 16.1 (1990): 115–50. Print.

Fernández Luzón, Antonio. "Profecía y transgresión social. El caso de Lucrecia de León."
   Historia social 38 (2000): 3–15. Print.

Fradenburg, L. O. Aranye. *Sacrifice Your Love: Psychoanalysis, Historicism, Chaucer*.
   Minneapolis: U of Minnesota P, 2002. Print.

Gallop, Jane. *The Father's Seduction: Feminism and Psychoanalysis*. Ithaca, NY: Cornell UP,
   1982. Print.

Garber, Marjorie, and Nancy J. Vickers, eds. *The Medusa Reader.* New York and London: Routledge, 2003. Print.

Holland, Peter. "The Interpretation of Dreams in the Renaissance." Brown 125–146. Print.

Kagan, Richard L. *Lucrecia's Dreams: Politics and Prophecy in Sixteenth-Century Spain.* Berkeley: U of California P, 1990. Print.

Kamen, Henry. *The Spanish Inquisition: A Historical Revision.* New Haven, CT and London: Yale UP, 1997. Print.

Kruger, Stephen. *Dreaming in the Middle Ages.* Cambridge, UK: Cambridge UP, 1992. Print.

McLuskie, Kathleen. "The 'Candy-Colored Clown': Reading Early Modern Dreams." Brown 147–67. Print.

Ostlund, DeLys. *The Re-Creation of History in the Fernando and Isabel Plays of Lope de Vega.* New York: Peter Lang, 1997. Print.

Stroud, Matthew D. *Plot Twists and Critical Turns: Queer Approaches to Early Modern Spanish Theater.* Lewisburg, PA: Bucknell UP, 2007. Print.

———. *The Play in the Mirror: Lacanian Perspectives on Spanish Baroque Theater.* Lewisburg, PA: Bucknell UP, 1996. Print.

Vega Carpio, Lope de. *El niño inocente de La Guardia.* Ed. Anthony J. Farrell. London: Tamesis Books, 1985. Print.

———. *El mejor mozo de España.* Ed. and trans. David M. Gitlitz. Tempe, AZ: Bilingual Press, 1999. Print.

Voros, Sharon D., and Ricardo Sáez, eds. *"Aquel breve sueño": Dreams on the Early Modern Spanish Stage.* New Orleans: UP of the South, 2004. Print.

Wright, Elizabeth. *Psychoanalytic Criticism: A Reappraisal.* 2nd ed. New York: Routledge, 1998. Print.

Mirror Neurons and Mirror Metaphors: Cognitive Theory and Privanza *in* La adversa fortuna de don Alvaro de Luna

BARBARA SIMERKA
Queens College/CUNY

Matthew Stroud's pioneering study, *The Play in the Mirror*, demonstrated the utility of the Lacanian mirror paradigm for *comedia* studies. In Lacanian psychoanalysis, the mirror stage is a concept that serves both literal and metaphorical purposes, designating both the development of self awareness among infants or toddlers who recognize themselves in reflective surfaces and also the life long process of creating and maintaining a stable coherent subject. Cognitive theory has emerged as the newest psychological paradigm to be incorporated into literary analysis. This discipline has many different branches, including the study of mirror neuron function. Where Lacan (and Freud) use the mirror as a metaphor for the ways that the human mind understands its own individual subjectivity, studies of the mirror neuron network provide new insights concerning how human beings understand and influence one another's actions. The mirror neuron network is responsible for Theory of Mind and Machiavellian Intelligence, the cognitive activities that underly complex social interaction. In my recent study, *Knowing Subjects,* one chapter focuses on the way that courtier manuals conceptualize the most efficient uses of Theory of Mind for social advancement. In this essay I will turn to *privanza* drama, the subgenre that studies the relationship between Kings and their *privados* [ministers] in order to study the ways in which plays such as Mira de Amescua's *La adversa fortuna de don Alvaro de Luna* [*The Adverse Fortune of Don Álvaro de Luna*] represent the complex cognitive interplay among Kings, *privados* and *hechuras* [the band of supporters that a *privado* gains by bestowing favors], with a focus on Theory of Mind.[1] I will use these insights in order to trace the connections between cognitive processes and Early Modern Court culture.

The mirror serves as a primary metaphor in many types of discourses. Since classical antiquity, handbooks written for a newly ascended monarch or advisor have been entitled *speculae*; such works based their precepts on historical examples of successful and virtuous predecessors whom rulers and ministers of later ages were to emulate or mirror. The metaphor of the mirror also circulated widely in idealized depictions of aristocratic male friendship from Ancient Greece through the Early Modern era. Recent studies of such discourses have demystified the paradigm of mirror friendship, offering instead the model of "homosociality" as a less benign force, one that serves to secure and perpetuate patriarchal power (Sedgwick 1–3; Simerka, "Homosociality" 522). In *Plot Twists and Critical Turns*, Stroud employs this concept to explore the gender dynamics at work in several plays (121–40). Scholars also use the model of homosociality as a prism through which Early Modern depictions of masculinity and mirror friendship can be reconsidered. Juan Pablo Gil-Oslé has proposed the term "imperfect friendship" to conceptualize a transitional phase between the traditional model of mirror friendship and the modern bourgeois notion of honest interpersonal commerce (169). Analysis of mirror metaphors concerning cognition, friendship and advice manuals will help to illuminate the scrutiny of the *privado* system of governance found in *La adversa fortuna de don Alvaro de Luna*.

In *Mind Reading: An Investigation into How We Learn to Love and Lie*, Sanjida O'Connell describes Theory of Mind (ToM) or Mind Reading (MR) as a universal cognitive activity, "thinking about what is going on in [another's] head" (6). Since the 1980s, ToM has been a focus of studies in cognitive philosophy (Goldman), developmental psychology (Baron Cohen), primatology (Byrne and Whiten) and neuroscience (Gallese). This form of "Mind Reading" is completely different from the occult activity known as mental telepathy; it entails the study of how humans conceptualize the thoughts and rationales behind other people's actions and use those insights to negotiate social relationships. This capacity is a necessary precursor to a wide variety of human interactions—both positive and not—including projecting and empathizing as well as lying and cheating. When ToM is used for deceptive or manipulative purposes, it is known as Social Intelligence (SI) or Machiavellian Intelligence (MI). ToM transforms into SI as people (and primates) in hierarchical social units seek to understand and shape rivals' mental processes in order ascend the social ladder (Byrne and Whiten 1–23). Neurological studies of ToM activity became possible when improvements in brain imaging technology led to the 1996 discovery of the mirror neuron function: in the human brain, the very same neuron networks fire both when subjects per-form an activity and also when they observe that activity being performed by another (Gallese et al. 593). Mirror neurons serve as the basis for the human ability to first mirror and then simulate—or manipulate—the thoughts and feelings of others. Mirror neurons have been found to play a very active role in the cerebral activity of subjects who engage in ToM; for example, basic experiments have documented that mirror neuron networks fire differently when a subject interprets the grasping of a cup as a drinking activity rather than as a clean-up activity (Gallese 284). Further neurological studies have identified mirror neuron activity in many types of social interactions, espe-cially those that entail the ascription of intentions or emotional states (Frith 304–05). Imaging technology has revealed a "hardwired" tendency to detect and mirror emotions (Frith 305). However, we are generally not aware of such mirroring activities as ToM, because they occur in premotor areas of the brain that are below the level of consciousness. A growing body of cog-nitive-oriented literary studies indicates that, long before researchers labeled this phenomenon, texts written during moments of significant social transi-tion often foregrounded ToM, MI and SI (Zunshine 10; Leverage and Manc-ing; Simerka, *Knowing* 5–140). In applying the concept of ToM to Early Modern *privanza* drama, I am interested in highlighting specific types of social intelligence behaviors that are depicted as playing a key role in political friendships. Cognitive theory emphasizes the importance of SI for survival during periods of environmental change; anthropologists refer to such factors as droughts and ice ages. However, this model can also be used to explore the re-emergence of the *privado* in the early 17th-century Court as a source of equally drastic social dislocations, which elicited an increase in concerns about the convergence of friendship and politics, and about the cognitive behaviors that govern public and private forms of intimacy. In Mira de Amescua's depic-tion of Court relationships, the use of Theory of Mind helps both to forge and to unravel intimate friendships.

The first act of *La adversa fortuna de don Alvaro de Luna* foregrounds ToM as crucial for governing the relationship of patronage and friendship between Don Alvaro and the *hechuras* [supporters given official positions] he selects to hold high offices and carry out his policies, as well as between the favorite and his sovereign. During the reign of King Juan II, the net-works of patronage and rivalry were both complex and fluid, encompassing factions that represented: family members who governed Portugal, Aragon and Navarre; the hereditary aristocracy of grandees who held ceremonial palace offices; and the *letrado* [jurist] class of educated second-tier noblemen who formulated and carried out policy (Round 7–10; MacCurdy 93–107; Boyden 27–30). The first act presents in rapid albeit chronologically inaccurate succession, a series of historical incidents in which Don Alvaro grants patronage or performs a significant favor. In his encounters with *hechuras* and Princes alike, he devotes significant effort to shaping the intentions of his new protégés in order to maintain control of the unstable and treacherous milieu he inhabits. After he appoints Hernán Alonso de Robles and Alonso Pérez de Vivero to top posts within the Treasury, he emphasizes that he is not gratified by flattery or adulation. Rather, he implores loyalty and gratitude, "solo os quiero agredecid[o]" (I.400 [I want only gratitude] because his ToM concerning all beneficiaries of patronage is highly pessimistic. He then quotes a famous maxim, "those who do the most good for others are the most likely to have enemies," to highlight his skepticism about fidelity and thus his need to use SI to shape the future actions of his allies (I.405–08).

In the next scene, the valiant *privado* rescues Enrique, Infante of Aragon, from a murder plot. The Prince offers great material reward, but Alvaro again asks only for gratitude, "Que no me pagues / como suelen todos" (I.683–84) [that you don't repay me / as all are accustomed to]. This encounter concludes with another declaration of Don Alvaro's gloomy ToM; when Enrique assures him, "No temas que ingrato sea" [have no fear that I will be ungrateful] Luna responds, "Si temo, porque eres hombre / y tal es su naturaleza" (I. 694–96) [yes I fear, because you are human / and such is human nature]. In these early scenes, his ToM seems to indicate that extracting verbal promises might serve as the guarantor of future loyalty. However, the astronomer who serves as the *gracioso* in this play had already confirmed Luna's worst projections when he prognosticated, "todos aquéllos a quien / hará en este mucho bien / le serán ingratonazos" (I.314–16) [all those for whom / you have done favors / will be supremely ungrateful]. The 17th-century spectators had access to a wide variety of chronicles, poems and ballads documenting betrayal on the part of each of these historical figures, so from their perspective the protagonist's doomed attempts to use ToM to forestall typical patterns of perfidious Court behavior would accentuate the character's tragic status. It is likely that the audience would view Luna's SI machinations in these cases as pathetic rather than Machiavellian because of their foreknowledge that they failed. Less predictable is the way that an Early Modern audience member would weigh these scenes against their awareness of Luna's long history of previous success with MI.

When Luna returns from exile in the second act, he seeks to use SI to protect himself from further disappointments. Upon discovering that Robles was a leader in the conspiracy to topple him, his ToM had attributed the *hechura*'s disloyalty to his inferior social classes, "Quien hace bien a un villano / ... a un traidor favorece" (I.862–63) [whoever promotes a commoner / ... favors a traitor]. When he confronts Robles, his interrogation implies a very personal ToM concerning betrayal from below; the query "... ¿Qué causa / os he dado ...?" (I.1126–27) [What cause have I given you ... ?] focuses on individual interactions and ignores the larger dynamic of factions and rivalries as a possible motivating force. Now, instead of advancing lower cadre men to serve and defend him, Don Alvaro seeks to perform services for and win gratitude from his superiors. His implicit ToM is that higher born nobles will not let him down; in particular he anticipates that having arranged a marriage between the King and Isabel, the daughter of a Portuguese aristocrat, will secure his position and security at Court, "con esto fija a mis pies / a la Fortuna, si es / Isabel agradecida" (II.1718–20) [Fortune / will be under my heel / if Isabel is grateful]. However, the historical record indicates that the new Queen soon allied herself with rival factions, as part of a plan under which the King would allow them to topple his friend and then accrue for himself the system of centralized power that Alvaro had created for their mutual benefit over four decades (Round 41, 50–57).

Don Alvaro discovers the complete failure of his SI and the disintegration of his web of powerful supporters within the space of four short sequential scenes: each in turn, the King, Queen, Infante and Vivero reveal that they will not or cannot withstand the pressure of the factions that have conjoined against the favorite (III.2200–65). At this point, Luna abandons all thought of using ToM to salvage his situation. For the remainder of the play, the *privado* analyzes his fall within the context of tragic and Christian discourses:

> para ejemplo universal
> de los hombres que confían
> en los hombres ... (III.2261–63)

> [as a universal example / of men who trust / in other men ...]

If Fortune and God are against those who stake their fortune and place their trust in human alliances, then no amount of cognitive skill can save them; this is the foundation upon which *privanza* drama depicts well-intentioned ministers as predestined to become tragic heroes (MacCurdy 133–40).

As many scholars have noted, Mira's play follows the outlines of the highly sympathetic *Crónica de don Alvaro de Luna* [*Chronicle of Don Alvaro de Luna*] (attributed to Alvar García de Santa María or Gonzalo Chacón), rejecting the critical perspective found in most other histories of the age that present him in a less flattering light. However, narratives written by supporters and vilifiers alike were unanimous in their depiction of a man who accumulated great power precisely because of his skill at social intelligence, his uncanny ability to hold and augment his power and to increase royal revenues, despite competition from so many different factions (Round 34–60, Boyden 27). In order to function in a tragic mode and to depict the fallen favorite as an appropriate hero, Mira's play must ignore all of the success that Luna enjoyed in employing his SI to build and modify his support system over the course of an extremely long reign. The plot model of *in medias res*, focusing on the peak moment and subsequent heroic downfall, requires Mira to depict the incidents when the favorite's MI fails him. Significantly, the first play in this diptych chronicles the fall of the previous favorite Ruy de Avalos and implies but does not show Alvaro's rise. The political machinations linked to SI that enable courtiers to gain power are not narratable within the scope of Early Modern literary genres. Even in the picaresque novel, Lazarillo's narration of his life story is mostly silent concerning the details of how he managed to win the favor of influential men. The text implies but does not actually show that Lazarillo made use of the SI tactics the third master had described so vividly (Simerka, *Knowing* 118–19, 150–53). If even the most vulgar genre of the age throws a veil over the moments when the protagonist engages in Machiavellian politics, it is not surprising that dramatists would follow suit. MacCurdy implies that it is not possible both to represent the favorite as successful at MI and also to create a true (Neo-Aristotelian) tragic hero; plays that represent well known Machiavellian ministers such as Sejanus or Phillipa de Catania are denigrated as Senecan revenge drama or simply unsuccessful tragedy (195–219).

It is worth a brief detour to consider Mira's depiction of King Juan II and his use of ToM. As MacCurdy notes wryly, both the real life figure and the dramatic persona seem "unmindful" when it comes to understanding the way that various political factions will react to the immense concentration of wealth and power that resulted from the largesse he bestowed upon his *privado* (85). And although Luna has been his companion since childhood, the monarch is represented as completely incapable of MR even with this closest acquaintance. He instructs Juana de Pimentel, Alvaro's future wife, to deliver the news of impending exile, explaining that "… es bueno / que al amigo se dé dulce el veneno; / cuando es la causa fuerte" (I.767–69) […it is best / if a friend gives bitter news]. As the farewell scene of the first act makes abundantly clear, Alvaro's love for the King is the primary emotional connection in his life. If one takes seriously that the King chose Juana to be his messenger out of a desire to reduce his friend's grief rather than simply to escape an unpleasant task, then his MR is highly faulty in not recognizing which bond is the strongest. In addition, as the King heaps more and more titles on Luna over the course of the first two acts, Alvaro responds with increasing discomfort, noting that, "un privado es infelice /con el pueblo cuanto suele / ser dichoso con su rey" [the luckier a privado / is with his King, / the more unlucky in the eyes of the people] (II.1066–68). He is much better than his ruler at using ToM to anticipate the negative public reaction to the flow of favors—and to understand upon whom the blame will fall, "En mí lla-man ambición / el recibir galardones / de las manos liberales / de mi rey" (II.1073–76) [when I receive favor / from a generous King, / they condemn / my ambition]. The King also ignores Luna's plea not to be made Duke of Trujillo after his military victory there (III.2030). Portraying the King as a cognitive naïf who suffers because of his poor ToM abilities serves the pur-poses of a drama that prioritizes tragic form over historical reality. The King's last minute *anagnorisis* and failed attempt to save Alvaro conform both to the logic of tragedy and to the sentimentalized perspective found in the Don Alvaro chronicle. Mira de Amescua is able to portray both characters as tragic heroes only because they appear as pawns in the SI strategies of others; according to this play, nearly all of the wrongs committed at this Court stem from other conniving courtiers.

Within the plot trajectory of the play, Don Alvaro sets the stage for his own downfall at the moment when he uses ToM incorrectly and misreads his ruler's true feelings concerning his remarriage. Early Modern discourses about *privanza* inscribe the bond between a King and his favorite as extremely inti-mate. Such intimacy can be idealized in accordance with the aristocratic model of mirror friendship, which *should* render ToM superfluous. So, although it was normal for best friends to act as go-betweens in arranging marital con-tracts, even the highest idealism did not suppose that a friend could know the feelings of another without consultation. This is precisely the error that Luna commits in his negotiations with the Portuguese ambassador, when he declares: "... No lo he tratado / con él, pero está bien el casamiento / a Castilla, y así doy la palabra" (II.1415–17) [... I have not discussed this / with him, but the marriage benefits / Castille so I give my word]. Although it does occur to Luna that he may have crossed a line when he sees the King gazing fondly at a miniature of another woman, he assuages his concerns by citing the very law of *perfect friendship* that he himself has just broken,

¿si tuviese otra intención
cuando de casarle trato?
Mal hice en no darle cuenta
primero de mi deseo.

Empeñada en esto veo
mi palabra; mas, ¿qué intenta,
qué pretende, qué imagina,
sin que yo lo sepa? Nada. (II.1563–70)

[What if he had other plans / when I arranged his marriage? / I was wrong not
to notify him / of my plan beforehand. / My word is at stake here. / But, what /
has he ever planned / without my knowledge? Nothing.]

Even though Luna confesses to an impropriety, "Confié, engañéme, erré"
(I.1661)[I trusted, I was wrong, I erred], he nonetheless continues to stretch
the bonds of friendship when he threatens to resign his posts and leave Court
rather than lose face with his Portuguese allies. This scene is of course the
imaginative creation of a dramatist, but it conveys an incident that is confirmed in every document of Juan's reign. Several chronicles also indicate that
Luna's influence over his monarch declined soon after the marriage, either
because of resentment at this violation of friendship or because Isabel managed to win her husband's affection (Round 42–45). Although many factors
converged when Luna was executed in 1453, most sources concur that Juan
did not submit passively to the will of rival factions; rather, he coerced the
council that he had convened to declare a death sentence against his lifelong
confidant (Round 35–50).

Documentation concerning the lives of Luna, Lerma and Olivares confirms that in a Court setting, SI is unreliable and thus perfect mutual understanding and perfect friendship are difficult to maintain. James Boyden notes
that in cases where the advisor enters the life of a youthful future King as a
tutor or page, a sort of equality is possible during those early years, because a
boy could be easily impressed by the "dashing" young men who served him
(33). However, as an awestruck youth matures into a sitting monarch, he
becomes aware of his own "power and prerogatives" and it is inevitable that
the original friendships would be recalibrated (Boyden 33). In this context, it
is noteworthy that Juan remained under the sway of Luna well into adulthood.
Mira's play reflects the historical reality that even when arranging his second
marriage, the King allowed Don Alvaro to overrule his wishes in selecting
a bride. However, as indicated above, the play depicts the SI Don Alvaro
deploys at that moment as a violation of the bonds of mirror friendship.

In *Amistades imperfectas* [*Imperfect Friendships*], Juan Pablo Gil-Oslé
traces the network of competing sentimental and practical considerations
(political, social, and economic) that conjoined to undermine the mirror ideal
of passionate bonds among elite males over the course of the 17th century.
Gil-Oslé documents the shifting socio-economic reality of the *privado* governed society, in which allegiances based on aristocratic networks of blood

ties wane in influence, while new webs of paid offices, bought titles, favors and patronage emerge (1–43). Although Mira de Amescua's play completely omits references to economic factors, Round indicates that Luna's early rise was due in part to an improved system of tax collections, which enabled him to bestow new favors and win support for himself and the new King (14–20). Similarly, Round points to declining economic conditions, which limited royal displays of splendor and reduced the annual stipend received by office holders, as a crucial factor when both the King and Luna's *hechuras* deserted him in 1453 (58–60). Although the play itself attributes the defections on the part of Don Alvaro's supporters to abstract moral failings, Gil-Oslé's model of imperfect friendship offers a relevant pragmatic context.

Across 17th-century Europe, depictions of ideal friendship circulated in counterpoint not only to literary representations of *amistad imperfecta* but also to writings that demonized the intimate nature of *privanza*, often through allusions to sodomy and enchantment (Hutcheson 222; Weimer 265; Levin 64; Worden 163; MacCurdy 94–96). As Steve Hutcheson has shown, nearly all of the contemporary narratives about the reign of Juan II—chronicles, ballads, and poems alike—emphasized the extreme and unusual closeness between the King and his favorite (222–29). Alonso de Palencia provided direct accusations of sexual misconduct (MacCurdy 94–96). Hutcheson links discourses about sexuality and *privanza* with Jonathan Goldberg's paradigm of "sodometries": situations where the actual truth of the bodily act is irrelevant because discourses of sodomy are so ubiquitous as to completely shape public perception of a personal relationship (Goldberg xv–xvi; ctd. in Hutcheson 229). Over a century after Luna's death, attacks against Felipe IV's favorites repeated accusations of sodomy. Christopher Weimer notes that in Early Modern Spain, "discourses of sexual anxiety could and did converge, an intersection that was not only logical but very possibly inevitable" (265). Weimer observes that sodomy and *privanza* were "imbricated" as relationships that transgressed hierarchical norms and as such were viewed as inherently deviant (258). Although Mira de Amescua avoids direct references to sexual activity, the extended parting scene that closes Act I is among the most passionate declarations of eternal devotion in all of the *comedia*; moving Luna's future wife Juana de Pimentel, who was watching their farewell from the sidelines, to exclaim "… amor extraño" (I.952) [… strange love].

In this play, Mira de Amescua deconstructs the ideal of mirror friendship from two opposing directions. On the one hand, the early scenes depict the two men as excessively devoted friends; it may be that playwright sought to reference to the "sodometries" concerning Felipe IV that were in circulation at the time the play was written. As shown above, the very midpoint of the play stages the moment when political ambitions cause Luna to prioritize diplomacy and personal ego over the wishes of his true friend, thus reducing their relationship from mirror perfection to *amistad imperfecta*. Although the closing scene depicts Juan's change of heart and his failed attempt to rescue his friend, audience members were aware that most historical evidence pointed to a vastly different truth. As the play progresses, the relationship shifts from one pole of excess, the homoerotic, to the opposite pole of betrayal. There is not a single moment where the relationship between the two men occupies the golden mean of a devoted but measured bond.

This depiction of national leaders as men who are equally flawed in maintaining a mirror friendship and in using their mirror neurons to manage Machiavellian forms of interaction, presents a double-edged sword. At this historical moment, traditional discourses of the ideal Christian Prince were being challenged by more pragmatic writings (Feros 212). The new genre of *specula* for favorites emphasized not only a new class of political leader but also a newly realistic approach to politics. It is worth noting that the intended reader for these writings was not merely the small circle of Court advisors, but rather the entirety of the vast network of courtiers and aspirants. Across Europe in the 17th century, *privanza* drama arose in tandem with this new didactic genre aimed at ministers rather than Princes (Elliott, "Intro" 1–4; MacCurdy 55). The homologies among the fractious Courts that were guided by Luna, Lerma, and Olivares would have been obvious to those spectators (Boyden 26–37). If Juan and Luna are to be seen as an analogy for Felipe III or IV and their ministers, then the lack of SI skills would constitute an unpractical and even disadvantageous "virtue." From this perspective, the fact that the honorable intentions of a virtuous ruler and his faithful minister can be overset due to the Machiavellian machinations of a Grandee class guilty of the ambition attributed to the *privado* could be viewed as tragic in the more colloquial sense of the term. The realities of 17th-century imperial Courts, in Spain (and in Europe as a whole) necessitate a larger bureaucracy of ministers and *hechuras*, which inevitably leads to rivalries and factionalism (Thompson 13–15).

There are serious ideological implications in this attempted erasure of the role of SI in Court politics for the 17th-century audience looking to apply dramatic insights to the *privado* situation of its own historical moment. The original audience would have been well aware of the discrepancies between this idealized depiction of the most famous fallen favorite, and the myriad texts of many different genres that had foregrounded Luna's extraordinary proficiency in those very skills. Viewed not as a tragedy but as a *specula* for favorites, the emphasis on cognitive skills can be seen as didactic in nature.

This play stages the Court as a locus where SI and even MI are indispensable if regrettable tools for monarch and *privado* alike, in order to maintain networks of power and influence within an unstable and evolving Court culture.[2]

Notes

1. Antonio Feros describes the phenomenon of "royal favorites" across Europe during the 16th and 17th centuries as a multivalent situation which entailed factors such as: the need for a father figure on the part of the monarchs who ascended the throne at a young age; a disguised outlet for sexual desire on the part of female or homosexual rulers; the dynamics of power vacuums; increasingly complex bureaucracies; the personal proclivities of reclusive or self indulgent rulers, etc. He notes that the rise of notably powerful favorites (called *privados* in Spanish) nearly always generated a backlash.
2. A grant from Professional Staff Congress, City University of New York supported research for this essay.

Works Cited

Baron Cohen, Simon. *Mindblindness: An Essay on Autism and Theory of Mind*. Cambridge, MA: The Massachusetts Institute of Technology P, 1997. Print.

Boyden, James A. "'Fortune Has Stripped You of Your Splendor'; Favorites and Their Fates in Fifteenth- and Sixteenth-Century Spain." Elliott and Brockliss 26–37. Print.

Byrne, Richard, and Andrew Whiten, eds. and pref. *Machiavellian Intelligence: Social Expertise and the Evolution of Intellect in Monkeys, Apes, and Humans*. Oxford: Oxford UP, 1988. Print.

Elliott, John Huxtable. Introduction. Elliott and Brockliss 1–12. Print.

———. and Laurence W. B. Brockliss, eds. *The World of the Favourite*. New Haven, CT: Yale UP, 1999. Print.

Feros, Antonio. "Images of Evil, Images of Kings: The Contrasting Faces of the Royal Favourite and the Prime Minister in Early Modern European Political Literature, c. 1580–c. 1650." Elliott and Brockliss 205–22. Print.

Frith, Chris D. "The Social Brain?" *Social Intelligence: From Brain to Culture*. Ed. Nathan Emery, Nicola Clayton, and Christopher D. Frith. Oxford: Oxford UP, 2007. 297–312. Print.

Gallese, Vittorio, Luciano Fadiga, Leonardo Fogassi, and Giacomo Rizzolatti. "Action Recognition in the Premotor Cortex." *Brain* 119.2 (1996): 593–609. Print.

Gil-Oslé, Juan Pablo. *Amistades imperfectas. Del Humanismo a la Ilustración con Cervantes*. Madrid: Iberoamericana; Frankfurt: Vervuert, 2013. Print.

Goldman, Alvin. "Interpretation Psychologized." *Folk Psychology: The Theory of Mind Debate*. Ed. M. Davies and T. Stone. 1st ed. Oxford: Blackwell, 1995. 74–99. Print.

Leverage, Paula, Howard Mancing, et al, eds. *Theory of Mind and Literature*. West Lafayette, IN: Purdue UP, 2010. Print.

MacCurdy, Raymond R. *The Tragic Fall: Don Álvaro de Luna and Other Favorites in Spanish Golden Age Drama*. Chapel Hill, NC: U of North Carolina P, 1978. Print.

Mira de Amescua, Antonio. *La adversa fortuna de don Alvaro de Luna*. The Association for Hispanic Classic Theater. Web. 24 June 2014. <www.comedias.org/mira /advdal. html>.

O'Connell, Sanjida. *Mindreading: An Investigation into How We Learn to Love and Lie*. New York: Doubleday, 1998. Print.

Peck, Linda Levy. "Monopolizing Favour: Structures of Power in the Early Seventeenth-Century English Court." Elliott and Brockliss 54–70. Print.

Round, Nicholas G. *The Greatest Man Uncrowned. A Study of the Fall of Don Alvaro de Luna*. London: Tamesis, 1986. Print.

Sedgwick, Eve Kosofsky. *Between Men: English Literature and Male Homosocial Desire*. New York: Columbia UP, 1985. Print.

Simerka, Barbara. *Knowing Subjects: Cognitive Cultural Studies and Early Modern Spanish Literature*. West Lafayette, IN: Purdue UP, 2013. Print.

———. "Homosociality and Dramatic Conflict: A Reconsideration of Early Modern Spanish Comedy." *Hispanic Review* 70.4 (2002): 521–33. Print.

Stroud, Matthew D. *Plot Twists and Critical Turns: Queer Approaches to Early Modern Spanish Theater*. Lewisburg, PA: Bucknell UP, 2007. Print.

———.The *Play in the Mirror: Lacanian Perspectives on Spanish Baroque Theater*. Lewisburg, PA: Bucknell UP, 1996. Print.

Thompson, I. A. A. "The Institutional Background to the Rise of the Minister-Favorite." Elliott and Brockliss 13–25. Print.

Zunshine, Lisa. *Why We Read Fiction: Theory of Mind and the Novel*. Columbus: Ohio State UP, 2006. Print.

The Calderonian Aesthetic Experience: Plot, Character, Politics, and Primal Emotions in El alcalde de Zalamea

(What Neuroscience and US Presidential Campaigns Might Tell Us about the Spanish Comedia)

ROBERT M. JOHNSTON
Northern Arizona University, *Emeritus*

In his article, "The Director's Cut: Baroque Aesthetics and Modern Staging of the *Comedia*," Matthew Stroud considers the aesthetic effect of directorial editing of Spanish *comedias* to adapt them for modern audiences. He draws examples from modern productions of Calderón's *Celos aun del aire matan* [*Even Baseless Jealousy Can Kill*] and Moreto's *El lindo don Diego* [*Dandy Don Diego*] but he aims his comments at contemporary productions of *comedias* in general. He maintains that: "In most modern stagings, plot and character (i.e. narrative) are preserved while structure and image (poetry) are sacrificed to the supposed demands of audiences more accustomed to television and film" (81). Unfortunately, in Stroud's view, modern directors too often cut the very passages of Baroque lyric poetry that are most richly imbued with the aesthetic "essence" of the original plays. As a consequence, the *comedia* playwright's poetic intention yields to the modern director's dramatic vision, and "aesthetics" loses out to "practicality" (91).

The dilemma, of course, has two sides. From a scholar's perspective, one must agree with Stroud that much of the *comedia*'s unique identity resides in the poetic texture of the verse. On the other hand, directors such as Lee

Mitchell and Jonathan Miller, both cited by Stroud, argue persuasively that modern productions of classical plays need the director's creative intervention if they are to span historical and cultural difference and engage today's audiences. Miller advocates careful preservation of the original play's scenes, plot, and characters, but recommends smoothing out tangled syntax and eliminating excess verbiage to produce "speakable" lines that will be effective for live performance (12–16). For Mitchell, plays depend for their existence on their audience, which inevitably changes and evolves with time. Attempts to preserve canonical interpretations and representations will likely render them "odd and stilted" (36).

The issue is too complex to resolve in this brief article. I would like, however, to offer some consolation for those who share Stroud's disappointment with modern productions of *comedias* that privilege plot and character over poetic language. To do this, I will ask that we make two adjustments in the way we assess the "aesthetic essence" of a *comedia*. First I would like to shift the focus from the stylistic features of the poetic text to the affective response a *comedia* playwright may have designed for the audience. Most *comedia* scholars will agree that the emotional responses a playwright sought to evoke in spectators mattered a great deal in the design of a play. The "passions" were an essential aspect of human psychology as understood since Ancient times. Aristotle's prescription for fear and pity in tragedy and the classical and Renaissance formula for poetry, *delectare, docere, movere* [to delight, to teach, to move] where instruction and delight depend on "moving" the affects, figured prominently in 17th-century dramatic theory. "Poetry," of course, as understood by Renaissance writers and theorists included all forms of creative writing, epic, lyric, and dramatic, and prose as well as verse. All of these, it was assumed, should "please, instruct, and move" the reader or spectator.[1]

The second adjustment will be to reconsider the role of plot and character in achieving this end. The narrative structures of 16th- and 17th-century Spanish plays may invite comparison to film and television today, but they should not as a consequence be dismissed as purely conventional and lacking in artistic value. They provided, after all, the structure in time and space for the other elements of a play. And, as Albert Sloman showed in his *The Dramatic Craftsmanship of Calderón*, for a master such as Calderón, the skillful recrafting of previous playwrights' plot structures and characters comprised an important aspect of his artistic genius. In what follows, I will try to show some ways that Calderón used plot design and character in one of his most famous *comedias*, *El alcalde de Zalamea* [*The Mayor of Zalamea*] to "move" the affects of the spectator.[2] I will argue that this is central to the "poetic essence" of the play and that the aesthetic experience it offers should be similar for popular as well as sophisticated audiences, both 17th-century and modern alike.

For an approach to this question, I will draw on the work of two research-ers in neuroscience, an area that has recently begun to interest some scholars in theater studies, including the *comedia*.[3] The first of these is Drew Westen, a clinical and political psychologist and professor at Emory University. In *The Political Brain,* Westen considers the neurological bases for human emotions as a way to understand the 'art of political persuasion' as practiced in US presidential campaigns from the 1960s up until 2004. The second is Marco Iacoboni, a neurologist and neuroscientist at the UCLA medical school and Director of the Transcranial Magnetic Stimulation Laboratory at the Ahman-son-Lovelace Brain Mapping Center. Iacoboni's *Mirroring People* describes research on a particular type of brain cell called "mirror neurons," which have a major role in how we perceive and interact with other humans. They are responsible, among other things, for the feeling of empathy, essential for com-passion and for vicarious identification with other people, whether they are political candidates, or characters on television, on a movie screen, or on stage.[4]

I first will explain a few of Westen's and Iacoboni's findings about politics, brain function, emotions, and "mirror neurons." I will then offer Calderón's El *alcalde de Zalamea* as a case study of how some of their ideas might apply to *comedias.*

One might agree that politics in the US today has something in com-mon with theater: both employ imagination and skillful acting, and both aim, in one sense or another, to engage and win over their audience. This last point is the focus of Westen's book: "the science and practice of persuasion in American politics" (17). His overall question is why Republicans have won so many elections when, as Westen believes, Democrats have reason, a better argument, and positions with which more voters actually agree. To answer this he combines recent findings in clinical and laboratory research on brain functions with detailed analyses of ads, speeches, debates, and other events from US presidential campaigns over a span of forty years. His main charac-ters include the likes of Lyndon Johnson, Jimmy Carter, Ronald Reagan, Bill Clinton, John Kerry, Bushes Sr. and Jr., and well-known political strategists such as Lee Atwater and Karl Rove. He finds that while Democrats have appealed to voters' reason, Republicans have moved voters' emotions. "*The political brain*" Westen argues, is "*an emotional brain*" (xv). The conventional idea of "a *dispassionate mind* that makes decisions by weighing the evidence and reasoning to the most valid conclusions—bears no relation to how the mind and brain actually work" (ix). Republicans have understood this, he says, Democrats have not.[5]

The power of emotions over reason derives from the way the human brain evolved over the past 2.5 million years. The brain's "creation," says Westen, was "an elegant patchwork of circuits" with each one added on to the previous ones as organisms' brains became more elaborate. At every step along the way as creatures developed ever more sophisticated neural structures, the original ones remained. The process did not allow starting over from scratch with a more elegant design (50). Thus the deeper one looks into the human brain and spinal cord, the more one discovers the ancient structures that first evolved. Westen continues, "Most of us would be truly embarrassed if we realized the extent to which the more primitive structures of our brains, particularly the structures that regulate basic motives such as sex and hunger, resemble those of a sheep" (51). In this evolutionary trajectory, rudimentary feelings were guiding behavior millions of years before the appearance of the activity we call "reason" (57). Prehistoric organisms survived because they developed the ability to dodge negative stimuli and seek positive ones (88). This simple adaptive process describes the evolutionary history of thought processes in living creatures today, including humans. Reason developed as a complement to, not a substitute for, prehistoric behavioral systems.[6]

The primitive reactions to stimuli that promoted evolutionary adaptation and contributed to the development and survival of our species are the origins of what we today call emotions. In the process of natural selection, in addition to the feelings that promote behavior aimed at individual survival, feelings that aim at protecting and caring for offspring also contribute to a species' success. This concept extends to care and protection of family and community. Feelings of "fear" or "anger" when one's family is threatened, "pride" for success of one's children, "gratitude" to those who support us, "admiration" for selfless and courageous action, "guilt" when we have done wrong—these emotional responses serve our own survival and the survival of our community (49–50). Achievement of power and status, and values such as honor and shame also fit in this scheme, since they relate to protection of family and to 'kin selection.' We might use the term "primal emotions" to describe these fundamental responses which we have acquired through evolution. These feelings are not specific to a given culture, race, or historical context, since they are embedded much more deeply in the neurophysiology of the human brain.[7] In addition, they are unconscious, automatic, and much more powerful than rational thought processes.[8]

These "primal sentiments" have strong influence on our behavior, but they do not solve moral or ethical problems. They do not tell us, for example, if we should we feel stronger allegiance to self, family, community, tribe, nation … or to all humanity. The emotions can also hijack our reasoning process, and they can motivate the worst of human behavior (Westen 50). This is true especially with what Westen calls the "underground emotions" of sex and aggression. He argues: "… if we strip males in particular of the inhibitions of conscience—either by blasting a hole through their frontal lobes around the eyeballs, or sending them off to war with even the slightest ambiguity about the rules of engagement—we always see the same things: rape, murder, and torture. We need look no farther than Abu Ghraib to see the naked (male) human instincts, shorn of the shackles of conscience. We have seen the same footprints in Uganda, Bosnia, Rwanda, Burundi, and Darfur" (81).

Westen's formula for the successful political campaign depends on constructing a campaign "storyline" based on themes that resonate with primal emotions: security, children, family, "reproduction," and community (73). As a classic example, he offers Ronald Reagan's famous television ad "Morning in America," which subtly but effectively elicits positive emotions associated with "reproductive success" (home, security, children), "kinship" and "inclusive fitness" (marriage, family), "reciprocal altruism" (patriotism), "national pride," and the flag as "symbol of our common fate and identity" (76).

The basic formula of Westen's "emotional story line" looks remarkably like the prescription for a good play. It should have a simple setting, "once upon a time," one or more protagonists, a problem to solve, obstacles (often these are other characters … or candidates), and a "denouement" which provides a solution. The story may have complex variations and a moral, but the "rhetorical power" comes from this simple, basic structure. In fact, a political party's theme story should be so simple and direct that it could be told as a children's story. Westen uses "The Little Engine That Could" as an example of this structure (146–47). We might add: "Yes We Can!," the slogan of Obama's 2008 campaign. In addition to carefully selected themes and story line, visual elements can be especially powerful: Westen's examples include a television ad with "young Bill Clinton shaking hands with John Kennedy" (6), Lyndon Johnson's infamous "Daisy ad" with a child picking daisies in the foreground and a mushroom cloud rising behind her (55), and Bush Sr.'s Willie Horton ad, which showed black male inmates entering and leaving prison by a revolving gate, and which effectively erased Dukakis's 17-point lead and tipped the election to Bush (63–68). Finally and especially important, Westen notes voter identification with the candidate. Again, Reagan provides a compelling example: "people were drawn to Reagan because they *identified* with him, liked his emphasis on values over policy, trusted him, and found him authentic in his beliefs. It didn't matter that they disagreed with most of his policy positions" (13).

We will turn to *El alcalde* in a moment, but I want first to touch briefly on Iacoboni's research at UCLA, since it has great relevance to these last two points: sensory stimulation and vicarious identification or empathy. For the past two decades, Iacoboni and other researchers have used some impressive technology (procedures such as functional magnetic resonance imaging, transcranial magnetic stimulation, positron emission tomography, and magnetoencephalography) to study a particular type of brain cell, which they call 'mirror neurons.' The remarkable thing about these cells is that they activate and fire in the same manner, whether we carry out an action ourselves, such as kicking a soccer ball, or just observe someone else kicking a ball, or hear a ball kicked, or hear the word "kick." In like manner, when we see someone else kiss their lover or experience pain, some of the same brain cells fire in our brains as if we were experiencing these actions ourselves (4–5). This phenomenon holds for actions observed first hand as well as for watching sporting events on the television, seeing movies, and reading. For Iacoboni, the term "vicarious" does not fully describe the power and the significance of this "internal imitation" or "simulation" (30).

Indeed, our simulation and internal imitation of others' actions and expressions actually enables us to feel others' emotions. We do this automatically and unconsciously and prior to comprehending cognitively what we are observing. This mirroring also enables us to understand the intentions of others, since our own brain cells associated with carrying out our intentions fire when we observe another's actions. Iacoboni hypothesizes that imitation and mirroring establish a relation between the self and the other that leads to empathy, a feeling essential for developing social skills, and indeed a fundamental aspect of a successful social order (70). It is this very remarkable neurological phenomenon that is involved when we talk about vicarious identification with another person, a political candidate, or a character on stage.

Calderón thought deeply about politics in theory, in moral terms, and in the practical dimensions of human interactions and relationships; we see this both in his *autos sacramentales* [one-act religious plays] and in his secular plays for the Court and for the *corrales* [public theaters].[9] In his characters we also see evidence of his deep understanding of human psychology, a knowledge he employed in designing his plays to engage and to move his spectators. In *El alcalde de Zalamea* he melds politics and psychology in an emotional storyline about family values, patriotism, individual rights, and a father's fight to protect his children from aggression and sexual abuse in the guise of intrusive government. The story starts, "there was once a man in Zalamea"; the problem develops in terms of one's obligation to family versus nation. The *cargo de aposento* [housing requirement], whereby villagers were obliged to lodge soldiers in their homes, pits national, royal and military power against the local, civil authority of Zalamea, and against community, home, and family. Pedro Crespo seeks to reconcile his duty to King and country and his responsibility as a father by receiving the soldiers but at the same time hiding his daughter from them. The soldier Captain, an embodiment of sexually motivated aggression, first penetrates the innermost sanctuary of Crespo's house to see her. He returns later to kidnap and rape Isabel, and in the process he destroys Crespo's family. Calderón's resolution for this outrage has Crespo elected *alcalde* just when his misfortune and disgrace have reached their nadir, and just when the Captain comes within his grasp. Crespo defies royal authority and has the Captain imprisoned, judged, and garroted under the civil authority of Zalamea. The solution has a price—Crespo's daughter, though rescued, will spend the rest of her life in a convent, and his son Juan leaves home to become a soldier, albeit under the protection of Don Lope de Figueroa, in real life a national hero, and in this story also an alter-father figure. Crespo breaks the King's law, but he preserves Natural Law and the spirit of justice, and in the process he restores his and his family's honor.[10] His struggle costs him personally, but his and his children's service to community, nation, and the Church assures their kind will survive. In a cameo appearance at the end, King Phillip II approves Crespo's action and names him *alcalde* of Zalamea for life. This, indeed, is the story of "the mayor that could." And it derives its compelling, persuasive power from the evocation of a combination of deeply felt primal emotions: fear, anger, compassion, the instinct for personal survival and protection of offspring, and loyalty to community in the face of violent aggression.

Calderón endowed his characters with considerable psychological interest, but more than this their qualities and the pattern of their interrelationships show a clear design to stimulate the spectator's emotional response and channel his or her vicarious identification and sympathy toward Pedro Crespo. Crespo has a serious work ethic, a stubborn adherence to traditional values, and a solid sense of self. He is comfortable with his station as an independent farmer (*labrador*), and he disdains the idea of buying a title of nobility, even though it would excuse him from the obligation to house soldiers in his home. His labors produce wealth and sustenance for both his family and his community. He is a diligent host, a devoted father and a model citizen: quick to fulfill his legitimate duties to family, community, and country, slow to trust others with the security of his home, and fierce in defense of his family. He is the keeper of traditional values, a guardian of domestic security, as well as a symbol of paternal honor and patriotic loyalty. Crespo's daughter and son also vie for the spectator's empathy and sympathy. Isabel is as chaste, reserved, and beautiful as a daughter could be. Juan compensates for faults of youth and immaturity (his attraction to gambling) with eagerness and courage. For Calderón's audience, both in the 17th century and today, Crespo and his family display the timeless values and moral character that define the best of "common folk."

The other principal characters serve as antagonists, foils to propel the spectator's emotional attachment toward Crespo and his family. The effete and silly *hidalgo* [minor nobleman], Don Mendo, who loiters by Crespo's house, hoping to make Isabel his mistress and then abandon her, offers both a ridiculous opposite to Crespo and a hollow, impotent threat to Crespo's family. The soldiers, and particularly the captain, on the other hand, represent a powerful force totally opposed to the survival of Crespo's home and hearth. Though slower to kindle, at first he disdains the idea of making love to a village girl, the Captain's obsession with possessing her takes on all the power of primal sentiments run amok. Instead of promoting the survival of the species, these sentiments aim toward its destruction, indeed they converge into the blind primal drives of sex and aggression. The Captain is the full "antithesis" of Crespo (Díez Borque, ed., "Introducción" 69): the aggressive rogue male, determined to overthrow Crespo's family and by extension the social and political order. He is the specter of Willie Horton in uniform.

Don Lope de Figueroa, with whom Crespo initially butts heads, later in the play displays the depth of his loyalty to the positive values of family and honor. Díez Borque calls him Crespo's "replica" in military guise ("Introducción" 69). Figueroa and the King, who pardons Crespo and makes him *alcalde* for life, with their presence and approval—like the blessing of the founding fathers—reaffirm the security and paternal honor of the community and the nation. Beyond a compelling emotional storyline and a field of characters designed to encourage the spectator's empathetic vicarious identification with Crespo, Calderón arranges scenes, stage movement of characters, and visual and other effects so as to maximize the emotional stimuli for the spectator. Time and space will not permit here a full description of what we might call the play's "emotional dramatic structure." I will describe a few scenes and some of the visual devices to illustrate what I have in mind.

Perhaps the most emotionally stimulating moments of the play occur when the Captain forces his way into Isabel's hiding space. We know of Crespo's fear of allowing the soldiers to see and interact with his daughter, and we also know of the Captain's disdain for everything associated with the family's integrity and honor. In the first act, the Captain's ruse, feigning an argument with the sergeant, results in their violent intrusion, swords in hand, into Isabel's hiding place. The commotion draws Crespo and Juan, both also with swords drawn. For the spectator who identifies with Crespo and his daughter, this should be enough to start their mirror neurons firing. The explicit threat of bodily harm represented by the use of swords in this scene and several others to follow provides a strong emotional stimulus.[11] As visual symbols the swords also infuse these scenes with the suggestion of male potency. These features of Calderón's staging seem precisely designed to stimulate the spectator's emotional reaction: exhilaration, alarm, fear, and simultaneous preparation to either fight or flee.

In the second act, the Captain again breaks into Isabel's hiding place, this time to kidnap and rape her. Crespo rushes in, but without his sword he cannot stop the kidnapping. As the soldiers carry Isabel away, we hear her plaintive cry from backstage, "¡Padre mío!" (II.868)[12] [Father!], while Crespo calls back: "¡Hija mía!" (II.868) [My daughter!], but the soldiers subdue him and carry him away also. Their echoing cries from off stage: "¡Ay de mí!" (Isabel, II.872), "¡Ay de mí!" (Crespo, II.873), represent their overwhelming feelings of fear, anguish, and despair. If these scenes are performed in a manner consistent with the stage directions and the storyline of Calderón's original design, for the spectator who has come to identify with Crespo and his family there is a compelling stimulus to share, or "mirror," these feelings of fear, anguish, and despair.

Many other elements of the play provide strong visual evidence of emotion, which the empathetic spectator is invited to share with Crespo and his family. At the beginning of the third act, when she kneels before her father, who has been tied up by the soldiers in the discovery space, Isabel's tears convey fear and despair. Later, in Crespo's own tears, when he himself kneels before the Captain and begs him to take all his belongings and marry Isabel, we can see a father's devotion, deep to the point of absolute self-sacrifice. There is hope to be felt in Crespo's receiving of the mayor's staff (*vara*) upon his election as *alcalde*, which replaces his sword as a symbol of power. This time it is the power of community and cooperation rather than of competition between individuals. And we can feel gratification upon seeing both justice and revenge in the image of the Captain, properly garroted and dead, in the same discovery space where previously we saw Crespo tied with his daughter kneeling and pleading before him.

The emotional storyline of *El alcalde* as described here offers the spectator opportunity and encouragement to take pleasure both in the vicarious involvement with Crespo and his family and in the emotional stimulation this and other features of the play provide. Calderón, it would seem, understood that the spectator's brain is an emotional brain. Since the emotions involved are rooted deeply in the human psyche, we may fairly assume that this experience would be similar for spectators both in Calderón's time and ours.[13]

For Calderón and other 17th-century playwrights, this engagement and stirring of the spectators' "passions" would have been the first step in achieving the desired aesthetic goals. The second step, that of moral instruction and the deeper pleasure this was thought to provide would have depended, at least in part, on the spectators themselves. The final scene of the play, with the Captain garroted in the discovery space and Crespo receiving the King's blessing and approval, offers a compelling image of justice, closure and the restoration of order. This straightforward interpretation, however, relies heavily on the momentum of the emotional storyline. Voters today may find that the emotional fervor of a political campaign can obscure the complexities and contradictions in candidates' positions. *El alcalde* involves a similar situation: Crespo's honor has been restored, but his family has been fragmented; the King has blessed Crespo's actions, but Crespo will bear the burdens of making judgment and administering justice the rest of his life. The idyllic vision of peaceful rural life, which at the beginning of the play Crespo and his family seem to represent, has given way to a life of self-denial, hardship and service. Justice as shown in the final scene seems conclusive, but it is also imperfect: the soldiers who aided the Captain go unpunished, as does Crespo's son who sought to kill his sister for honor's sake. Scholars have pointed out these and other apparent contradictions that emerge from the play's ending and from perceived "defects" in Crespo's character.[14]

Considering this aspect of *El alcalde* in the context of 17th-century emblem theory, Bradley Nelson has explained how the visual and linguistic signs deliver a contradictory message, which produces "wonder" and unsettles the spectator's faculties. The play's action, he maintains, relies on "intuited ideas of justice and honor which refuse absolute definitions," and which challenge the spectator actively to use his or her moral intuition to reach a solution. This "emblematic mode of representation," he concludes, "points toward a solution outside of language, where paradoxes and enigmas do not find logical obstacles" (51). The effect seems to involve what the theorist Alonso López Pinciano in his *Philosophia antigua poética* [*Ancient Poetic Philosophy*] (1596) describes as "perturbación," an agitation of the "passions," caused in different ways by both comedy and tragedy, which disturbs and moves the faculties of the soul. The intended result is moral edification (II.53–54); Pinciano characterizes the process as a battle—"lid"—between the rational and the sensual appetites (I.93–94). Although the outcome is not predetermined, in Pinciano's Christian worldview certain fundamental, eternal truths, which the soul's "understanding" naturally comprehends (I.73–74), should help assure a favorable, moral outcome.

This result, which causes the spectator to look more deeply and beyond the signs delivered by the play, Nelson suggests, exemplifies the Baroque *topos* of *desengaño* [disillusionment] (51). Others have seen reflections of the Baroque in Crespo's character (Ruano compares it to the perspectivism in Velázquez's paintings 2001: 230), and in the play's exposure of "the complexity of the simple" (Fox 268). These ways of seeing the play point toward a design that works paradoxically to unify disparate elements and that reflects the Baroque theme of *discordia concors*.

Today's spectators may or may not choose to understand their experience of *El alcalde* in terms of the Christian worldview. They, like Calderón's spectators, can still feel the power of the emotional storyline and face the contradictions the ending of the play presents. They may find an answer in the innate truths of Natural Law, in their intuitive sense of justice, perhaps drawn from their primal emotions, or through a more rational thought process. But in any case, Calderón hands them the responsibility. It seems fair to suggest that we might find this same aesthetic design in other *comedias*, especially those with themes that speak to primitive human sentiments (personal survival, protection of offspring and family, kin selection, service to community and nation, as well as the "underground" emotions of sex and aggression) and that end problematically with unlikely marriages and imperfect justice. These criteria fit many Spanish Golden Age *comedias*, and they may help account for a quality of universal, lasting appeal.

If modern productions of such *comedias* follow Mitchell's advice and adhere carefully to the original structures of scenes, plot and characters, they might plausibly be expected to offer spectators an emotionally engaging aesthetic experience similar to that had by *corral* spectators. This does not account for the additional intellectual stimulus and pleasure knowledgeable spectators may take from hearing Baroque poetry recited onstage. But the aesthetic experience to be had would still follow the same design, offering pleasure and instruction through a process that moves the emotions, produces wonder, and provides the opportunity for edifying moral reflection. Stroud and those of us who share his desire for authenticity may find some consolation in this.[15]

Notes

1. Phillips Salman offers an excellent survey of Medieval and Renaissance theorists' descriptions of the process; see especially his pages 320–32 on the 17th century.
2. For his *El alcalde* Calderón reworked an earlier play of the same title by Lope de Vega, but Sloman shows how he completely transformed the plot, characters and structure (217–49).
3. In *Engaging Audiences: A Cognitive Approach to Spectating in the Theater*, Bruce McConachie explores how recent findings in neuroscience challenge traditional views on audiences' experience of theater performances. Similarly, in a series of articles

Catherine Connor-Swietlicki has shown how this same body of scientific research can be applied to a new understanding of the ways *comedias* engage their spectators ("Preceptistas," "Bridging," "Hacia una poética," "The Scientific Arts," "Creative Cognition," and "Embodying Rape"). Simerka's *Knowing Subjects: Cognitive Cultural Studies and Early Modern Spanish Literature* also devotes sections to *comedias* (27–79, 144–54, 162–96).

4. McConachie's section, "Mirror Neurons and Empathy" (65–75) and Connor-Swietlicki's articles "Embodying Rape" and "Creative Cognition" (74) cite earlier studies on mirror neurons. See also Simerka 68–79.

5. The Obama campaigns of 2008 and 2012, however, seem to have gotten this point.

6. Westen notes: "The capacity for rational judgment evolved to augment, not replace, evolutionarily older motivational systems. The emotional systems of simpler organisms are 'decision-making' systems that initiate approach, avoidance, fight, or flight. The neural circuits activated during complex human decision-making do not function independently of these more primitive systems" (62). McConachie explains how this fact undermines the foundational assumptions of post-modern critical theories in his section, "Falsification Theories" (6–11).

7. McConachie notes, "...the major emotional systems are unconscious and universal to all average humans at the neuronal and chemical levels of operation, although their expression in behavior will vary among different cultures and individuals" (94).

8. Westen remarks, "Freud analogized reason to a hapless rider on a horse, who does his best to channel and control the large beast—pulling it this way and tugging it that way—but ultimately, the power resides in the horse, not the rider" (62–63).

9. For Calderón's use of political themes see, for example, Greer on his Court plays and Rupp on his *autos sacramentales* and *comedias*.

10. P. N. Dunn's article, "Patrimonio del alma," exemplifies this traditional reading of the play applying the notion of honor as "patrimony of the soul."

11. In his section, "Of Props and Puppets" (82–87), McConachie explains how objects manipulated by actors onstage stimulate spectators' mirror neurons and their perception of a character's intentions and emotions.

12. Calderón, ed. J. M. Díez Borque II, 833. All citations are from this edition.

13. Connor stresses that scientific findings about individuals' potential responses are valid also for 16th-and 17th-century spectators, since evolution of "basic bio-chemical and neurological processes of our brains" moves so slowly that five centuries is insignificant ("Bridging" 28). She also notes that scientists agree that culturally acquired behaviors become encoded genetically very slowly, "even a small change in human genetic codings takes at least 50,000 years" ("Creative Cognition" 76).

14. Ruano, for example, sees ambiguity and complexity in Crespo's character, honor and virtue matched by pride and stubbornness, and suggests that the play leaves open the possibility that Crespo's own choices contribute to his misfortune ("Introducción" 23–40, "Pedro Crespo" 221–30). Díez Borque notes the polarity of good and evil between Crespo and the Captain, but he also sees evidence of pride, arrogance, and "excessive prudence" on the part of Crespo ("Introducción" 66). Fox offers a strongly negative view of Crespo as proud, arrogant, deceptive, and cunning. She sees the trial and execution of the captain as a "Machiavellian" act, a "sham with the appearance of legality" ("Quien tiene" 263). Edwards has perhaps the darkest view of Crespo and the play as a whole. In his analysis, Crespo becomes trapped in a "closed

world," a "maze," of his own "inflexible ideologies" and damned whichever way he moves. For Edwards the play is "...the despairing spectacle of men seeking to assert themselves, striving to defend integrity in a world which demands the sacrifice of individuals to implacable rigid codes" (65).
15. An earlier version of this paper was read at the Association for Hispanic Classical Theater's Annual Golden Age Drama Symposium in El Paso, TX in March 2009.

Works Cited

Calderón de la Barca, Pedro. *El alcalde de Zalamea*. Ed. and Introd. José María Díez Borque. Madrid: Castalia, 1987. Print. Clásicos Castalia.

Connor-Swietlicki, Catherine. "Bridging the Performance Gap: The Body, Cognitive Theory, and *Comedia* Studies." *Bulletin of the Comediantes* 55.2 (2003): 11–53. Print.

———. "Creative Cognition for Staging *Comedia*." *Comedia Performance* 4.1 (2007): 67–96. Print.

———. "Embodying Rape & Violence: Your Mirror Neurons & 2RC Teatro's *Alcalde de Zalamea*." *Comedia Performance* 7.1 (2010): 9–52. Print.

———. "Hacia una poética de los oyentes/espectadores de la comedia." *Actas del XIV Congreso de la Asociación Internacional de Hispanistas, II: Literatura española, siglos XVI y XVII*. Ed. Isaías Lerner, Robert Nival, and Alejandro Alonso. Newark, DE: Juan de la Cuesta, 2004. 119–25. Print.

———. "The *Preceptistas* and Beyond: Spectators Making 'Meanings' in the *Corral de Comedias*." *Hispania* 82.3 (1999): 417–28. Print.

———. "The Scientific Arts of Theater: The Bio-Social World-Theater with Examples from Lope, Calderón, and Others." *Bulletin of the Comediantes* 58.2 (2006): 457–67. Print.

Dunn, Peter N. "Patrimonio del alma." *Bulletin of Hispanic Studies* 41.2 (1964): 78–85. Print.

Edwards, Gwynne. "The Closed World of *El alcalde de Zalamea*." *Critical Perspectives on Calderón de la Barca*. Ed. Frederick A. de Armas, David M. Gitlitz, and José A. Madrigal. Lincoln, NE: Society of Spanish and Spanish American Studies, 1981. 53–67. Print.

Fox, Dian. "'Quien tiene al padre alcalde ...': The Conflict of Images in Calderón's *El alcalde de Zalamea*." *Revista Canadiense de Estudios Hispánicos* 6.2 (1982): 262–68. Print.

Greer, Margaret Rich. *The Play of Power: Mythological Court Dramas of Calderón de la Barca*. Princeton: Princeton UP, 1991. Print.

Iacoboni, Marco. *Mirroring People: The New Science of How We Connect with Others*. New York: Farrar, Strauss and Giroux, 2008. Print.

López Pinciano, Alonso. *Philosophia antigua poetica*. Ed. Alfredo Carballo Picazo. 3 vols. Madrid: Artes Gráficas, 1953. Rpt. Biblioteca de Antiguos Libros Hispánicos. Madrid: Consejo Superior de Investigaciones Científicas, 1973. Print.

McConachie, Bruce. *Engaging Audiences: A Cognitive Approach to Spectating in the The-ater.* New York: Palgrave Macmillan, 2008. Print.

Miller, Jonathan. *The Afterlife of Plays.* Fifth Distinguished Graduate Research Lecture, San Diego State University. San Diego: San Diego State UP, 1992. Print.

Mitchell, Lee. *Staging Premodern Drama: A Guide to Production Problems.* Westport, CT: Greenwood P, 1983. Print.

Nelson, Bradley J. "*El alcalde de Zalamea*: Pedro Crespo's Marvelous Game of Emblem-atic Wit." *Bulletin of the Comediantes* 50.1 (1998): 35–57. Print.

Rupp, Stephen. *Allegories of Kingship: Calderón and the Anti-Machiavellian Tradition.* University Park: Pennsylvania State UP, 1996. Print.

Ruano de la Haza, José María. Introducción. *El alcalde de Zalamea.* By Pedro Calderón de Barca. Madrid: Espasa Calpe, 1988. 9–57. Print. Colección Austral.

———. "Pedro Crespo." *Cuadernos de Teatro Clásico* 15 (2001): 217–30. Print.

Simerka, Barbara. *Knowing Subjects: Cognitive Cultural Studies and Early Modern Spanish Literature.* West Lafayette, IN: Purdue UP, 2013. Print.

Stroud, Matthew. "The Director's Cut: Baroque Aesthetics and Modern Staging of the *Comedia.*" *Comedia Performance* 1.1 (2004): 77–94. Print.

Salman, Phillips. "Instruction and Delight in Medieval and Renaissance Criticism." *Renaissance Quarterly* 32 (1979): 303–32. Print.

Sloman, Albert E. *The Dramatic Craftsmanship of Calderón: His Use of Earlier Plays.* Oxford: Dolphin, 1958. Print.

Westen, Drew. *The Political Brain: The Role of Emotion in Deciding the Fate of the Nation.* New York: Public Affairs, 2007. Print.

Gendered Gazing: Zayas and Caro Go Back to the Future of the "Artful Brain and Body"

Catherine Connor-Swietlicki
University of Vermont

> "Only in theater are real human beings with real bodies integral to the communication of the literary message from text to recipient ... [T]he body is the material agent of the subject through which one deals with others ..."
> —Matthew D. Stroud[1]

Introduction: Reexamining the Bio-Cultural Gendered "Gaze"

In recent decades, *comedia* studies have refocused scholarly attention back to our bodies and minds in their bio-cultural roots. Matthew Stroud and his generation of *comedia* scholars continue to revolutionize how we understand our embodied minds today and, as a consequence, what occurred during the *comedia*'s heyday. We continue probing the interdependence of biology and culture in Caro's and Zayas's art and, simultaneously, in how we might connect with them. In effect, we can now greatly improve on the performance-oriented metaphor "the gaze." Rather than a social control mechanism, we can now analyze "gazing" within a range of interactive tendencies. These include understanding how gender and sexuality—like "gazing"—are continuous bio-cultural processes, not set categories. Rather than being *the* method of perceiving, "the gaze" is but one means of an individual's adaptation across a continuum. Because the dramatic arts intensify all bio-cultural processes of becoming, they are now studied by neuroscientists as well as performance scholars. In fact, Caro's and Zayas's arts are one of the best means available for illustrating how individuals develop differently within a range of biological and cultural networks. Caro and Zayas thus help us know ourselves in art and life.

Major breakthroughs in the neurobiology of culture are making this progress possible.[2] They are most fully summarized by the term *autopoiesis*, meaning "self-organizing," "self-realizing" and other synonyms such as "self-adaptation," "re-creation" or "re-connecting." These explain how perceiving, learning, memory, creativity, emotions and any other body-brain activities really operate.[3] Indeed, each individual only knows what she thinks or feels via her body-brain's re-connections. Because *autopoiesis* is the only means anyone has of knowing anyone or anything, it is *the* organizing system of everything in life and in the arts—with the latter offering the greatest concentration and variety of life experiences available (Connor, "Bridging," "Beyond").

The second major breakthrough from neuroscience studies demonstrates that no one's inner connections of self-organization fit neatly into categories such as subject, object, male and female. This revolutionary development affects all theories of literature, drama, psychology, political philosophy and especially performance studies. It is why we must change what we think it means to gaze or to perceive and conceptualize. Because living beings are *autopoietic*, each of us emerges from our personal range of experiencing neurobiological and cultural connections. When performances and other arts incite spectators, each adapts new and individual bio-cultural reflections within when realizing the outside stimulus. Thus, each one's perceptions, memory, behavior and sex-to-gender notions will reorganize personally and internally before gender distributions can be represented across a societal continuum. These body-brain differences within and between selves occur at the microscopic levels in all our interconnected organs. This means that each of us self-organizes across her personal algorithm in life and art. Her algorithm of self-realization necessarily precedes any societal algorithm researchers might construct.

Gender and sexual classifications of brains are an excellent example of how societies ignore the "trans" nature of every aspect of an individual's being. In fact, every internal contributor to self-realization depends, like sex and gender, on each individual's particular neuronal connections. Indeed, the majority of female-male characteristics substantially overlap in how these are distributed in anyone's brain (Fine 2014). These supposedly feminine and masculine characteristics *are only weakly inter-correlated*, if at all. Both male and female brains possess a *complex mosaic* of sex and gender indicators. This mutability of gendered behavior is what Caro's and Zayas's characters confirm in performance. Cordelia Fine's summary of neurological discoveries parallels what *comedia* scholars detect in culture. "Female-male differences and individual behavior vary across time, place, group and context" (915). In sum, this is how *comedia* scholarship and neuroscience need each other to validate the evolved aesthetic practices of our individual body-brains.

Ana Caro de Mallén and María de Zayas y Sotomayor were ahead of their time in how they stimulated spectators' feelings about individual experiences, especially gender-related ones. Long before current neuroscience discovered how our individual bodies, brains and minds develop together, Caro's and Zayas's creative characterizations showed them. By the 1990s, Stroud's generation of *comedia* scholars had recognized in Caro's and Zayas's characters a diversity of ways of being "rational" and "gendered" (Soufas, Campbell). By investigating the interactive meanings created by the *autopoietics* of individuals' bodies and minds, scholars began connecting their observations to the whole selves and not just to the parts most easily observed. The new evidence establishes that Caro's and Zayas's characters were not just fictional fantasies or just critics' irrational notions of subjectivity or gender.[4] New, bio-cultural evidence of *autopoieisis* invalidates naïve and false assumptions that hormones, genitalia or brain sex alone are determinant. Rather, all our interconnected contributors of an individual's body-brain must be examined together.

Today art and science agree that one's body *is* a body of proof. It is time for *comedia* scholars to take up the banner that neuroscientists are helping us create. Today's leading neuroscientists look to the arts to demonstrate how we humans have always self-realized in our body-brains (Ramachandran, Kandel, Zeki). They need our interpretive leadership, however, to help more spectators and readers discover the individual *autopoiesis* of Caro's or Zayas's characters in the process of experiencing them. This realization of self in art and life is interdependent proof that we are necessarily diverse in the details of our emotions, aesthetics and sexualities. Thus, as we engage Caro's and Zayas's characters more profoundly, they lead us back to the future of analysis and criticism, grounding them in bio-cultural history.[5]

Theaters of Self-Organization and Art

Comedia scholars and critics have been active in performance studies since the last quarter of the 20th century. By uncovering *comedia's* complex semiotics, we have been able to theorize that spectators' means of processing a performance were necessarily multiple and individual. But without bio-cultural proof, we could not validate any ideological or aesthetic differences among individual spectators. The discovery of individual self-organization, however, documents how individuals necessarily process "universal" human experiences differently—even in becoming gendered.[6] All our senses, all our organs in all their degrees of difference participate in our constant becoming. Every aspect of someone's bio-cultural *autopoiesis* contributes to sex and gender. Similarly, one's brain has no cognitive center to which our sensory-motor systems report. All individual neuronal contributors, from emotional to rational components, are required continually to reorganize their relations to each other. In short, humans always necessarily recreate their connections of self in life and art (Ramachandran).

Each individual reorganizes herself like a theater or network of distributed, interworking body-brain connections to the world. Even if your body parts feel like "they are you," you are only *what you can remember* you are. You can only self-realize your memory and "make up your mind" *if* your body's chemistry can turn on and off your billions of neurons and their networks. A brief survey of a few areas will help describe how each individual's body-brain adapts "artful" solutions in becoming one's self even at the cellular level (Sapolsky). Like theater, the mind-brain is each human's internal space for coordinating multiple interactive systems. In art, as in our body-brains, self-realization necessarily transpires in the proximity of spaces, movement and time. Because everything in our minds evolved within these integrated organic media, they are also the essential building blocks of our aesthetics. For example, newly discovered *entorhinal grid neurons* indicate how crucial anyone's hippocampus (basic memory organ) and nasal areas are to the artful overlapping of spatial relations inside us. Although located deep within the evolutionarily older area of the brain, these spatial neurons are essential to the most sophisticated contributors of individuality. Grid neurons establish one's sense of place, movement, balance, memory and the rhythms needed for dance, song and language (Moser). We depend on these for all life's performances onstage or off. In fact, these neurons explain how Proust created his memorable opening description of scent in *Remembrance of Things Past* (Lehrer, Moser). Similarly, readers and spectators mirror the neuronal connections they perceive in narratives or performances and thus activate their memories, completing a cycle of self-organization (Iacoboni).

Caro's *Courage, Betrayal and Woman* (Williamsen) and Zayas's *Friendship Betrayed* (Larson) provide excellent examples of body-brain stimulation in action. They ignite emotional processes of remembering, thereby creating new thoughts and feelings. Their performances might cleverly apply neuro-aesthetic principles of peekaboo, exaggeration and audio or visual groupings (Ramachandran, Levitin). These naturally evolved for pleasure and survival in our daily processes of reorganizing memories. Our eyes and ears evolved to abstract and identify friends and foes from among incomplete images hidden by branches or noise. Our mind-brains enjoy solving these puzzles and are rewarded when they can correctly reassemble visual patterns and auditory arrangements from dissonance. For example, we delight in reworking memories from real life simultaneously with perceptions of Caro's Leonor/Leonardo in performance. But this can happen only if our brain areas can first abstract movements, colors, pitch, rhythms, etc. After sensing these parts, our brains reorganize all their contributions before identifying what is seen and heard. And only when these signals reconnect with memory networks does anyone realize the joy or the despair of her perceptions and conceptualizations.

Regardless of what our body-brains might organize, we humans evolved to enjoy figuring things out! Our brains are rewarded with a shot of dopamine to further enforce our successful connections of perceptions and memory into a new image. That is just one example of our natural and most basic-level "chemical dependence." Without all our hormones and neurotransmitters to connect all areas of our mind-brain, we cannot be cognizant of our delight! There is no memory or mind in the usual sense unless one's varied types of neuronal structures can realize new connections, i.e. concepts, feelings, and memories.

Other newly discovered neurons significant to life and theater are called "grandmother neurons" (Quian Quiroga). Also referred to as "Luke Sky-walker neurons" and "Jennifer Aniston neurons," these reveal that a single "personalized" neuron can spark connections, memories, thoughts and feelings responding to a particular person. When some individuals saw photos of or merely thought about the "Luke actor" or "Jennifer" or their grand-mother, specialized neurons particular to the individual would light up brain scans. First called "category neurons," they are now more accurately named "concept neurons." That is because they do not strictly categorize an image or sound but instead conceptualize it by linking together as many additional emotional and "rational" brain areas as possible. Thus our concepts of memory are reworked and self-realized among any contributors an individual can muster in response to inside or outside stimulation. That means that we do not recognize someone onstage or off unless we can reignite memories of the experiences and emotions that we originally associated with that person. Our visual cortex does not see anything until our memories are reconnected to the images perceived (Raichle, Edelman, Kandel). The same thing happens when individuals listen to or even just imagine familiar sounds, voices and especially music (Levitin). These discoveries demonstrate that we do not just hear with our audio cortices or see with our occipital cortex. It is why "the gaze" is not singular or unified as originally assumed. An individual necessarily makes her own conclusions by connecting her multiple interior-to-exterior contributors of self-realization.

These constituents of *autopoiesis* are excellent illustrations for how *comedia* spectators' thoughts and feelings about actors or their characters arise when an individual body-brain recreates memory connections. Only individuals who have experienced Caro's Leonor or Zayas's Fenisa and Marcia might already have the neurons to reignite memories of the characters and of their actors. Just as those who are inattentive to or uninterested in contemporary popular cultures would not have specialized neurons for Luke or Jennifer, so too spectators past and present would not have neurons for particular actresses or Fenisa and Leonor. That is especially the case of the performance critics and drama scholars not interested in reimagining Fenisa or Leonor. If a reader or spectator does not want to perceive the actors or characters as more unconventional than most female protagonists of *comedias*, he won't. These facts demonstrate how our bio-cultures, i.e. our individual body-brains, interact within our particular experiences in becoming ourselves in aesthetic experiences as well as in everyday life.

Mirror neurons are the most significant discovery now revolutionizing how body-brains map together cultures and biology in their individual ways (Iacoboni, Ramachandran, Connor "Embodying" 2010). Caro's or Zayas's varied female creations and their actresses' embodied characterizations demonstrate how spectators diversely imitate others in order to connect with them, thus creating their own individual-levels of meanings of their performance experiences. Starting with brain-based evidence, we can see how these neurons have become so essential to humans because of their locations and their tendencies to ignite all possible connections of one's memory. Significantly, most humans have a concentration of mirror neurons on the left side of the brain—precisely where other contributors connect to make meaning. The left side is where visual input (occipital cortices), diverse touch sensations (parietal lobe) and our capacities for hearing, balance and facial recognition (temporal lobes) overlap with our basic language areas, named for their discoverers Wernicke and Broca (Ramachandran). Their proximity enhances overlapping connectivity in these amazing neural concentrations! This is how essential areas for perceiving performances get a boost from mirror neurons and better connect memory, imagination, and language all at once! Mirror neurons activate neuronal linkage if I hear, see, or just think about someone or something previously experienced and organized into my brain's mappings. These neurons thus stimulate me to imitate or mirror perceptions and to reshape them into my new memories. And because one's memory functions *autopoietically*, each individual's mirroring is also reflecting her particular conceptual blending of feelings and thoughts she has been realizing about the performer perceived. This is how one's body and cultural experiences always work together by connecting at the individual level.

A contemporary television example will emphasize how different individuals' mirror neurons contrast in their capacities to connect. Like a good *comedia* cast, plot and performance, the award-winning sit-com series "The Big Bang Theory" stimulates spectators to mirror within themselves and to develop diverse levels of insight and empathy. Characters in the series differ in their abilities to interpret the social and personal signals expressed in faces, voice tones, gestures and every bodily indication possible. In doing so, their individualized capacities mirror their understanding of others. These in turn allow spectators to consider their own interpretive abilities in theater and in everyday *autopoiesis*. The lead "Big Bang" character, Sheldon Cooper, is like some people we know in *comedias* and especially in academe. Sheldon believes he is a highly rational and systematic thinker, but he is largely unable to mirror others' body-mind language enough to read their minds or to feel their emotions. Although experiments on mind-reading or Theory of Mind (ToM) show that ToM abilities correlate positively with empathy (Baron-Cohen), the two are not synonymous and they do not necessarily coexist. In fact, an actor needs strong ToM abilities to act well, but she must control her empathy to protect her own emotional system from overload (Goldstein et al., Petersen).

This aesthetic game of bodily communication, mind-reading, and mirroring levels of empathy is essential to human relationships in life as well as in theater. Contemporary stagings of *Friendship Betrayed* and of *Courage, Betrayal and Woman* exemplify how mirroring and perception are just as interdependent now as in the times of the two female dramatists.[7] From the neurological and humanistic perspectives, gendering and sexing are necessarily always a part of the interdependence of body and brain. The behavior of Zayas's Fenisa is a clear example of weak social empathy camouflaged by clever ToM acting abilities. In her asides and body language, the character/actress displays insincere friendship. Fenisa's strategic betrayal begins when her body and facial signals trigger the empathic but misread readings of her friends Marcia, Belisa and Laura. Similarly, in Caro's play, Leonor's clever vocal and bodily gestures complement her adopted "male" identity and send ToM signals that elicit much more than empathy in Estela. The latter's ToM and empathy reconnect in her imagined concepts of sexual attraction and even love. Estela's reading of Leonor/Leonardo demonstrates how mirroring, like gazing and gendering is always based on individualized processes of *autopoiesis*. In turn, spectators' potential ToM and empathy also depend on their individual bio-chemical and cultural connections.

These examples of using mirror neurons indicate how we humans differ in our connective abilities to feel, to think, and to "sex or gender" in any situation. We do not gaze at an attractive person with our eyes but with all contributing body-brain regions working together. In effect, we see what we want to believe or already believe. Thus, our neuronal memories contribute more to how we conceptualize and realize our perceptions than do our eyes alone (Connor "Beyond"). Marcia, Belisa and Laura try not to see Fenisa as a traitor, because they want to believe she is a friend. Estela wants to believe her mind-reading of Leonardo. But her desire for and concepts of "him" are more powerful than the messages her eyes and amygdala can connect to her frontal cortex's better judgment.

When we participate as scholars or popular spectators in performances of *Friendship Betrayed* and *Courage, Betrayal and Woman*, we ignite individually developed connections by experiencing the plays' concepts in the flesh. Thus when we engage the performance, we can only participate at our own individual levels of mind-reading and empathizing. We necessarily make our own *autopoietic* interpretations in the only way possible for our remembered selves. These multilayered yet individual processes range from socially ill-adapted "rationality" to excessive and misplaced empathy. This is why literary critics and theoreticians produce diverse feelings and analyses about the same plays and performances.

The "Trans" Organization of Everything and Everyone

In exploring the new evidence for how we become ourselves in all ways bio-cultural, I have been indicating how the term "trans" helps us comprehend our personal variations of selfhood across an internal spectrum of body-brain contributors. In effect, the transformations in our own algorithms of internal connectivity contribute to our social groups' algorithmic realizations as we engage with them. These varying manners of self-realization correspond to how spectators differently engage in a *comedia* performance. Thus the potential polysemy of Zayas's and Caro's characters multiplies as their performances stimulate our individual body-brains. *Comedia* critics have signaled how Zayas and Caro employ a wide range of female and male characterizations in a greater-than-normal variety of sex-to-gender distributions. This multiplicity is substantiated by the diversity of body-brain connectivity I have been outlining in this essay. The "trans" nature of our individual connections explains how critics can differently interpret plays (Fine). In neuroscience as well as performance arts we show how differences in concepts, values and definitions are not fixed word categories but plastic meanings in the process of change, just as *caballero* and *hidalgo* [minor nobleman] were in the times of Caro and Zayas. In their performance contexts "woman" and the other thematic concepts require each spectator to reimagine her embodied aesthetics and sexual-cultural politics.

As I have outlined, *autopoiesis* explains how we are always becoming ourselves and that necessarily includes sexing and gendering. These, like our notions of friendship, betrayal, courage and woman are quite literally "mirrored" and truly "self-realized" within and across each actor and spectator. Traditionally, spectators and critics have been obliged to accept "universal" definitions of words such as "friendship, betrayal, courage, and woman." Our critical analyses and aesthetics have had to settle for the prison house of language. Until now, we could not span the bio-cultural gap between one individual's and another's self-realizations of each word (Connor "Bridging"). From the perspective of our bodies, brains and language, however, George Lakoff, often with Mark Johnson, has been able to demonstrate how linguistic usage evolves from our body-brain networks. Words and concepts are real, physical connections within and across spaces and time in one's body-brain. Metaphors are truly connectors of body-brain experiences and therefore of memory. They are prime examples of the coevolution of aesthetics and our "trans" bio-cultural selves. These metaphorical mappings are how leading neuroscientists explain that our thoughts and feelings arise across networks and within our overlapping brain areas. (Edelman, Ramachandran, Zeki, Sapolsky).

This is how each spectator's experience in mirroring and gendering the actresses gives rise to her individual trans-realization of what "friendship, betrayal, courage" and even "woman" mean to her. Each person's hermeneutics of "woman" in the plays are a plastic transitioning and blending of her performance experience with her own bio-cultural algorithms of sexuality and gender. Like the neurochemical reactions that enable eyes, ears and all other organs to reorganize memory, so too sexing and gendering are neuro-chemical adaptations within our concepts experienced "in the flesh." This happens over the course of our lives, from fetus and neonate to the grave. Literally, the *neurotransmitters* that contribute to our daily self-realization are the same "makers" of our daily sexing and gendering of self. A lifetime of neuronal rehearsals constantly reworks and bio-culturally recreates each one's *autopoieisis*. The developmental and aesthetic processes of gazing, mirroring and gendering or sexing are thus inseparable from one's neurological *autopoiesis*. But just as ToM and empathy differ among actors and spectators, so too our individual variations of sexing and gendering experiences relate differently to key words like "woman," "valor," "friendship" and "betrayal."

In effect, performance experiences stimulate spectators to recreate internally their bio-cultural evidence for the "trans" and multiple distributions of those words. Each spectator or critic, past or present, will only sense what she is capable of reimagining, whether the experiences are sexualized or not. If her neuronal memory circuits have not practiced using his new bio-cultural connections, it is unlikely that she can create such new meanings within herself or in her sense of society.

All the actresses, especially those playing Zayas's Fenisa and Caro's Leonor and Estela, motivate "trans" or multiple realizations of selves. These processes are documented by current bio-cultural contributions to understanding sex and gender as body-brain connections. Our neuro-aesthetics demonstrate that no single chemical-hormonal formula and no genital pattern can produce brain gender or sex. In coming decades, researchers from neuroscience and the arts will cooperate in documenting and valorizing complex algorithms for all individual selves—whether in terms of sex and gender or any other bio-cultural traits. Their research will recognize Zayas and Caro as keen observers of how sexing and gendering are inseparable from other multiple and variant, body-brain indicators of our individual *autopoiesis*. This bio-cultural evidence should testify to Caro's and Zayas's contributions, not only in *comedia* history, but also to bio-cultural scholarship and the humanities' long revolution (Fausto-Sterling, Fine, Halpern, Hines, Maturana and Verden-Zöller).

Notes

1. Stroud's book represents a synthesis of his extensive critical contributions.
2. Each of us develops our *individual ontogeny* in the process of our evolved human phylogeny. Today's humans still begin with body-brains that have not changed for millennia. Their artistic instincts are as verifiable as all other evolved means of being personal, logical, emotional, social and linguistically expressive. The evidence is stronger than ever for how human body-brains co-evolved in culture and "nature." See Richerson and Boyd; Ramachandran, particularly "No Mere Ape" and "The Neurons that Shaped Civilization."
3. *Autopoiesis*, the term coined by neurobiologists Maturana and Valera, is widely used by artists, social scientists, neuroscientists and literary scholars to describe how an individual's body-brain creates its own inner-outer exchanges of becoming throughout life. Each living being—or a work of art or a society—is continually self-realizing or *autopoietically* connecting itself and its surroundings. Just as one's bio-cultural identity grows by living, so too literary characters, paintings or songs develop in the very process of creation. This does not mean that we are independently empowered by a self-fashioning "individualism" in the sense of a unified mind-self. Rather, the healthy brain needs to think that it is unified. Our body-brain regions evolved organically, giving us the illusion that we are directly processing the world around

us. Maturana compared this to how Alonso Quijano believes that he is self-realizing a new identity as Don Quixote. In fact it is an *autopoietic* result of his slowly connected self.

4. No matter how rational one might think her ideas are, there is no such thing as "rationality" in opposition to emotional (Damasio). Emotions always impact one's thought processes, especially in their absence from social emotions in decision-making. One can only realize and experience anything because all her body-brain organs, including everything "emotional," contribute to reworking what the mind has already remembered. Nothing we call cultural, artful or environmental in any form—verbal, material, intuitive or "spiritual"—can be imagined or injected into a mind without a brain in a body. An individual's organic media are the only ways that anyone can "make up her mind" about the messages being self-connected and realized inside/outside the self. These largely unconscious processes are what each of us always does in "real life" and in aesthetic experiences such as performances. Because Caro and Zayas depict so many individually gendered characters going through these bio-cultural processes, they provide attractive examples for the merging methodologies of neuroscience and *comedia* performance scholarship.

5. I do not hesitate in claiming the viability of what I write about body-brain and minds, individuality and more in this essay. Leading neuroscientists now rely on humanistic artifacts to demonstrate how different body-brains create culture and its individual social interpretations. See Note 3 above. No combination of previous psychological, cultural, sociological and cultural evidence can establish authoritative and verifiable answers to questions about how individuals necessarily think and feel differently. See Edelman, Sapolsky, Ramachandran, Kandel, Damasio, Zeki, and Varela, Thompson and Rosch.

6. *Comedia* criticism of recent decades has increasingly been based in concepts of bodymind. Our individual publications form a diverse yet integrated series of prismatic reflections. Together they are an *autopoietic* expression of human experience in life and art. In joining the editors of this volume, I uphold that there is no essential universality of human experience and identities but rather a range of ever-developing individuals who continually contribute to one *autopoiesis* and that can never be socially or personally monolithic.

7. My personal experience with the two plays in performance was at the 2006 conference of GEMELA in Georgetown University where Caro's *Valor, agravio y mujer* was presented with Amy Williamsen's subtitles and Zayas's *Traición en la amistad* was staged with Catherine Larson's translation. I am indebted, however, to the insightful analyses *comedia* scholars on the diversity of "woman" portrayed in both works.

Works Cited

Baron-Cohen, Simon. *The Essential Difference: Male and Female Brains and the Truth about Autism.* New York: Basic Books, 2003. Print.

Campbell, Gwyn E. "(En)Gendering Fenisa in María de Zayas's *La traición en la amistad*." *Romance Language Annals* 10.2 (1998): 482–87. Print.

Connor (Connor-Swietlicki), Catherine. "Beyond Cognition: Don Quijote and Other Embodied Minds." *Cervantes* 32.1 (2012): 231–61. Print.

———. "Bridging the Performance Gap: The Body, Cognitive Studies and *Comedia* Theory." *Bulletin of the Comediantes* 55.2 (2003 [2004]): 11–53. Print.

———. "Creative Cognition for Staging *Comedia.*" *Comedia Performance* 4.1 (2007): 67–96. Print.

———. "Embodying Rape and Violence: Your Mirror Neurons and 2RC Teatro's 'Alcalde de Zalamea.'" *Comedia Performance* 7.1 (2010): 9–52. Print.

Damasio, Antonio. *Looking for Spinoza: Joy, Sorrow, and the Feeling Brain.* New York: Harcourt, 2003. Print.

Edelman, Gerald. *Bright Air, Brilliant Fire. On the Matter of the Mind.* New York: Basic Books, 1992. Print.

———. *The Remembered Present: A Biological Theory of Consciousness.* New York: Basic Books, 1989. Print.

Fausto-Sterling, Anne. *Sex/Gender. Biology in a Social World.* New York: Routledge, 2012. Print.

Fine, Cordelia. *Delusions of Gender. How Our Minds, Society and Neurosexism Create Difference.* New York: W. W. Norton, 2010. Print.

———. "His Brain, Her Brain?" *Science* 346.6212 (2014): 915–16. Print.

Halpern, Diane F. *Sex Differences in Cognitive Abilities.* 4th ed. New York: Psychology P, 2012. Print.

Hines, Melissa. *Brain Gender.* New York: Oxford UP, 2004. Print.

Goldstein, Thalia R., Katherine Wu, and Ellen Winner. "Actors Are Skilled in Theory of Mind But Not Empathy." *Imagination, Cognition and Personality* 29.2 (2009–2010): 115–33. Print.

Iacoboni, Marco. *Mirroring People: The New Science of How We Connect with Others.* New York: Farrar, Straus and Giroux, 2008. Print.

Kandel, Eric. *The Age of Insight. The Quest to Understand the Unconscious in Art, Mind and the Brain from Vienna 1900 to the Present.* New York: Random House, 2012. Print.

Lakoff, George. *Women, Fire and Dangerous Things. What Categories Reveal about the Mind.* Chicago: U of Chicago P, 1987. Print.

———. and Mark Johnson. *Philosophy in the Flesh: The Embodied Mind and Its Challenge to Western Thought.* New York: Basic Books, 1999. Print.

Larson, Catherine, trans. *Friendship Betrayed.* By María de Zayas y Sotomayor. Lewisburg, PA: Bucknell UP, 1999. Print.

Lehrer, Jonah. *Proust Was a Neuroscientist.* Boston: Houghton Mifflin, 2007. Print.

Levitin, Daniel J. *This Is Your Brain on Music. The Science of a Human Obsession.* New York: Dutton, 2006. Print.

Maturana, Humberto, and Gerda Verden-Zöller. *The Origin of Humanness in the Biology of Love.* Exeter, UK: Imprint Academic, 2008. Print.

———. and Francisco Varela. *De máquinas y seres vivos. Autopoiesis: La organización de lo vivo.* 6th ed. Santiago de Chile: Editorial Universitaria, 1994. Print.

Moser, Edvard I., and May-Britt Moser. "Grid Cells and Neural Coding in High-End Cortices." *Neuron* 80.3 (2013): 765–74. Print.

Petersen, Elizabeth Marie Cruz. "Building a Character: A Somaesthetics Approach to *Comedias* and Women of the Stage." Diss. Florida Atlantic University, 2013. Print.

Quian Quiroga, Rodrigo. *Borges and Memory. Encounters with the Human Brain.* Trans. Juan Pablo Fernández. Cambridge, MA: The Massachusetts Institute of Technology P, 2012. Print.

Raichle, Marcus E. "The Brain's Dark Energy." *Scientific American* 202.3 (2010): 44–49. Print.

Ramachandran, V. S. *The Tell-Tale Brain: A Neuroscientist's Quest for What Makes Us Human.* New York: W. W. Norton, 2011. Print.

Richerson, Peter J., and Robert Boyd. *Not by Genes Alone: How Culture Transformed Human Evolution.* Chicago: U of Chicago P, 2006. Print.

Sapolsky, Robert. *Biology and Human Behavior: The Neurological Origins of Individuality.* 2nd ed. Chantilly, VA: The Teaching Company, 2005. Print.

Soufas, Teresa Scott. *Dramas of Distinction. A Study of Plays by Golden Age Women.* Louisville: U of Kentucky P, 1997. Print.

Stroud, Matthew D. *Plot Twists and Critical Turns. Queer Approaches to Early Modern Spanish Theater.* Lewisburg, PA: Bucknell UP, 2007. Print.

Williamsen, Amy, trans. *Courage, Betrayal and Woman.* By Ana Caro de Mallén. Forthcoming.

Zeki, Samir. *Splendors and Miseries of the Brain. Love, Creativity and the Quest for Human Happiness.* Walden, MA: Blackwell, 2007. Print.

Act Three

Gender Games: Plotting Women

Of Love and Labyrinths: Feminism and the Comedia

EDWARD H. FRIEDMAN
Vanderbilt University

> El que solo busca la salida no entiende el laberinto, y aunque la encuentre,
> saldrá sin haberse enterado, o como si no se hubiese enterado.
> —José Bergamín ("Molino de razón," *La cabeza a pájaros*)

> [One who only looks for the exit does not understand the labyrinth, and will
> leave without understanding or as if he had not learned anything.]
> ["Reason's Windmill," *Featherbrained*]

> Love's a conundrum. Love is a strain.
> Love is a trap set to bring you disdain.
> Love is a gamble. Love is a test.
> Love is a killing field of infinite jest.
> But there's something about love that you can't resist,
> a feeling that grabs you—there's no cease and desist—
> and you enter the quicksand instead of the mist,
> and you take it on the chin when you want to get kissed.
> —Anonymous Tennessee ballad

The social structure of Early Modern Spain consists of rigid hierarchies and restraints of many persuasions. Strict censorship and inquisitorial practices were facts of life, and the more one deviated—consciously or unconsciously—from a prescribed center, the more precarious one's safety and security. Certain groups, including New Christians and the poor, figured most conspicuously among the disenfranchised and demeaned, and it hardly would be an exaggeration to add women to a list of those marginalized in a strongly patriarchal environment. The prominent (and positive) status of women in comic drama of the period, then, becomes paradoxical, for here—if only briefly—women enjoy a power that eludes them in the so-called real world. This essay will explore the role of women in Golden Age Spanish comedy and will focus on a particular application of the conventions of characterization. In *The Labyrinth of Love* (2013), inspired by Cervantes's *El laberinto de amor*, one of the *ocho comedias* published in 1615, I attempted to inscribe the feminine and feminist sensibility of comic theater while underscoring both the irony implicit in the late 16th- and 17th-century plays and further ironies wrought by time. I want to demonstrate that writing an adaptation is, at once, a critical reading and an example of what Harold Bloom has labeled "the anxiety of influence," a necessary confrontation with tradition and the literary and cultural past. The product is a refashioning that cannot—nor would it wish to—elide its models nor remain fully faithful to them. As in the case of *Don Quijote*, the text is a flexible entity, standing in the middle of refurbished sources, on one end, and mindsets of the present and glimpses into the future, on the other. *The Labyrinth of Love* is about, among other things, how Cervantes and contemporary and subsequent playwrights portray women and how the interpretation of society is revealing, concealing, and, ultimately, an exhibition of irony.

It is a commonplace of discussion of comedy to stress the license of the writer to escape the boundaries of reality. Comedy, like deconstruction, tends to favor those who are more often than not off-center in the normal order of things. In narrative, the picaresque turns the literary world upside-down by depicting life in the lower depths and by featuring a narrator/protagonist of the most undesirable lineage. The earliest readers may have been inclined to laugh at—rather than sympathize with—the outcast, but the satire is double-edged, with the *pícaro* [rogue] and society as joint objects. In Early Modern Spanish drama, the Old Christian villager, noble of spirit if not of blood, is given space in which to challenge hierarchical authority. Servants can be wiser and cleverer than their masters and mistresses, and their plotting can help lead to happy endings. On stage, however, the leading ladies in comic (or tragicomic) works may represent the largest and most striking contingent of de-marginalized characters and may demand the biggest leap of faith on the part of the audience. The women dominate the proceedings. This is a comic blueprint that dates from classical Antiquity, but the Spanish playwrights create remarkable personalities, situations, and a poetic discourse that is sharp, hard-hitting, and persuasive. Lope de Vega and his formula for the *comedia nueva* [new comedy] lead to prolific dramatic production, by Lope himself and by his followers. The *dramaturgas* of the day—María de Zayas, Ana Caro, and, in Mexico, Sor Juana Inés de la Cruz—add what may be termed a feminine sensibility to the model, but that Early Modern feminism was in the air, that is, in the contributions of the men, although support for the women's cause may have been unintentional.

Some years ago, Bruce W. Wardropper made the crucial observation that female protagonists in comic plays almost always are unmarried, whereas those in serious or tragic plays are married. This fact is not unrelated to the idea of comedy as a vacation from reality, from the status quo. The most prevalent gauge of the happy ending is a marriage or a betrothal, and commonly multiple promises of marriage, among *galanes* [gentlemen] and *damas* [ladies], and, in parallel fashion, their servants, maids, and lackeys. The announcements frequently have a measure of spectacle about them, which works ironically, for matrimony brings with it the transfer of familial honor and an increased isolation of women. The freedom that they enjoy in the comedies is lost at the moment in which they tie the nuptial knot. The motivating drive of honor pertains to men who must preserve their good name at all costs. There is nothing positive about strong-willed, independent, and rule-breaking women within this frame. Cross-dressing to make one's way in society is no longer an option. The Saturnalian impetus is completely lost in this milieu, which is dead-serious (quite literally, in the wife-murder plays). The comedies about liberated women have special value in a limited context, not as the first parts of two-play cycles of pre-marriage and marriage but as autonomous works of wish-fulfillment and projections into the future. The comic texts are funny, hopeful, and prescient. Those by male dramatists—by far the majority, with respect to plays and playwrights—allow men to voice equality and to enter the domain of social transformations and transgressions. Those by female dramatists, in a strangely appropriate manner, "follow the protocol," while providing supplements of their own. In Golden Age literature, women are habitually trapped, notably in the plays of uxoricide (see Stroud, *Fatal Union*) and in the novellas of María de Zayas, wherein female characters who are aggressive and female characters who are passive are equally likely to suffer death. The structure and the tone of the comedies offer dramatic scenarios that run counter to prescribed social rules and regulations.

Lope de Vega's emphasis on the *tragicomedia* has substantial bearing on the comic vision of the plays under scrutiny, those in which articulate, headstrong, and indomitable female protagonists *se salen con la suya* [come out on top]. Early Modern Spanish drama is unavoidably bittersweet, because honor is never written out of the argument, and any lightness in the approach veils momentarily the atmosphere of distrust, discrimination, censorship, and paranoia that reigns in the society of the era. Even when the dramatic occasions are most festive, something unpleasant lingers as a reminder of reality, of the realm in which appearances can be masked as truth and innocence can

be deemed—or treated as—guilt. The female protagonists acknowledge the
dangers and the potential repercussions of their actions, but they are motivated by a yearning for release from the strictures that apply to their gender.
The stratagems that they devise are decisively theatrical, or metatheatrical.
They re-script marriage proposals and suits, they adopt disguises, they leave
the confines of their fathers' or brothers' homes to venture onto the street
or road, and they switch from the pursued to the pursuers. Cross-dressing is
a convention and a metonym for the ironic self-determination that defines
the female protagonists. In order to realize their objectives, women have to
conduct their negotiations as men, for only then can they have a say in whom
and under what circumstances they will marry. In brief, their challenge is to
out-man their male counterparts, to conspire against them, and to overlook
temporarily the modi operandi and the customary space allotted to women.
The act of walking out the door in male attire is equivalent to taking the
offensive and attempting to gain control by emulating the rival. A certain
type of practical education is about to begin. Adversarial politics become rhetorical maneuvers that complicate and, to an extent, invert the premises of
appearances turned reality. If the women are successful in their endeavors,
the endings are comic, but tragedy looms in the background. That may be a
portent, conscious or unconscious, of things to come.

The paradigm for the love comedy is tripartite, divided neatly into three
acts. The female protagonist, electing to go against the wishes of her father or
brother(s), chooses the man whom she would like to marry and takes charge
of outwitting those who would point her in other directions. Role-playing,
confusions, miscalculations, setbacks, questionable pairings, and errors of
communication intensify the hurdles and the humor. In the end, "girl gets
boy," and the victory is strengthened regularly by the matching of other ladies
with appropriate men. The variations on the theme can be skillfully plotted
and poetically resonant, with an eye on the intriguing dialectics of similitude
and difference. The setting up of dilemmas and the fabrication of metadramas,
clothed in Baroque language, give the plays an element of suspense, a heavy
dose of mishaps and near-misses, which blend effectively with the feminist
thrust. Pedro Calderón de la Barca's *La dama duende* [*The Phantom Lady*],
to cite but one of many examples, illustrates the archetypal plot and appends
such features as a young widow brought back to her brothers' home, a case of
divided loyalties, the mysteries of a secret passage, scenes that take place in the
dark, and a scaredy-cat *gracioso*, all complemented by poetry that harmonizes
with the intricacies of the story line. Here, physical comedy mixes with social
and psychological issues and with a metaphorical system that equates women
with phantoms, simultaneously present and absent, whose impact can be felt

one minute and can dissipate the next. In the comedies themselves, women are forces to be reckoned with, but the wedding bells are destined to chime and threaten to disrupt the newly acquired confidence in feminine wiles and wisdom. The plays bring laughter with an edge.

Women's space in drama is, by its nature, symbolic. In honor plays such as Calderón's *El médico de su honra* [*The Surgeon of His Honor*] and *El pintor de su deshonra* [*The Painter of His Dishonor*], women are "phantoms" in a different sense than in *La dama duende*. They are at the mercy of the men whose honor depends on the honor—and the public perception of the honorability—of their wives. A fundamental distinction between the comedies and the tragedies is point of view. The audience sees comedy from a woman's perspective and tragedy from a man's. In one case, freedom is at stake; in the other, honor, likened to life itself, is in jeopardy. One of the most fascinating aspects of the comic plays is the inscription of the women into the protagonist position. These characters defend themselves by concocting schemes, commanding the stage, and uttering words that reverberate and that may convince the listeners. Men write women who masquerade as men as a means of appearing in public and as a form of self-protection. Lope, Tirso de Molina, Calderón, and their fellow playwrights masterfully bestow the gifts of inventiveness and eloquence onto their heroines. The female dramatists expand the irony by writing themselves into the picture, through extremely expressive protagonists and self-referential passages about the audacity of women as authors for the stage. In *La traición en la amistad* [*Friendship Betrayed*], for example, María de Zayas puts on display the saving grace of a community of women, which can permit its members to unite against the dog-eat-dog mentality and the hypocritical morality of men. Zayas inserts into her dramatic casserole, as it were, the flamboyant, highly-sexed, and licentious Fenisa, obviously evoking Don Juan Tenorio, a profligate to contrast with upstanding citizens; and the foul-mouthed *gracioso* León, possibly to show that she can thrive in an implicit battle of survival of the fittest, or *¿quién es más macho?* Leonor, the protagonist of Ana Caro's *Valor, agravio y mujer* [*Courage, Betrayal, and Woman*], retains male clothing and her identity as Leonardo during most of the play. She is adept at subterfuge, sword fighting, and feminine psychology. She enamors a woman who is passionately courted by at least three gentlemen, including Leonor's brother, because it is she who understands how women think and feel. The unequivocal intelligence and the boldness of Doña Ana in Sor Juana's *Los empeños de una casa* [*The House of Trials*] link her to the author, who seems to want to "out-Baroque" her Calderonian model in plot and discourse. Sor Juana's gender-bending exercise contains scenes of the *gracioso* Castaño in drag.[1] In sum, comedy clears paths for women while reflecting the institutions, the prejudices, and the intolerance of 16th- and 17th-century Spain.

Literature and theater mirror the dichotomies of the time: urban and rural life, the rich and the poor, honor and dishonor, Old Christians and New Christians, the Old World and the New World, written and oral cultural traditions, sacred and secular texts, history and fiction, and, of course, men and women. Drama depends on conflict, and gender roles and questions of agency supply unlimited prospects for the dramatization of conflict. It is admirable that hundreds of *comedias*, written mainly by men, give careful attention to the concerns and viewpoints of women: courtship rituals, social restrictions, education, relationships, conformity (and nonconformity), exposure to ideas, patterns of behavior, and so forth. Female characters voice their grievances, excel at metatheatrics, and perform—if not, like Ginger Rogers, in high heels and dancing backwards—in uncomfortable postures and in male garb. Naturally, accepting the actresses as men, no matter how talented the thespians, would have required suspension of disbelief from the spectators, but the plays facilitate entry into an imaginative zone, where the participant—audience member or *dramatis persona*—cannot ignore considerations of gender or the restraints imposed on women by society.

Technique and motif come together in the comedies by virtue of *metatheater*, a term brought into vogue (and later into *Comedia* circles) by Lionel Abel's *Metatheatre: A New View of Dramatic Form* (1963).[2] This elucidation of role-playing and identity accentuates self-conscious theatricality, by way of characters who become figurative dramatists and actors in the scripts that they formulate for their own purposes. On the whole, women in comic works initially are bound by standards that prohibit them from what we now may call direct interface with a patriarchal society and thus with their respective destinies. Metatheatrical ploys enable them to fight for their rights; metatheater becomes an assertiveness training ground. Lope de Vega and Miguel de Cervantes were celebrated competitors and enemies, yet each brings the process of composition—and, consequently, the constructedness—of the text into the literary object, with far-reaching results. Books, plays, and the characters that inhabit them reflect and refract reality; they function reciprocally to deal with make-believe as if it were real and to heighten the fictional illusion. Self-referentiality bursts through the seams, but never forsaking the real-world correlatives that are inseparable from the textual messages. *Don Quijote* tells many stories. Two encompass the entire narrative: (1) the anachronistic knight errant's journey to combat evil and injustice, to serve his conjured lady Dulcinea del Toboso, and to be worthy of a chronicle that will proclaim his fame; and (2) the writing of said chronicle, a patently (and palpably) complex task that involves a corps of narrators and coauthors. Cervantes punctuates the acts of reading and writing as he analyzes human nature and the dynamics of experience and personal development. He differentiates between the making of history and the making of historiography, between observation and expression, and between direct and indirect means of access to concepts and to the truths behind them. He shows that the relative generally poses as absolute and the subjective as objective. Even with all mechanisms in place for ironic detachment, Don Quijote can win reader sympathy, because the narrative balances metafiction with realism.

Don Quijote, be it through madness or method acting, is one of literature's most enduring—if not its most enduring—metatheatrical characters. He is so engrossed in his role that he concurrently acts, writes, directs, and critiques. The world is his stage, and macrocosm and microcosm are fused and confused. Few phenomena seem mutually exclusive. Others follow the knight's lead, entering his tableaux and creating their own. Acting becomes the mediating factor between reading and writing. On the Spanish stage, one form of acting merges with another, and scripts are constantly under revision. The theater as mirror is itself mirrored, a replication replicated until the starting point becomes vague or indecipherable. The characters are cognizant of the theatricality of their enterprises, but the "real world" for them is still, "in reality," only the tenor, the signified, of a metaphor. Cervantes, Lope, and other Early Modern writers close gaps by maintaining that fiction and fiction-making are essential parts of life, and vice-versa. In *Don Quijote*, the linear plot is doubled when the knight's quest is accompanied by the writer's—or (pseudo-)historian's—testimony and search for materials. Don Quijote contemplates an account of his adventures the instant he sets forth from a village in La Mancha. In Part 2, he is privy to commentary on Part 1, and he holds a copy of the false sequel in his hands and later meets a character from that tome. The book goes out into the world, and the world comes into the book. In the theater, variations on the theme of the play-within-a-play juxtapose levels of fiction with levels of reality, depending on context and perspective. Don Quijote reaches the pinnacle of metatheater, but the novel is filled with metatheatrical characters, including—alongside Sancho Panza, Sansón Carrasco, Basilio, and Maese Pedro—Marcela, Luscinda, Camila, Zoraida, the Duchess and her supporting players, and Claudia Jerónima. The ducal palace and Barataria, Sancho's island, are the most elaborate of numerous stage settings in *Don Quijote*. Cervantes, the frustrated playwright, triumphantly engages the recourses of theater and the impulses of metatheater in his narrative.

In chapter 48 of Part 2 of *Don Quijote*, the priest from Don Quijote's village and the canon from Toledo discuss the state of drama, and in the course of the conversation they praise playwrights of the 16th century, among them Cervantes himself. The self-appointed critics famously malign the *comedia nueva*, and, without naming its primary proponent, cast aspersions on a design for playwriting which fails to respect the unities of time and place. They argue that playwrights pander to those most poorly qualified to recognize and appreciate quality. They go on to specify other flaws in the new art of writing plays and, to top it off, they advocate more rigorous censorship. Despite the vicarious ranting and raving over Lope's model, Cervantes responds, in his own way, to the tastes of the public when he publishes the unproduced *Ocho comedias y ocho entremeses* [*Eight Plays and Eight Interludes*] in 1615. The prologue to the volume is restrained; one can detect no venom beneath the words. Cervantes lauds Lope's prolific output and the excellence of his plays, while he refers to his own dramatic texts with the utmost humility. Although in the introductory remarks he seems to separate his works from those of Lope, the texts themselves indicate some modification of his thoughts, or a concession to practicality. In the saint's play *El rufián dichoso* [*The Fortunate Rascal*], for example—which does not adhere to the unities of time and place—the personified *Comedia*, in a speech that begins "Los tiempos mudan las cosas / y perficionan las artes" (Cervantes, *Teatro completo* II, 326) [Time changes everything / and perfects the arts] takes the position that it is advisable to join the best of the past with innovations of the present. Before 1605, Cervantes had been a failed artist. By 1615, he was known by the public and the literati as the author of a masterpiece, and Part 2 would be published that same year. 1614 marked the fateful intrusion of the Avellaneda continuation, thought to be retaliation by defenders of Lope for the condemnation of the *comedia nueva* in the first part of *Don Quijote*. Cervantes addresses the insults in the prologue and in the closing chapters of his Part 2, but shows no animosity in the prologue to the plays. On the contrary, he flatters Lope by employing the basic outline of the *comedia de enredo* [of intrigue] in selected plays.

La entretenida [*The Distracted Lady*] and *El laberinto de amor* can be paired as nods to Lope and as winks of the eye. Their complicated plots highlight amorous intrigues and showcase the female characters.[3] In *La entretenida*, all efforts are for naught. The confusion of names, differences in social rank, and changes of heart lead to disappointment. The stage business promises multiple betrothals, but the main characters exit empty-handed. Interestingly, the central character of *La entretenida* is the kitchen-maid Cristina, attractive and wooed by three men, but a bit too haughty for her own good. Her reward is comeuppance rather than a marriage pledge. The women of the play are crafty, yet, because Cervantes chooses to amuse himself with the intertext, they are fated to lose in the game of love; this *fregona* [washer-woman] is not illustrious. *El laberinto de amor* counters the disillusionment of *La entretenida* with the accomplishments of three capable and resolute female figures—Rosamira, Julia, and Porcia—who struggle to wed the men of their dreams. They face setbacks, the threat of dishonor, and imprisonment, but their ingenuity (*industria*), individual and collective, and their good fortune save the day. The student Tácito declares at the end of *El laberinto de amor*, "Éstas son, ¡oh amor!, en fin, / tus disparates y hazañas; / y aquí acaban las marañas / tuyas, que no tienen fin" (Cervantes, *Teatro completo* III, 542) [These are—oh, Love!—in the end / your madness and deeds; / and here stop your entanglements, / that know no end]. In *El laberinto de amor*, Cervantes takes role-playing to hyperbolic lengths. There are rapid costume changes and changes of locale, dizzying shifts in gender and social status, impersonations within impersonations, and metaplays within metaplays. Only in the dénouement do the characters reveal their true identities. Cervantes seems to want to exhaust the world-as-stage motif. The road to alterations in the social system and to self-knowledge is paved, in this instance, with the machinations of cross-dressing and misrepresentation. One can acquire self-knowledge only by taking risks and by placing personal needs in broader contexts. Theater becomes the medium and the message. Comedy can venture into harm's way because it pretends not to take life seriously, while doing precisely the opposite. Society can progress through productive adjustments to the status quo, and sometimes the softer touch is advisable. The women of *El laberinto de amor* intuit that, by taking the initiative, they can improve their lot. The conventions of comedy give them, and Cervantes, a chance to discover their potential and to shape their destinies. With *El rufián dichoso*, *El laberinto de amor* best evinces a willingness by Cervantes to admit the unqualified pull of Lope's model. As in all his literary undertakings, Cervantes the playwright never writes without rewriting, and *El laberinto de amor* is, in the end, a comedy about the juncture of truth and identity and about how each is conceived, reconfigured, and interpreted.

In envisioning a play inspired by—as opposed to a translation or an adaptation of—*El laberinto de amor*, I wanted to bring out what I regard as the salient points of Cervantes's text and to capture, as well, the core of Early Modern feminism embedded in the *comedia nueva*. My goal was to re-create patterns and topics and to update the operating principles, that is, to build upon the ironic foundation of *El laberinto de amor* and other plays by placing 17th-century views of women against contemporary feminism. I liked Cervantes's decision to complicate and crisscross the role-playing and to have three women as the leads, and I wanted to make the precocious female characters even more precocious. The visual analogue would be, logically, the labyrinth, a locus of confusion and lost souls, who would find each other, with all parties assembled on stage, only at the conclusion. I wanted to experiment with Baroque excess, so to speak, through metatheater, cross-dressing, transfers of authority, and general bedlam. The female protagonists would challenge and try to change the men's outlook toward women by confronting them directly, but also indirectly, in effect, disguised as men. I sought means of generating suspense and humor and of modulating the events so that everything would fall into place in the closing scene. Not surprisingly, as I prepared my version of the play, I hoped that a reader or spectator of *The Labyrinth of Love* would be entertained and edified.

   The Labyrinth of Love is set in the province of Cáceres in the region of Extremadura (a word that hints of borders and boundaries) in the early years of the 17th century. I used the names of nearby towns as homes of the various characters. The first scene of Act I introduces Julia and Porcia, cousins and confidantes. They have an extensive collection of books, but they complain that they have been confined to their homes and sheltered from the excitement of life. They yearn to have contact with the world, and they want to aim beyond the prospective husbands within their current grasp. They hatch a plan to run away, to forge a ransom note that will make it seem as if they had been kidnapped, to dress as shepherds so as to roam freely around the countryside, and to hire a male guide and protector when they are on the road. Male clothing and new identities will give them a practical education. Elsewhere, Don Gonzalo, an emissary of the young nobleman Don Manfredo, appears before the wealthy and powerful Count Federico, to propose a marriage between Manfredo and Rosamira, the Count's daughter. All is going well until the Count is interrupted by a visit from Don Dagoberto, who discloses that Rosamira has been sighted in a series of rendezvous with an unknown male subject. Dagoberto advises the Count to be watchful of his honor and promises discretion. Count Federico confronts Rosamira, who refuses to give an explanation. Without conveying the reason, the Count reluctantly dismisses the puzzled Don Gonzalo. As Don Gonzalo reports to Manfredo the mysterious disruption of his meeting with the Count, Manfredo's friend Don Anastasio arrives. When Manfredo remarks on the glitch, Anastasio comforts him. Left alone, Anastasio expresses his love for Rosamira, on whom he has looked lovingly at mass. He decides to travel to the Count's palace to seek employment as a servant, thereby positioning himself close to his beloved. The scene shifts to Julia and Porcia, now Blas and Rutilio, with their escort, the impecunious but kindhearted Nonada. They meet Anastasio, who was denied a job at the palace because he was spotted as an aristocrat.

Identity shows through, he insists, as he fails to notice that his interlocutors are women and is only mildly aware of their lofty discourse. He persuades "Rutilio" (Porcia) to apply for the post at the palace as his undercover agent. Julia is flabbergasted by her cousin's decision, but Porcia confesses that she is attracted to Anastasio, despite his braggadocio. The distraught Manfredo resolves to pursue Rosamira on his own, and he comes across "Blas" (Julia), "Enrique" (Porcia's new name as an employee of Anastasio), and Nonada, who is telling his companions the story of the protean Pedro de Urdemalas. Manfredo is struck by the "philosophizing shepherd" Blas and hires "him" as a factotum, under the name of Camilo. Julia feels something for Manfredo, but his thoughts are on Rosamira. Porcia, as Enrique, is hired to work in Count Federico's palace, and "he" delivers food to Rosamira. Rosamira tells "Enrique" that she desperately needs to escape and begs "him" to exchange clothes with her. Porcia is hesitant, but agrees. Camped outside the palace, Nonada and Julia see Rosamira in flight and think that she is Porcia. Their reaction of bewilderment ends Act I.

As Act II commences, Rosamira is alone on the road, afraid of what faces her. Manfredo passes by, and she identifies herself as Ramiro, a poor worker on the way to visit "his" family. He asks her about public opinion of Rosamira, and "Ramiro" answers cautiously and tactfully. Manfredo takes his leave, and who should come along but Anastasio, who laments his lack of news from "Enrique." Anastasio, impressed by the intelligence of the courteous and modest lad, offers Ramiro a temporary position as secretary. At Count Federico's palace, Julia has been hired as the servant Camilo. She is amazed to find Porcia in Rosamira's room. They will trade places, and Porcia will enlist Anastasio's aid. Porcia, as Enrique, appears at the home of Anastasio, who introduces "him" to Ramiro. "Enrique" informs "his" master that Rosamira's unhappiness is evident. Left by themselves, the two women compare notes; Rosamira believes that she is speaking with a young man. Anastasio announces that he will return to Count Federico's palace in hopes of furthering his suit of Rosamira. "Ramiro" will continue to help with the business affairs, and "Enrique" will accompany Anastasio. Manfredo mentions to Don Gonzalo that he has heard nothing from "Camilo." Nonada arrives, and reports that "Camilo" is safely ensconced in the palace; he says that rumor has it that Rosamira may be imprisoned there. Manfredo will return to the palace with Nonada, who has the opportunity to soliloquize on his intermediary role. Rosamira is busy with secretarial duties when Don Gonzalo appears at Anastasio's home. Don Gonzalo is confounded, but pleased, by the sagacity of the humble scribe. He asks "Ramiro" to go with him to interrogate Dagoberto about gossip that has been spreading about Rosamira. Ramiro agrees.

On their way to the Count's palace, Manfredo and Nonada come upon Anastasio and Porcia (as Enrique). In their rivalry as suitors to Rosamira, Manfredo and Anastasio barely contain their hostility.

In the seventh and final scene of Act II, Manfredo, Anastasio, "Enrique," and Nonada are assembled outside the palace. Manfredo goes off to request a meeting with Count Federico. The Count understands Manfredo's predicament; he suggests that they talk with Rosamira. Julia (as Camilo as Rosamira) is caught in a trap. The Count is stunned that there is a "man" in his daughter's bedroom, and Manfredo is stunned that his page Camilo has been posing as Rosamira. Under grilling, "Camilo" explains that "Enrique" asked her to assume the role of Rosamira. Manfredo notes that "Enrique" is at the palace entrance with "his" master Anastasio. The Count, recognizing the name of Anastasio as the stalker of his daughter, demands that he and Enrique be brought inside. Porcia (as Enrique) details the exchange of clothes and the exit of Rosamira from the palace. The Count worries about his daughter and about his honor. Rosamira and Dagoberto, with their faces covered, enter the palace. Nonada follows them. Rosamira takes off her male garments and, at her father's insistence, narrates her story. Those in attendance are astounded. Recounting the visit to Dagoberto, Rosamira says that Don Gonzalo was satisfied that Dagoberto's record was clean, and, obsessed with unraveling the deception, he went off in search of the culprit. Rosamira clarifies the situation: she had met Dagoberto in the chapel and had immediately fallen in love with him. His statement to the Count was her idea. The Count is livid; he feels that his honor has been destroyed. Rosamira attempts to comfort him by divulging that she and Dagoberto have been married in an official church ceremony. Count Federico accepts the inevitable. Rosamira would like to reward the two "boys," Enrique and Camilo, who have acted so selflessly. Porcia and Julia do not want to disrobe, and their identities are exposed. They enlighten Anastasio and Manfredo, whose respective hearts they have won. The men will lead them home, and the two couples assure Nonada that they will look out for him in the future. Don Gonzalo hurries in, out of breath and exasperated, for he has not been able to solve the mystery. Informed of the events that have transpired in his absence, he somewhat begrudgingly congratulates the three couples. The final words belong to Nonada, who refers to the confusions that unremittingly erupt in the labyrinth of love, which, as in this case, can lead to happiness.

The byzantine, or labyrinthine, plot—with gender-, name-, and identity-changes—demarcates the formal structure of *The Labyrinth of Love*. In the game, and war, of sexual politics, I wanted the women to be bookish and brilliant, but with much to learn, and the men to be good-spirited, but, in many ways, clueless and primed to be dis-illusioned. The most sensitive and benevolent male character is Nonada, significantly the person of lowest rank.

There is a learning curve for Manfredo and Anastasio, who must prove their merits and their amended attitudes. First and foremost, in this play about women in literature and in society, I wished to underline irony, humor, and, a catch-all and *primus inter pares*, language. Under the rubric of metatheater, I strove to emphasize metacritical and metalinguistic codes and to place self-image against the rhetoric and the mores of society. The fact that women have "come a long way," as the ad slogan of the late 1960s decreed,[4] adds to the irony of *The Labyrinth of Love*, as does the fact that there is still, four centuries after Cervantes published his play, room to grow. Like my far more illustrious predecessors in Spain, I gave extra space in the dialogue and on the stage—real or hypothetical—to women, and I aspired to eloquence and to a spot of poetry in the prose of the characters. Porcia notes in the first scene of the play that women "are sequestered, secluded, and policed, reduced to consuming art created by men, who, whether by design or coincidence, have taught us to reason. They are our jailers and our facilitators, and, of course, the paradox is entirely lost on them" (21). Things go well, and Nonada concludes, "To find our way, we have to trust men's word of honor, women's innate goodness, and the value of a trace of social rebellion. That is the stuff of happy endings" (114). Let us all work toward bringing about happy endings in the great theater of the world.

Notes

1. See Stroud, "The Demand" and "'¿Y sois …?'". On the plays by Zayas, Caro, and Sor Juana, see my essays "Order and Disorder," "Clothes Unmake the Woman," and "Sor Juana." For more general considerations, see McKendrick, *Women and Society.*
2. For theoretical issues related to metatheater, see also Hornby and Witt.
3. See Friedman, *The Unifying* Concept 103–17. See also Carrasco Urgoiti, the three listings under Zimic, and the two essays of Anderson, who focuses on *El laberinto de amor* and female characters in Cervantes's *comedias.* Students of Cervantes's theater are indebted to the work of such scholars as Joaquín Casalduero, Jean Canavaggio, and Nicholas Spadaccini, in collaboration with Jenaro Talens. For a brief survey of Cervantes's dramatic production, see McKendrick, "Writings."
4. "You've come a long way, baby" was used in the advertising campaign of Virginia Slims, a brand of cigarettes developed exclusively for women. Feminists (and perhaps even antifeminists) might have noted the irony.

Works Cited

Abel, Lionel. *Metatheatre: A New View of Dramatic Form.* New York: Hill and Wang, 1963. Print.

———. *Tragedy and Metatheatre: Essays on Dramatic Form.* Intro. Martin Puchner. New York: Holmes and Meier, 2003. Print.

Anderson, Ellen M. "Mothers of Invention: Toward a Reevaluation of Cervantine Dramatic Heroines." *Bulletin of the Comediantes* 62.2 (2010): 1–44. Print.

———. "Refashioning the Maze: The Interplay of Gender and Rank in Cervantes's *El laberinto de amor.*" *Bulletin of the Comediantes* 46.2 (1994): 165–85. Print.

Bergamín, José. *El cohete y la estrella. La cabeza a pájaros.* Ed. José Esteban. Madrid: Cátedra, 1981. Print.

Bloom, Harold. *The Anxiety of Influence: A Theory of Poetry.* New York: Oxford UP, 1973. Print.

Calderón de la Barca, Pedro. *La dama duende.* Ed. Fausta Antonucci. Intro. Marc Vitse. Barcelona: Crítica, 1999. Print.

———. *El médico de su honra.* Ed. Jesús Pérez Magallón. Madrid: Cátedra, 2012. Print.

———. *El médico de su honra. El pintor de su deshonra. Dramas de honor.* Ed. Ángel Valbuena Briones. Vol. 2. Madrid: Espasa-Calpe, 1967. Print. Clásicos Castellanos 142.

———. Canavaggio, Jean. *Cervantès dramaturge: Un théâtre à naître.* Paris: Presses Universitaires de France, 1977. Print.

Caro, Ana. *Valor, agravio y mujer.* Ed. Lola Luna. Madrid: Castalia, 1993. Print.

Carrasco Urgoiti, María Soledad. "Cervantes en su comedia *El laberinto de amor.*" *Hispanic Review* 48.1 (1980): 77–90. Print.

Casalduero, Joaquín. *Sentido y forma del teatro de Cervantes.* Madrid: Gredos, 1966. Print.

Cervantes Saavedra, Miguel de. *Don Quijote.* Ed. Tom Lathrop. Newark, DE: Juan de la Cuesta, 2012. Print.

———. *Teatro completo.* Ed. Florencio Sevilla Arroyo and Antonio Rey Hazas. Barcelona: Planeta, 1987. Print.

Cruz, Sor Juana Inés de la. *Los empeños de una casa.* Ed. Celsa Carmen García Valdés. Barcelona: Promociones y Publicaciones Universitarias, 1989. Print.

Fernández de Avellaneda, Alonso [pseud.]. *El ingenioso hidalgo don Quijote de la Mancha, contiene su tercera salida.* Ed. Fernando García Salinero. Madrid: Castalia, 1987. Print.

Friedman, Edward H. "Clothes Unmake the Woman: The Idiosyncrasies of Cross-Dressing in Ana Caro's *Valor, agravio y mujer.*" *Confluencia* 24.1 (2008): 162–71. Print.

———. *The Labyrinth of Love.* Newark, DE: Juan de la Cuesta, 2013. Print.

———. "Order and Disorder in María de Zayas's *La traición en la amistad.*" *Tradition and Innovation: Essays in Memory of Carroll B. Johnson.* Ed. Sherry Velasco. Newark, DE: Juan de la Cuesta, 2008. 107–30. Print.

———. "Sor Juana Inés de la Cruz's *Los empeños de una casa:* Sign as Woman." *Romance Notes* 31.3 (1991): 197–203. Print.

———. *The Unifying Concept: Approaches to the Structure of Cervantes' Comedias.* York, SC: Spanish Literature Publications, 1981. Print.

Hornby, Richard. *Drama, Metadrama, and Perception.* Lewisburg, PA: Bucknell UP, 1986. Print.

McKendrick, Melveena. "Writings for the Stage." *The Cambridge Companion to Cervantes.* Ed. Anthony J. Cascardi. Cambridge, UK: Cambridge UP, 2002. 13–59. Print.

————. *Women and Society in the Spanish Drama of the Golden Age: A Study of the* Mujer Varonil. Cambridge, UK: Cambridge UP, 1974. Print.

Spadaccini, Nicholas, and Jenaro Talens. *Through the Shattering Glass: Cervantes and the Self-Made World.* Minneapolis: U of Minnesota P, 1993. Print.

Stroud, Matthew D. "The Demand for Love and the Mediation of Desire in *La traición en la amistad.*" *María de Zayas: The Dynamics of Discourse.* Ed. Amy R. Williamsen and Judith A. Whitenack. Madison, NJ: Fairleigh Dickinson UP, 1995. 155–69. Print.

————. *Fatal Union: A Pluralistic Approach to the Spanish Wife-Murder* Comedias. Lewisburg, PA: Bucknell UP, 1990. Print.

————. "'¿Y sois hombre o sois mujer?': Sex and Gender in Tirso's *Don Gil de las calzas verdes.*" *The Perception of Women in the Spanish Theater of the Golden Age.* Ed. Anita K. Stoll and Dawn L. Smith. Lewisburg, PA: Bucknell UP, 1991. 67–82. Print.

Vega Carpio, Lope de. *Arte nuevo de hacer comedias.* Ed. Enrique García Santo-Tomás. Madrid: Cátedra, 2006. Print.

Wardropper, Bruce W. "Lope's *La dama boba* and Baroque Comedy." *Bulletin of the Comediantes* 13 (1961): 1–3. Print.

Witt, Mary Ann Frese. *Metatheater and Modernity: Baroque and NeoBaroque.* Lanham, MD: Fairleigh Dickinson UP, 2012. Print.

Zayas, María de. *Desengaños amorosos.* Ed. Alicia Yllera. Madrid: Cátedra, 1983. Print.

————. *Novelas amorosas y ejemplares.* Ed. Julián Olivares. Madrid: Cátedra, 2000. Print.

————. *La traición en la amistad.* Ed. Barbara López-Mayhew. Newark, DE: Juan de la Cuesta, 2003. Print.

Zimic, Stanislav. "Cervantes frente a Lope y a la comedia nueva (Observaciones sobre *La entretenida*)." *Anales Cervantinos* 15 (1976): 19–119. Print.

————. *De esto y aquello en las obras de Cervantes.* Newark, DE: Juan de la Cuesta, 2010. Print.

————. "El laberinto y el lucero redentor: Estudio de *El laberinto de amor* de Cervantes." *Acta Neophilologica* 3 (1980): 31–48. Print.

Woman, Learning, and Fear: Racial Mixing in Diego Ximénez de Enciso's Juan Latino

BALTASAR FRA-MOLINERO
Bates College

In his introduction to *Fatal Union,* the trailblazing study of the wife-murder plays of the Spanish Baroque period, Matthew Stroud warns against monolithic interpretations of the "truth." Paraphrasing Roland Barthes, he claims that critical readings must approach meaning without attempting to be totalizing in their apprehension (20). Stroud has championed a critical approach to the study of the Spanish *comedia* that tries to decenter meaning, that is, that accepts and celebrates these 17th-century plays—all cultural manifestations in fact—as rich in contradictions and paradoxes. This is also the case of Spanish Baroque *comedias* in which the protagonist is a Black character.

Written during the early period of modern-day slavery in the Atlantic world, Spanish *comedias* with main Black characters—whether the protagonist is a saint, a Biblical Queen, a common soldier or a princely character—deal in one way or another with the dis-ease of Spanish society in regards to race, and in particular, the Black race. Spain and Portugal were setting the intellectual stage of modern racist thought through the justification of the enslavement of Blacks even if they were converted to Christianity, or born of Christian parents (Sweet 158). Old ideas were renewed and adapted to the new social circumstance of the new capitalist society being formed on Iberian soil, not just across the Atlantic in the overseas empire. The Iberian Peninsula was a slave society. No other western European monarchy was experiencing anything similar. Spaniards, a "mongrel race" in the words of Sir Edmund Spenser because of its African and Muslim historical roots, were building an empire of contradictions.[1] On the one hand Spain was perhaps—with Portugal—the most ethnically diverse country in Western Europe. On the other hand—and also because of this—Iberian society established a caste system of exclusions based on religious ancestry and phenotype, what we now would call "race."

The racial discourse that developed in Spain and Portugal possessed a "grammar" that underlies its practice, as defined by David Theo Goldberg (298 and ff). In 17th-century Spain social exclusion based on the skin color of a person was a matter of fact. The word *negro,* applied as a noun to a human being, was practically synonymous with that of slave. To be free and Black— two contradictory categories—required the presence of an adjective, such as *libre* or its synonym of Arabic origin, *horro.*

Contradiction is at the heart of Spanish classical theater. The more contradictory premises a play contained, the better. A learned white woman [*bachillera*], a Black man who knows Latin yet he is still a slave, a Christian city where the majority of the population is suspected of not being exactly Christian—all these are the elements and pre-texts of Diego Ximénez de Enciso's play *Juan Latino* (c. 1625, published in 1652). Common to all three elements is the fear they engender. This *comedia* exploits the tensions and anxiety of a fearful group, an elite of old Christians in Granada at the time of the *Morisco* uprising of the Alpujarras in December of 1568. The anxiety had given place to a series of royal decrees that encroached upon the *Moriscos,* the people of Muslim descent that had been forced to convert to Christianity after the conquest of 1492, prohibiting them the exercise of their cultural difference. This conflict, staged as the secondary action of the play *Juan Latino,* constitutes the intractable contradiction that has to be dealt with in a violent exercise of military power.

The other contradictions are more manageable by contrast. A *bachillera* called Ana de Carlobal will fall in love with a Black slave man, called Juan Latino, thus tarnishing the honor of her family. Juan Latino, the protagonist of the *comedia,* is the first historical individual of African origin to serve as the protagonist of a piece of fiction in European literature, as well as the first Black person to be the author of a published literary work in the Renaissance, his Latin epic poem *Austrias Carmen* [*Song of the Scion of the House of Austria*], dedicated to the Christian victory over the Ottoman empire in Lepanto. The play *Juan Latino* works, in fact, as a pre-text of the epic poem dedicated to Don Juan de Austria, the victor of Lepanto but also the commander-in-chief of the royal armies that defeated the *Moriscos* in Granada between 1569 and 1570.[2]

Fear is present in the intellectual life of Granada. Juan Latino, the Black man, threatens the academic establishment by aspiring to a Latin chair at the university. His opponent is a white man of Jewish descent. Fear of this confrontation will result in an exchange of mutual accusations: anti-Black prejudice evokes anti-Jewish diatribe (Panford 4). These two discourses have the charm of cancelling one another and being resolved through the offices of Castillo, the *gracioso*, who mocks the victorious Black man in the end.

The other fear that is ill-resolved in *Juan Latino* originates in Doña Ana de Carlobal, who reveals herself as the love interest of the Black protagonist. This *comedia* presents as a means for his love the academic exploits of the famous 16th-century Afro-Hispanic humanist Juan Latino, celebrated by different writers including Miguel de Cervantes, who compares himself with Latino in a mock poem in the preface of the First Part of *Don Quijote*.[3]

As much as the play highlights the social elevation of the Black male protagonist as an ambivalent occasion, it also presents the dilemma of its female counterpart, Ana de Carlobal, who has to choose between two "monsters" as objects of her desire. On the one hand, she feels inclined towards a Black man, and a slave, which will ruin her honor. On the other, she detests the seemingly more favorable suitor Don Fernando de Válor, the historic Aben Humeya, who led the *Morisco* rebellion of the War of the Alpujarras (1568–1570).

Juan Latino is a case study in the formation of Early Modern consciousness, as freedom and agency in a woman is compared to the attempts of an enslaved Black man to gain manumission through scholastic prowess. The playwright, Diego Ximénez de Enciso, was himself a member of a prominent family in Seville that participated in the Atlantic slave trade, with ties in Cartagena de Indias. Ximénez de Enciso had to fight during his life to defend himself and his family against accusations of Jewish and even Muslim ancestry (Pike 131).

Ana de Carlobal, as a character, had been studied by Vern Williamsen years ago as an example of Baroque *admiratio* (205). She combines the type of the *bachillera*, the one who challenges the male rule that restricts her access to books and the world of formal learning, with a second challenge, that of the threat of race-mixing. As a *bachillera*, Ana de Carlobal privileges her desire for humanistic learning over her gendered and racialized social status. Most moralists in Early Modern Spain had an ambivalent attitude towards the relation of women with reading and writing. The opinion of humanists like Luis Vives and Fray Luis de León are well known, admonishing parents of aristocratic young ladies against allowing them to read the accursed books of chivalry or even the poems of Garcilaso that would fill their heads with ideas of love and put their honor in peril. These admonitions, however, implied that humanism considered the education of women of a certain status a necessity, following in many ways the advice of Erasmus.[4] Lope de Vega, with considerable humor, put the dilemma more openly in *La dama boba*

[*A Woman of Little Sense*]. What is worse, a perfectly ignorant "beast" like Finea, who cannot even read at the age of fourteen, or her insufferable sister Nise, whose main conversation topic is philosophy and books of entertainment in Latin as well as in Spanish? Where was the limit in the education of a woman of the upper classes in the early 17th-century? Spain, like other western European countries, had already seen the establishment of the first schools for girls in some cities, a testimony that for the sector of society that wielded institutional power, illiteracy in women was not desirable. In *La dama boba*, learning in a woman is equivalent to sexual impropriety, and even racial defilement, as Nise's father brings up the case of Juan Latino, the enslaved Black man who married the white woman he was hired to teach Latin. As representative of the patriarchal principle that is going to be questioned and toyed with—but not necessarily threatened—Octavio equates learning in women with the opening to new sources of authority. In *La dama boba* and *Juan Latino* mastery over the Latin language is a form of challenge to a patriarchal conception of knowledge and social order.

The other two forms of knowledge that appear to unsettle the established patriarchal Christian order are Muslim religious prophecy and magic. The latter proves powerful as love has a special occasion for mischief in the festivities of St. John's eve, the moment in which Ana de Carlobal will see her future Black husband, Juan Latino, thus establishing an uncanny connection between her desire for human letters and sexual knowledge in the person of a "racially inferior" male. Her servant induces her to say the prayer to catch a husband, one of those prayers the Inquisition did not look favorably on: "... no querría / que te sacasen en el auto, Juana" (Ximénez de Enciso I, 154) [... I don't want / you to end up in the Inquisition, Juana]. As the comedy progresses immediately, the man who fits the definition of ideal husband and the one who is the answer to the heretical prayer is one and the same: the Black slave Juan Latino. On that night, right at the beginning of the play, Ana de Carlobal pronounces fateful words that define her as a *bachillera*: "... del ingenioso / a las letras les soy aficionada; / solo el que sabe, para mí, es hermoso" (Ximénez de Enciso I, 153) [A savant famed for learning and for wit. / The love I have for letters is so deep / that I make synonymous of "fair" and "wise" (Spratlin 76)].[5] The already canonical definition of the *bachillera* or scholarly woman established decades ago by Melveena McKendrick makes this type of women in the *comedia* a variant of the *mujer esquiva* [disdainful woman] the woman who will not yield easily to her gender obligations to become a wife (219). Ana de Carlobal is "difficult," and this poses a problem and a threat.

Ana de Carlobal's desire for humanistic learning is heretical, as it is set against the time's notions of gender, race and even religious practice.

Humanist education in a woman was always a source of contamination, pollution and a threat to patriarchal principles of authority. Her social interaction with poets and students puts her honor in jeopardy, something her brother, Dr. Carlobal, makes clear. Her answer will seal her fate, as she transacts with her brother to dispense with the cohort of literary suitors in exchange for a teacher. The choice her brother makes is the very Black slave Juan Latino of St. John's Eve, a rising star in the literary circles of Granada, and not a likely menace to his sister's reputation, or so he thinks.

Humane letters in a Black slave and in a white woman will generate unwanted results. To dispel the initial horror Ana de Carlobal shows for a Black teacher, her brother mounts a spirited defense of his abilities—"no enseña con el color" (Ximénez de Enciso II, 242) [His color's not the text he teaches with (Spratlin 132)]. The text plays with the issue of contamination of racially opposed bodies that mingle as well as contamination of meaning as used by the two future lovers in the scene that marks the beginning of their love for each other:

LATINO.	(*Tómale Juan la mano y escribe en ella*)
	¡Ay mano bella y cruel!
DOÑA ANA.	¿Qué hecistes?
LATINO.	Escrebí.
DOÑA ANA.	¿Pues en mi mano?
LATINO.	Entendí
	que era mano de papel.

(*Tómale la mano para ponelle la pluma y desvíale y él vuelve a llevarla.*)

	Así ha de tomar la pluma
	Vuesa merced.
DOÑA ANA.	Bien lo hacéis;
	Quitad, que me tiznaréis. (Ximénez de Enciso II, 260–61)

[L: (*He places his hand on hers and directs her writing*) If it were mine to touch her hand! Ah hand, / so beautiful and cruel! / DA: What have you done? / L: I wrote. / DA: Your hand on mine? / L: I dreamed it was / A scroll of vellum white and soft to touch. / (*Juan tries to place pen in her hand, which she draws away. He persists.*) / L: The pen is grasped in this wise. / DA: Hey, what's this? / Release my hand; I would not have it stained. (Spratlin 143–144)]

To the traditional notion of woman as a tabula rasa on which the male principles inscribes law, norm, and knowledge, Ana de Carlobal counters with the discourse of racial contamination that she has the power to utter as a white person. If the male principle that legitimates humanistic knowledge in a Black man is the key to Juan Latino's speech, it is the racial discourse of white supremacy that gives Doña Ana leverage and the capability to speak her own fears.

Speaking saves and speaking condemns. Eloquence is the measure of humanity in the Renaissance. The speech by Fernando de Válor (Ximénez de Enciso I, 213–15) is a defense of the right to speak of the Morisco minority that is being threatened into political silence: "¡Mandarnos que la lengua en que nacimos / mudemos en tres años y dexemos / los vestidos y trajes que vestimos / cosa inhumana es!" (Ximénez de Enciso I, 213) [It is inhuman to command that we / forget the language that we learned from birth / and in three years perfect a foreign tongue! (Spratlin 113)].[6] The leader of the rebel *Moriscos* makes a spirited defense of the right to speak and be culturally different, but to no avail. Equally, the speech by Juan Latino requesting his freedom to be able to teach and marry Ana de Carlobal will receive no positive response. It is striking, then, that Ana de Carlobal's words are capable of advancing the action of the *comedia*, as Melveena McKendrick remarked years ago ("Breaking the Silence" 19). In *Juan Latino* Ana de Carlobal captures her dilemma between learning and keeping her white woman's honor, knowledge and its consequence of becoming the source of racial contamination— just as Eve is the purported source of sin for humanity. It is all because her desire to acquire the tools that allow someone to speak in public is the direct consequence of acquiring a humanist education. In a woman, this is akin to running against the Pauline dictum that commands her to silence:

> Yo soy tan aficionada
> a las letras, que en Granada
> no hay persona de buen gusto
> que no me conozca y vea.
> Y en todas las ocasiones
> me hallo en las conclusiones
> que yo puedo; en fin, soy fea
> y tengo este privilegio
> de libertad en la cara,
> y, a ser lícito, cursara
> cada día en el Colegio. (Ximénez de Enciso I, 189)

> [My love of letters is so passionate, / That I am known to all Granada's wits. / Announce a forum, and you may be sure / That I'll be there to drink in all that's said. / I have a homely face, you know, and hence / Am free to move among the erudite. / If women were admitted to the schools, / Each day would find me in the sacred halls. (Spratlin 98)]

The irony of self-recognition as an ugly woman makes her the opposite of Juan Latino. Her homely face gives her freedom, she says, as she will not be the object of erotic desire among men of letters. This is precisely the miscalculation her brother had made earlier when he thought the blackness and slave condition of Juan Latino would render him equally unappealing.

Freedom and slavery compose the leitmotiv of this *comedia*. Both are presented as paradoxes in which each simultaneously defines and deconstructs the other. Freedom and slavery are shadows of each other. Freedom can only be understood in modern terms in opposition to slavery, which is its utter negation, the very condition of social death, in Orlando Patterson's definition. In this *comedia*, Ana de Carlobal, Juan Latino, and Fernando de Válor see their wishes constantly undermined and this causes them anxiety.

Ana de Carlobal's two choices are shadows of each other. Juan Latino represents the racial other that has chosen Christian humane letters and puts his learning at the service of anti-Muslim forces. A Muslim triumph would make his fate as a slave even worse. The *Morisco* Fernando de Válor, after being rejected by the learned lady, becomes the leader of the historical rebellion and war of 1568–1570. He fears his *doppelganger* in the Black scholar and in Cañerí, a Black character and first leader of the rebellion who appears to him in his dreams and announces his future death in the form of prophecies written in Arabic. Don Fernando embodies the very literary material against which the historical Juan Latino will write in his epic poem *Austrias Carmen*. His double is not just the Black scholar in the play, but his own position in history, that he fatefully misreads:

> DON FERNANDO. (*Aparte*)
> Y éste es el rostro y talle
> Del negro que yo vi. Vence mi suerte.
> Si reino, he de matalle
> Y asegurar mi vida con su muerte,
> Que el hombre que repugna
> Su hado, es oficial de su fortuna. (Ximénez de Enciso II, 237–38)

> [DF: (*Aside*) The face and figure of the very black / Who threatened me. I mean to nullify / The dire prediction of the stars. As King / I will command his death and thus insure / My life. The man who laughs at what is writ / Is master of his fortune and the world. (Spratlin 129)]

This is the fear that will not be resolved in this *comedia*, thus ending with the death—in the play and in historical events—of Don Fernando de Válor. Don Fernando de Válor's fate is not written in the Arabic prophetic texts he has in his hands—they are heretical and thus false—but in the text of the *Austrias Carmen*, a text not yet written during the events of the play, that will sing the Christian victory over Islam and announces Don Fernando's ultimate tragic end, written by a Black man he seems to misrecognize.

The notion of modernity as interruption through the presence of a double is a constant presence in literature (Vardoulakis 100). In *Juan Latino* the main characters are constructed dialogically as fearful doubles of one another. Ana de Carlobal's whiteness is interrupted by the shadow of her desire to be free and to learn through the body of a Black slave. Juan Latino's scholarship is interrupted by the shadow of Dr. Villanueva—a person whose last name denotes Jewish ancestry—and his anti-Black rhetoric, on the one hand, and by the blackness of his own body, which expresses his enslavement to the Duke of Sessa, who wants him to be a precious jewel in his possession rather than give him freedom. The third protagonist in the triangle, Fernando de Válor, sees his love for Ana de Carlobal interrupted by the rebellion he is about to lead, and by his fateful allegiance to non-Latin letters written in the secret documents full of anti-Christian prophecies the Black-skinned ghostly Cañerí presents to him.

Hidden in a typical happy ending of sorts, Ana de Carlobal's choices are equally negative in as much as she has to make herself the vehicle of racial impurity, either by bearing children from a Black slave or from a religious and political enemy, the *Morisco*, the figure that is historically destined to be enslaved and later expelled from the national/Catholic *ecumene*. As Matthew Stroud has demonstrated in his study of wife-murder plays in 17th-century Spain, Ana de Carlobal embodies the cultural *melancholia* of the Spanish Golden Age, its political restrictions of *limpieza de sangre* [purity of blood], and the ultimate dilemma of freedom as choice between (always) imperfect objects.

In Ximénez de Enciso's *Juan Latino* there is fear of racial mixing in the main action. In the secondary plot, connected to the main one, there is fear of taking the spirit of the anti-Muslim crusades to its ultimate end, which is the conquest of Jerusalem and the destruction of Islam. The destruction of Islam was tantamount to the destruction of Granada itself, represented in the play in the defeat of the *Moriscos*, that "doubtful" victory, according to Diego Hurtado de Mendoza (68). The wife-murder plays studied by our admired Matthew Stroud were a reflection of a generalized anxiety about new social formations in which capitalism could buy (and destroy) honor, marriages, and social standing. The racial mixing in *Juan Latino* that will result from the marriage of white Ana de Carlobal and Black Juan Latino is the unstated point of anxiety of a slave society. This is the "decentered" meaning of the "unusual" thirst for humanistic learning that envelops the desire between a white woman and a Black man in the modern era.

Notes

1. The use of the religious racialization of Spaniards as a mixed race of people appears in Spenser's writings about the Irish invasion of 1602 in which he participated so

prominently (Fuchs 52). Spenser compared the Irish Catholics and their claims to Spanish ancestry to the Spanish *Moriscos.*

2. Juan Latino was a sort of literary folk hero in the early 17th century. Lope de Vega at times compared himself to him in his letters to the Duke of Sessa, his master and a member of the aristocratic house that had owned Juan Latino. Different scholars from Granada referred anecdotes of his life that would find their way into Ximénez de Enciso's play. Such were the cases of Bermúdez de Pedraza or Ambrosio de Salazar (Marín Ocete 7).

3. "Pues al cielo no le plu- / que saliera tan ladi- / como el negro Juan Lati- / hablar latines rehu-" [Since Heaven did not wish / for me to be as clever / as Black Juan Latino / I refuse to use all that Latin].

4. Erasmus found his friend Vives' *Institutio foeminae christianae* [*The Formation of Christian Women*] too harsh on women, and too preoccupied with issues of honor and honesty that limited women's actions. Or as he pointed, the text was "too Spanish" (Capel Martínez 89).

5. From this point onward, I will use Velaurez B. Spratlin's 1938 translation of the play *Juan Latino.* An African American scholar of the Harlem Renaissance generation, Spratlin's essay on the historical figure of Juan Latino is a veritable archeology of a forgotten figure. It contains the first extensive analysis of Juan Latino's epic poem. It also analyzed the textual and anecdotal sources Ximénez de Enciso used in the play.

6. Don Fernando de Válor's speech is a version of Don Fernando Núñez Muley's famous "Memoria" to the Granada authorities in protest for the royal *Pragmática* of 1566 that ordered the *Moriscos* of Granada to abandon almost every aspect of their culture, including the use of the Arabic language, dress, public baths, dances, and even the ownership of Black slaves in *order* to stamp out heresy.

Works Cited

Capel Martínez, Rosa María. "Mujer y educación en el Antiguo Régimen." *Historia de la educación* 26 (2007): 85–110. Print.

Cervantes Saavedra, Miguel de. *El ingenioso hidalgo don Quijote de la Mancha.* Ed. Luis Andrés Murillo. Madrid: Castalia, 1986. Print.

Fuchs, Barbara. "Spanish Lessons: Spenser and the Irish Moriscos." *Studies in English Literature* 42.1 (2002): 45–62. Print.

Goldberg, David Theo. "The Social Formation of Racist Discourse." *Anatomy of Racism.* Minneapolis: U of Minnesota P, 1990. 295–318. Print.

Hurtado de Mendoza, Diego. *Guerra de Granada hecha por el Rey Don Felipe II contra los moriscos de aquel reino, sus rebeldes. Historia escrita en cuatro libros.* Digital edition from Biblioteca de Autores Españoles. Madrid: Rivadeneyra, 1852: 65–122. Biblioteca Virtual Cervantes. Web. 9 December 2014. <http://cervantesvirtual.com>.

Latinus, Joannes. *Austrias Carmen. Ad Catholicum pariter et invictissimum Philippum Dei gratia Hispaniarum Regem, de foelicissima serenissimi Ferdinandi Principis nativitate epigrammatum liber.* Granada: n.p., 1573. 1–35. Print.

Marín Ocete, Antonio. *El negro Juan Latino. Ensayo biográfico y crítico.* Granada: Librería Guevara, 1925. Print.

McKendrick, Melveena. "Breaking the Silence: Women and the Word in the *Comedia*." *Revista Canadiense de Estudios Hispánicos* 29.1 (2004): 13–30. Print.

———. *Women and Society in the Spanish Drama of the Golden Age. A Study of the Mujer Varonil*. Cambridge, UK: Cambridge UP, 1974. Print.

Núñez Muley, Francisco. "Memoria de Francisco Núñez Muley." *Revue Hispanique* 6 (1899): 205–39. English translation as *A Memorandum for the President of the Royal Audiencia and Chancery Court of the City and Kingdom of Granada*. Ed. Vincent Barletta. Chicago: U of Chicago P, 2007. Print.

Pike, Ruth. "The Converso Origins of the Sevillian Dramatist Diego Jiménez de Enciso." *Bulletin of Hispanic Studies* 67 (1990): 129–35. Print.

Panford, Moses. "La *Comedia famosa de Juan Latino*: el discurso hegemónico como artefacto socio-político." *Afro-Hispanic Review* 18.2 (1999): 3–9. Print.

Spratlin, Velaurez B. *Juan Latino, Slave and Humanist*. New York: Spinner P, 1938. Print.

Stroud, Matthew D. *Fatal Union: A Pluralistic Approach to the Spanish Wife-Murder Comedias*. Lewisburg, PA: Bucknell UP, 1990. Print.

Sweet, James H. "The Iberian Roots of American Racist Thought." *The William and Mary Quarterly* 3rd Series 54.1 (1997): 143–66. Print.

Vardoulakis, Dimitris. "The Return of Negation: The Doppelganger in Freud's 'The 'Uncanny.'"" *SubStance* 35.2.110 (2006): 100–16. Print.

Vives, Juan Luis. *Instrucción de la mujer cristiana*. Trans. Juan Justiniano. Intro., ed. Elizabeth Teresa Howe. Madrid: Fundación Universidad Española and Universidad Pontificia de Comillas, 1995. Print.

Williamsen, Vern G. "Women and Blacks Have Brains Too: A Play by Diego Ximénez de Enciso." *Studies in Honor of Everett W. Hesse*. Ed. William C. McCrary and José A. Madrigal. Lincoln, NE: Society of Spanish and Spanish-American Studies, 1981. 199–206. Print.

Ximénez de Enciso, Diego. *Comedia famosa de Juan Latino. Segunda Parte de comedias escogidas de las mejores de España*. Madrid: n.p., 1652. Print.

———. *Comedia famosa de Juan Latino. El encubierto y Juan Latino*. Ed. Eduardo Juliá Martínez. Madrid: Aldus, 1951. Print.

Antona García: *A* Mujer Varonil *for the 21ˢᵗ Century*

KATHLEEN REGAN
University of Portland

One *comedia* playwright noted for portraying fascinatingly unconventional women is Tirso de Molina. Clearly, this important detail has not gone unnoticed in the history of criticism dedicated to Tirso's work. In *Spanish Drama of the Golden Age,* Margaret Wilson noted, "What he [Tirso] does give to the best of his *Comedias*—and it is now high time to credit him with the real contribution which he did make to the development of this genre—is a new vitality and heightening of interest in the female character" (98). Surely, one of the most intriguing characters in the corpus of Tirso's works is Antona García, loosely based on the historical figure of the same name. This female protagonist provides a good example of Tirso's dynamic view of female identity, despite occasionally having been mistaken by critics as a parody of the conventional *mujer varonil* [manly woman]. Many critics have focused on the supposed love between the nobleman Penamacor and Antona García and have examined the class issues that this relationship highlights. Yet, such a reading fails to recognize the way Tirso skillfully subverts the gender norms imposed by the patriarchal system of his time. This essay will examine the mastery and humor with which Tirso interrogates gender identity, thereby providing a unique representation of the *mujer varonil* character that continues to resonate with contemporary audiences.

Tirso's *Antona García* stands apart from standard *comedias* in its abundance of *mujeres varoniles*, among them the titular protagonist, the antagonist María Sarmiento, and most notably, the historical figure of the Queen, Isabel of Castile. In his study of this *comedia*, P. R. K. Halkhoree strongly objects to this excessive proliferation: "The fact that three *mujeres varoniles*

are presented [María indirectly] right at the beginning of this play is itself
grotesque" (250).[1] Nonetheless, Halkhoree recognizes the significance of this
"embarrassment of riches." Indeed, Tirso wastes no time creating an interesting triangle including the aforementioned would-be lovers and María. From
the very beginning the playwright focuses on the tension between the "laws"
that dictate gender behavior and the actions that invalidate and contradict
them. Furthermore, Tirso carefully manipulates the representation of Queen
Isabel, María Sarmiento, and Antona García to foreground these issues.

The familiar figure of Queen Isabel, as beloved in the 17th century as in
her own time, opens the *comedia* with a speech that serves to introduce to the
audience the military campaign around which the action centers. In this manner, the playwright establishes Isabel's power. The audience also recognizes
that as a warrior woman and leader of her own armed forces, Queen Isabel is a
very strong-willed and unconventional woman. As the Queen begins to speak
to her soldiers, she names the enemy. Among those mentioned in her litany,
she lists María Sarmiento, the wife of the mayor of Toro, whom the Queen
accuses of "… vituperando / su misma naturaleza, / en el acero templado /
trueca galas mujeriles; / plaza de armas en su estrado, / sus visitas centinelas, y
sus doncellas soldados" (I.18–24) [… inveighing against / [female] nature, /
she exchanges feminine finery / for hardened steel; / military arms surround
her, / her guest sentinels, and her ladies-in-waiting soldiers]. In this opening
statement, the Queen directly attacks the irregular gender behavior of María
Sarmiento. Yet, the monarch's attack is both puzzling and contradictory. This
opening criticism sets an ironic tone for the entire play, for surely had Isabel followed her own counsel, she would have passed through history unre-
marked and unremarkable. Queen Isabel, it could be argued, is as guilty of
reviling her nature as is María Sarmiento. Hence, the Queen's own flaunting
of the prescribed norm of gender behavior—ironically a trait she vilifies in
María—deconstructs this denunciation.

The inclusion in this *comedia* of Queen Isabel, who appears infrequently
after Act I, proves crucial: she represents a positive example of a *mujer varonil*,
thus serving to make the character type more accessible and acceptable to a
17th-century audience. Furthermore, as other critics have noted, she functions as a role model for the other woman warrior in the play, Antona García.
The Queen encounters Antona shortly after her opening speech while the
peasant girl is celebrating her nuptials with her husband, Juan de Monroy.
Impressed by a commander's description of Antona, which highlights the
peasant girl's unusual characteristics, the Queen asks to meet the young bride.
Antona truly stands outside the norm of gender behavior and identity in the
way she brings together masculine and feminine attributes. The commander

notes, "... experimenté / en la novia dos contrarios / de hermosura y for-taleza ..." (I.219–21) [... I witnessed / in the bride two contrary [natures] / of beauty and strength ...]. Futhermore, one notes the duality of Antona's nature through her community's overt references to her as a "gentilhombra" [gentlewoman] a regendered neologism in which the final "e" of "hombre" becomes the feminine "a." This detail, at first sight, may seem trivial, yet proves telling in that the language itself mirrors Antona's unconventional behavior. Even more, this play with words correlates Antona's own irregular birth, for she was born: "... nací de pies, / dando a la comadre espanto" (I.298–99) [... I was born feet first / horrifying the midwife"]. In this man-ner, her origins prefigure her destiny.[2]

In the initial meeting between the Queen and Antona, the interaction between the two women eclipses the marriage celebration. In an unusually dramatic departure from a typical *comedia* wedding, the scene ends not with an exchange of vows between Antona and her husband, but rather with Anto-na's celebration of the Queen, which deliberately evokes and simultaneously subverts the image of a courtly lover praising his beloved. The metaphors of adulation that Antona employs include farm and field imagery, thus humor-ously reminding the audience of her own humble background:

> ... vuesos dos ojos parecen
> dos matas de perejil
> ...
> En las dos mejillas solas
> miro, según son saladas,
> rosas con leche mezcladas,
> o cebollas y amapolas.
> ...
> Estas cuatro higas os doy
> que a la fe que loca estoy
> viendo vuesa catadura. (I.267–68, 277–80, 287–90)

> [... your two eyes / look like parsley plants / ... / in your two salty cheeks / I see roses mixed with milk / or onions and poppies / ... / I give you these four figs / and swear that upon seeing / your beauty I go crazy.]

Antona's celebration of the Queen both parodies conventional metaphors of beauty and creates an earthy variant that startles as it pleases with its freshness and humor. Tirso deliberately uses one conventional metaphor to remind the audience of how peculiar these new images really are: Antona cites the famil-iar milky skin and rosy cheeks of Petrarchan verse, only to immediately replace these tired metaphors with the unexpected image of onions and poppies. The startling changes highlight Antona's rusticity while they also directly evoke

Isabel's humanity. Other characters and the audience alike are reminded that
the Queen's popularity stemmed not only from her success as a leader but
from the fact that despite her regal stature she was very much in touch with
the simple life.

Whereas the nature of the imagery is startling, the most striking feature
of this exchange is the fact these words of "courtly love" are proffered by one
woman to another. Thus, the subversion of a courtly love scene is complete:
the pseudo-poetic discourse, the gender of the participants, and the setting in
a wedding celebration. The bond between the two women is further heightened when Queen Isabel gives a chain to Antona as a sign of their friendship.
Like the panegyric, this gift evokes *comedia* conventions only to overturn
them. Here, one expects a man to give a gift to a woman, his beloved, as a
reminder of his devotion and love for her. In another subversive inversion, the
Queen confers the chain to Antona so that Queen, the giver, will remember
Antona after battle: "Tomad esta joya, Antona, / que si salgo de cuidados, /
yo me acordaré de vos" (I.321–23) [Take this jewel, Antona / so that if I
survive the battle / I will remember you]. The gift is readily accepted by
Antona, who emphasizes the union between the leader and herself: "la sarta
que al cuello llevo / nos encadena a los dos" (I.393–94) [the necklace that I
will wear / unites the two of us].

The irony in this interaction between the Queen and Antona is clear.
The scene is framed by the heterosexual ritual of marriage, yet that ritual is
subverted when this unique bonding between the two women is represented
instead of the wedding itself. Praise, which distinctly parallels yet completely
fails to resemble heterosexual wooing, is exchanged first, followed by vows
of loyalty sealed with a gift. The chain itself resembles a wedding ring to the
degree that Antona's panegyric resembles a courtly speech: while the chain
and the tribute do not duplicate norms, neither do they ignore them. Like a
wedding ring, the Queen's gift symbolizes a bond, meant to represent not a
constricting eternal union, as a ring does, but a looser loyalty signaled by the
less restrictive necklace.

The unusual exchange between Queen Isabel and Antona is not lost on
the *gracioso* Bartolo. After witnessing the Queen's gift to Antona, he begins
to complain that he did not receive a similar gift from the Queen: "Media
cadena la pido / hasta que Gila me chera; / pues si Antona es novia entera, /
Bartolo es medio marido" (I.341–44) [I request half a chain / until Gila
loves me; / if Antona is a whole bride, / Bartolo is half a husband]. Bartolo's
lament highlights exactly how irregular the exchange between the Queen
and Antona is by playfully exploring the problematic nature of matrimony
and sexuality that this scene seeks to subvert. Bolstering his request is the

presumption that the Queen has given the chain to Antona in celebration of her marriage, when, in fact, far from delivering it as a wedding gift, the Queen clearly says that the chain should serve to recall Antona were she to need Antona's protection. Bartolo's rudeness thus reminds the audience that the scene they have just witnessed is truly peculiar; his next words suggest that the underlying suspect sexuality accounts for its peculiarity. When Bartolo characterizes himself as a "medio marido" [half husband],[3] he raises the specter of the powerless or cuckolded husband, which by extension includes both King Ferdinand and Juan de Monroy. The friendship between the two women clearly supersedes their relationships with their husbands, who have stepped back in this scene. Although King Ferdinand and Juan de Monroy are not specifically portrayed as effeminate, their absence suggests their more passive roles. Bartolo defines what he means by a half husband and, in turn, suggests a critique of the King and Juan de Monroy:

> Pintadas vi muchas veces
> figuras (verdad os digo)
> como hombre hasta el ombligo
> que allí abajo son peces;
> y yo en viéndolo decía:
> «medio maridos serán,
> que de noche huera están
> y en casa duermen de día.» (I.351–58)

> [Often I have seen painted / representations (and I tell you the truth) / figures that were men from the navel up, / and below the navel fish-like; / and while looking at this I have said: / 'these must be half husbands, / who are out all night / and sleep by day.']

Certainly, Bartolo's reference to "mermen" brings up a cast of associations for the well-read Early Modern spectator. Sebastián de Covarrubias's description further provides important insight into Bartolo's references. Covarrubias notes that the *murena*, an eel that is long, scaly, and hard to hold, easily slipping through the hand, has an association with male effeminacy.[4] Thus, the concept of a half-man, half-fish is doubly suspect. Bartolo's lines move from his own lack of virility in being unable to win Gila's affection, through the reference to two other half-husbands (King Ferdinand and Juan de Monroy), toward a peculiar definition of the term which raises the specter of homosexuality and, finally, to the accusation that half-husbands engage in questionable, possibly homosexual, practices when they slip out at night, leaving their wives to sleep alone and catching their own rest during the day.

In one of the more telling allusions included in this complicated play, an extremely minor character in Act III—referred to in the play simply as

Castilian #8—boasts of his profession as an "eye-dyer," noting that blue and green eyes have been banned and now only black eyes are approved:

> Celebran los amantes
> los verdes y azules antes;
> ya solamente se aprueba
> el ojo negro rasgado.
> De aquéllos soy tintero (III.223–37)
>
> [Before, lovers celebrated / greens and blues / but now only approve / slanted black eyes. / I am the eye-dyer of those.]

By way of explanation, Ruth Lee Kennedy notes that in 1623, about the time Tirso was writing this *comedia*, the Spanish government imposed sumptuary laws that were intended to tone down some of the fashions and lifestyles at Court. Because the color blue in men's clothing was associated with male effeminacy, and male effeminacy was viewed as threat to the norms of gender behavior, blue was banned:

> Blue had, as a color, become so linked with the dainty young things (male) of the time that even blue eyes were sufficient to condemn one to the category of *lindo* and to justify the authorities in forbidding him the privilege of dagger or sword—or even freedom of movement. (108–09)

The Castilian's playful discussion of dyeing eyes is amazingly farcical, but the underlying metaphor clearly indicates that dyed or standardized eyes are analogous to the discourse of gender or class that is used to blindly standardize reality, making events and people conform to one reading, regardless of how irrelevant it may be. A close comparison of different utterances and subsequent actions, in conjunction with the commentary offered by the *gracioso* Bartolo, suggests that far from defending the status quo by reiterating conventional plot elements and characters, Tirso sought to subvert it. In the course of his experiment he overturns the notion, prevalent in his day and repeated in narrative and persuasive texts alike, of a static norm of gender comportment and female identity.

The historical context in which the play unfolds provides further evidence of the way in which Tirso communicates the idea of male weakness. Indeed, the playwright's critique of the patriarchal system is clearly signaled in that the historical background to the action of the play concerns the *Guerra de la Beltraneja* [*The War of the Beltraneja*] fought between 1475–1479. In her introduction to this play, Margaret Wilson notes:

> On the death of Enrique IV in 1474, most of the Castilian nobles declared in favour of his sister Isabella and her husband Ferdinand as their new sovereigns,

instead of Enrique's ostensible heir Juana, since the latter was widely reputed to be the daughter, not of the King, but of the Queen's lover Don Beltrán de la Cueva. (xi)

Juana's questionable heritage suggests that the King was cuckolded, which places his virility in question. Thus, the very basis of *Antona García* highlights the passivity of this male ruler. Furthermore, the succession in question involves not two men, nor a man and a woman; rather, two women are vying to take control of Enrique's territory. From the beginning, then, Tirso situates his play within a crisis of leadership, which by extension suggests a lack of strength in the patriarchal structures and the men who ordinarily might benefit from them.

One such character of this *comedia* is Penamacor, who serves as a foil to the three *mujeres varoniles*. Wilson reads this character as fulfilling an "important dramatic function as the link between the opposing bands, and the ultimate factor in both conflicts" (xiv). Halkhoree extends Wilson's argument and reads Penamacor as a savior to Antona, who redeems her and raises her social status (264). Both critics offer strong arguments yet fail to provide a thorough assessment of Penamacor and his failed interactions with Antona. Penamacor is shown to be so self-absorbed, so taken with his great love for Antona, that he becomes passive and ineffective as a soldier/advisor for the Portuguese, thus truly reducing himself to his role as a suffering lover.

In her analysis of Penamacor Wilson notes, "The count is the very embodiment of the Portuguese quality of love-sickness, or *sebocidad*, as Tirso so often describes it" (xiv). Antona's treatment of Penamacor makes it hard to view him as a noble or even useful figure. Preceding each encounter between the Count and Antona is a scene that prefigures the comic elements in this unlikely match. Similarly, the gap between the language used by Antona and that of Penamacor signifies their unsuitability for one another.

Not only is the ongoing exchange between Antona and Penamacor very comical, but from the start it undermines Penamacor's attempts to woo her. The Count is introduced in Act I after Antona's wedding. Although he is en route to meet with the Portuguese forces, he is instantly distracted from his mission by the sight of Antona. He sees Antona combing flax outside her home and orders his servants to continue without him. The Count approaches Antona and immediately alienates her with his lofty rhetoric. Recalling Calisto and Melibea from *La Celestina*, the ludicrousness of Penamacor's suit adds comic relief by comparison. Both Calisto and Penamacor attempt to have "impossible" loves, but Calisto speaks a language of love that Melibea comprehends while Penamacor is speaking a language that Antona does not. Calisto successfully seduces Melibea because she is a typical young maiden who is naïve, passive, and coy. Penamacor attempts to pigeonhole Antona into a role that she has rejected and employs an ineffective strategy that fails to win her affections. His struggles to normalize Antona prove fruitless and ridiculous.

In every encounter the Count has with the protagonist, Tirso ridicules the courtly love convention by contrasting Penamacor's sophisticated language with Antona's down-to-earth parlance. The socioeconomic and cultural divide between these two characters is masterfully revealed in their first exchange. When Antona invites Penamacor to sit down, he replies, "Mal puede amor reposar / cuando comienza a penar" (I.640–41) [Love cannot rest / when it begins to suffer]. When Antona asks if the Count is sick, he replies, "… lo desea / mi dicha …" (I.643–44) [… such is my fate]. Again, deflecting the rhetoric of love, the heroine informs the Count that he is out of luck because the town has no doctor.

Penamacor's association with the Court also detracts from his credibility, since the Court was a place of deception and lax morals. Furthermore, males associated with the Court were usually seen as being effeminate.[5] Penamacor's focus on love dramatically contrasts with the protagonist's hunger for war and her defense of Queen Isabel's territory. Furthermore, the Count's soft love discourse constrasts with Antona's aggressive activity as she forcefully combs the flax. A short chorus highlights this facet of Antona's activity through repetition: "Rastrillába*lo* la aldeana, / y ¡cómo *lo* rastrillaba!" (I.755–56; emphasis mine) [The peasant girl combed it (the flax), / oh how she combed it!]. The pronoun *lo* refers to the *lino* [flax] Antona is combing but also can be read as a direct object pronoun that refers to the Count. The double meaning reiterates the two communicative levels at play in this scene: Antona is using unadorned language as she attends the humble task of combing flax, and she is simultaneously attacking the Count with her comb in a metaphorical fashion.

By Act III, rather than entering into a symbolic union, Antona and Penamacor have created a friendship. Penamacor is brought to the inn where Antona is giving birth to her twins. Between birthings, Penamacor arrives with two Castilian soldiers: he is their prisoner. When Antona sees him, she frees him from his captors and insists on hearing the news from the front. Unable to resist her, near the end of their meeting, Penamacor asks:

PENAMACOR.	En fin, ¿prometéis ser mía?
ANTONA.	Sí, con una condición.
	… ¿Juráis vos de cumplirla?
PENAMACOR.	Claro está.
ANTONA.	¡Que vos paráis
	los hijos y yo las hijas! (III.886–92)

[P. In the end, do you promise to wed me? / A. Yes, with one condition … Do you promise to fulfill it? / P. Of course. / A. That you birth / the sons and I the daughters!]

Antona's final statement is anything but a "Yes," and in light of the way the interaction between these two characters has been portrayed throughout the play, the last laugh is surely on him. Tirso builds a type of suspense into the situation: Antona has finally accepted him, but the conditions under which Penamacor has agreed are impossible for him to complete. The protagonist makes it clear that the Count has been deceived yet again, and rather than indulging in his desires, he will have to content himself with a strong friendship with this woman whom he refers to as "… prodigio de Castilla" (I.830) [… marvel-monster of Spain]. A conventional love between Antona and the Count is impossible in the end because this prodigious protagonist is herself anything but conventional.

Antona García challenges the hierarchy of terms that a rigid patriarchal system imposes in order to create a sense of coherence and social order. The protagonist proves herself to be stronger and braver than any of her male counterparts. This portrayal is emphasized by the inclusion of Queen Isabel in the *comedia*. Ultimately, what is represented is the arbitrary nature of the borders that separate male from female. While many moralists of the 17th-century in Spain argued that women were inferior to men because of their supposedly physical weakness, fragility, and passiveness, Tirso and many of his contemporaries offered dynamic representations of female identity that broke away from the rigid prescriptions imposed by the conservative patriarchy in place. Antona, on the one hand, embraces a typical representation of wife and mother. However, she is not limited by those social roles since she proves herself a brave warrior and a loyal subject to her Queen.

The time is ripe to invite more critical studies related to this dynamic *comedia* penned by Tirso. Thus far, the studies of *Antona García* have tended to suppress the problematic contradictions that arise because of the blending of terms typically read in opposition to each other (such as, male/female, country life/courtly life, low/high class). The artificial borders between the terms are collapsed and new meanings are created. Many of the critical studies referred to in this analysis, ones that still figure prominently in the scholarship on this play, attempt to forge an imaginary coherence, forcing the text to adhere to something familiar and recognizable. *Antona García* defies such a confining reading and lends itself to a more contemporary reading grounded in postmodern feminism, given that familiar terms are purposefully decentered and reinterpreted. By foregrounding the contradictions in the text, it is possible to "liberate the plurality of the text, to reject the 'obvious' and to produce (new) meaning" (Belsey 55). Tirso questions the nature of one absolute truth by showing contradictory discourses in competition. Furthermore, accepted discourse regarding gender roles is constantly subverted by Antona and Queen Isabel, who employ the discourse but also defy it through their actions. To force a coherent reading onto this play is to erase and undermine the very contradictions that make it fascinating to a 21st-century audience.

Notes

1. Wilson, P. R. K. Halkhoree, and McKendrick all make note of the parallelism established between Queen Isabella and Antona García.
2. During the 16th century in Spain, many believed that a difficult birth, especially for females, signaled an irregular sexuality. Consult Antonio Torquemada's work *Jardin de flores curiosas* [*Garden of Rare Flowers*], 118.
3. Covarrubias in *Tesoro de la lengua castellana* states: "...los egiptos significaron con ellas la crueldad oculta de los hombres afeminados y flacos..." (820).
4. The term *medio marido* recalls Laurencia from Lope's *Fuenteovejuna*, who chastises the weak men in the village for their failure to protect the women from the Comendador. She accuses them of being "hilanderas, maricones / amujerados, cobardes" (III.1781–82) [spinners, homosexuals / effeminate, cowards], and continues to accuse them of being "medio-maridos" as she wishes for the return of "aquel siglo de amazonas" (III.1794) [that century of the Amazons].
5. Cristóbol Suárez de Figueroa was a staunch critic of the Court of Philip III. He was particularly upset by what he saw as young men appearing feminine. For more information consult Maravall, 38.

Works Cited

Belsey, Catherine. *Critical Practice*. New York: Methuen, 1980. Print.

Covarrubias y Orozco Sebastián de. *Tesoro de la lengua castellana o española*. Madrid: Ediciones Turner, 1984. Print.

Halkhoree, P. R. K., José M. Ruano de la Haza, and Henry W. Sullivan. *Social and Literary Satire in the Comedies of Tirso de Molina*. Ottawa: Dovehouse, 1989. Print.

Kennedy, Ruth Lee. "Certain Phases of the Sumptuary Decrees of 1623 and Their Relation to Tirso's Theater." *Hispanic Review* 10.2 (1942): 91–115. Print.

Maravall, José Antonio. *Culture of the Baroque*. Trans. Terry Cochran. Minneapolis: U of Minnesota P, 1986. Print. Theory and History of Literature 25.

McKendrick, Melveena. *Women and Society in the Spanish Drama of the Golden Age*. Cambridge, UK: Cambridge UP, 1974. Print.

Molina, Tirso de (Gabriel Téllez). *Antona García*. Ed. and introd. Margaret Wilson. Manchester, UK: Manchester UP, 1957. Print.

Torquemada, Antonio. *Jardín de flores curiosas.* Ed. Giovanni Allegra. Madrid: Castalia, 1982. Print.

Vega Carpio, Lope de. *Fuenteovejuna.* Web. 14 Jan. 2014. <http://www.wordpress.comedias.org/play-texts/lope-de-vega>.

Wilson, Margaret. *Spanish Drama of the Golden Age.* Oxford: Pergamon P, 1969. Print.

"Más valéis vos, Antona": Worthy Wives in Lope, Tirso, and Cañizares

SUSAN PAUN DE GARCÍA
Denison University

As scholars engaged in dramaturgical analysis, we face important choices in our attempts to provide ways to connect readers, directors, and audiences with Early Modern plays. How can we uncover ways in which the written text intersects with daily lived experiences? The authors of *The Process of Dramaturgy. A Handbook* recommend assembling a production history, a resource that allows us "to get a quick sense of what was happening within both global society and popular culture at the time the show opened ... so that the director, performers, and designers alike can see what might have had direct influence not only on the play text but also the performance text at any given time" (Irelan, Fletcher, and Dubliner xii). This imperative becomes doubly important when the play in question is itself based on history.

To paraphrase Lawrence Raw, most historical plays make reference to common cultural elements, even if they are intended for specialist audiences (68). However, a historical play comprises several different histories: the "source" history, the history told on the stage, and the histories of individual audience members witnessing the play. Not only do we need to construct the narrative that comprises the "story" in the "history," but we also need to attempt to make sense of the past in terms of the present—both the present for the contemporary audience and our own. This was the task I set before myself with three plays by Lope, Tirso, and Cañizares. My research began with a play by José de Cañizares: *La heroica Antona García* [*The Heroic Antona García*]. At the very beginning of the play, the villagers of Tagarabuena sing the praises of the heroine at her wedding: "Más valéis vos, Antona, / que la corte toda" (I.223–24) [You are worth more, Antona, / than the whole

Court]. This sounded like a popular song, but I was aware that it could be something invented to sound like one. (For example, Lope's propensity to sprinkle his plays with popular songs and rhythms, along with others of his own creation, makes it difficult to determine whether any particular song is traditional or original.)

As a matter of fact, the song "Más valéis vos, Antona" [You are Worth More, Antona] appears in two plays by Lope, *El cuerdo en su casa* [*The Sane Man at Home*] and *Más valéis vos, Antona*, as well as in Tirso's *Antona García*. Angel López, citing Henríquez Ureña, suggests that "Más valéis vos Antona" might have been a popular *seguidilla* [strophic poem and dance tune] that inspired both Lope and Tirso to include the song in their plays (53). As the *seguidilla* was used for all happy occasions, it was particularly suited to weddings, the context in which it appears in the plays under consideration. The *seguidilla's* popularity was particularly strong at the beginning of the 17th century, as Gonzalo Correas remarked in *Arte grande de la lengua castellana* [*The Great Artistry of the Castillian Lanugage*] (1626).

Another possibility was that "Más valéis vos, Antona" did not come from a song but instead represented a saying well known in the waning years of the 16th century, judging by its inclusion in López de Ubeda's *La pícara Justina* [*Justina The Rogue*]: "y de quando en quando dauale [al tamborino] golpezitos, y dezia: Más valéis vos, Antona, que la corte toda" (Puyol y Alonso 89) [and from time to time he would strike the tambourine and say: You are worth more, Antona, than the whole Court]. Despite the fact that the quote refers to a saying, Julio Puyol y Alsono remarks that it sounds like the beginning of a popular song (104).

In fact, the origin seems not to be popular but instead literary. As it turns out, Vicente Espinel composed a polymetric piece called "Boda," ["Wedding"] in which two rustics, Gil and Antona, celebrate their wedding, feted by the guests with the following song:

> Mas valéis vos Antona
> que la corte toda
> Mas vale vuestra gala
> gracia y bizarria
> que otra çagala
> desta serrania
> si viniese el dia
> que sera la boda. (Haley 67. vv. 78–85; No punctuation in original)[1]

> [You are worth more, Antona, / than the whole Court. / Your elegance, grace, valor / are worth more / than any other lass / of these hills / who might come / the day of your wedding.]

In fact, its theatrical manifestations in the 17th and 18th centuries seem not to have been so much as a saying or *dicho* but as a *refrán cantado* [sung refrain]. Subsequent appearances as a full-blown song appear in Lope's *El cuerdo en su casa*;[2] in his *Más valéis vos, Antona, que la corte toda*;[3] in Tirso's *Antona García*;[4] and in Cañizares's *La heroica Antona García*.[5]

The multiple versions of the song both evoke the past and tie it to the present. With the exception of *El cuerdo en su casa*, the historical context to which the action of each of these plays alludes is one of threat, external or internal.[6] While Lope's *Más valéis vos, Antona* makes vague references to strained relations between the Kingdom of Navarre and France (specifically the Duchy of Brittany) as a framing device to the plot, both Tirso's *Antona García* and Cañizares's remake are based on specific and well-known historical characters and events. All three plays, I suggest, are written in moments that make the re-telling of these events relevant to the contemporary audience; the song links the characters and their contexts within the play to the audience and their own circumstances.

The three plays share elements beyond the obvious: namely, the use of the song to praise a main character named Antona, a country lass who, as referenced in the song, is worth as much as or more than any lady of the Court. In all three plays, the comparison and contrast is between a humble Antona and a royal Isabel or Isabela. But the differences are significant. In Lope's play, Antona is an assumed name, and therefore does not refer to a historical figure, whereas Tirso's and Cañizares's Antona García was celebrated in historical chronicles and later in legends. On the other hand, all three Isabels were historical figures. Although Lope's Isabela would probably not ring any bells for 21st-century audiences, Tirso and Cañizares bring to their plays none other than the Catholic Queen, a recognizable figure even in our own age of historical unenlightenment.

What I explore in this essay goes beyond the normal function of the song in each of the plays, although this is interesting in and of itself. Songs inserted into *comedias* are not purely decorative, and can assume an important function in developing or advancing the plot, often providing a structural frame—either as an introduction to the plot or a recapitulation, not to mention a dramatic or comic climactic moment.[7] Beyond its narrative functions, the value of the traditional song can be seen as its atemporality, its evocation of a moment in the past, often a rural, uncomplicated past, an idyllic society supposedly innocent and free from social or political perturbations. In particular, the popular and rustic elements of a wedding scene constitute a very useful instrument to entertain the spectators in the courtyard theaters (Florit Durán 218). At the same time, the lyrical local color of a rustic scene provides

an edifying contrast, a confrontation of two opposite worlds; the world of the
Court, its unhealthy desires, and its abuses are clearly condensed in the refrain
"Más valéis vos, Antona, que la corte toda."

But why would each playwright use this refrain to evoke a circumstance
of history? Why at that moment? To what current events or present circumstances might they have been pointing in order to connect past to present?
What familiar historical "story" would take on additional meaning when jux-
taposed to current events? What would have been the context in which Lope's
Más valéis vos, Antona, que la corte toda would have been seen? The plot,
grossly reduced and simplified, begins with Isabela, Duchess of Brittany, making a pilgrimage to Santiago to fulfill a promise before her marriage to Juan,
Infante de Navarra, whom she has never met. In a convenient concurrence of
shipwrecks, they meet in Asturias, both adopting rustic names to hide their
status and their true nature, she as "Antona" and he as simply "el Serrano"
[the Mountain man]. After the required anagnorisis at the end of the play,
they marry, along with the secondary characters. In this play, "Antona" is the
assumed identity of a royal personage. The song is ironic because "Antona"
is really Isabela in disguise; the country wife judged to be as worthy as any
noble is, in reality, a noble.

"Vaguely historical" is how Fermín Sierra Martínez describes the plot
(239).[8] A preliminary web search for Isabella, Duchess of Brittany revealed
an intriguing reference to "Isabella Stewart (1426–1499), a Scottish Princess, the second daughter of James I of Scotland ..., and the second wife of
the Duke [of Brittany] Francis I."[9] An even more intriguing but undocu-
mented statement seemed to fit the bill perfectly: "Upon her husband's death
in 1450, there were talks of Isabella's marrying Charles, Prince of Viana, heir
to the disputed Kingdom of Navarre, but this proposal fell through due to
the disapproval of Charles VII of France" ("Isabella"). More digging turned
up two articles devoted to the marital politics between Scotland—specifically
James's six daughters—and Continental royal houses, a series of six Scottish marriage alliances concluded with Franco-Burgundian princes between
1428 and 1449, according to Fiona Downie (174), who suggests that Scotland's "political and marital attractions lay outwith her borders, namely in her
hostility to England and alliance with France" (174n14). Furthermore, the
marriage of Stewart princesses to French allies proved even more significant
following the Anglo-French truce of 1444, shortly after Isabella's marriage
to Duke Francis (Downie 177). In fact, after the death of the Duke of Brittany in 1450, there was talk of a marriage between Isabella and Navarre,
but it was James Stewart who objected, not Charles VII. It is possible that
James wanted Isabella to return to Scotland, but she maintained her desire to

stay in Brittany, "effectively ruling out her remarriage to Navarre or within Scotland ... It seems clear that she did not wish to remarry and had the legal and economic independence, not to mention the will, to reject any marriage plans put to her" (Downie 185–86).

In the second article, Priscilla Bawcutt and Bridget Henisch stress that "[l]ike other great ladies of her period, Isabella was devout, and from the evidence of the books she collected it is possible to trace the pattern of her piety" (48). While the various Books of Hours she possessed, commissioned, and passed on to her daughters are of enormous interest to art historians today, it is doubtful that Spaniards of the early 17th century would have knowledge of them or interest in them. But her origins as a Stewart and, more probably, her Catholic piety might have been known, given her connection to the Carmelites by her marriage and her personal sympathies with the Franciscans. As Bawcutt and Henisch characterize Isabella, "[b]eneath the splendid trappings and ceremonial routine appropriate for her rank, Isabella attempted an internal pilgrimage as a private soul, a day by day progress on a path to spiritual enlightenment" (50).

Would Isabella Stuart ring any bells for Lope's audience of 1601 (or 1608)? What was happening at that time in Spain that could resonate with Lope's audiences? One possible connection might have to do with the peace treaty signed in 1604, bringing an end to the Anglo-Spanish war (1585–1604) and the military tensions between the two countries. The death of Elizabeth I of England (another "Isabel") in 1603 brought to the throne her nephew, James VI of Scotland, son of Mary Stuart, uniting the crowns of Scotland and England and bringing to England the House of Stuart. Catholic Europe had favored James as successor to the throne of England in the hope that the new monarch would show tolerance and clemency to Catholics at the very least, and some dared hope that he might even convert. In 1604, the treaty was signed in London between Philip III and James I, or Jacobo I, as he is known in Spain. The Jacobean Age begins with the end of the hostilities between the two countries, just as Lope's play begins on the Jacobean pilgrimage route and ends with the marriage between two nobles that will bring an end to hostilities between their respective crowns. It could be; but then again, the historical reference could be a simple framing device that would not have resonated at all.

Antona García is another matter entirely. In Tirso's play, the character's name and circumstances suggest and recall the song, which defines (without any irony at all) the genuine essence of the character. Antona is really Antona, but her worth and valor in battle compare favorably with that of Queen Isabel, unsurpassable in her excellence and exemplarity. The plot of the play is fairly well known, as is the historical episode recreated by Tirso. The so-called *Guerra de la Beltraneja* [War of the Beltraneja] (1475–1479)[10] pitted Isabel against Juana, and Castilians against Portuguese. Scholars point to the chronicles of Fernando del Pulgar as the most likely source, although Eva Galar finds echoes of other sources, in particular Manuel Faria e Sousa's *Epítome de las historias portuguesas*, [*Epitomy of Portuguese Stories*], in Tirso's dialogue as well as the elevated protagonism of María Sarmiento and her harangue from the walls of Toro, and Galar is quick to point out the many liberties taken by Tirso in altering the historical facts to suit his sense of theater:

> ... en la comedia no se desarrolla la historia de Antona sino una recreación artística. La Antona de Tirso es una mujer aldeana, de Tagarabuena, en vez de la ciudadana de Toro de la que hablan los historiadores. En su primer enfrentamiento con los portugueses resulta herida y su esposo muerto, si bien los hechos sucedieron al revés. En la ficción Antona y Penamacor mantienen una estrecha relación y llegan a comprometerse: el caballero portugués estaba casado desde 1467 y Juan de Monroy no murió hasta 1486, diez años después que su esposa. La Antona de la comedia participa en el asalto de Toro del 19 de septiembre, al lado de Bartolo y Alvaro de Mendoza, cuando la verdadera Antona ya había sido ejecutada en julio de ese mismo año. (495)

> [... in the play it is not the history of Antona that is developed but rather an artistic recreation. Tirso's Antona is a villager from Tagarabuena and not the citizen of Toro that historians describe. In her first confrontation with the Portuguese, she is wounded and her husband is killed, but the facts are just the opposite. In the fictional account Antona and Penamacor maintain a close relationship and eventually become engaged. In fact, the Portuguese gentleman was married in 1467 and Juan de Monroy, Juana's husband, did not die until 1486, ten years after his wife. The Antona of the play takes part in the attack on Toro on September 19, at the side of Bartolo and Alvaro de Mendoza, whereas the real Antona had been executed in July of that same year.]

The playwright accomplished his mission of providing a dramatic humanization of the political and historical ideas that defined the creation of the work; one can find various political messages throughout. The *Reyes Católicos* come off as perfect monarchs, in contrast to the corrupt nobles who rebel against them. The Catholic Monarchs show evenhandedness—even serenity—in their actions and repress their ire, in sharp contrast to the cruel vengeance meted out by María Sarmiento and her band. And the *Reyes Católicos* reward their faithful followers, which is of capital relevance to this play.

Antona García, we might say, is worth more than the Court, but not more than the Queen. She is better than María Sarmiento, who has been depicted as cruel and ultimately ineffectual, whereas Antona shows a natural nobility and epic valor. She describes herself as "Hidalga no, pero sí / sin raza y Cristiana vieja" (I.301–02) [Not noble but definitely / pure in blood and an Old Christian]. She accomplishes prodigious feats of strength, most notably mowing down four Portuguese men with a wooden bench in a scene that McClelland and Halkhoree have seen as parody, but which Galar sees as a sort of popular and folkloric "vengeance" against a Portuguese heroine, the so-called Forneira, who killed seven Spaniards with a wooden bread peel; Antona breaks the bones of four Portuguese with a wooden bench (502). But this behavior is not applauded by Queen Isabel, who urges Antona to attend to her husband and her house: "No os preciéis de pelear, / que el honor de la mujer / consiste en obedecer / como el del hombre en mandar" (I.361–64) [Do not pride yourself on fighting; / a woman's honor / consists of obeying, / just as a man's consists of commanding]. This might seem ironic to a public who knew well Isabel's actions in the wars of la Beltraneja and Granada, and all would know by heart the motto "Tanto monta, monta tanto" that sums up the equality of Isabel and Fernando: "as much as the one is worth, so too is the other."

In recognition of the worthiness of Antona García's heroic actions, the monarchs declared that all her descendants would enjoy the status and privileges of *hidalguía* [petty nobility]. Scholars have placed the date of the play as between 1623 and 1625, based on a supposed coincidence with the prolongation of a lawsuit conducted against the descendants of Antona García "who claimed exemption from taxes in accordance with the privilege granted to Antona and her heirs by the *Reyes Católicos*" (Wilson viii). According to Wilson, Ruth Lee Kennedy surmised that the latter date was thus probably *ad quem* for the play, "which could very well have been composed in support of the claims of Antona García's descendants, and would hardly have been written after the government had decided the matter in high tribunal" (viii). Would members of the audience have been aware of the legal suits, the virtue of which would seem unquestionable in light of the exploits of one so worthy? I submit the possibility that the historical incident is more than a narrative device; it establishes lateral dialogical reminders, pointing the audience to the relationship between the characters in the play and contemporary descendants, whose social status devolves from the worthiness of Antona García.

In a similar fashion, Cañizares's version of Antona García demonstrates to all what the essence of nobility, loyalty, and virtue should be. The play begins with the song, coming even earlier than it had in Tirso's version. Cañizares follows Tirso, but adds an ironic twist of a different sort, in a scene in which Antona dons one of the Queen's dresses that the monarch has given her as a present and as a result is mistaken for Isabel. Consequently, she is kidnapped by María Sarmiento, but Antona escapes, acquitting herself as well as Isabel might have. In my article "Bride in the Battlefield," I have dealt at length with Cañizares's remaking of Tirso's story but here I want to speculate as to why he would bring this plot to the stage almost one hundred years after Tirso. Why in 1709 would it make sense to revive and adapt *Antona García*?

Obviously, it was a good story and probably known by all, but it strikes me that there might have been echoes of a different sort. In *La heroica Antona García*, Cañizares is mindful of the cultural memory embodied in the historical person of Antona García as well as in Tirso's literary text, itself based on history and legend. In effect, Cañizares forges the latest link in a chain of intertextuality and intervocality. First, the chronicles convey the voice of the historical persons involved in the incidents or events in question; then Tirso's play takes over the voice of history and embodies the persons into characters who, in turn, through the actors, give voice and substance to the historical/legendary ones; finally, we have Cañizares's play, which subsumes the voice of Tirso's characters. In this chain of historical and literary events, the Cañizares version is at the service of the times, evoking and embodying the voice of the Bourbon monarchs, who are emerging victorious from a civil war with striking parallels to the dynastic struggle portrayed in the Antona García plays. In cultural terms, Antona speaks and acts for her side of the struggle, and her victories celebrate the rightful succession of "her" King and Queen, just as Cañizares speaks for his side of the forces engaged in the War of Succession. That Cañizares chose to rewrite this play is probably due as much to the political message he sends by bringing to life the historical person of Antona as to the dramatic attractiveness of Tirso's eponymous character. Cañizares evokes a moment in Spain's history that presents parallels to his own recent present. By taking over the voice of Antona, he maintains a link to the political and literary traditions that he supports. Through Antona (and through Tirso), Cañizares speaks for the supporters behind the pretender to the throne, named as legitimate by the last will and testament of the recently deceased monarch.

Comparing the three plays in question, Lope uses vaguely familiar characters from the past and places them in a likely location to set off a plausible tale of mistaken identity and anagnorisis, but at the same time, a tale of reconciliation and hope. Tirso and Cañizares are bound by the renown of their characters and the temporal and political circumstances surrounding them. In all three instances, the saying or song is the vehicle or means of suggestion— of a bygone time and of a rural genuineness that embody the spirit of the people, of the folk. For Tirso and Cañizares, the steadfast invincibility of this spirit is an evocation meant to celebrate the present circumstances of kinship to the worthy heroine (in Tirso) and victory of the "right" side in the recent civil war (in Cañizares).

The song "Más valéis vos, Antona, que la corte toda" is a wedding tribute, setting Antona apart as a worthy wife. The message is that the humble, imperfect country lass is valued as highly by her own as the grand lady is by the Court. In Lope's play, a second, ironic message is understood as well: that you can't judge a book by its cover; a seemingly lowly lass might really be a grand lady—or conversely, a seemingly grand lady might really be a lowly lass, for clothes don't make the woman. And Tirso and Cañizares convey a third message: that a woman's worth or value is determined by her actions as much as by her origins. Antona, humble but pure, can defend the claims of Isabel, the sovereign, with whom she identifies. The audience members, reveling in the happy ending—and perhaps unaware of the license taken with history—can congratulate themselves for being on the winning side.

Notes

1. Haley admits it is hard to determine the date of this polymetric piece. Espinel's *Diversas rimas* [*Selected Verse*] appeared in 1591, but his reputation preceded this by at least a decade (65n49).
2. Probably written sometime between 1606 and 1612, but most likely between 1606 and 1608, according to Morley and Bruerton (220).
3. Placed between 1620 and 1623 by Morley and Bruerton, but dated at least a decade earlier by Sierra Martínez. According to Morley and Bruerton (307), if the play was indeed by Lope, it would have probably been written around 1620. Fermín Sierra Martínez ("Aproximación" 243–44) has studied the question through examination of available manuscripts and copies, and through comparison with *El cuerdo en su casa*, probably written sometime between 1606 and 1612, but most likely between 1606 and 1608. If we accept Sierra Martínez's assertion that *Cuerdo* and *Mas Valéis Vos, Antona* are close metrically, then we could surmise that they were close chronologically.
4. It is dated as 1621 by Ruth Lee Kennedy (198) but 1625 by Margaret Wilson (viii–ix).
5. The work was published in 1755, but probably written in 1708 or 1709, given the fact that it premiered on October 3, 1709 at the Cruz, according to Andioc and Coulon (667).
6. Since *El cuerdo en su casa* lacks a specific historical setting, I do not include it in my exploration. For a discussion of the use of proverbs in Lope's titles, see Hayes.
7. As well, in the introduction to his study of songs in Lope's plays, Gustavo Umpierre observes that "[t]he multiple activities accompanied by music in Lope's theater reflect clearly the pervasive influence of music in the daily life of his contemporaries" (1). For additional studies of songs in Lope see Alín and Barrio Alonso, and also Bras. For a more general study of traditional songs in Europe, see Frenk.
8. Sierra Martínez refers to the heroine as "la Duquesa de Borgoña;" however, Lope's text reads "Duquesa de Bretaña."

9. Duke Francis I of Brittany married Isabella Stewart in 1442 (Downie 174). The Duke of Brittany had been betrothed to Bonne of Savoy and married to Yolande of Anjou before marrying Isabella Stewart in 1442 (Downie 180).
10. Interestingly, this is roughly the same time period of Isabella Stewart. I am indebted to Eva Galar's introduction to Tirso's play, *Antona García* (492–93).

Works Cited

Alín, José María, and María Begoña Barrio Alonso. *Cancionero teatral de Lope de Vega.* London: Tamesis, 1997. Print.

Andioc, René, and Mireille Coulon. *Cartelera teatral madrileña del siglo XVIII: (1708–1808).* Toulouse: Presses Universitaires du Mirail, 1996. Print.

Bawcutt, Priscilla, and Bridget Henisch. "Scots Abroad in the Fifteenth Century: The Princesses Margaret, Isabella, and Eleanor." *Women in Scotland, c. 1100–1750.* Ed. Elizabeth Ewan and Maureen M. Meikle. East Linton, Sotland, UK: Tuckwell, 1999. 45–55. Print.

Bras, María Julia. "Recreación de la lírica popular en las comedias de Lope de Vega." *Lírica tradicional europea.* Ed. Eva Silvia Capelli and Josefa Zamudio de Predan. Buenos Aires: Universidad Nacional del Sur, 1999. 9–34. Print.

Cañizares, José de. *La heroica Antona García. Obras escogidas.* Vol. 2. Madrid: Ortega, 1838. Print.

Correas, Gonzalo. *Arte grande de la lengua castellana 1626.* Madrid: Real Academia Española, 1903. Print.

Downie, Fiona. "'La voie quelle menace tenir': Annabella Stewart, Scotland, and the European Marriage Market, 1444–56." *The Scottish Historical Review* 78.2.206 (1999): 170–91. Print.

Faria e Sousa, Manuel. *Epítome de las historias portuguesas.* Madrid: Francisco Foppens, 1677. Print.

Florit Durán, Francisco. "La escenificación de lo popular-villanesco en el teatro de Tirso de Molina." *La comedia villanesca y su escenificación: Actas de las XXIV Jornadas de teatro clásico.* Ed. Felipe Pedraza Jiménez, Rafael González Cañal, and Elena Marcello. Almagro: Ediciones de la Universidad Castilla-La Mancha, 2002. 217–36. Print.

Frenk Alatoree, Margit. *Corpus de la antigua lírica poular hispánica: siglos XV a XVII.* Madrid: Castalia, 1987. Print.

Galar, Eva E. Introduction. *Antona García. Obras completas. Cuarta parte de comedias de Tirso de Molina, I.* Madrid-Pamplona: Instituto de Estudios Tirsianos, 1999. 492–93. Print.

Haley, George. "Hacia el canon poético de Vicente Espinel. Atribuciones nuevas, poemas inéditos, textos recuperados." *El canon poético de Vicente Espinel. Sátiras, romances, lírica cantada, composiciones neolatinas.* Coord. José Lara Garrido. Málaga: Fundación de la Universidad de Málaga/Analecta Malacitana, 2009. 13–75. Print.

Halkoree, P. R. K. *Social and Literary Satire in the Comedies of Tirso de Molina.* Ed. José M. Ruano de la Haza and Henry W. Sullivan. Ottawa: Dovehouse, 1989. Print.

Hayes, F. C. "The Use of Proverbs as Titles and Motives in the Siglo de Oro Drama: Lope de Vega." *Hispanic Review* 6.4 (1938): 305–23. Print.

Irelan, Scott R., Anne Fletcher, and Julie Felise Dubliner. *The Process of Dramaturgy. A Handbook.* Newburyport, MA: Focus/Pullins, 2010. Print.

"Isabella of Scotland, Duchess of Brittany." Wikipedia. Web. 20 Jan. 2011. <http://en.wikipedia.org/wiki/Isabella_of_Scotland,_Duchess_of_Brittany>.

Kennedy, Ruth Lee. "On the Date of Five Plays by Tirso de Molina." *Hispanic Review* 10.3 (1942): 183–214. Print.

Lara Garrido, José, ed. *Vicente Espinel: historia y antología.* Málaga: Diputación Provincial de Málaga, 1993. Print.

López de Úbeda, Ángel. *La pícara Justina.* Ed. J. Puyol y Alonso. Madrid: Fortanet, 1912. Print.

McClelland, Ivy L. *Tirso de Molina: Studies in Dramatic Realism.* New York: AMS P, 1976. Print.

Molina, Tirso de (Gabriel Téllez). *Antona García.* Ed. Margaret Wilson. Manchester, UK: Manchester UP, 1977. Print.

Morley, Sylvanus Griswold, and Courtney Bruerton. *The Chronology of Lope de Vega's Comedias.* New York: Modern Languages Association; London: Oxford UP, 1940. Print.

Paun de García, Susan. "The Bride on the Battlefield: Cañizares' Antona García." Association for Hispanic Classical Theater Golden Age Theater Symposium. Cliff Inn, El Paso, TX. 5 Mar. 1997.

Puyol y Alonso, J., ed. and Intro. *La pícara Justina.* Madrid: Fortanet, 1912. Print.

Raw, Lawrence. "Retelling European History on Film." *Film and History* 41.2 (2011): 64–68. Print.

Sierra Martínez, Fermín. "Aproximación a Lope de Vega (III). *Más valéis vos, Antona, que la corte toda*: ¿atribución o autoría?" *Actas del XII Congreso de la Asociación Internacional de Hispanistas: 21–26 de agosto de 1995, Birmingham.* Ed. Aengus M. Ward, Jules Whicker, and Derek W. Flitter. Vol. 3. Birmingham, UK: Dept. of Hispanic Studies, The U of Birmingham, 1995. 238–46. Print.

Umpierre, Gustavo. *Songs in the Plays of Lope de Vega. A Study of Their Dramatic Function.* London: Tamesis, 1975. Print.

Vega, Lope de. *Más valéis vos, Antona, que la corte toda. Obras.* Ed. Emilio Cotarelo y Mori. Vol. 7. Madrid: Revista de Archivos, Bibliotecas y Museos, 1930. Print.

Wilson, Margaret, ed. *Antona García.* By Tirso de Molina (Gabriel Téllez). Manchester, UK: Manchester UP, 1977. Print.

Tried and True: *Leonor de la Cueva y Silva's Tirso Connection*

SHARON D. VOROS
United States Naval Academy

Piecing together literary influences on Leonor de la Cueva y Silva (1611–1705) presents a number of challenges. Unlike many of her sister dramatists, there are no contemporary commentaries on her work, with only two funereal sonnets published in her lifetime (Olivares and Boyce 105). However, in her will, which I located in Valladolid (Voros, "Leonor's Library" 498), Leonor includes titles of her small collection of books, among them Juan Pérez de Montalbán's *Para todos* [*For Everyone*], a miscellany with his own plays and novellas, and a list of writers and dramatists, including Tirso de Molina and María de Zayas.[1] While she draws on plays by several dramatists, such as Lope de Vega (Voros, "Leonor" 192) and Montalbán (Voros, "Leonor's Library" 503), Jonathan Ellis has shown her indebtedness to Cervantes's tale "El curioso impertinente" ["The Impertinent Meddler"][2] with the implementation of a test. With the notion of a test in mind, I will explore still another influence on her writing, Tirso de Molina. I find similar dramatic structures in both Tirso and Leonor with help by a concept developed from structural linguistics to trace recurrent patterns in the plot, linguistic structure or characterization, called "narremes" by Eugene Dorfman and Henri Wittman (Bonheim 1).[3] Although the narreme accounts for narrative aspects of the text, it can also account for dramatic constructs because of the recurring patterns of action, place and time, similar to Aristotle's three unities, in what Helmut Bonheim calls the "scenic narreme" in his analysis of Shakespeare's adaptations of his prose source material. The narreme is a kind of binary set, with "macro-narremes" or repeated structures or "patterns" and "micro-narremes," although there may be also single events or "solitaires" to use Bonheim's term.

One narreme then brings about the occurrence of another narreme, thus providing the dramatic frame or pattern for stage action. Thus a narreme is not simply the statement of a theme, but an indication of dramatic or narrative structure. Since we often look for the unique aspects of language, such as metaphor, the narremic structural underpinning often goes unnoticed or underappreciated.

Why Tirso? While Leonor probably became familiar with him through the *Para todos*, I came to Tirso in a roundabout way. Thanks to Barbara Mujica, I began reading French women dramatists, especially Marie-Catherine Desjardins (1640–1683), known as Madame de Villedieu, who based her play, *Le favori* [*The Favorite*] (1665),[4] on Tirso's *El amor y el amistad* [*Love and Friendship*]. The master narreme for *Le favori* involves a fall from grace of the Court favorite who unwittingly transgresses against his King, followed by a test and reconciliation. Moncade, the King of Barcelona's Court favorite, becomes despondent since he does not know if his friends and lady love are loyal to him for himself or for his power and influence. The King, however, interprets Moncade's melancholic state as treasonous and orders him arrested. Not only Moncade but his lady Lindamere are put to the test. Clotaire, for whom Moncade had secured political asylum, and the coquette Elvire conspire to secure his downfall. They lie to the King that Lindamere and Moncade plan to escape together. The accusation of treason, however, is the King's own fabrication, for he reveals in the final act that this scheme was actually designed to rid Moncade of the cause of his chagrin. It has all been an act, a Court drama, yet Moncade triumphs in the end and marries his lady love. Is the King another impertinent meddler? Villedieu is careful to show the monarch as acting within his rights. However, only four months before this play's performance at Versailles in 1665, in which Molière himself probably played Clotaire,[5] Nicolas Foucquet, the King's favorite finance minister, was tried as a traitor and never saw the light of day (Hogg 48).

Tirso de Molina's El amor y el amistad

The overarching narreme for Tirso's play, *El amor y el amistad,* adapted by Villedieu, and, as I will argue, by Leonor, is quite similar. Transgression by a Court favorite is followed by a test and eventual reconciliation. While these plays are not tragedies, they nevertheless take on the tone and manner of tragic discourse. The Court favorite, often the best warrior, falls from grace and is removed from Court by his monarch. However, the fall is only the first segment of the narreme which is then followed by a second segment, the trial or test. In the implementation of this narreme in Tirso and Leonor, the test ends up being an ordeal for all three principal characters involved, the reigning aristocrat, the Court favorite and the lady. Each dramatist emphasizes different aspects of this recurrent structure. Leonor shifts emphasis away from the warrior favorite, for Don Juan becomes less important dramatically than Armesinda, his lady love. However, the narreme of the fall from grace explains why Leonor places the exploits of Don Juan in the key dramatic position at the play's opening with his *fanfarrón* [braggart] boasting. His style changes when he gets orders to lead the attack against the invading French, for he sees his being sent to war by King Filiberto as a means to remove him from Court: "por vengar su desprecio / me ausenta, con la occasion / de la Guerra del de Francia" (II.276–79, 201) [To avenge her rejection / he (the King) sends me away / with the pretext of a war against the French].[6] He has become the King's rival for Armesinda and even for the best warrior in the land; hence, being the King's rival is a position of peril.

In Tirso, after overhearing a conversation between his beloved Estela and rival Don Grao, Guillén de Moncada, the *privado* [favorite] to the Count of Barcelona, begins to doubt her love and his friendship. He devises an elaborate test to assess the mettle of courtiers who represent friendship (*amistad*) and ladies who represent love (*amor*), two coquettes here instead of one as in Villedieu's version. Guillén had distinguished himself in battle, so the Count of Barcelona feels indebted to him for his rise to power (Gethner, "Power" 212). However, the fall from grace of the Court favorite, a device instigated by Guillén himself to test friends and lovers, three in each group, appears at the beginning. Villedieu holds off until the last act to reveal the truth that the arrest is merely the King's device to test Moncade, while in Tirso, the audience knows from the outset that the test is Guillén's fabrication. The Count of Barcelona even is in on the act. He lavishes wealth on Guillén, who then becomes anxious and edgy; he is much more impulsive and unpredictable than Villedieu's Moncade and resembles Leonor's *gallardo rey* [gallant King] Filiberto. The Count at first is reluctant to put Guillén in prison, since he fears that rival enemies would perceive him as inconstant: "Han de llamarme inconstante" (II.1886, 279) [They will call me inconstant].[7] The test involves everyone, as it turns out. Of course Grao and Estela prove true to Guillén, while the two coquettes (Gracia and Victoria), who had attempted to gain his favors, reject him, as do the two so-called friends (Gastón and Dalmao), who decline to support him.

The Count, however, has his own ideas, for he plans a trial of his own and turns the tables on his Court favorite. At first I thought that the mention of the "tribunal de amor" [Courts of love], the courtly-love trial of the lover's fidelity that the Count discusses (II.1217, 256), was enough to connect these two plays. The Courts of love, a phrase Leonor uses (Voros, "Al tribunal" 167), led me to believe at first that Leonor could have understood this play as a model. Further evidence of a connection appears when the reigning aristocrat becomes the rival of his Court favorite, just as King Filiberto becomes a rival of his best warrior, Don Juan. Rivalry between King and Court favorite does not occur in Villedieu's play, more centered on political power than on love. In Tirso, however, the Count unexpectedly proposes to Estela, with Guillén listening in, convinced that his own lord, whom he has swept into power, has betrayed him by stealing his lady love. The Count then explains that this marriage proposal was indeed a test: "que ya bastan tantas pruebas" (III.3138, 327) [for enough already with so many tests]. We never get a good explanation from the Count as to why he does this, other than that he is curious to find out what will happen to Guillén when he attempts to woo Estela. In a very brief aside, the Count says: "Hoy he de probar más bien / lo que tiene don Guillén" (III.2938–39, 321) [Today, however, I will test / what Guillén is made of]. So, Tirso provides an interesting dramatic twist to the narreme of the fall from grace and the inevitable test. The Count plays his role convincingly and even mentions to Guillén that he has to rehearse his part: "Esperadme, pues, que quiero / ensayarme de enojado" (II.1924–25, 280) [Wait for me then, for I want / to rehearse the role of the angry one]. He plays the role of the *enojado*, as does Guillén himself. As with Cervantes's impertinent meddler, Guillén finds that the trial he sets up for others of his entourage becomes his own dilemma. Yet this is not just idle curiosity, but a serious matter of loyalty to one's liege lord and true love.

This narreme also explains the presence of the coquettes in Tirso, the two ladies of the Court who attempt to attract Guillén but desert him when he falls from grace, for they are part of the test. Madame de Villedieu included the term coquette in the subtitle of her play *Le favori*, yet scholars puzzle over this (Ekstein 220). Ekstein considers the coquette Elvire superfluous at the beginning (219), yet Villedieu apparently read Tirso with this character type in mind. Not only is this coquette extremely important as part of the narreme of the test, but she also deflects some of the dramatic action away from the tyrannous monarch, part of tragic discourse, and introduces some comic relief into the work. Elvire's flippant remarks conclude the play with assurances that despite her failed scheming, she is moving on: "Tout cela ne vaut pas la peine d'en parler / Et Dom Lope m'attend qui va m'en consoler" (V.1435–36, 126) [All this is not worth any conversation. / Don Lope's waiting; he's my consolation (Gethner, *Favorite* V.1435–36, 88).] Leonor, however, omits the coquette altogether, and replaces her with the King's sister Celidaura, who is not a help to Armesinda, but a hindrance, for she attempts to convince her to submit to her brother Filiberto. Both Leonor and Tirso bring in rivalry between a warrior/Court favorite and a lady love as way to implement this recurring pattern. Removal from Court of the favorite or warrior then follows sequentially the narreme of the test, although that removal can involve a variety of dramatic possibilities, jail in Tirso, the threat of jail in Villedieu, or war in Leonor.

Leonor de la Cueva's La firmeza en la ausencia [Steadfastness in Absence]

With the "tribunal de amor," or Courts of love, as a key phrase in Leonor's play, her heroine Armesinda (a name used by Tirso in *Cómo han de ser los amigos* [*What Friends Should Be Like*]) is the only character to call for justice in her despair and isolation: "¿Qué haré? Que estoy dudosa, / sin que pueda cuadrarme alguna / cosa que traiga remedio" (II.1601–03, 215) [What shall I do? I am in turmoil. / Nothing pleases me, / nothing brings relief] and "Mas, pues falta del cielo / remedio, al tribunal de amor apelo; / él me le dé, pues es mi resistencia / la más rara firmeza en la ausencia" (II.1609–12, 215) [But since there is no help from Heaven, / I appeal to the courts of love. / May they give me release, / for my resistence / is the rarest loyalty. / And despite myself I always knew: / I am tried, tried and true].[8] While Armesinda's fidelity is certainly tested, the test here is also a fabrication, as it is in both Tirso and Villedieu. In this instance, the test is an elaborate scheme to conceal the actions of a predatory, tyrannous monarch intent on seducing the lady after having successfully sent her true love Don Juan to the battlefield. Leonor's play focuses on the sexual harassment of Armesinda. In a kind of reworking of the David, Bathsheba, Uriah story, the King sends his best warrior Don Juan, now his rival, to battle the French. While this war is a real danger to the realm, Don Juan does not interpret the King's motives as concern for the security of the Kingdom of Naples, for this narreme of transgression and the fall from grace involves also the King's true motives. The exigencies of war simply provide a legitimate means to send Don Juan away, since prison or death would not be possible for the best warrior in the land. This narreme explains why Leonor begins her play with the warrior hero and the tournament during which he perceives the King's unwanted attention towards Armesinda and her reluctance to acknowledge him. Leonor, as does Villedieu, uses an historical personage as her model, *El gran capitán* [The Great Captain], Gonzalo Fernández de Córdoba, Court favorite of Isabel la Católica and viceroy of Naples, until his fall from grace after her death (Voros, "El actor" 203). References to the Great Captain's exploits abound in this play. Villedieu, as mentioned, uses the imprisonment of Louis XIV's finance minister Nicolas Foucquet, charged with treason and embezzlement. Thus the narreme of the fall from grace has numerous historical antecedents that apparently both women were familiar with. Tirso certainly was aware of conflicts between reigning aristocrats and their favorites. Leonor changes the dynamics of the testing narreme, for her heroine, not the monarch, calls for justice, since she is isolated and marginalized in what appears to be a scheme for the King's seduction of her.

There is even an attempted rape that Jonathan Ellis calls the coercive narreme based on the Lucretia story.[9] In the dream scene in Act III, Filiberto enters the lady's bedchamber and is inches away from accosting her. Although she is unaware of the danger in her dream state, she is rescued by Don Juan's friend Don Carlos, also a loyal courtier to the King, just as Filiberto attempts to grab her. Carlos says in an aside, "Mi industria salió valiente / y cumplí famosamente / con la ley de buen amigo" (III.1917–19, 218) [My efforts were successful / and I fulfilled my obligation famously. / Such is the law of the good friend], a recasting of the theme of Tirsian friendship.

The rape never happens and this play is not a tragedy. It is "disnarrated," a concept from Gerald Prince that involves aspects of a narration mentioned but not really happening. In fact, great portions of *Firmeza* are disnarrated, including the battery of lies concocted by the King and his courtier about Don Juan in his absence, as a way to persuade Armesinda to submit. Leonor also modifies or "disnarrates" the David, Bathsheba, Uriah story, since the warrior returns home with a victory and a bride for his King, and the lady Armesinda is unwilling to submit to the King's predatory advances. She struggles to remain virtuous in a hostile environment in which even her own maid, named ironically Leonor, appears to betray her. Don Juan begins and ends the play with the recurrent structure that involves the narreme of the fall from grace, followed by his victory against the French and reconciliation with his King. While this narreme offers the structure and devices of tragedy, with dream sequences in which Armesinda rejects the King and calls him a tyrant in her dream discourse, this play does not work itself out as tragedy, for order of the realm is restored with the fidelity and constancy of one lady and the successful campaign of the warrior hero, who also returns with a French bride for his King.

That Leonor bases her resolution of this narreme on Tirso is also shown in the concluding scenes of both plays. While what she endures amounts to a trial of her *firmeza* [steadfastness], Armesinda finally has her day in Court and reveals to the entire King's entourage that she has had a secret relationship, albeit chaste, with Don Juan for six years. She demands permission to leave the Court or die. Then she becomes impatient when he does not respond and tells him: "¿No respondes? ¿En qué tardas?" (III.2121, 221) [You do not respond? What are you waiting for?], while the King mutters asides such as "¿Hay semejante mujer? / Callen griegas y romanas" (III.2110–11) [Is there any woman like her? / Let Greeks and Romans keep silent!], a topic that recalls Armesinda's list of exemplary strong women (Voros, "Calderón's" 128–29). He then turns the tables, just as Tirso's Count did, and proposes marriage: "Mi esposa has de ser" (III.2123, 221) [You are to be my wife]. When she refuses the offer, the King attempts to grab her by force in the presence of the entire Court, just as Don Juan makes his grand entrance, triumphant from war with the French. Filiberto receives Don Juan as conquering hero: "Levanta, don Juan, levanta, / que bien mereces mis brazos" (III.2143–44, 221) [Arise, don Juan, arise, / for you deserve my embrace] in what must be one of the quickest turnarounds in dramatic history. It becomes clear that all is forgiven with a military victory.

This scene parallels Tirso's revelation scene also at the end of the play. When the Count proposes to marry Estela (Guillén's lady love) himself, Guillén steps out from behind the discovery space and reveals his true love for her and his fear that the Count has betrayed him. All ends well, as in Leonor's play. Both Tirso and Leonor invoke the famous Courts of love, part of the courtly love tradition in which lovers' actions and true affections are submitted for scrutiny usually to a lady judge, even Eleanor of Aquitaine. The Courts of love apparently had some influence in Cataluña, the setting of Tirso's play, with early translations into Catalan (Perry 23). Trials, revelation scenes, and judgments provide the dénouement for each play here and keys to the understanding of stagecraft in both Tirso and Leonor.

Leonor de la Cueva y Silva's literary heritage clearly involves several major dramatists of the Spanish Golden Age. However, we also see Tirso de Molina's influence cross the Pyrenees, and not just for Molière, since his *El amor y el amistad* is a foundational text for Madame de Villedieu. Both women had connections to the Court, although Leonor has no known stage history, unlike Villedieu, whose relationship with Molière allowed her not only to publish her work but to see all three of her plays on the stage. *Le favori* was her last stage production and, unfortunately, there is no evidence that she actually attended the performance at Versailles. As with Leonor, she remained somewhat ignored until the 20th century. Both women, however, were keen observers of life in Court and found Tirso's play, with narremes on a fall from grace and the test, a model for their own dramatic concerns. Leonor shifts the emphasis to her female lead Armesinda, while Villedieu provides a notion of the King's pardon of a favorite, unlike their historical antecedents, but very much like Tirso de Molina's dramatic vision.

Notes

1. I refer to Leonor by her first name, since many of her relatives have the same surname. Thomas Finn's excellent study of Spanish influence on Molière inspired my title.
2. All translations are my own unless otherwise indicated.
3. My thanks to Jonathan Ellis for suggesting the usefulness of narremes in analyzing dramatic structure.
4. Translations for Villedieu are from Gethner's edition. All translations for Leonor de la Cueva y Silva are my own.
5. Thanks to Molière, Madame de Villedieu's play has a stage history. *Le favori* was performed in Paris in April 1665 and then again at Versailles in June 1665 (Hogg 46–48). Villedieu is the only woman playwright whose work was performed at Versailles itself and Molière himself probably played the role of Clotaire, according to Henriette Goldwyn and Aurore Evain in their Introduction, 20.
6. All citations for Leonor de la Cueva's play are from the Teresa Soufas edition.
7. All citations for Tirso are from María Teresa Otal's edition.
8. I added a rhyming couplet to emphasize Armesinda's plight and recall the title of my translation *Tried and True* for Leonor's *La firmeza en la ausencia* [*Steadfastness in Absence*].
9. See Ellis, "The Question of Female Solidarity and Female Honor in Leonor de la Cueva's *La firmeza en la ausencia.*"

Works Cited

Bonheim, Helmut. "Shakespeare's Narremes." *Shakespeare Survey 53: Shakespeare and Narrative.* Ed. Peter Holland. Cambridge, UK: Cambridge UP, 2000. 1–11. Print.

Cueva y Silva, Leonor de la. *La firmeza en la ausencia. Women's Acts.* Ed. Teresa Soufas. Lexington: The U of Kentucky P, 1997. 198–222. Print.

Dorman, Eugene. *The Narreme in the Medieval Romance Epic: An Introduction to Narrative Structures.* Toronto: U of Toronto P, 1969. Print.

Ellis, Jonathan. "*Cervantine* Curiosity and Impertinence in Leonor de la Cueva's *La firmeza en la ausencia.*" *Romance Notes* 49 (2009): 35–46. Print.

———. "The Question of Female Solidarity and Female Honor in Leonor de la Cueva's *La firmeza en la ausencia.*" Association for Hispanic Classical Theater Symposium on Golden Age Theater. Camino Real Hotel, El Paso, TX. 4 Mar. 2011. Address.

Ekstein, Nina. "The Second Woman in the Theater of Villedieu." *Neophilologus* 80 (1996): 213–24. Print.

Finn, Thomas P. *Molière's Spanish Connection: 17th-century Spanish Theatrical Influence on Imaginary Identity in Molière.* New York: Peter Lang, 2001. Print.

Gethner, Perry, trans. *The Favorite Minister. The Lunatic Lover and Other Plays by French Women of the 17th and 18th Centuries.* Portsmouth, NH: Heinemann, 1994. 40–88. Print.

———. "Power Grabbing and Court Opportunism: From Spain to France." *Echoes and Inscriptions. Comparative Approaches to Early Modern Spanish Literatures.* Ed. Barbara Simerka and Christopher B. Weimer. Lewisburg, PA: Bucknell UP, 2000. 210–19. Print.

Goldwyn, Henriette, and Aurore Evain. Introduction. *Théâtre de femmes de l'Ancien Régime*. Vol. 2. Saint-Étienne: Publications de l'Université de Saint-Étienne, 2008. 17–28. Print.

Hogg, Chloé. "Staging Foucquet: Historical and Theatrical Contexts of Villedieu's *Le favori*." *A Labor of Love. Critical Reflections on the Writings of Marie-Catherine Desjardins (Mme de Villedieu)*. Ed. Roxanne Decker Lalande. Madison, WI: Associated UP, 2000. 43–63. Print.

Montalbán, Juan Pérez de. *Para todos. Obra no dramática*. Ed. José Enrique Laplana Gil. Madrid: Fundación José Antonio de Castro, 1999. 461–889. Print.

Molina, Tirso de (Gabriel Téllez). *Cómo han de ser los amigos y El amor y el amistad. (Dos comedias palatinas)*. Ed. María Teresa Otal. Pamplona: Instituto de Estudios Tirsianos, 2007. Print.

Olivares, Julián, and Elizabeth S. Boyce, eds. *Tras el espejo la musa escribe. Lírica femenina de los Siglos de Oro*. Madrid: Siglo XXI Editores, 1993. Print.

Perry, John Jay, trans. Introduction. *The Art of Courtly Love*. By Andreas Capellanus. New York: Frederick Unger, 1959. 3–24. Print.

Prince, Gerald. "The Disnarrated." *Style* 22 (1988): 1–8. Print.

Villedieu, Madame de (Marie-Catherine Desjardins). *Le favori. Femmes dramaturges en France (1650–1750): pièces choisies*. Ed. Perry Gethner. Vol. 1. Tübingen: G. Narr, 1993. 71–126. Print. Biblio 17.

———. *The Favorite Minister [Le favori]*. In *The Lunatic Lover and Other Plays by French Women of the 17th and 18th Centuries*. Ed. and trans. Perry Gethner. Portsmouth, NH: Heinemann, 1994. 40–88. Print.

Voros, Sharon D. "'Al tribunal de amor apelo:' Leonor de la Cueva and the Language of Law." *Women's Voices and the Politics of the Spanish Empire*. Ed. Jeanne Gillespie. New Orleans: UP of the South, 2008. 159–75. Print.

———. "Calderón's Women Writing and Women Writers: The Subversion of the *Exempla*." *Looking at the Comedia in the Year of the Quincentennial. Proceedings of the 1992 Golden Age Drama Symposium at the University of Texas, El Paso. March 16–21*. Ed. Barbara Mujica and Sharon D. Voros. With Matthew Stroud. Washington, DC: UP of America, 1993. 121–32. Print.

———. "El actor como soldado en *La firmeza en la ausencia* de Leonor de la Cueva." *Del texto al espectáculo. Homenaje a Francisco Portes*. Ed. Ysla Campbell. Ciudad Juárez, Mex.: Universidad de Ciudad Juárez, 2008. 201–18. Print.

———. "Leonor's Library: The Last Will and Testament of Leonor de la Cueva y Silva." *Hispanic Studies in Honor of Robert Fiore*. Ed. Chad Gasta and Julia Domínguez. Newark, DE: Juan de la Cuesta, 2009. 497–510. Print.

———. "Leonor de la Cueva y Silva Rewrites Lope de Vega: The Subversion of Silence in *La firmeza en la ausencia* and *La corona merecida*." *Engendering the Early Modern Stage: Women Playwrights in the Spanish Empire*. Ed. Amy Williamsen and Valerie Hegstrom. New Orleans: UP of the South, 1999. 189–209. Print.

Act Four

Performative Possibilities:
From Actors to Audiences

Actresses as Athletes and Acrobats

Barbara Mujica
Georgetown University

Comedia audiences were composed mostly of men, and actresses[1] were the main attraction at the theater for many of them. Melveena McKendrick writes that, "The presence on stage of women playing female roles was one of the *comedia*'s great box-office draws" (82), and Lola González lists twenty-one actresses for whom plays were specifically written (135).[2] The mostly male audience was undoubtedly fascinated with the lithe female bodies onstage, and the configuration of the *corral* [public] theater, with *gradas* [grand-stand] for paying customers contiguous to the performance space, gave them a close-up view. But there were also censors in the audience. Actresses had to demonstrate that they were talented and professional, not just pretty and seductive. The Jesuit Giovan Domenico Ottonelli (1584–1670) was one critic who defended the importance of an actress's skill over her appearance (Rodríguez 579).

    Comedia actresses distinguished themselves as different from other women not only because they had a public persona, worked for a salary, and were generally more literate than their sisters of a comparable social class,[3] but also because they had to discipline their bodies in ways that other women did not. All actors, male and female, had to remain in excellent condition, as rehearsals and performances were regularly long and arduous.[4] Women, like men, had to master basic acting techniques that required physical skill and stamina. Some roles were exceptionally strenuous, entailing leaping or climb-ing or even flying through the air on treacherous stage devices. The centrality of female roles in many plays meant that actresses were under particular pres-sure to stay in top form. McKendrick notes that when the actress Jerónima de Burgos became seriously overweight, she met with derision when she played Doña Juana in Tirso de Molina's *Don Gil de las calzas verdes* [*Don Gil of the*

Green Breeches] (82). Although, according to the *Genealogía, origen y noticias de los comediantes de España* [*Genealogy, Origin and Records about Spanish Comedia Performance*] some actresses worked past forty, Evangelina Rodríguez Cuadros notes that, "La edad ... se mostraba un cruel condicionante en la carrera de una actriz" (588) [Age imposed cruel limitations on an actress's career]. She cites the example of "Amarilis," who attempted to play the *dama joven* [young lady] past her prime and was ridiculed for doing so by Juan de Tassis, Count of Villamediana (588–89). Until Moratín began creating roles for older women at the end of the 18th century, few were available on the *comedia* stage.[5] However, some actresses who retired from performing continued in the theater as *autoras* [producers, impresarios], often taking over the company of their husband after his death.

As they do now, actors had to create the illusion of emotion, perception, sensation, transformation or movement by creating visual images with their bodies (Lust 99). By the 17th century, stage movement and gesture were highly codified in Spain. Actors of both sexes were required to learn the gestural language of the stage—movements based on natural or instinctive physical responses, but codified by society and then further refined for theater—in order to bring their characters to life. Evangelina Rodríguez-Cuadros notes that, "al sumergirse el rito en la imitación y en la expresión nace el concepto moderno de *interpretación*" (342) [the modern concept of *interpretation* is born of submerging oneself in the rite of imitation and expression]. In his *Philosophía antigua poética* [*Ancient Poetic Philosophy*] (1596), Alonso López-Pinciano describes positions of the hands, feet, body, lips and eyes that serve to communicate diverse psychological states. Although these descriptions of poses were originally intended for orators, actors scrutinized them to hone their communicative skills. Duncan Moir affirms that Lope de Vega undoubtedly knew López-Pinciano's treatise and it is likely that he recommended it to his actors or shared its counsel with them (195). Jusepe Antonio González de Salas, friend of Lope de Vega[6] and author of *Nueva idea de la tragedia antigua* [*The New Concept of Classical Tragedy*], also provided detailed advice on movement and elocution for actors. Elizabeth Petersen provides evidence that, in addition, Early Modern actors studied other oratory manuals such as Quintilian's *Instituto Oratoria* [*Institutes of Oratory*] for information on exercises and breathing techniques that would enable them to improve the quality of their voices and projection. She notes that Quintilian is quoted by both López-Pinciano and González de Salas, so even if actors didn't read the classical author directly, they would have been familiar with his teachings (52–53). Mastering the communicative codes of theater required discipline and years of practice. Technique was particularly important for actresses because, as Rodríguez Cuadros affirms, "La actriz ... es un centro o un cuerpo donde convergen miradas sociales" (574) [The actress ... is a focal point or a body for the convergence of social gaze]. This meant that censors would be constantly scrutinizing the women onstage for objectionable material.

The dance origins of many theatrical gestures offered one source of concern. Laura Vidler has demonstrated possible influences of fencing and dance guidebooks on stage movement. Rodríguez Cuadros notes that dance moves performed by actresses onstage, often in actual dances, were often the basis for censure by moralists. Several complained that such moves should be modified to avoid lasciviousness. For example, González de Salas insisted that movement for the theater, although inspired by courtly dance, must be measured and controlled rather than uninhibited (Rodríguez Cuadros 39).

Among the most challenging roles for women were those in which actresses appeared dressed as men. Such roles gave dramatists the opportunity to explore controversial themes, for which Early Modern audiences had tremendous appetite, and of flaunting conventional decorum. Lope de Vega "made no mystery of the importance of teasing the limits of conventional decorum" (Cañadas 19). His comment in *Arte nuevo de hacer comedias* [*The New Way of Writing Plays*] that "... suele / el disfraz varonil agradar mucho" (vv. 282–83) [masculine costume usually pleases (the public)] shows that he consciously and deliberately sought to create dramatic appeal by defying social norms. Cross-dressed *damas* not only wore revealing garments, they engaged in decidedly unladylike behavior, traveling alone, carrying swords, provoking fights. The audaciousness of their conduct was always titillating and provoked the wrath of moralists, who evoked the Bible to argue against the practice.

Comedias de bandolera [bandit plays] such as Mira de Amescua's *El esclavo del demonio* [*The Slave of the Devil*] and Calderón's *La devoción de la cruz* [*Devotion to the Cross*] and plays in which women don male garb to redeem their honor, such as Ana Caro's *Valor, Agravio y mujer* [*Woman Aggrieved, Woman Avenged*], often required constant and strenuous movement. Lisarda, female protagonist of *Esclavo*, uses images of power and velocity in her self-description to convey her own dynamism: "Un delfín cortando el mar, / una cometa encendida, / un caballo en la carrera, / en alta mar un navío, / el veloz curso de un río, / rayo que cay de su esfera; / una flecha disparada ..." (II.3–10, 117) [A dolphin cutting through the sea / a blazing comet / a racing horse / a ship on the high seas / the rapid course of a river / a bolt of lightning that falls from the sky / a shooting arrow ...]. She is a blind force, governed by directionless passion, and her gestural language mirrors her words. She terrorizes her victims not only with threats, but also handles a

crossbow and a pistol. Similarly, in *Devoción*, Julia exhibits wildness and ferocity. She descends a ladder to escape from her convent through the window
while still dressed in a skirt, and then, dressed as a man, terrorizes wayfarers
and threatens them with the sword. And Leonor, protagonist of Caro's comedy, not only engages in fencing and fighting, but also in exaggerated, carica-
turesque male movements when she "metamorphoses" into a man.[7]

Mimma de Salvo notes that actresses distinguished themselves by the kinds
of roles they played, and several excelled at these grueling "breeches" roles
(4). Among them was Luisa de Robles, who played Guzmán in Juan Pérez
de Montalbán's *La monja alférez* [*The Lieutenant Nun*]. The play depicts
the exploits of an historical character, the Basque noblewoman Catalina de
Erauso, who as a girl escaped from the Convent of San Sebastián el Antiguo,
shed her nun's habit for male garb, and went to fight Araucano Indians in
South America, earning the moniker *monja alférez*. By the time Juan Pérez
de Montalbán wrote his play in 1626, Erauso was a celebrity, and a curious
public was anxious to learn more about her. Pérez de Montalbán knew how
to exploit the market. The play was performed in Madrid shortly after it was
written, just when curiosity about Catalina was peaking and she was in Rome
petitioning the Pope to allow her to wear male garb permanently. The sen-
sationalist appeal of the play was undoubtedly heightened by casting Robles
as the lead. Known for her lurid personal life,[8] she was also famous for her
intrepidness and ingenuity.

The role of Erauso, called Guzmán in the play, requires exceptional dexterity with a sword. In some cases the swordfights are presented through
dramatic synecdoche. For example, in Acts I and II, Guzmán engages first
the Field Marshall and then an unsavory character known as El Nuevo Cid,
both of whom s/he[9] kills. In both scenes the actors move offstage to fight,
and Guzmán's victims die out of the sight of the audience. The playwright
probably made the decision to stage these scenes synecdochically for reasons
of decorum—to avoid showing the deaths onstage rather than to deprive the
actress of the opportunity to display her fencing skill—for she does exhibit her
dexterity with a sword elsewhere, for example, in Act I, when Guzmán fights
and wounds his/her brother Miguel.

Pants would surely have facilitated the movement of actresses in such
roles, but for one of the most demanding bandit roles on the Spanish stage,
the actress wears a skirt. *La serrana de la Vera* [*The Mountain Woman of La
Vera*], by Luis Vélez de Guevara, revolves around Gila, a kind of hermaphroditic character whose beauty identifies her as a woman, but whose tastes,
physical strength, and hunting and fighting skills identify her as a man. The
role of Gila was written for Jusepa Vaca, who is mentioned specifically in the

stage directions: "lo hará muy bien la Señora Jusepa" (92) [*Señora* Jusepa will perform it well]. One of the most celebrated actresses of her time, Vaca was known for her physical prowess and daring as well as for her introspection and lyricism. Her reputation, combined with the popular type of the *serrana bandolera* and the integration of colorful regional folklore, would have been enough to guarantee the success of the play (Peale 43).

Before Gila's appearance, Vélez de Guevara builds audience anticipation through the observations of the local people about the protagonist: She can run faster than any farmhand, and she can jump, wrestle, and throw a javelin. Gila's spectacular entrance underscores her dual identity and is contrived to elicit expressions of *admiratio* from the public. The country folk sing her praises as she arrives on horseback from the hunt, her hair loose and flying in the wind. She brings with her a wolf skin, a bear skin, and a wild boar—evidence of her extraordinary skill at bagging dangerous prey. Her gun and hunting knife underscore her manly prowess, yet she wears a wide skirt, dangling *patenas* [religious images], a plumed hat, and feminine boots that highlight her womanly charms. As soon as she dismounts, she picks up her shotgun. Gila is, as her costume indicates, a paradox. The violence of Gila's description of the hunt foreshadows her future persecution of men, but also reveals a powerful sensuality. Intrigued by this exotic creature, a Captain who is enraged by the refusal of Gila's father to quarter troops in his house, vows to get even by dishonoring her. As a result, Gila becomes a bandit and takes to the mountains.

The role calls for extensive fighting. Gila picks a fight with two men, one of them a fencing master, defending herself admirably with the sword. Then she participates in a bullfight. Although the audience sees only the head of the bull—an actor with a bull headpiece—the actress would have had to master some of the basic moves of bullfighting. Elsewhere she will have to demonstrate her skill with not only a sword and a shotgun, but also a slingshot. After Gila takes to the mountains and becomes a bandit, she continues to wear feminine garb to seduce and dispatch travelers. Vélez makes a point of Gila's feminine appearance in the *Caminante*'s [Traveller's] song, which itemizes her articles of apparel: "botín argentado, calza / media pajiza de seda, / alta basquiña de grana / que descubre media pierna, / sobre cuerpos de palmilla / suelto airosamente lleva / un capote de dos faldas / hecho de la misma mezcla" (III.2206–13, 71) [she wears little silver boots / silk straw-colored stockings / a high-waisted, crimson skirt / that reveals half her leg / over a bluish bodice / and a gracefully flowing double cape / made of the same medley]. Matthew Stroud has elucidated the limits of clothing to determine gender signification. Here, clothing corresponds to Gila's sex (woman), but not her gender (man). Stroud notes that Gila uses "heterosexual desire to punish men for their homosocial objectification of women" (137). The *Caminante*'s song emphasizes the role costume plays in enabling her to do this. The actress playing Gila would have to convey gesturally both her gender and sexual identities. Costuming might also have complicated the role by depriving the actress of the freedom of movement that breeches would have afforded her. It is significant that in the film version of *La serrana de la Vera*, Gila wears pants.

The role of Gila requires tremendous physical strength. The playtext calls for Gila to pick up the *Caminante* and then the Captain and hurl them off cliffs. Of course, the heave could have been accomplished through stage machinery, mime, or through fight choreography. The actress may have pushed her colleague off the second level of the *corral* onto a stage device, or else onto an offstage platform or a straw heap behind the stage.

Actresses playing this kind of role, whether in pants or skirts, would have to be knowledgeable about stage combat, including fight choreography. Stage combat is "stylized mime" that uses "codified movement techniques that create the illusion of fighting, often violently," without causing harm to the performers (Lust 7). Not only the aggressor but also the recipient of blows must be trained in the proper mime techniques.[10] Stage combat includes unarmed skills such as illusory slapping, punching, kicking and throwing, as well as armed skills such as fencing. Such techniques involve carefully choreographed movements based on real fighting techniques, which are modified to protect the actors. Fight choreography is related to stunt performance, acrobatics and gymnastics, and requires training exercises designed to increase flexibility and agility. As William Hobbs points out, earlier audiences possessed firsthand familiarity with fencing and would have been far more critical than modern spectators of actors' handling of the sword (13). Therefore, Early Modern actors—and actresses—engaged in swordplay had to know what they were doing. Furthermore, both then and now, costume (skirts, full sleeves, boots) could be an impediment (Hobbs 27). Actresses fighting in flouncy feminine garb had to be especially skillful. Finally, as Richard Lane points out, "Stage combat swords aren't toys" (52). Although they lack the sharp edge of real swords, they have points and can maim and kill. "In the old days," writes Lane, "a lack of 'point awareness' could mean injury or death in a fight" (52). Today's stage weapons are safer, but Early Modern men and women playing fencing roles required extensive training.

The actress playing the *Serrana* would have had to master other kinds of "masculine" movement as well. Act II opens with Gila plowing, and although the plow itself remains invisible behind the dressing room curtain, the actress would have to engage in energetic mime to play the scene convincingly.

Likewise, she would have to be familiar with a number of movements involved in conventional male games, such as rolling dice and shuffling cards.

Farce and slapstick comedy can be as demanding on actors of both sexes as stage combat because, like choreographed fighting, they require highly stylized and strenuous mime techniques. Prior Aphter writes that "one of the most important skills to master if you wish to delve into comedy acting is physical comedy ... Physical movements are vital for the success of a character as comedy requires more than simply delivering dialogue in a humorous manner. Including physical comedy makes your performance interesting and engaging." Vélez incorporates physical comedy into *La monja alférez* in a slapstick scene in which Guzmán tries to put on women's clothes. Guzmán's true sex discovered, s/he is ordered to wear a skirt. In the funniest scene of the play, s/he trips around, putting on the dress backward, messing up the headdress, and stumbling over the shoes—only to throw off the garments, grab a weapon, and go running out to join the ruckus when swords clang outside. The actress playing the role must convey the character's awkwardness through clumsy movements, twisting, tripping, lurching and hopping as Guzmán tries to wriggle into the dress. The actor must then interrupt her contortions abruptly and leap into action when swordplay becomes audible. Similar mime techniques are required in Act II of Ana Caro's *El conde Partinuplés* [*Count Partinuplés*], much of which takes place in the dark. Here, the actress playing Rosaura must grope around furniture and other objects pretending to lurch, stagger and stumble.

Not only acting codes and techniques, but the very structure of the *corral* theater made physical demands on actresses. Located in the patio of a house, a *corral de comedias* consisted of a raised platform in the shape of an apron stage, with dressing rooms located below and behind it. The stage itself had two levels. On the bottom level there were three doors, probably closed with curtains rather than wooden planks (Ruano, "Actores" 96). Actors entered and exited through the doors on either side, while the door in the middle opened onto the "discovery space." On each side of the stage a ladder or stairs led to the second level, which could be used to depict balcony scenes, mountains, towers, and so forth.

Because of the two-level structure, actors had to climb up and down ladders and stairs or, in some cases, jump from a rung or step. For example, at the beginning of Calderón's *La vida es sueño* [*Life is a Dream*], Rosaura, who is dressed as a man and has fallen from her horse, finds herself lost in the mountains. The stage direction that precedes Rosaura's entrance states: "*Sale en lo alto de un monte* ROSAURA *en hábito de hombre de camino, y en representando los primeros versos va bajando*" (85) [Rosaura enters at the top of a

wooded mount, dressed as a man in traveling clothes; she descends reciting
the first verses].[11] John Varey notes that in a *corral* performance, this scene
would require a ladder fixed at one side of the stage for the duration of the
play (232). Ruano de la Haza clarifies that there would have been a walkway
extending over the women's dressing room and the discovery space, with a
second corridor above it. Rosaura's twenty-two-line monologue would give
the actress time to step onto the *corral* balcony and descend the ladder to
the stage in front of the audience ("Introducción" 31–32). Rosaura's fall
takes place offstage and is represented by means of theatrical synecdoche. The
actress begins her speech before she appears onstage and continues it as she
moves into a position of prominence before the public. This produces a sense
of expectation in the spectators and allows for the depiction of Rosaura as an
active, energetic woman.

In Calderón's play, Rosaura is wearing pants, which would have facilitated
her movement up and down the ladder, but in Ana Caro's *Valor, agravio
y mujer*, Estela and Lisarda climb down a ladder wearing hunting clothes,
which, for women, would have consisted of an ankle-length skirt and a man-
nish coat. The stage directions state: "*Han de estar a los dos lados del tablado
dos escalerillas vestidas de murta, a manera de riscos, que lleguen a lo alto del
vestuario: por la una dellas bajen* ESTELA *y* LISARDA, *de cazadoras, con
venablos*" (61) [On either side of the stage there will be a small ladder covered with vegetation, like bushy crags, which go all the way up the dressing
room. Estela and Lisarda climb down one of them dressed as huntresses,
with bows and arrows]. In other plays, women had to climb up and down
in full-length skirts and farthingales. For example, in Tirso de Molina's *The
Balconies of Madrid,* Leonor appears on one balcony and moves across a walkway to another. Shortly after, Doña Elisa appears on another balcony and is
intercepted by Doña Ana on the walkway. Whether the actors had to access
the balconies from stage machinery called *tramoyas* or stairs, they would have
had to be nimble and daring to negotiate the elevation and then cross narrow
walkways during every performance.

The verticality of the *corral* structure was extended through the use of
stage machinery, which could be used to raise actors above the upper stage
or move them below floor level through the use of trapdoors. *Tramoyas*
to elevate actors, male and female, were hung in the air near the balcony
and hidden from the audience by curtains that were suspended from the
ceiling and could be opened and closed as needed. When such *tramoyas*
were used, the balcony guardrail was removed to allow room for the actors
to rise from floor level to above the second level of the *corral* (Ruano,
"Actores" 95). In some cases, they descended from above to the stage.

Tramoyas usually moved vertically or diagonally, but could also extend horizontally across the patio, as in Moreto's *La renegada de Valladolid* [*The Renegade from Valladolid*] (Ruano, "Actores" 94). Stage machinery in *corrales* was relatively simple, but as Kings and noblemen began to build elaborate theaters in their palaces, scenic effects became more complicated and costly (Rennert 101).

As Court dramatist, Calderón often included *tramoyas,* especially in theological and mythological plays, which use machinery to stage angels flying or ascensions into Heaven. For example, at the end of Calderón's *La devoción de la cruz,* Julia, who in spite of her banditry remains devoted to the Cross, ascends into Heaven grasping a cross from the sepulcher of her dead brother Eusebio. Often angels were played by young girls—or boys—who were still in training and not yet ready for speaking parts.

Calderón also sometimes used sophisticated devices in his *autos sacramentales,* religious plays that were performed in the street during Corpus Christi. *¿Quién hallará mujer fuerte?* [*Who Will Find the Strong Woman?*], one of Calderón's more complex *autos,* calls for four *carros,* or carts, that serve as the backdrops for the stage action below and out of which characters emerge. The four carts are described in detail in the *Memoria de las apariencias* [*Documentation on Stage Devices*] prepared for the performance. Of particular interest are the third and fourth. The third *carro* shows, at its juncture or seam, storm clouds packed with stars and roses. Later in the play the seam will open into two large doors to reveal a garland of flowers in which a woman is seated. She will be lowered at a diagonal through a canal, pulled by plaster lions with silk ribbons for reins, and then, without getting down, she will be pulled back up. The fourth *carro* is identical to the third and engages in the same movements, except that instead of lions, two coiled snakes will do the pulling. Calderón places his actresses in a precarious position, high above the floor and in constant motion. The women playing these roles would have to be able not only to climb or be lifted to the interior of the cart, where they get into position, but also able to jump, should the apparatus malfunction.

Ana Caro must have had ample confidence in the ability of women to perform rigorously demanding roles, as she created characters that had to use all manner of stage devices. In her *El conde Partinuplés* [*Count Partinuplés*], the actresses playing Rosaura and Aldora are both required to use *tramoyas.* Rosaura appears above the stage to the Count during a hunt, then disappears. A moment later, Aldora appears in the trees, and then disappears. In Act III, the actress playing Aldora disappears through a trapdoor and, later, both women climb stairs to a low balcony.

Roles such as these were not only physically demanding, but also dangerous. Melveena McKendrick notes that accidents involving stage machinery could be fatal. She mentions that Josefa de Medina fell from a *tramoya* while performing in Seville and died (82). Operated by pulleys much like an elevator, stage machinery could easily malfunction. Some women were notoriously audacious when it came to *tramoyas*. Luisa de Robles, in particular, was known for her daring and ingenuity. In a 1623 production of Alarcón's *El Anticristo* [*The Anti-Christ*], the lead actor playing an angel suddenly took fright at the prospect of using a *tramoya* to stage an ascent into Heaven. The intrepid Luisa grabbed his crown and robe and flew upward in his place, much to the delight of the audience. Then she dropped from a cloud machine into a trapdoor below. The incident was recounted originally by Luis de Góngora in his sonnet, "Contra Vallejo, autor de comedias" ["Against Vallejo, The Theater Director"], and then by Quevedo in a poem called "A Vallejo, cuando no quiso bajar en una nube" ["To Vallejo, When He Refused to Come Down From a Cloud"].

Early Modern Spanish actresses could sometimes even be required to ride animals. Gila enters on horseback at the beginning of *La serrana*. In *El conde Partinuplés*, Libella enters on horseback, dismounts, and approaches Rosaura via a ramp that, when needed, could rotate to extend from the floor of the theater to the stage. However, horses onstage could be dangerous. Mary Elizabeth Perry notes that Ana Muñoz, the first lady of the acting company of Andrés de Claramonte, appeared onstage while pregnant astride a horse. The cheering of the audience caused the horse to shy and toss Muñoz to the ground, which caused a premature birth. Moralists interpreted the accident as divine punishment for Muñoz's aberrant behavior (133).

As these examples illustrate, Early Modern women actors had to be in excellent physical condition in order to meet the demands of scripts that sometimes called for nearly acrobatic feats. They had to be daring enough to jump from platforms and balconies and cloud machines, lithe enough to work with stage equipment, and strong enough to pick up or push a male actor. In spite of the demands on their bodies, some actresses worked even when they were pregnant, and many performed well past the age when they could play the ingénue comfortably. By performing such active and demanding roles, they demonstrated that women were not necessarily physically limited by their sex. Women could do more than sew and spin, the activities prescribed by moralists such as Juan Luis Vives. They could take their place alongside men onstage as actors, athletes and acrobats. Perhaps this suggested to at least some viewers that they could take their place alongside men offstage as strong, vibrant members of society.

Notes

1. Although it is now common to use "actor" to refer to both men and women and many theater professionals prefer this term, I have chosen to use "actress" in order to distinguish easily from male actors and to avoid the cumbersome term "female actor."

2. Women did not appear onstage in England until the Restoration, the period beginning in 1660 during which the English, Scottish and Irish monarchies were restored after the Interregnum that followed the Wars of the Three Kingdoms.

3. Melveena McKendrick writes: "Actresses … worked with texts, they memorized dialogue and speeches, often extremely long and intricate ones, and I think we can assume that those who played all but very small parts must have been able to read, as was the case with most, they came from very humble stock" (89).

4. Agustín Moratín describes the long days of actors in *El viaje entretenido* [*The Entertaining Journey*] *II:* "Pero estos representantes, / antes que Dios amanece, / escribiendo y estudiando / desde las cinco a las nueve, / y de las nueve a las doce / se están ensayando siempre; / comen, vanse a la comedia / y salen de allí a las siete. / Y cuando han de descansar, / Los llaman el presidente, / los oidores, los alcaldes, / los fiscales, los regentes, / y a todos van a servir, / a cualquier hora que quieren" (Qtd. in McKendrick 90) [But even before God arises / these *comedia* actors / are already writing and studying / from five o'clock until nine / and from nine until twelve / they're always rehearsing / then they eat and go to the theater / not leaving until seven. / And when they're supposed to rest / the president of the provincial Council summons them / or the judge of the royal Courts / or the members of the town Council / or the tax collector / or the regents / and they have to go attend to them / at whatever hour they are called]. Josef Oehrlein notes that "La duración de los ensayos para cada nueva pieza fue de unas dos semanas, más o menos" [the length of rehearsals for each new play was about two weeks], which means that actors were under tremendous pressure to learn lines in a short period of time (23).

5. See Dowling, "Moratín's Creation of the Comic Role for the Older Actress."

6. González de Salas is best known for his posthumous edition of the poetry of Francisco de Quevedo.

7. See my article, "*Comedia* Actresses, Then and Now: The Case of Ana Caro's *Valor, agravio y mujer.*"

8. She married two men, but lived with neither, even though all three remained friends (*Geneología* 523).

9. Whether to refer to Guzmán, Erauso's male persona, as "he" or "she" is one of the themes of the play and the source of one very humorous passage.

10. See J. D. Martínez, *Combat Mime: A Non-Violent Approach to Stage Violence.*

11. Stage directions are identified by page number, as they do not correspond to line numbers.

Works Cited

Aphter, Prior. "Comedy Acting Preparation—What Physical Movements Should I Incorporate into the Material?" Web. 15 Oct. 2013. <http://voices.yahoo.com/comedy-acting-preparation-physical-movements-11421950.html>.

Calderón de la Barca, Pedro. *La devoción de la cruz.* Ed. Manuel Delgado. Madrid: Castalia, 2000. Print.

——. *¿Quién hallará mujer fuerte?* Ed. Ignacio Arellano and Luis Galván. Kassel, Ger.: Reichenberger, 2001. Print. Autos sacramentales completos 35.

——. *La vida es sueño.* Ed. Ciriaco Morón. 30th ed. Madrid: Cátedra, 2007. Print.

Cañadas, Iván. *Public Theater in Golden Age Madrid and Tudor-Stuart London: Class, Gender and Festive Community.* Aldershot, Hampshire, UK: Ashgate, 2005. Print.

Caro, Ana. *El conde Partinuplés.* Ed. Lola Luna. Kassel, Ger.: Reichenberger, 1993. Print.

——. *Valor, agravio y mujer.* Ed. Lola Luna. Madrid: Castalia, 1993. Print.

De Salvo, Mimma. "Mujeres en escena: las primeras damas en el teatro español de los Siglos de Oro." *Midesa* (2008). Web. 10 Oct. 2013. <http://www.midesa.it/cgibin/show?art=De%Salvo%20Primeras-%20damas.htm>.

Dowling, John. "Moratín's Creation of the Comic Role for the Older Actress." *Theatre Survey* 24 (1983): 55–63. Print.

Escudero, Lara, and Rafael Zafra. *Memorias de apariencias y otros documentos sobre los autos de Calderón de la Barca.* Pamplona: Universidad de Navarra; Kassel, Ger.: Reichenberger, 2003. Print.

Genealogía, origen y noticias de los comediantes de España. Ed. N. D. Shergold and J. E. Varey. London: Tamesis, 1985. Print.

González, Lola. "Mujer y empresa teatral en la España del Siglo de Oro: El caso de la actriz y autora María de Navas." *Teatro de Palabras: Revista sobre teatro áureo* 2 (2008): 135–58. Print.

González de Salas, Jusepe Antonio. *Nueva idea de la tragedia antigua.* Ed. Luis Sánchez Laílla. Web. 1 Oct. 2013. <http://books.google.com/books?id=y1GV-guIUKUC&printsec=frontcover&source=gbs_ge_summary_r&cad=0#v=onepage&q&f=false>.

Hobbs, William. *Fight Direction for Stage and Screen.* London: Heinemann/A & C Black, 1995. Print.

Lane, Richard. *Swashbuckling: A Step-by-Step Guide to the Art of Stage Combat and Theatrical Swordplay.* New York: Limelight, 1999. Print.

López-Pinciano, Alonso. *Philosophia antigua poética.* Web. 8 Aug. 2013. <http://books.google.com/books/about/Philosophia_antigua_poetica_del_doctor_A.html?id=x-rm2NjTyLp8C>.

Lust, Annette. *Bringing the Body to the Stage and Screen.* Lanham, MD: Scarecrow P, 2012. Print.

Martínez, J. D. *Combat Mime: A Non-Violent Approach to Stage Violence.* Chicago: Nelson Hall, 1982. Print.

McKendrick, Melveena. "Representing their Sex: Actresses in 17th-century Spain." *Rhetoric and Reality in Early Modern Spain.* Ed. Richard Pym. London: Tamesis, 2006. 72–91. Print.

Mira de Amescua, Antonio. *El esclavo del demonio.* Ed. Ángel Valbuena Prat. Madrid: Espasa-Calpe, 1971. Print.

Moir, Duncan. "The Classical Tradition in Spanish Dramatic Theory and Practice in the 17th century." *Classical Drama and Its Influence; Essays Presented to H. D. F. Kitto.* Ed. Michael Anderson and H. D. F. Kitto. New York: Barnes & Noble, 1965. 191–228. Print.

Mujica, Barbara. "*Comedia* Actresses, Then and Now: The Case of Ana Caro's *Valor, agravio y mujer.*" *Remaking the Comedia.* Ed. Susan Paun de García and Harley Erdman. Woodbridge, Suffolk, UK: Tamesis, in press. Print.

Oehrlein, Josef. *El actor en el teatro español del Siglo de Oro.* Madrid: Castalia, 1993. Print.

Peale, George. "Estudio bibliográfico y métrico." *La serrana de la Vera.* By Luis Vélez de Guevara. Fullerton: California State Fullerton P, 1997. 41–62. Print.

Pérez de Montalbán, Juan. *La monja alférez.* Ed. Luzmila Camacho Platero. Newark, DE: Juan de la Cuesta, 2007. Print.

Perry, Mary Elizabeth. *Gender and Disorder in Early Modern Seville.* Princeton: Princeton UP, 1990. Print.

Petersen, Elizabeth M. "Building a Character: A Somaesthetics Approach to Comedias and Women of the Stage." Diss. Florida Atlantic University, 2013.

Quintilian. *Institutes of Oratory.* Web. 1 Aug. 2013. <http://rhetoric.eserver.org/quintilian/>.

Rennert, Hugo Albert. *The Spanish Stage at the Time of Lope de Vega.* New York: Hispanic Society of America, 1909. Print.

Rodríguez Cuadros, Evangelina. *La técnica del actor español en el Barroco: Hipótesis y documentos.* Madrid: Castalia, 1998. Print.

Ruano de la Haza, José María. "Actores, decorados y accesorios escénicos en los teatros comerciales del Siglo de Oro." *Actor y técnica de representación del teatro clásico español.* Ed. José María Díez Borque. London: Tamesis, 1989. 77–97. Print.

———. Introducción. *La vida es sueño.* By Pedro Calderón de la Barca. Madrid: Castalia, 1994. 7–90. Print.

Stroud, Matthew. *Plot Twists and Critical Turns: Queer Approaches to Early Modern Spanish Theater.* Lewisburg, PA: Bucknell UP, 2007. Print.

Tirso de Molina (Gabriel Téllez). *Los balcones de Madrid.* Web. 15 Aug. 2013. <http://mgarci.aas.Duke.edu/celestina/MOLINA-TD/BALCONES-MADRID-II/>.

Varey, John E. *Cosmovisión y escenografía: El teatro español en el Siglo de Oro.* Madrid: Castalia, 1987. Print.

Vega Carpio, Lope de. *El arte nuevo de hacer comedias en este tiempo.* Madrid: Teatro Español, 2009. Print.

Vidler, Laura. "Bordieu, Boswell and the Baroque Body: Cultural Choreography in *Fuenteovejuna.*" *Comedia Performance* 9.1 (2012): 38–64. Print.

Vives, Juan Luis. *The Education of a Christian Woman: A Sixteenth-Century Manual.* Ed. and trans. Charles Fantazzi. Chicago: U of Chicago P, 2000. Print.

Stages of Passing: Identity and Performance in the Comedia

AMY R. WILLIAMSEN
University of North Carolina Greensboro

Tales about passing—stories of attempted transformation across lines of social identity categories—have been analyzed largely for what they can teach us about the workings of race or gender in the United States. The term is usually associated with the tensions between phenotype and racial categories in the post-Civil War US, as represented, for instance, in Nella Larsen's 1929 novel, *Passing*. More recently, Judith Butler, Nadine Ehlers and others have theorized passing and its relationship to the performativity of identity. Useful as it is for an understanding of individual subjectivity, current US-based work on passing inevitably constrains and even predetermines the possible theoretical models of passing and its representations. Sean McDaniel and Joyce Tolliver's forthcoming book, *Writing Counterfeit Subjects: The Representation of Passing in Spain*, suggests that passing stories arise at times of anxiety about changes in the reliability of certain social categories for determining social meaning and individual identity.[1] They demonstrate that "passing tales are powerful: not only is tension created by the imminent possibility that the pass will be exposed, but the examination of how passing acts are represented and received reveals the contours and power of the social categories that are transgressed" ("Introduction"). Their work reveals that it is not a cultural universal that race is the fundamental category determining social station and privilege; in cultures such as that of 17th-century Spain, religion as an identity category takes on a crucial role. Even in cases where the social category most obviously transgressed is that of class, the workings of gender and religious categories impinge repeatedly on those of class, and at times are inextricable from them.

In this brief study, I will focus on how staged acts of passing (involving intersections of social rank, religion and ethnicity) in the *comedia* challenge notions of social stability, with special attention to Lope's *Los melindres de Belisa* [*Belisa's Whims*] (1606–1608), published in 1609.[2] The representation of passing in Spain's Early Modern theater proves much more complex than critics might anticipate based on general assumptions. To the surprise of many scholars, we know a great deal about the material realities of the acting troupes thanks to the pioneering work of Thornton Wilder, who meticulously studied Lope and the theater of his period from the perspective of a theater professional.[3] By carefully tracing the plays purchased and works commissioned by "autores" [theater/stage managers] and their companies, Wilder demonstrates that in addition to women and children, troupes included actors of color. Mary Blythe Daniels' dissertation, *Re-Visioning Gender on the 17th-century Spanish Stage: A Study of Actresses and Autoras*, also represents a crucial contribution to our understanding of the complex intersections of gender, class, race, ethnicity and religion on/off the stage.

In addition to historical figures such as Juan de Sesa, who inspired the play *Juan Latino*, it seems some *comedias* were created especially to showcase the talents of a gifted black actor who played the lead role in several plays and who, throughout his career, worked for different acting companies.[4] In other instances, as in Tirso's *Quien no cae no se levanta* [*He Who Does Not Fall, Does Not Rise*], stage directions indicate that actors appear "tiznados de negro" [blackened].[5] Thus, the diversity of the actors themselves contributes to the complexity of representations of passing.

Even in the most studied type of pass found in the *comedia*, cross-gendered dressing, critics often oversimplify. I vividly remember during graduate school being taught that there were no cases of men who would dress as women—that would be, as my distinguished professors told their eager students, simply unthinkable. When I pointed to the case of the *gracioso* in Lope's *La discreta enamorada* [*In Love but Discreet*] who disguises himself as a lady to help his master make his beloved jealous, the professor seemed startled. Then he stated that no noble character would cross-dress. In fact, the Early Modern stage in Spain was a site of great experimentation. As demonstrated by Sherry Velasco in *Male Deliveries*, Peter Thompson in *The Triumphant Juan Rana*, Matt Stroud in *Plot Twists and Critical Turns: Queer Approaches to Early Modern Spanish Theater*, Sturgiss Leavitt in "Striptease in Golden Drama" and other scholars, gender and sexuality were explored in multiple ways, although few go as far as Juan Rana in the *entremés* [interlude] where he gives birth on stage.[6] Calderón's *Las blancas manos no ofenden*

[*White Hands Don't Offend*], as succinctly summarized by Vern Williamsen, provides ample evidence of nobles cross-dressing: the Prince, César, "dressed as woman pretends to be Celia who then dresses as a man. At the same time, a woman dresses as a man and claims to be César—then, one of the *criadas* [maidservants] dresses as a man; only the *gracioso* has the sense to recognize her identity" (*Notes* 3).

Even with scripts as rich as these, the way the actors/directors stage the scenes can either heighten or mitigate the transgressive potential of the works. For example, in one production of Sor Juana's *Los empeños de una casa* [*The House of Trials*], the actor playing the role of Castaño portrayed a macho figure even when in female garb; in contrast, John Fletcher, cast as Castaño for the Pasto production, obviously relished the sensations as he donned the woman's finery (the transformation in Sor Juana takes place center stage and is the subject of great asides and metatheatrical commentary)—he delighted in performing woman. Yet, equally as important, Castaño affects a class pass—other men pursue him, convinced that he is a noble *dama*—and he exits the stage betrothed to another man.

Interestingly, the main character in Ana Caro's highly metatheatrical work, *Valor, agravio y mujer* [*Courage, Betrayal and Woman*] also performs her male identity with such success that she wins favor as the "best" of the male suitors vying for the ladies's affections. She even wields a sword better than they do—wounding the errant Don Juan who betrayed her. When her servant attributes her new-found valor to her male attire, she states "Engáñaste Ribete / si imaginas que soy mujer, / mi agravio mudó mi ser" (I.510–12) ["You err, Ribete, / if you think I am a woman / my offense changed my being]. In some way, this statement anticipates current scientific insights. Cognitive science problematizes the division between gender and sex—it has been proven that experiences, especially traumatic ones, can trigger changes in hormones that affect the brain and the "sex" typing of the brain. As Hines argues, the distinction between biologically determined sex and socially constructed gender "assumes that we know the causes of various behavioral and psychological differences between males and females. Second, it implies that the causes are either biological or social/cultural when in many cases they are both. Third, it assumes that biological and social/cultural processes are separate or even separable" (213). In fact, research into the interplay between stress and hormones documents bodily responses to emotional trauma in hermaphrodites—those Early Modern Spaniards who attributed Elena's transformation into Eleno to the body's response to traumatic events might be closer to today's scientific understanding than previously believed.[7] This same research might prompt a re-reading of several *comedias* and their treatment of gender and sexuality. Indeed, as Leonor asserts, her very being may have been changed by her experience.

Critics have often interpreted the ending of *Valor* as a return to the established order. Yes, Leonor dons a dress; however, she redresses the wrong done to her. Moreover, the Condesa carefully arranges the inevitable marriages, emphasizing that she will wed Leonor's brother, in order to guarantee an ongoing intimacy with Leonor as her loving sister. In fact, on stage, all of the elements of Caro's ending (a disgruntled Tomillo excluded from the so-called "happy" matches, the noble *galanes* depicted as interchangeable, and the clever Ribete accepting Flora's hand only because of the promised dowry) serve to underscore the nature of marriage as economic transaction, thereby undermining the conventional pairing of couples so typical of *comedias de enredos* [comedies of intrigue]. Finally, the play concludes with a twist on the traditional "disculpas" [apology] voiced by Leonor herself—"Aquí, senado discreto, / valor, agravio y mujer / acaban. Pídeos su dueño, / por mujer y por humilde, / que perdonéis sus defectos" (III: 2753–57) [Here, esteemed audience, / courage, betrayal and woman ends. / Its author, as a woman, / and a humble one at that, asks / that you forgive its shortcomings]. In a work that repeatedly employs metatheatrical elements to foreground the role of the woman as poet/creator, this final coda proves remarkably double-voiced— these lines have elicited marked examples of gender-inflected responses. Some men, who unquestioningly accept male authors' self-deprecation as a *topos* of false humility, have read Caro's words as her frank acknowledgement of the limitations of her "weaker" sex. Women, on the other hand, tend to interpret the same verses as a blatant reminder of Caro's successful "pass" into the male dominated public sphere of commercial theater. They delight in the strategic activation, also found in María de Zayas's prologues to her works, of the social expectation that chivalrous men would hesitate to speak ill of women or women's works.

As mentioned earlier, when we think of gender passes in the *comedia*, attention immediately turns to myriad *mujeres vestidas de hombre* [cross-dressed women]. Yet, more compelling in terms of what we learn about cultural construction of identity are the less frequent *hombres vestidos de mujer* [cross-dressed men]. In Angela de Azevedo's lesser-known work, *El muerto disimulado* [*The Fake Dead Guy*, as per the performance by Brigham Young University], Clarindo takes advantage of the fact that he is presumed dead. This nobleman dresses as a merchant woman—thus engaging in a double pass. (It is interesting to note that a popular current Mexican *telenovela* [soap-opera], *Por ella soy Eva* [*For Her Sake, I'm Eve*] employs this same premise). Though women, including his cross-dressed sister, note the incredible resemblance to the dead man, they accept Clara as a woman; yet, they treat her as a fellow noblewoman despite her attempt to sell them wares. This suggests that, in the period, a convincing "class pass"—a transgression against social rank—was more difficult to sustain than a gender pass. This may indeed reflect the dominant culture's necessary fiction that one's nobility/ one's blood "will tell" no matter what one's circumstances. As in Tirso's *El vergonzoso en palacio* [*The Shy Courtier*, or *The Outcast In*] and in *El perro del hortelano* [*The Dog in the Manger*], successful class passes are normalized by the revelations of noble blood. None of these works, despite many apparently transgressive elements, overtly threatens established norms regarding social rank because individuals end up where "they belong," thus perpetuating the illusion that social rank is a "natural" essence rather than a social construction. Yet, one cannot deny that these texts provide fertile territory for exploring the boundaries of passing.

In terms of staged passings, Lope de Vega's *Los melindres de Belisa* proves much more problematic. Originally, I was drawn to this work because of the mother—one of the creative crones/contestatory cougars that populate the world of the *comedia* despite critics' continued avowal of the absence of the mother. In fact, an allusion to the clay that women eat—either for their complexion or because of mineral deficiency during pregnancy—raises the remote possibility that there may in fact be two mothers here: Belisa's *melindres* may have a physical cause—representing cravings rather than mere whims. (Vestiges of this practice remain in contemporary rural Mexico: visiting a family-owned tack store outside Saltillo, I inquired about some unusual clay figures. The men blushed and left quickly—the "abuelita" [grandmother] then came into the store and explained "que es barro estampado con la Virgen que comen las mujeres embarazadas" ["it is clay stamped with the image of the Virgin that pregnant women eat"] (Illustration 1).

Upon further reflection, I realized that the most fascinating aspects of this play are, without question, the elements dealing with passing.[8] In Nadine Ehlers's compelling book, *Racial Imperatives: Discipline, Performativity, and Struggles against Subjection*, she considers the performativity of race. She asserts that, "race has operated as a literal and figurative vehicle of containment to imprison individuals within a discursive designation based on a supposed 'essence.' And this racial essence has been made evident in two corporeal sites: color and blood, which have become the fictive loci of race" (27). In Counter Reformation Spain, the concept of blood, specifically purity of blood, is powerfully inflected by religion. In her review of John Beusterien's *An Eye on Race: Perspectives from Theater in Imperial Spain,* Susan Paun de García explains: "Because one's religion might or might not be immediately evident, because one might be able to conveniently assimilate or mimic the dominant religious practices, this "invisibility" is the source anxiety, and the only way to make this invisibility visible is to bring to the surface the essence of the difference: the blood" (202). Others—*moriscos, conversos, guineos* [the people of Muslim and Jewish descent that had been forced to convert to Christianity, Guineans]—are marked by their religion as much as by their race or ethnicity.

Early in the play, Belisa, as she catalogues the reasons for rejecting her many suitors by cruelly highlighting their shortcomings, explicitly states that she refuses to say anything that might lead her to be taken for black. She says she cannot consider a one-eyed man since she could not refer to him with the endearment "mis ojos" [my eyes]—and the alternative would be unacceptable "Pues llamarle yo 'mi ojo'/ era ser negra ..." (I.228–29). [For me to call him 'my eye' / would make me black ... ']. Here she alludes to the "lenguaje de negros" ['black language'] codified on stage, and characterized by the elision of the final "s" and other phonological markers.[9] In his article, "Playing the Moor," Israel Burshatin addresses the use of this marked discourse; yet, he does not consider how the actor's own ethnicity might literally and figuratively color this aspect of performance.

A few scenes later, two noble lovers seek refuge in Eliso's home—when the law knocks on the door, their host suggests that they assume the role of two of his trusted Moorish slaves, Pedro and Zara. Pedro, as a Christian, is trusted with the horses; Zara works in the kitchen. This is all the two lovers know about their respective roles when they initiate their "pass." Ironically, the officers were not chasing the man for his dueling; instead, they had come to collect on a debt Eliso owes to Lisarda, Belisa's mother. When Eliso instructs them to take whatever goods they want to satisfy the balance, the officials seize the two "slaves." The play thus underscores that by assuming the roles as slaves the two have moved immediately from personhood to possession.

Once Pedro and Zara enter Belisa's home, Pedro catches Belisa's eye ... and her mother's. Both women want him; both are jealous of Zara. (The servant woman, however, contents herself with "testing" his "Christianness" by asking stereotypical questions that would supposedly uncover abstemious Muslims—Do you drink wine? Do you eat bacon?) Meanwhile, Belisa's brother, Don Juan, desires Zara. In an effort to make Pedro and Zara less appealing, the women order them branded on the face with the S / clavo—the most frequent marking inflicted on slaves of the time and one that graphically underscores their status as merchandise. (In fact, some scholars trace the origins of the money sign "$" to this brand. See Illustration 2).

The play sounds several salacious notes in rather quick succession. First, the women are even more attracted by Pedro's marked body, thus fetishizing the exotic otherness of the branded face. (Interestingly, Zara and Pedro also find each other's "branded" faces appealing.)

Then, in a fit of jealous rage, Belisa accuses Zara of stealing a jewel she herself planted on Zara, and demands that she be punished. Specifically, she orders that she be "pringada," a practice condemned by Covarrubias: "*Pringar* es lardar lo que se asa, y los que pringan los esclauos son hombres inhumanos y crueles" [*Pringar* is to grease what one roasts, and those who grease and roast their slaves are inhuman and cruel]. Carrillo, charged with carrying out the torturous punishment adds insult to injury, relentlessly demanding that Zara strip naked, calling her "galga," "perra" [hound, dog] and threatening that "ha de haber azote y tocino ardiendo" (II, 333) [there will be whips and sizzling bacon]. Not only would he whip her, and grease her to increase the pain of the fire, he specifies bacon grease—to debase her and her purported religion further. Frantic, Zara calls for Felisardo (Pedro), but Don Juan appears first and stops Carrillo.

Though Zara comes to no physical harm—the brand has been painted instead of burned—the threatened violence, erotically charged with elements of sadism where the audience plays voyeur, proves destabilizing. Pedro and Zara's "otherness" exposes them to the cruelest, basest treatment—at any moment the comedy could have veered into tragedy. In addition, the fact that their nobility was not/could not be immediately recognized produces tremendous anxiety. For, what happens when the dominant culture cannot distinguish between its own and its others? The observation that Ehlers proffers regarding race, "Passing raises pressing challenges to the disciplinary regime of race. The simple possibility of passing 'works' to expose the tenuous foundations upon which this system rests" (61), would aptly describe the impact of Pedro and Zara's passing for the regime of religion. Their successful pass (the failure of others to see through their assumed roles) reveals the fragile artificiality of the culturally constructed "differences" that have been reified as "natural" and used as unquestioned/unquestionable guarantees of one group's superiority over others.

Passing in all these plays coincides with heightened meta-theatricality. Not only are the players playing roles within their roles (and, at times, a series of roles), theatrical asides regarding the dramatic, literary and social conventions abound. At every turn, the works foreground the performativity of identity and its inherent instability. Thus, these texts anticipate the theoretical formulations of Butler and the creative representations of contemporary performance artists like Lady Gaga as they attempt to frame and reframe categories of meaning. The very impossibility of "fixing" an individual's illusive/illusory identity through intangible terms may well have contributed to the legislation enforcing the expulsions of the *moriscos*. Eerily, we seem to be witnessing the same dynamic in legislation enacted along our Arizona/Mexico border. The preoccupation with "limpieza de sangre" [purity of blood] flourishes under a new guise.[10] We must actively resist discourses that objectify human beings as "other" for this is the first step in constructing the psychological and sociological conditions for abuse. Greater understanding of the power (and limits) of performativity empowers us to transcend the socially constructed barriers that would otherwise divide us.

Notes

1. I am most grateful to Joyce Tolliver and Sean McDaniel, who generously included me in the session they organized on passing at the 2011 SAMLA conference. Their work has been fundamental to my thinking on this subject, a topic that has fascinated me ever since I realized I myself have sometimes unwittingly "passed" across social categories.
2. In a more extensive study, I consider the various markers, including linguistic discourse markers, associated with each of these categories and how individuals or, in the case of plays, characters in certain roles, manipulate these markers in their attempts to pass. For related discussions, see Larquier, Mariscal, Martín Casares, Martín Márquez, and Weber de Kuralt.
3. I have explored the relationship between Wilder and the *comedia* in depth in a forthcoming study.
4. In *El negro del mejor amo* [*The Best Master's Black*], by Mira de Amescua, the cast also included a black woman who played the role of a slave who becomes possessed. Ironically, one element of her demonic possession is that, instead of communicating in the only dialect she knows, she suddenly speaks in fluent standard "castellano."
5. The contemporary performance of plays that call for the actors to appear "tiznados" can prove very problematic. For example, at the 2014 Chamizal, a Spanish troupe employed "black face" to the chagrin of the US audience. In the roundtable discussion afterward, it became clear that they were unaware of the politically charged nature of this staging choice in our current context.
6. That the actor himself had been charged with "unnatural acts" yet remained in the good graces of the Court attests to a certain social fluidity one might not automatically associate with Counter Reformation Spain.
7. For a fascinating discussion of such issues, see Sherry Velasco's study of *The Lieutenant Nun* and Anne Moir and David Jessel's *Brain Sex*.
8. I wish to thank all of those involved in the American Society for Theater Research panel in Puerto Rico, especially Mindy Badia, for her stimulating presentation.
9. Quevedo quipped that "sabrás guineo en volviendo las rr ll y al contrario" ["By switching 'rr's with 'll's and the reverse, you'll speak Guinean"].
10. For more on "limpieza de sangre" and its legacy, see Martínez.

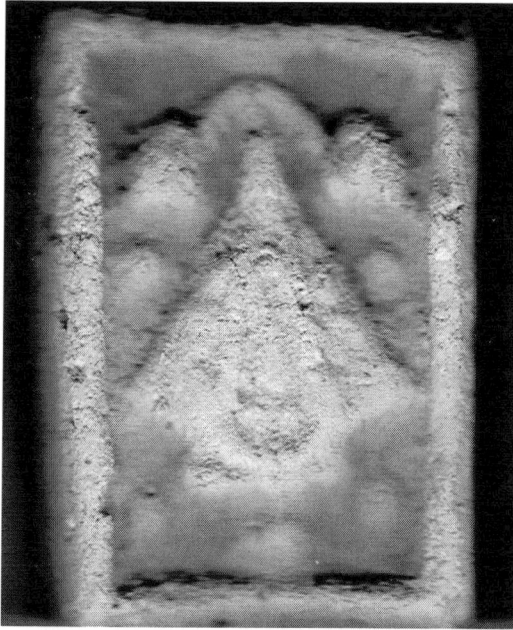

Illustration 1: Clay Virgen

Illustration 2: "S" + clavo = $?

Works Cited

Azevedo, Angela. *El muerto disimulado*. *Women's Acts*. Ed. Teresa Scott Soufas. Lexington: U of Kentucky P, 1996. 91–131. Print.

Badia, Mindy. "*Los melindres de Belisa*." American Society for Theater Research, 2009. Condado Plaza Hilton, San Juan, PR. 14 Nov. 2009. Round-table presentation.

Beusterien, John. *An Eye on Race: Perspectives from Theater in Imperial Spain*. Lewisburg, PA: Bucknell UP, 2006. Print.

Burshatin, Israel. "Playing the Moor: Parody and Performance in Lope de Vega's *El primer Fajardo*." *Modern Language Association* 107.2 (1992): 566–81. Print.

Butler, Judith. *Gender Trouble*. New York: Routledge, 1990. Print.

———. "Passing, Queering: Nella Larsen's Psychoanalytic Challenge." *Bodies That Matter: On the Discursive Limits of "Sex."* New York: Routledge, 1993. 417–35. Print.

Calderón de la Barca, Pedro de. *Las manos blancas no ofenden*. Web. 14 Oct 2014. <www.comedias.org>.

Caro, Ana. *Valor, agravio y mujer*. Web. 14 Oct 2014. <www.comedias.org>.

Covarrubias, Sebastián de. *Tesoro de la lengua castellana*. 1611. Madrid: Editorial Castalia, 1994. Print.

Cruz, Sor Juana Inés de la. *Los empeños de una casa* [*The House of Trials*]. Web. 14 Oct 2014. <www.comedias.org>.

Daniels, Mary Blythe. "Re-Visioning Gender on the 17th-century Spanish Stage: A Study of Actresses and Autoras." Diss. U of Kentucky, 1998. Print.

Ehlers, Nadine. *Racial Imperatives: Discipline, Performativity, and Struggles against Subjection*. Bloomington: Indiana UP, 2012. Print.

Gaga, Lady. "Born This Way." Visual from *Gagastigmata* March 2010. Web. 14 Oct 2014. <http://gagajournal.blogspot.com/>.

Garcés, María Antonia. *Cervantes in Algiers: A Captive's Tale*. Nashville, TN: Vanderbilt UP, 2002. Print.

Hines, Melissa. *Brain Gender*. Oxford: Oxford UP, 2004. Print.

Lanini y Sagredo, Francisco Pedro. *El parto de Juan Rana*. Ed. Peter Thompson. *Comedia Performance: Journal of the Association for Hispanic Classical Theater* 1.1 (2004): 219–37. Print.

Larquié, Claude. "Les esclaves de Madrid à l'époque de la decadence (1650–1700)." *Revue Historique* 244.1 (1970): 41–74. Print.

Leavitt, Sturgis E. *Strip-tease in Golden Age Drama*. Madrid: Castalia, 1966. Print.

Mariscal, George. *Contradictory Subjects: Quevedo, Cervantes and 17th-century Spanish Culture*. Ithaca, NY: Cornell UP, 1991. Print.

Martín Casares, Aurelia, and Marga G. Barranco. "Popular Literary Depictions of Black African Weddings in Early Modern Spain." *Renaissance and Reformation* 31.2 (2008): 107–21. Print.

Martín Márquez, Susan. *Disorientations: Spanish Colonialism in Africa and the Performance of Identity*. New Haven, CT: Yale UP, 2008. Print.

Martínez, María Elena. *Genealogical Fictions: Limpieza de Sangre, Religion, and Gender in Colonial Mexico*. Stanford, CA: Stanford UP, 2008. Print.

McDaniel, Sean, and Joyce Tolliver. *Writing Counterfeit Subjects: The Representation of Passing in Spain*. Forthcoming.

Moir, Anne, and David Jessel. *Brain Sex: The Real Difference between Men and Women*. New York: Dell Books, 1991. Print.

Molina, Tirso de (Gabriel Téllez). *El vergonzoso en palacio*. Web. 14 Oct 2014. <www.comedias.org>.

Paun de García, Susan. Rev. of *An Eye on Race*, by John Beusterien. *Cervantes* 28.1 (2008): 202–05. Print.

Stroud, Matthew D. *Plot Twists and Critical Turns: Queer Approaches to Early Modern Spanish Theater*. Lewisburg, PA: Bucknell UP, 2007. Print.

Soufas, Teresa Scott. *Dramas of Distinction*. Lexington: U of Kentucky P, 1997. Print.

Thompson, Peter. *The Triumphant Juan Rana: A Gay Actor of the Spanish Golden Age*. Toronto: U of Toronto P, 2006. Print.

Vega Carpio, Lope de. *El perro del hortelano*. Web. 14 Oct 2014. <www.comedias.org>.

———. *Los melindres de Belisa*. *Comedias escogidas, I*. Ed. Juan Eugenio Hartzenbusch. Madrid: Biblioteca de autores españoles, 1946. 317–40. Print.

Velasco, Sherry. *The Lieutenant Nun: Transgenderism, Lesbian Desire, and Catalina de Erauso*. Austin: U of Texas P, 2000. Print.

———. *Male Deliveries: Reproduction, Effeminacy, and Pregnant Men in Early Modern Spain*. Nashville: Vanderbilt UP, 2006. Print.

Weber de Kuralt, Frida. "El tipo del negro en el teatro de Lope de Vega: Tradición y creación." *Nueva Revista de Filología Hispánica* 19.2 (1965): 337–52. Print.

Wilder, Thornton. *American Characteristics and Other Essays*. New York: Harper and Row, 1979. Journals. Web. 14 Oct 2014. <http://www.theparisreview.org/interviews/4887/the-art-of-fiction-no-16-thornton-wilder>.

Williamsen, Vern G. "Miscellaneous Notes: *Las blancas manos no ofenden*." Web. 14 Oct 2014. <http://www.comedias.org/misc/vernsno.html>.

Zayas y Sotomayor, María de. *La traición en la amistad*. Ed. Valerie Hegstrom. Trans. Catherine Larson. Lewisburg, PA: Bucknell UP, 1999. Print.

The Spanish Golden Age Entremés in English: Translating the Juan Rana Phenomenon

PETER E. THOMPSON
Queen's University

Born Cosme Pérez (1593–1672), the most famous actor of the Spanish Golden Age was better known by his stage name Juan Rana. Specializing in the era's extremely popular *entremés* [theatrical interlude], he became the star of this genre for over four decades. Some of the most famous *entremesistas* [*entremés* writers] and playwrights of the period wrote over fifty *entremeses* specifically for him. In many cases his name appears in the title of the work, which supports the theory that Juan Rana was the major drawing card for many performances and ensured the success of the theatre production as a whole. While adored by the masses, he was also greatly esteemed by the noble classes and the monarchy.[1] Overtime the Juan Rana persona obtained a mythical status similar to that of the Italian Harlequin and his legacy was maintained alive by generations of actors and allegorical references to him (Rodríguez Cuadros 566).

During his lifetime, however, one important episode stands out that would have a lasting effect on his life and theatrical career. As Rodríguez Villa documented, the already famous Juan Rana was arrested in 1636 for the *pecado nefando* [nefarious sin/homosexual activity], but the author bemoans the fact that the actor and his accomplice were swiftly set free, not receiving the appropriate punishment for such a severe crime (68). While under normal circumstances merely being accused of *pecado nefando* activity would have cost the actor his position, all his possessions and even his life, it would seem that having friends in high places saved Juan Rana and his "partner in crime" from the normal punishments for this crime.[2] Surprisingly, this life-threatening event ended up benefiting the actor's career and that of all those who wrote for him and produced theatre at this time. This incriminating event set the stage for the evolution and refinement of his famed persona. From this point on, *entremesistas* took full advantage of Juan Rana's double/dual personal life as a base for his onstage double/dual persona. The actor's ambiguous identity, gender and sexuality became the base for many of the works written especially for him after his arrest. Indeed, Juan Rana as a person and actor ideally fitted the era's need for spectacular novelty, its obsessive questioning of the meaning of life, and its *mundo al revés* [topsy-turvy world] perception of the world gone absurdly awry. Within the permissive *entremés*, he was an ingenious vehicle used to parody Spanish Baroque society seen to be full of inherently ambiguous and ambivalent incongruities. Considering Juan Rana's long and successful career and the melding of his on- and off-stage life, of his real life and his fictional one and the twists and turns in his life, one can confidently say that he is not only unique in the annals of Spanish theater but also those of all of Europe.[3] This is what I call "the Juan Rana phenomenon."

After writing various articles concerning the Juan Rana *entremeses* and *The Triumphant Juan Rana: A Gay Actor of the Spanish Golden Age* (2006)— or in other words, metaphorically dissecting "John Frog" over a long period of time—and reading research from other colleagues on this extraordinary actor, my next step was to make the astonishing Juan Rana phenomenon better known to a larger audience in both the Spanish and English speaking world. Considering that most of the original Spanish *entremeses* had not been published since the 17th-century and no collection of Juan Rana *entremeses* existed, I decided to take on the at times daunting task of writing *The Outrageous Juan Rana Entremeses: A Bilingual and Annotated Selection of Plays Written for This Spanish Golden Age Gracioso* (2009).

The first task was to choose a selection of plays. My criterion was to select, as the title of the edition indicates, the most outrageous of the Juan Rana plays. I use outrageous in the sense of a spectacular manner of questioning gender and sexual identity, social norms, marital status and queerness that made this actor so famous. As such, the works would appeal to the 21st-century Spanish and English student and researcher and provide material for possible theatrical productions. Also important was to select a variety of works that dealt with the major topics and themes that were part of the Juan Rana repertoire. In the end, I selected the most fitting works from those that I had initially analyzed in my monograph study of the actor, with the exception of two *entremeses*.[4] I based my edition on the original published manuscript of the *entremés*, as it was never my intention to provide a critical edition of these works. As such, this edition was intended as a textbook for students, a resource for researchers and a source for plays for theater directors.

With regards to methodology, as the texts present a great complexity in the use of language, close reading was the main apparatus employed. It was imperative to use a wide variety of specialized dictionaries and glossaries. Fundamental to the translating of complex word play was the Spanish Royal Academy's *Diccionario de autoridades* [*Dictionary of Authorities*] (DA), a period dictionary. Surprisingly, many of the nuances of wordplay so frequent in these *entremeses* were to be found in this most basic of reference tools. The same can be said of Covarrubias' dictionary. However, in the case of slang, popular speech, erotic and sexual connotations, which pepper the Juan Rana *entremeses*, a number of sources were used. Alzieu's glossary was an extraordinary source for erotic and risqué language, as was the case for Cela's dictionary. Chamorro's incredible dictionary specializing in criminal and lower-class vocabulary shone the light on many an obscure reference. Herrera's dictionary of older medical terms was also fundamental in deciphering difficult passages dealing with medical conditions.

Another important decision was how to write the text itself in the English version. I choose to write in prose, as replicating the original 17th-century Spanish rhyme scheme and the convoluted Baroque style would be next to impossible. As far as the original language is concerned, it must be stressed that even for native Spaniards the texts pose a great challenge not only because they are written in 17th-century Spanish and the Baroque style of writing but also because of many historical, topical and complex semantic references. The endnotes would, therefore, serve both the Spanish and English speaking public in explaining the text and its subtext and historical context. In the case of the English text, I choose to use modern English and turns of phrases that best suited each particular text but reflecting the original tone as much as possible. As much of the erotic, queer, sexual and other risqué vocabulary was written euphemistically, I replicated this in the English text. But as Stroud has justly written in his review,

> … it would be impossible for any translation to convey all the connotations of the original. In addition to the usual problems that face translators of Early Modern Spanish dramas, these comic plays present additional challenges because of the intensely layered meanings of so many words. In some instances, it is simply impossible to render into English sentence the varied meanings found in the Spanish which means that the footnotes are essential if one hopes to appreciate the connotations that come in rapid succession. (145–46)

Stroud has, in a nutshell, identified the major challenge of translating the twelve *entremeses* that are included in this edition. That said, every translation of a complex work from whatever language or era holds its own special challenges for the translator and the receptor and never can fully capture all that is contained in the original. My goal, therefore, was to capture the essence and the essential message of the original text, and when possible replicate the multilayered comedic effect intended by the *entremesista*. Notwithstanding, the copious endnotes serve to delve into the complexity of the work, as explanatory references of the nuances in the original and as possible reference points for play directors. In other instances, the endnotes were also necessary to place the works in a historical context, as many texts are based on specific historical events of the era.

The two *entremeses* I will discuss in this paper, Luis Quiñones de Benavente's *Guardainfante I y II* (1645) / *Hoopskirt: Part One and Two* (Thompson, *The Outrageous Juan Rana* 21–61) are prime examples of the need to historically contextualize certain works. On the other hand, these mirror-image *entremeses* embody the majority of the themes, topics, and rhetorical figures found in the Juan Rana *entremeses* and therefore are excellent examples of the challenges of translating the Juan Rana phenomenon. As the title suggests, a specific type of female clothing is the central motor of these *entremeses*. As Bergman has explained, this large hoop skirt was used to conceal pregnancy. For this reason, ecclesiastic and civil authorities and moralists alike considered it immoral, hence controversial, and indeed its wearing was prohibited in 1639 (Bergman 48).[5] As such, the historical background information puts the hoopskirt controversy into perspective and adds depth to its raison d'être. The main rhetorical device used in these *entremeses* is the double, a device that is used in many Juan Rana *entremeses*. Indeed, the two *entremeses* are themselves doubles and within the sister works Juan Rana is faced literally and metaphorically with his female alter ego. As such, these mirror-image *entremeses* deal with questions of patriarchal power, sexual and gender identity and, ultimately, queerness.

In "Guardainfante I" Juan Rana plays his most common topos, the bumbling country mayor, which in and of itself represents a mockery of unjust and unwarranted power. At the beginning of the *entremés*, he is infuriated by the fact that a false and female mayor has tried to usurp his position or, in other words, his patriarchal power. She is wearing an exaggeratedly large hoopskirt, which allows for a meaningful comment by Juan Rana: "Que he de vengarme en las hembras, / pues no alegarán que pagan / los justos por pecadores / andando todas tan anchas" (24–25) [That I will revenge all those swollen women / who have to be given a wide berth, / that do as they please. / They have to pay / for all their sins]. It is important to note the special significance of the phrase "andar a sus anchas." *Ancho* or wide can refer to the fact that women are physically larger and wider when they are pregnant and, especially, if they are wearing the concealing *guardainfante*. Using the expression to *andar a sus anchas*, Juan Rana is, however, contesting the fact that women do as they please, moving freely about at their will. From the onset, therefore, this perceived affront to his municipal authority and the need to put women in their place due to their free-wheeling lifestyle and fashionably large attire sets the thematic tone for this parody of patriarchal power. His comments are also in tune with the moralists, who condemned the wearing of this garment. (Thompson, *Outrageous* 55–56n10).

We soon learn that this female double has been imprisoned, but in time she is unceremoniously dragged onstage with a large cable wrapped around her waist. This also allows for a communal male commentary on women seen to becoming "too big for their britches" in the physical and metaphorical sense: "Por sus condiciones, y por usos / ya no caben las hembras dentro del mundo" (28–29) [Now women just don't fit in this world / because of their character and ways]. These two complaints made by men will come to a head in the spectacular final scenes of "Guardainfante I." In theses scenes, the false female mayor is physically stripped of her clothing but it is her power that is truly and metaphorically taken away from her. A fisherman, a stable boy, old man winter and finally a cadaver, each take off a different layer of the hoop-skirt. Each layer (*costas*/baleen [30–31], *paja*/straw [32–33], *sayas*/skirts [32–33], *moño*/wig [34–35]) allows for a condemnation of the excesses of this garment but also of the female condition seen to be egocentric and weak.

Juan Rana's final dialogue places a more sinister slant on man's power over women:

JUAN.	En mi vida di más de jubones,
	si destos quisieren, escojan y tomen.
MUJER 2.	¿De qué tela son, Alcalde?
JUAN.	De cuero, que no se rompen.
MUJER 3.	Y, ¿de qué color, amigo?
JUAN.	Coloradas las labores.
JOSEFA.	Y, ¿qué guarnición les echa?
JUAN.	Mosqueado, y atrás los golpes.
JOSEFA.	¿Es buen sastre el que los hace?
JUAN.	Píntalos, que nos los cose.
JOSEFA.	Y, ¿tan bien abotonados?
JUAN.	Qué jamás se desabrochan.
TODOS.	Guárdelos, vístalos, póngalos, majaderote.
JUAN.	Estas sean las galas, y naguas
	que den a las hembras los señores hombres. (35–36)

[J: I've given more than a few cuffs in my time. / If you want some take your pick. / M2: What are they made of? / J: Of hide so that they won't rip or tear. / M3: What colour are they? / J: A reddish colour from whipping. / JOS: And what trimmings do they have? / J: Hand-beaten ones with visible marks. / JOS: Is the one who gives them good at what he does? / J: It as if he paints them rather than sews them on. / JOS: And do they stay on? / J: So well attached that you can't take them off. / ALL: Take them, try them, and wear them, you fools. / J: These are the fine fittings and adornments that men give to women.]

The full meaning of this at first innocent sounding reference to the preparation of leather and leather clothing is made clear at the end of the play when Juan Rana states "(p)alo, y azotes" (36) [Give them thirty lashes]. In other words, it is at the end that the audience realizes this section of the text actually is a euphemistic reference to physically "tanning the hides" of women or the domestic violence that women are forced to endure and the bloody scars that remain.

In "Guardainfante II," the false female mayor who was stripped of her power and of her multilayered hoopskirt seeks revenge in a gender bending fashion. Mirroring the actions and dialogue of Juan Rana in the opening scenes of "Guardainfante I," she takes center stage dressed as a man carrying the quintessential Juan Rana mayoral staff. She is now a Juan Rana double who will produce havoc for the unsuspecting Juan Rana. Juan Rana is puzzled by this double and wonders if he is looking in a mirror or if a portrait of him has been made. The false mayor is so convincing in her attire and actions that she is taken to be the real mayor and it is Juan Rana who is arrested as the false mayor. With this complete reversal of roles, the themes of gender and sexual identity and the abuses of patriarchal power take center stage like the cross-dressed false mayor herself. But just before escaping, Juan Rana speaks this revealing passage:

Yo me vo a volver galán,
y a traer en la cabeza
un gran canalón de fieltro.
Un tejarón de guedejas,
sóla una vaina en la espada,
en los calzones sesenta,
dos sábanas por lenzuelos,
cuatro colchones por piernas,
seis pabellones por ligas,
y por zapatos dos leznas,
que desfigurarme puedo ... (46–47)

[I know I'm going to come back as a gallant / wearing a huge furrowed felt hat / and a large crown of curls like a tiled roof. / I'm going to wear / a sheath for my sword, / and huge trousers. / I'll carry two bed sheets as hankies, / my legs will be stuffed with four mattresses, / for which I'll wear garters made of six canopies, / and for shoes, two pointy cobbler's awls. / I know I can escape and refashion myself ...]

In other words, Juan Rana's plan to differentiate himself from the false mayor amounts to dressing in an over-the-top effeminate foppish manner.

Apart from his exaggerated description of his refashioning, the word *guedejas* has special significance. Strictly speaking, *guedejas* is translated as ponytails but here it would seem to refer to ringlets. But more significantly for this *entremés*, Cartagena-Calderón explains that in the Spain of the Early Modern period, men found guilty of homosexual practices were sent to the gallows wearing women's clothing and with their hair curled. In this way, artificially curled hair was emblematically linked to effeminacy and homosexuality (159–60). Lehfeldt also reiterates this by citing moralists of the period who believed this obsession with hairstyling showed men to be effeminate, womanlike, weak, submissive and ultimately homosexual. She also notes that this male hairdo fashion statement became to be seen as so abominable that it was prohibited in 1639 (484–85).[6] In this way, Juan Rana's attempt to differentiate himself from the cross-dressed false female mayor is a description of a queer man. As such, he embodies in a jocular manner all the fears of many of the moralists of this period. His reentrance onstage dressed in an over-the-top manner, as he had promised, causes the false mayor to ask if this apparition is a man (49). The Juan Rana character, now identified as effeminate, is also seen as useless and false:

CATALINA.	Deste postizo galan
	damos las Viejas querella,
	pues no nos deja que hilar,
	sus pantorrillas por piernas.
JOSEFA.	Dadle luego que hile.
JUAN.	Busque, o perezca,
	que yo miro a los usos,
	si ella a las ruecas. (50–51)

[C: All of us old ladies / have complained about this / phoney gallant as he just spins a yarn. / All talk and no action. / JOS: Let's make him spin. /JN: I'm just interested in clothes / and not the yarn they're made of.]

In the end of an *entremés* where all is topsy-turvy or, in other words, women rule, the final moral, while denouncing the importance of appearances and falsehood, maintains a warning against the mistreatment of women: "Quedito, pasito, que son tales ellas, / que aun sin esas liciones no hay Diablos / que puedan sufrirlas sus impertinencies" (51–53) [Think before you act. / Even when put in their place women are capable of / making life hell for everyone]. While a jocular warning against the mistreatment and unjust treatment of women, it still remains current in the 21st century, where abuse of women, and power in general, still reigns.

This overview of the translation of *Guardainfante I y II/ The Hoopskirt I and II* has hopefully shed some light on the process of translating the Juan Rana phenomenon. I also trust that it has shown that the essence and essential meaning of original 17th-century *entremeses* can be kept and communicated to a 21st-century public. The footnotes, of course, are indispensible for students and researches of both Spanish and English to fully understand all the nuances and complexities of the text. However, what is important to remember is that these are theatre texts and therefore the ultimate goal is to have the Juan Rana *entremeses* staged. It is therefore up to play directors to find the best manner to transmit the message of each particular *entremés* to the audience. Many of *entremesil* nuances that have been explained in footnotes can be communicated through the actors' body/bawdy language, gestures, props, costumes and by other inventive means. With regards to the historical context, the setting and scenery of the play can convey a sense of the era. Of course, specific historical events or contexts will still have to be included in the explanatory notes of the playbill just as they are for the performance of older plays in any language. While no translation is perfect and most certainly some nuances are lost in translation, I can only hope that *The Outrageous Juan Rana Entremeses* has helped to make better known the extraordinary Juan Rana phenomenon to a wider audience.

Notes

1. See Lobato "Un actor en palacio; Felipe IV escribe sobre Juan Rana."
2. See Thompson, "Introduction: The Outrageous Juan Rana" 9–11 for an overview of the normal punishment for the *pecado nefando*.
3. This introduction includes material used in earlier publications. See also Lobato, Sáez Raposo, Stroud, Thompson and Velasco for more detailed biographical information on the life and career of Juan Rana.
4. Quiñones's "El guardainfante I" and "II" were not part of my monographic study of Juan Rana.
5. See Velasco 76–77 for further information about why this large hoopskirt was considered scandalous by moralists such as Carranza and Jiménez Patón.
6. See *The Outrageous Juan Rana Entremeses* 179–80n8 for further information on the controversies surrounding men's hairstyles in Early Modern Spain.

Works Cited

Alzieu, Pierre, Robert Jammes, and Yvan Lissorgues, eds. *Poesía erótica del Siglo de Oro*. Barcelona: Editorial Crítica. 1983. Print.

Bergman, Hannah E. *Luis Quiñones de Benavente y sus entremeses. Con un catálogo biográfico de los autores citados en sus obras*. Madrid: Castalia, 1965. Print.

Cartagena-Calderón, José. "'El es tan rara persona.' Sobre cortesanos, lindos, sodomitas y otras masculindades de la temprana Edad Moderna." *Lesbianism and Homosexuality in the Early Modern Spain: Literature and Theater in Context.* Ed. María José Delgado and Alain Saint-Saëns. New Orleans: UP of the South, 2000. 139–75. Print.

Carranza, Alonso de. *Rogación al Rey D. Felipe IV, y a sus supremos Consejos de Justicia y Estado, en detestación de los grandes abusos en los trajes y adornos nuevamente introducidos en España.* Madrid: María de Quiñones, 1636. Print.

Cela, Camilo José. *Diccionario secreto.* Madrid: Alianza, 1968. Print.

Chamorro, María Inés. *Tesoro de villanos. Diccionario de germanía. Lengua de jacarandina: Rufos, mandiles, galloferos, viltrotonas, zurrapas, carcaveras, murcios, floraineros y otras gentes de la carda.* Barcelona: Herder, 2002. Print.

Covarrubias y Orozco, Sebastián de. *Tesoro de la lengua castellana o española.* Ed. Felipe C. R. Maldonado. Madrid: Castalia, 1995. Print.

Herrera, María Teresa. *Diccionario español de textos médicos antiguos.* Madrid: Arco/ Libros, 1996. Print.

Jimémez Patón, Bartolomé. *Reforma de trages: Doctrina de frai Hernando de Talavera.* Baeza: Juan de la Cuesta, 1638. Print.

Lehfeldt, Elizabeth A., "Ideal Men: Masculinity and Decline in 17th-century Spain." *Renaissance Quarterly* 61.2 (2008): 463–91. Print.

Lobato, María Luisa. "Un actor en Palacio: Felipe IV escribe sobre Juan Rana." *Cuadernos de Historia Moderna* 23.5 (1999): 79–111. Print.

Quiñones de Benavente, Luis. "El guardainfante I." *Joco Seria. Burlas veras, o reprehension moral, y festiva de los desordenes públicos en doze entremeses representados, y veinte y quarto cantados.* Madrid: Francisco García Morras, 1664. Fols. 59v-64.

———. "El guardainfante II." *Joco Seria. Burlas veras, o reprehension moral, y festiva delos desordenes públicos en doze entremeses representados, y veinte y quarto cantados.* Madrid: Francisco García Morras, 1664. Fols. 69–75.

Real Academia Española. *Diccionario de autoridades.* Madrid: Gredos, 1990. Print.

Rodríguez Cuadros, Evangelina. *La técnica del actor español en el Barroco: Hipótesis y documentos.* Madrid: Castalia, 1998. Print.

Rodríguez Villa, Antonio. *La corte y monarquía de España en los años 1636 y 37.* Madrid: Luis Navarro, 1886. Print.

Sáez Raposo, Franciso. "La herencia de la Commedia dell'arte italiana en la conformación del personaje de Juan Rana." *Bulletin of the Comediantes* 56.1 (2004): 77–96. Print.

———. "El otro Juan Rana." *Nueva Revista de Filología Hispánica* 52.2 (2004): 389–408. Print.

———. *Juan Rana y el teatro cómico breve del siglo XVII.* Madrid: Fundación Universitaria Española, 2005. Print.

———. "III. Una máscara especial: Juan Rana." *Historia del teatro breve en España.* Ed. Javier Huerta Calvo. Madrid: Iberoamericana/Vervuert, 2008. 47–56. Print.

Stroud, Matthew D. "Gender, Genre and Class. The Theater of Juan Rana." *Plots, Twists and Critical Turns: Queer Approaches to Early Modern Spanish Theater.* Lewisburg, PA: Bucknell UP, 2007. 159–77. Print.

———. Rev. of *The Outrageous Juan Rana* Entremeses*: An Annotated and Bilingual Selection of Plays Written for this Spanish Golden Age Gracioso,* by Peter E. Thompson. *Bulletin of the Comediantes* 63.2 (2011): 145–46. Print.

Thompson, Peter E. *The Outrageous Juan Rana* Entremeses*: An Annotated and Bilingual Selection of Plays Written for this Spanish Golden Age Gracioso.* Toronto: U of Toronto P, 2009. Print.

———. "Pícaro guardainfante." *La Aventura de la Historia* 133 (2009): 76–78. Print.

———. "Why all the Hoopla About a Hoopskirt?: Quiñones de Benavente's *El guardainfante I* and *II* (1645)." *La violencia en el mundo hispánico en el Siglo de Oro.* Ed. Juan Manuel Escudero and Victoriano Roncero López. Madrid: Visor Libros, 2010. 337–50. Print.

———. "Juan Rana: Un actor gay en la corte de Felipe IV." *La Aventura de la Historia* 112 (2008): 50–55. Print.

———. *The Triumphant Juan Rana: A Gay Actor of the Spanish Golden Age.* Toronto: U of Toronto P, 2006. Print.

———. "La boda de Juan Rana." *Revista canadiense de estudios hispánicos. Ángulos y perspectivas: Reconsideración de la dramaturgia aurisecular* 29.1 (2004): 157–67. Print.

———. "Fencing and Fornication in Calderón's *El desafío de Juan Rana.*" *Revista de estudios hispánicos* 37 (2003): 497–507. Print.

———. "Crossing the Gendered 'Clothes'-Line: Lanini y Sagredo's *El parto de Juan Rana.*" *Bulletin of the Comediantes* 53.2 (2001): 317–33. Print.

———. "Juan Rana, A Gay Golden Age *Gracioso.*" *A Society on Stage: Essays on Spanish Golden Age Drama.* Ed. Edward H. Friedman, H. J. Manzari, and Donald D. Miller. New Orleans: UP of the South, 1998. 239–51. Print.

Velasco, Sherry. "Performing Male Pregnancy in 'El parto de Juan Rana.'" *Male Delivery: Reproduction, Effeminacy, and Pregnant Men in Early Modern Spain.* Nashville, TN: Vanderbilt UP, 2006. 28–49. Print.

Three Productions of El condenado por desconfiado: *The Devil's Polymorphism in Our Time*

Maryrica Ortiz Lottman
The University of North Carolina, Charlotte

El condenado por desconfiado [*Damned by Despair*] is a canonical play of the Spanish Golden Age but one that presents special challenges to the modern director, given its heady theological themes. Three recent productions have tried to make this *comedia* more accessible, in part by altering the character of its Devil. All three productions have a striking number of features in common. They unanimously treat the Devil as a comic character, experiment with the Devil's gender, and convert the character into a guide for the audience, sometimes greatly enlarging the role. While the productions of *El condenado* by Colombia's Teatro del Valle (2003) and by Spain's Centro Nacional de Teatro Clásico (2010) scored successes with their audiences, the Devil of *Damned by Despair*, an adaptation at London's National Theatre (2012) showcased a multifaceted Devil who was no less terrifying for exercising a wicked sense of humor.[1]

As Natalia Fernández Rodríguez notes, the entire plot of *El condenado* proceeds from the Devil's actions in the opening scene (208). The Devil convinces Paulo that his destiny will coincide with Enrico's, but Paulo despairs when he discovers that Enrico is a notorious gangster and hired killer. Paulo becomes a murderous bandit and is damned, while Enrico finally repents of his crimes and attains Heaven. Among the play's minor characters, the Devil has an out-sized impact; his entrances and exits call for special effects and his conversations with both protagonists are soul-searching. Tirso deliberately confines the Devil's appearances to just three instances, and one of them is very brief. In Act I, the Devil first converses with Paulo in the wilderness

(I.201–84), then pops up again to gloat about his successful deceptions (I.329–33).[2] He is not seen again until Act III, when he appears among the shadows of Enrico's prison cell (III.2239–317). Yet, despite the Devil's brief stints on stage, he can seem almost omnipresent. He is equally at home in the mountain fastness and among the dark shadows of Enrico's prison cell in Naples.

An evaluation of the modern tendency to interpret the Devil comically requires us to examine the 17th-century text and imagine how the role might have been performed in the playwright's own time. A mischievous, antic Devil is not a modern invention. *Graciosos* pretend to be devils in Juan de Timoneda's *Los menemnos* [*The Menaechmi*] and in Antonio de Zamora's *El hechizado por fuerza* [*The Forcibly Bewitched*] (Kallendorf 46–47, 57–59), but these are examples of characters who merely pretend to be devils. It is highly unlikely that the Devil of *El condenado* or of other *comedias* was played for laughs in the 17th century, though exceptions might be found in the *teatro breve* [one-act plays]. José María Ruano de la Haza and John E. Varey have both analyzed the probable staging of *El condenado* in the *corral de comedias* [public theater], and both scholars describe a dramatically colorful demon meant to frighten the audience. Yet, it is still possible that the play's early audiences laughed at an uproarious Devil. The *primer* [principal] *gracioso* in a theatrical company would have played Paulo's servant Pedrisco, and the *segundo* [second] *gracioso* could have acted the part of Enrico's sidekick Galván as well as the role of the Devil, as was done in the Teatro del Valle production in Colombia. In Early Modern theatrical companies that employed three *graciosos*, a comic Devil in *El condenado* might have become standard. We can imagine a staging in which a comic Devil chooses Paulo as his victim and instigates a huge practical joke and supernatural *burla* [trick] in Act I, while Paulo sees the universe as a cruel joke and a colossal example of black comedy.

Comedia scholars have so far neglected to examine the portrayal of the Devil in *El condenado* as a kind of third *gracioso*, one whose performance competes for laughs with Pedrisco and Galván. Serge Maurel's article about "La risa" ["Laughter"] in the play does not mention the Devil as a potentially comic figure, nor does Natalia Fernández Rodríguez's study of the Tirsian devils in *El condenado* and *La ninfa del cielo* [*Heaven's Nymph*]. The closest we have come to acknowledging the potentially comic character of the Devil appears in a 1948 article by I. L. McClelland. In the prison scene, McClelland notes, the Devil calls out "Enrico!" three times (III.2239, 2246, 2249) in what may constitute a "devilish parody of a sacred tradition," and thus the Devil shows that he "has almost the makings of a sense of humor, and, consequently, of personality" (160–61). In 1958, T. E. May pointed out several instances of Tirsian wit and word play in the Devil's instructions to Paulo. For example, the Devil refers to Enrico as a *gentilhombre*, a word that contains a pun on *gentil*, *meaning* "gentile" and "outside the law," so that in effect the Devil is secretly warning Paulo that Enrico is a rogue (Tirso, *Condenado* 268). May imagined the 17th-century Devil delivering such puns in a straightforward manner that deceives Paulo but not an alert audience (May 138–40). We can imagine the Devil delivering these witticisms with a wink and a nod without any aim at provoking laughter.

Three recent productions of *El condenado* have portrayed its Devil as a comic figure, sometimes under the mistaken assumption that a modern audience cannot take the Devil seriously. A comic demon can guide today's secular theatergoers when they are confronted with a theological drama over 400 years old, and he can display a more than ironic detachment from the religious beliefs of human characters. In 2003, Colombia's Teatro del Valle presented a greatly abridged, carnavalesque version of *El condenado* that was aimed at the theater's Afro-Colombian public, though the production also played in Mexico, Chile and at the Siglo de Oro Drama Festival in El Paso, Texas. The cast, consisting of four men and one woman, all acted multiple roles, and a marimba and other percussion instruments were played throughout. Like all the productions of *El condenado* examined in this study, the Colombian production expanded the modern notion of the Devil through its use of costume. In full view of the audience, the Colombian Devil (Felipe Pérez) made two red marks on his forehead to represent horns. A comic air so dominated the production that the whole project could be read as a near parody of Tirso's play. The director Alejandro González Puche defended his interpretation by noting that comedy does not necessarily detract from a work's gravity or spirituality, and he also explained that in Colombia the Devil is a carnavalesque rather than theological figure (Lee 247, 249).

The Devil was also portrayed comically in the 2010 production of *El condenado* by Spain's Compañía Nacional de Teatro Clásico (CNTC) under the direction of Carlos Aladro. In Act I, the Devil (Francisco Rojas) gives such a comically bad imitation of an angel that Paulo's credulity could not fail to amuse us even if clever harp music were not underscoring the Devil's bad acting. This charming and handsome Devil mischievously invades all three acts, for example, by hilariously tormenting Pedrisco. These funny bits overwhelm the many instances in which the smiling Devil escorts a dead man off to damnation. The production works hard to make Enrico a sympathetic character, and we never see him actually murder anyone, but the lack of violent bloodshed means that both death and the Devil lose their sting and the play its force and meaning.

In Tirso's text, almost none of the Devil's lines are comic in themselves, but a director of any era can give all of them an impish twist, as in the Colombian production, or a director can make the Devil a knee-slapping clown, as in the CNTC interpretation. But playing the Devil as a comic figure can have damnable consequences. It can kill off dramatic tension, rob Satan of his power, belittle the struggles of Paulo and Enrico, and dismiss Tirso's philosophical questions. If we define Hell as a state of mind (a concept dramatized in such Early Modern plays as Marlowe's *Doctor Faustus*), then a Devil who can laugh uproariously does not suffer sufficiently and this demon seems to have escaped from the Hell that he ought to carry within him.

Fortunately, the interpretive pitfall of providing too much comedy was avoided in *Damned by Despair*, the 2012 London adaptation of *El condenado* directed by Bijan Sheibani. Thanks to the vast resources of the National Theatre, this production was probably the most well-funded staging of Tirso's play in at least several decades.[3] The production itself received few enthusiastic reviews, but one of its most applauded features was the Devil, who replaced Galván as *segundo gracioso* (while Galván was rendered as little more than a thug). In the script by the Irish playwright Frank McGuinness, the Devil's Act I soliloquy contains many examples of comic alliteration and of colloquialisms that mock theological themes.[4] The production showcased a Devil with a deeply sadistic and restrained sense of humor. A pitiless deceiver, this demon is too bitter to laugh, even as he revels in the eternal joke of snuffing out a soul's salvation. He charms us with his wit; but when addressing Paulo, he feigns celestial seriousness and demonstrates truly terrifying powers of deceit.

Refashioning an Early Modern Devil into a comic figure can both inspire a contemporary director and guide a modern audience. In my extended interview with director Bijan Sheibani, he recalled that the Devil's presence attracted him to the play. Sheibani retained the male pronouns in the script, but he cast Amanda Lawrence as the Devil because of her "clown-like ability" to convey her own attractive personality while simultaneously portraying a dramatic character (Lottman 207). Lawrence's Devil puts us in the uncomfortable position of happily following a heinous demon. As Sheibani remarked, our modern aesthetic sensibility applauds those Tirsian moments when we laugh at horror (Lottman 205–06).

To a notable degree, the Devils portrayed in the Colombian, Spanish and British productions all acted as prominent guides for the audience. In the Colombian production, the Devil guides the action by announcing important changes of locale (Lee 249), and in the final scene, he shoves Paulo into Hell and then addresses us in verses taken from Tirso's dialogue for Pedrisco (III.2897–902; 2293–96). In the CNTC staging of *El condenado*, the Devil participates as an often silent yet always demonstrative guide in nearly every scene, for example, by making an enormous curtain drop to reveal an imposing platform. In the final scene, the Devil points Paulo to Hell, then returns to perform a happy little dance. As in the Colombian production, the Devil is the last actor on stage, facing us as if he were the star of the show.

The decision to make the Devil a clearly identifiable guide automatically enlarges his role on stage, an arrangement that has positive as well as negative consequences. Enlarging the Devil's role reminds us of his great influence in the popular imagination of Early Modern Spain. But the CNTC production transformed the Devil from a minor character to a major one. Its Devil is as tall and handsome as either of the lead actors. He appears in nearly every scene, and in the *comedia*'s final moments his reassuring presence undermines the impact of Paulo's damnation. A supernatural figure can lose its mystery through overexposure. But the London production of *Damned by Despair* successfully portrayed a prominent Devil that was no less terrifying. Sheibani enlarged the role of the Devil by inserting him as a silent, guiding presence in only two or three scenes in which he is absent in Tirso's script (and McGuinness's). Sheibani invented several telling moments; for example, when Paulo and Pedrisco begin their journey to Naples, the Devil literally opens a door for them and slams it shut once they have stepped through (Lottman 222–23). The Devil's added presence was especially effective in the long Puerta del Mar scene, which was staged as if Enrico and his criminal cohorts were meeting on the open-air terrace of a Neapolitan pizzeria. It is here that Paulo and Pedrisco first spy Enrico and learn that he is the lead murderer in a notorious gang. The Devil sits silently at a lone table against a wall, but this Devil is now a woman who is fashionably dressed all in black. Her pallid face can frighten us in its stillness, though at other times she appears to sample food or drink. We might uncomfortably notice that, like her, we are seated at a remove from the goings-on and that we too watch in anonymous silence.

Of course, inserting even this silent Devil into the Puerta del Mar scene changes the cosmos and structure of the play to some extent. In Tirso's text, the Devil appears to Paulo early in Act I, and when in Act III he speaks to Enrico from within the shadows of a prison cell, the Devil's sudden and surprising presence increases our terror. In Act I he had vanished into the natural, open space of the mountain wilderness, but now in Act III he has materialized inside Enrico's stifling prison cell. By introducing the Devil into the Puerta del Mar/pizzeria scene, Sheibani suggests that this demon is perhaps following Paulo. In Act III we might even sense that despite Enrico's life of crime, the Devil is stalking Enrico in prison largely because the Devil has been trailing Paulo; we might sense that the prideful, overconfident Devil has

heretofore devoted minimal energy to capturing Enrico's black soul and that
he has focused almost exclusively on Paulo, the former hermit.

All three productions of *El condenado* depicted the Devil as an androgynous being, at least in Act III. This practice coincides with the Medieval
tradition of imagining the serpent of Eden as ambisexual (Jager 110). Furthermore, tarot cards, which have been in use in Europe since at least the late
15th century, display a Devil that many scholars identify as androgynous, and
one study discusses the cards' likely Hermetic heritage and their influence on
Cervantes's *Numancia* [*The Siege of Numancia*].[5] Act I of the Colombian production presents the audience with a creature that is both man and woman;
an actress (Marleida Soto) faces the audience. Her face and full-skirted white
dress hide the Devil, who stands just behind her. This lithe actress has wound
her arms backwards over the Devil's shoulders and she has curled her legs
backwards around his hips. As the Devil speaks, her mouth silently moves, and
his own gesturing arms emerge from around her body. Spain's CNCT Devil
was portrayed as ultimately childlike or even gender-neutral, displaying little
comprehension of adult sexuality. In the opening scene, Francisco Rojas plays
a male Devil who is giving a mawkish and unconvincing imitation of a female
(or at least feminized) angel. At the Devil's next appearance, he has freed his
bare chest from his white gown—the better to show off the harness that holds
up his wings—and his manly chest and white skirt suggest androgyny. Then
the Devil becomes a wily gentleman in a fine black suit, though his bare feet
and naked chest betray his picaresque nature. In the prison scene of Act III,
he wears the monstrous, macho head of a black ram with huge twisted horns
and he speaks in electronically distorted bass tones. But as soon as Enrico
rejects the Devil, the Devil tosses his ram's head off stage and throws a child-
ish tantrum, demonstrating that his virile ferocity was a sham.

The London production of *Damned by Despair* added a pinch of androgyny to each of the Devil's scenes simply by casting a woman in this male role.
Shebani did not feminize the pronouns of McGuinness's script, nor did he
adjust the line in which the Devil introduces himself as "a man with a mission" (Lottman 207; Tirso and McGuiness 8). In the opening scene, Paulo,
Pedriso and the Devil all wear monkish robes, a nearly timeless costume. In
the 17th-century version of this scene, when the Devil disguises himself as an
angel, he merely removes his black cape to reveal the angelic dress beneath
(Ruano de la Haza 113). But the Devil created by Sheibani and Lawrence is
a thoroughly androgynous shape-shifter. When this modern Devil disguises
himself as a female angel, he turns his monkish robe inside out and wraps it
around himself in an impromptu ball gown; the smooth lining of the coarse
robe imitates fine fabric. This new, more feminized Devil ties the sleeves

together at the back of his costume, where they suggest a clumsy bow. He holds the impromptu gown against his body in a girlish gesture that implies both modesty and desire; one large open hand is clasped to his breast and the other to his genitals. The gesture exemplifies those moments when we humans tend to admire and embrace the Devil's wiles. With ingenious irony, the Devil has turned a monk's costume backwards and inside out, making of it a strapless, feminine gown that fools the hermit Paulo, who is himself wearing a very similar garment. The Devil's chalky, graying face and thick black brows are less than alluring, as is the sparse red hair on his skull. Yet Paulo thinks he beholds a female angel with long blonde locks. Paulo sees the beautiful version of Amanda Lawrence's face that is projected far above him in each of the three huge, window-like openings that recall a medieval triptych.[6] We in the audience simultaneously see three aspects of the Devil: an androgynous head, a black and erotic body, and a golden angelic face watching over us.

Casting an actress as the Devil opened up a rich vein of possibilities on stage. A female Devil can seem like an especially modern touch, though there is a long and solidly established tradition of linking Eve and Lilith (and therefore all women) to Eden's serpent. Assigning the role of the Devil to an actress created an implicit comparison between the Devil and Celia, who in one scene was fashionably dressed entirely in black, like the very Devil. While the young Celia was aggressively erotic, the Devil of the Puerta del Mar scene, who was at least twenty years senior to Celia, was portrayed as a secret sensualist and as what Sheibani described as "a fashionista" (Lottman 205). One reviewer spotted Lawrence seated at the pizzeria and using her finger to scoop up the sugar at the bottom of her espresso cup, and another reviewer watched her mercilessly consume a rather phallic frozen dessert called "a Zoom ice lolly" (Monks; Phil and Andrew). Audience members could envy this she-devil's fashion sense. The black dyes fashionable in Baroque Spain were the same ones that had been historically associated with demons (Pastoureau 100–04; 51–52), and the same midnight shades remain stylish today. The clothing designer Hugo Boss costumed selected characters in *Damned by Despair* in the latest trends and also dressed these actors for publicity events (White).

Perhaps the most potent result of casting an actress as the Devil was the effect it had on the characterization of Paulo. In Christian iconography, devils often take the shape of comely women before tempting desert hermits such as Saint Anthony. Tirso's Devil successfully tempts Paulo by giving him what he has deprived himself of—a taste of sexuality—though his words do not acknowledge the Devil's seductive charms. *Comedia* scholars such as R. J. Oakley have suggested that Paulo's sense of guilt and sin is related to sexuality. In Act I, Pedrisco fondly recalls a voluptuous woman, and this recollection prompts

Paulo to order Pedrisco to stomp on him—in a seemingly futile attempt to stomp out Paulo's lust (635–54; Oakley 31). In keeping with the Baroque theme of deceptive appearances, Lawrence embodied a Devil who convincingly portrays sensuality without actually feeling it. Her Devil has the sexual power to seduce and control Paulo, but her lust is all a metatheatrical put-on.

El condenado por desconfiado is a powerful dramatic work that continues to be performed for modern audiences. Its theological themes must be made completely real and palpable for today's theatergoers, and the Devil is key to theatricalizing those themes. The three productions we have examined all explore the tradition of Satan as a shape-shifter by experimenting with the character's gender, and they all use the Devil as a guide for the audience, sometimes expanding the Devil's role so significantly that he loses the power to truly menace either us or Tirso's protagonists. All three productions work hard to present us with a comic Devil, with varying degrees of success. Too much humor only further distances the spectator from the sobriety of the play's themes and fails to deeply frighten or move us. A trickster of folklore fame inhabits the carnavalesque production of *El condenado* by Colombia's Teatro del Valle. The CNTC's charming and handsome Devil laughs at every death and, unfortunately, he encourages us to undervalue the people on stage. But the Devil of London's *Damned by Despair* at the National Theatre cannot smile. He can only grimace, and his every reassuring gesture is full of Tirsian menace.

Notes

1. In 1991, Stephen Daldry directed an acclaimed production called *Damned for Despair* at London's tiny Gate Theatre, but so little documentation is available that even Daldry historian Wendy Lesser could describe it only very briefly (52–53). The published translation by Jonathan Thacker and Lawrence Boswell provides the Devil with some potentially comic lines in Act I.
2. All citations to *El condenado por desconfiado* refer to the 2000 edition by Ciriaco Morón Arroyo.
3. For the production history of *El condenado*, see <http://www.outofthewings.org>. 14 Dec. 2014.
4. All citations to *Damned by Despair* refer to the adaptation by Frank McGuinness.
5. Cf. Giles 12; Chevalier and Gheerbrant 287; Fris 49–60.
6. Regarding the overall set design of *Damned by Despair*, see Lottman 198–200.

Works Cited

Chevalier, Jean, and Alain Gheerbrant. *A Dictionary of Symbols*. Trans. John Buchanan-Brown. London: Penguin, 1996. Print.

Damned by Despair. By Tirso de Molina. Adapt. Frank McGuinness. Dir. Bijan Sheibani. Perf. Sebastian Armesto, Bertie Carvel, Rory Keenan and Amanda Lawrence. National Theatre, London. 10 Oct. 2012. Performance.

El condenado por desconfiado. By Tirso de Molina. Dir. Alejandro González Puche, La Corporación Teatro del Valle, Cali, Colombia. Perf. Néstor Durán, Manuel Viveros, Marleida Soto, Felipe Pérez. Chamizal National Memorial, El Paso, TX, USA. 1 Mar. 2003. Association for Hispanic Clasical Theater. DVD.

El condenado por desconfiado. By Tirso de Molina. Dir. Carlos Aladro. Perf. Ángel Ramón Jiménez, Arturo Querejeta, Daniel Albaladejo, Francisco Rojas. Compañía Nacional de Teatro Clásico. Teatro Pavón, Madrid, Spain. 2010. Centro de Documentación Teatral, Madrid, Sp. DVD.

Fernández Rodríguez, Natalia. "Demonología dramática en Tirso de Molina: *El condenado por desconfiado* y *La ninfa del cielo.*" *Ramillete de los gustos: Burlas y veras en Tirso de Molina.* Ed. Ignacio Arellano. Burgos, Sp.: Fundación Instituto Castellano y Leonés de la Lengua, 2005. 195–212. Print.

Fris, John. "The Devil, the Tower, and the Hanged Man: the Hermetic Tarot of the *Numancia.*" *A Star-crossed Golden Age: Myth and the Spanish Comedia.* Ed. Frederick Alfred de Armas. Lewisburg, PA; London: Bucknell UP, 1998. 46–61. Print.

Giles, Cynthia Elizabeth. *The Tarot: History, Mystery, and Lore.* New York: Paragon House, 1992. Print.

Jager, Eric. *The Tempter's Voice: Language and the Fall in Medieval Literature.* Ithaca, NY: Cornell UP, 1993. Print.

Kallendorf, Hilaire. *Exorcism and Its Texts: Subjectivity in Early Modern Literature of England and Spain.* Toronto: U of Toronto P, 2003. Print.

Lee, Christina H. "Rescatar a *El condenado por desconfiado* del teatro de museo: Una entrevista con Alejandro González Puche, Director del Teatro del Valle (Cali, Colombia)." *Comedia Performance* 1.1 (2004): 238–52. Print.

Lesser, Wendy. *A Director Calls.* Berkeley: U of California P, 1997. Print.

Lottman, Maryrica Ortiz. "Tirso's *Damned by Despair* at London's National Theatre: An Interview with Bijan Shebani." *Comedia Performance* 10.1 (2013): 195–226. Print.

Maurel, Serge. "La risa y su efecto de distanciamiento en *El condenado por desconfiado.*" *Homenaje a Tirso.* Madrid: Revista "Estudios," 1981. 433–38. Print.

May, T. E., *"El condenado por desconfiado:* I. The Enigmas. II. Anareto." *Bulletin of Hispanic Studies* 35 (1958): 138–56. Rpt. in *Wit of the Golden Age: Articles on Spanish Literature.* Kassel, Ger.: Reichenberger, 1986. 134–53. Print.

McClelland, I. L. "The Conception of the Supernatural in the Plays of Tirso de Molina." *Bulletin of Hispanic Studies* 19.76 (1942): 148–63. Print.

Molina, Tirso de (Gabriel Téllez). *El condenado por desconfiado.* Ed. Ciriaco Morón Arroyo. Madrid: Cátedra, 2000. Print.

———. *Damned for Despair, Don Gil of the Green Breeches: Two Plays by Tirso de Molina.* Trans. & adapt. Laurence Boswell, Jonathan Thacker, and Deidre McKenna. Bath, UK: Absolute, 1992. Print.

Molina, Tirso de, and Frank McGuinness. *Damned by Despair: A Version by Frank McGuinness from a Literal Translation by Simon Bredon*. London: Faber and Faber, 2012. Print.

Monks, Ben. "Defending Damnation." *Exeunt*. 25 Oct. 2012. Web. 14 Dec. 2014. <http://exeuntmagazine.com/search>.

Oakley, R. J. *Tirso de Molina, El condenado por desconfiado*. London: Grant & Cutler, 1994. Print.

Pastoureau, Michel. *Black: The History of a Color*. Princeton: Princeton UP, 2009. Print.

Phil and Andrew. "Review—*Damned by Despair*, National Theatre." *West End Whingers*. 9 Oct. 2012. Web. 14 Dec. 2014. <http://westendwhingers.wordpress.com/search>.

Ruano de la Haza, José María. "Una posible puesta en escena de *El condenado por desconfiado*." *La década de oro en la comedia española, 1630–1640: Actas de las XIX Jornadas de Teatro Clásico, Almagro, 1996*. Ed. Felipe B. Pedraza Jiménez and Rafael González Cañal. Almagro (Ciudad Real), Sp.: Universidad de Castilla-La Mancha, 1997. 103–26. Print.

Varey, John E. "The Use of Levels in *El condenado por desconfiado*." *Revista Canadiense de Estudios Hispánicos* 10.2 (1986): 299–310. Print.

White, Belinda. "Hugo Boss Team Up with National Theatre." *The Telegraph*. 9 Oct. 2012. Web. 14 Dec. 2014. <http://fashion.telegraph.co.uk.search>.

Adapting the Spanish Classics for 21ˢᵗ-Century Performance in English: Models for Analysis

CATHERINE LARSON
Indiana University

Increasing numbers of Early Modern dramas are finding audiences in the English-speaking world, which raises significant critical and theoretical questions for the academics and theater professionals who navigate the space between the page and the stage and between the present and the past. This study explores the English-language adaptation of 16ᵗʰ- and 17ᵗʰ-century Spanish plays in the 21ˢᵗ century, proposing a set of tools or frameworks for organizing approaches to the topic; it is based on the concern that although we may believe we mutually agree on the basic definitions of adaptation for the stage, the variety of critical and theoretical discussions generated in recent years would indicate that there is much left to consider, in great measure due to the relative lack of widely accepted models for approaching theatrical adaptation.[1] As interest in the subject increases, as more plays are adapted and staged, and as more research is published, it has become ever more imperative to further bridge the gap that sometimes separates the two groups who bring distinct perspectives to the field as the result of their training and experience, i.e., scholars who share their love of Early Modern dramas in the classroom and in publications and conference papers, and theater practitioners who transform the printed word into embodied practice onstage. In this essay, I suggest three possible models for analyzing the English-language performance of Spanish Early Modern plays.

The large number of terms associated with adaptation points to the need for a clarification of them and the connotations they carry with them.[2] Charles Ganelin describes the problem: "Publicity may call them 'versions,'

or 'updates,' or 'translations,' or *refundiciones*: those of us who engage the
comedia, at one time strictly academically, but now more often theatrically,
are concerned with what these products are because the terms, like those
above, do not carry the same value" (*"Refundición* Redux" 1). Ultimately, it
is clear that "adaptation" can fairly be described as contested and that a useful
way to categorize the various types of adaptions for the stage remains elu-
sive. Of the vocabulary describing adaptation, two terms, "translation" and
"tradaptation," merit special consideration, in part because translation and
adaptation are so intimately connected, both literally and metaphorically. On
the most basic level, every drama from the Spanish Early Modern era that has
been adapted for performance in English has been translated, and even the
most literal translation is not a word-for-word linguistic product; the result
would be an incomprehensible rendering of the source text.[3] Every translation bears within it the unmistakable mark of the translator in terms of both
language choice and cultural understanding: as David Johnston observes, "in
any attempt to recreate one language from another, to transpose stage worlds,
there lingers the flavor, the memory of difference" ("Historicizing" 54). Tensions resulting from that difference are, then, an inevitable by-product of the
translation/adaptation process.

    Even more, the initial "literal" translation is but one of many prior to the
performance. The idea of creating a design or outline for further transformation lies at the heart of considering how the written word from four hundred
years ago might work onstage in the 21st century. Johnston summarizes: "A
translator for performance, of course, writes for actors. And as actors, in turn,
construct their performance from these words so the blueprint of a playing
style is laid down" ("Historicizing" 52). The theater practitioners who prepare that translated text for the stage will transform it to make it playable for
their actors and audiences; moreover, the performance text often changes
from one performance to the other, as directors and actors continue to
modify the adaptation based on audience reaction, the actors' or director's
input on how the translated text works for them, or a host of other reasons.
Catherine Boyle posits:

> ... there is no original play, nor is there a final one. And the trust in the translated
> text is often expressed as a trust in the translation and its 'sounding' in English:
> the ability to understand it, to approach that space where alien concepts are not
> obscured by the jarring on the ear of language that insistently suggests the for-
> eign both linguistically and culturally. (63)

Johnston and Boyle are describing the process of creating the Royal Shakespeare Company's 2004 season of Spanish Golden Age plays (artistic director,
Laurence Boswell), which grew from the collaboration of academics and

theater professionals in crafting both literal translations and performance texts for the four plays ultimately selected for production.[4] Kathleen Mountjoy outlines the essential role translation played in this project and in the theater in general:

> Translation is negotiation. The reason that a literal translation, even if it is not very "literal," is a useful tool in the rehearsal room is precisely because of its imprecision; meaning is found in arguing with the text and teasing out more accurate ways of phrasing the ideas it conveys. In collaborations with the translator, it is in the search for the best words that the actors find their characters, and the director finds the play. Because the rehearsal process is where the characters are born, lines which generate the response "no, that's not quite right" and those of which we cry out "that's it!" are, for the actors and director as well as the translator, the generation process of a new play in the target language. (77)[5]

Translations for performance, then, function as interpretations negotiated by a varied group of participants. Consequently, we can easily imagine that an English-language theatrical adaptation of *La vida es sueño* [*Life is A Dream*] could appropriately also be termed a "translation" or a "tradaptation." The connections between translation and adaptation both blur the terminological lines and require that we remain cognizant of the inherent points of contact between them. In essence, we need to find a way of talking about adaptation for performance that moves beyond the role—albeit significant—of translation.

A related issue bears mentioning at this point. The last thirty years have marked a significant new direction in the performance of Early Modern Spanish Theater. First, many more English-language plays have been staged in the U.S., Canada and Great Britain during that time, thanks in great measure to initiatives such as the RSC productions of 2004 and productions at the Chamizal National Memorial in El Paso. The opportunity to see the classics performed onstage has been democratized, and in the process, it has created a different type of audience. As academics and English-speaking audiences have become more literate about Early Modern Theater, many formerly held assumptions have been replaced by other viewpoints: creative new approaches promote the acceptance of yet other approaches. The idea of the *comedia* as a museum piece has gradually been replaced; fewer spectators now come to the theater with the expectation that the play must look and sound onstage as it did in in the era in which it was originally created. Such a liberalization of performance expectations reflects a movement away from what had been a hotly debated topic, the relative importance of fidelity to the original, which now holds much less sway in the disciplines of adaptation studies, translation studies and performance studies, as well as Hispanic theater studies.[6] This does not mean that we must never consider connections between the source play and its avatar but, rather, that the degree of faithfulness to the source should not necessarily determine qualitative assessments of worth: an adaptation should be judged on its own terms as the new play it fundamentally is. Comparisons between source and target can be useful, even necessary; I simply argue that they be value-free, that challenges to the original text be neither privileged nor condemned *a priori*, and that we acknowledge that even "outrageous" adaptions for the theater could be seen as respectful.[7]

How, then, can we make sense of the terminology and find a useful way to talk about the variety of adaptions for performance? Many of the terms in the adaption lexicon could easily be described as synonymous: what, for example, differentiates a "reinvention" or "reimagining" from an "updating"? In what follows, I offer three possible models for "coming to terms" with what is now little more than a list of indiscriminate synonyms. My goal is to suggest possible strategies or approaches for considering what we see onstage and thereby help to navigate and organize the various intertextual layers that comprise the adapted text. I propose three models or approaches that might serve as useful tools for categorizing and describing adaptation for the stage: *Re-creation vs. Re-imaging, Performance Questions*, and *Relationship*.

The first approach, the *Re-creation vs. Re-imaging Model*, examines from different perspectives the same topic: the ways in which an adaptation enters into dialogue with its origins. This model looks non-judgmentally at the source/adaptation relationship in terms of an adaptation continuum, with various adaptations falling at different points along that line. A *re-creation*, like a version, reconstitution or rendition, more closely resembles the source play in a number of ways. Although the play is performed in English, in essence, a modern audience sees a drama that maintains many of its historical and socio-cultural markings, the nature and number of which could well provide fruitful material for analysis. Obviously, some re-creations would be closer to the original than others, but ultimately, the *Re-creation* category would contrast significantly with the *Re-imagining* type of adaptation.

In a *re-imagining*, the adaptation uses the original as an inspiration for other perspectives and creative actions. The synonyms that most closely resemble such a free or loose adaptation of the source text include "appropriation," "transformation," "re-writing," and "re-interpretation"; each term signals an intentional departure from the source play, in which the adaptor deliberately modifies the original in a substantive manner. A subcategory of re-imagination, "modernization" and "updating" emphasizes conscious efforts on the part of the adaptor to remake the Early Modern play in a new, 21st-century context.[8] Theater practitioners' attempts to free the original text (ideologically or in form or language) from the constraints of the age in which it was written point towards the construction of modernized versions. A modernization calls attention to the creative contributions of the adaptors, who function as collaborative co-participants in taking the play from page to stage, and highlights the relationship between the reincarnation and the contemporary audience's tastes and expectations, especially with regard to cultural change over time.[9] It is also often called a response to the source play; at times, new characters (and characterizations) appear; at other times, the ending is completely changed as the adaptor challenges the original writer's worldview by heading in a decidedly different direction.

The *Re-creation vs. Re-imagining Model* offers a general, relatively straightforward way of approaching adaptations, allowing audiences of varying types a structure for talking about what they have read or seen onstage without having to frame the discussion as merely a list of elements that are or are not faithful to the original play. The adaptor's decisions may then be evaluated on their own terms. Moreover, this model allows for discussions of the freedom and constraints that all adaptors—both text- and performance-based—face in transforming a classical play for the modern stage and facilitates consideration of both the process and product of adaptation.

A second model for categorizing adaptations for the theater, which I describe as the *Performance Questions Model*, asks us to consider key questions that focus attention on adaptation as the blueprint for performance in a time and place—and language—far from the original, treating the decisions the adaptor made, often in collaboration with translators, directors and actors, to create a playable text for 21ˢᵗ-century, English-speaking audiences.[10] Although it could be argued that some plays are adapted for reading purposes only, the focus of this model (and, I would submit, of most adaptations) emphasizes their potential for performance, which might lead to the consideration of some or all of the following questions: How did this adaptation fare when directors and actors took ownership of the written text and began to prepare for performance? Are interviews with the theater practitioners who further transformed the text for the stage—or actual rehearsal notes—available to better describe the process? What made the adaptation playable? How did dramatic discourse unite with physical action to create the theatrical experience? Did it maintain the original length, or did it include drastic cuts—and for what purpose and with what results? What decisions went into writing in verse or prose (or in contemporary, colloquial language, as opposed to language more reflective of the time of the play's setting), and how did those decisions ultimately affect the production and audience response to it? Did the adaptation contain clues for stage properties, sets, costumes, music, light, or darkness that affected the text in performance? In what ways did the adaptation consider the comic characters that figure so prominently in many dramas of the era? How did the adaptation treat the socio-cultural or ideological ethos from which the target text originated? In what ways did the adaptation incorporate music or include other performance material such as a *loa* [prologue], *mojiganga* [farce], or *fin de fiesta* [finale], and with what goals in mind? Did the adaptation appear to draw attention to the differences between the time and place of the source text and those of the adapted text, and if so, in what ways? How did the audience react to decisions that were carried out in the performed adaptation? Certainly, such performance-oriented questions open the adapted text to nuanced, extended commentary. The *Performance Questions Model* allows those analyzing the adaptation a great deal of freedom in selecting which topics offer the most fruitful avenues for exploration and exegesis, while still providing a central focus for approaching the adaptation. Because the model would most likely be employed to discuss what happened in actual performances or on the path to those performances, the questions might be explored from the perspective of the spectator/reviewer, or they might be complemented by adding the views of the adaptor, director, or actors.

A third possible approach to examining the adaptation of Spanish classical theater, the *Relationship Model*, derives from a metaphor underscoring both the author/adaptor relationship and that of the source and target texts.[11] The model, inspired by José Rivera's introduction to his adaptation of Calderón's *La vida es sueño*, focuses attention on these relationships from a decidedly self-reflexive and intimate point of view. Rivera describes the story of his adaptation from the perspective of the connections between the adaptor and source author: "It's either a dance, a dialogue, a duet, or a duel between you the adaptor and the original creator" ("A Dance" 8).[12] The metaphor offers an ideal way to study the evolution of such relationships and the perceptions that guide responses to them, and it serves as a marker for representing both partnerships and confrontations and for illuminating the range of possibilities inherent in the act of (re)creation. *Duels* thrive on antithesis, with winners and losers in a ritual that foregrounds danger, life and death. The duel is therefore clearly antagonistic, with the adaptor actively working at being "not him or her." Allegiance to the source text is minimized, and the creation of a new play for modern audiences results from the deconstruction of the original. The *dance* implies an intimate, often physical connection, with the participants moving closer and then further apart. The experience of the relationship is frequently positive, enjoyable, and sometimes even seductive. Nonetheless, the expression "dancing around a topic" connotes another side of the issue, the lack of direct engagement with it. The simultaneous closeness and separation that define a dance can afford an apt metaphor for the relationship between a source text and its avatar and open the discussion of the adaptation to more nuanced readings. In a relationship described as a *dialogue*, we move from the physical, corporeal experience of the dance to that of the voice. Talking with one another suggests relative equality in the interaction, with less emphasis on either the lack of connection (the monologue) or fights for power. In terms of theatrical adaption, we might characterize this phase as one of balance and respect, moving towards partnership. The idea of seeing the relationship as a true partnership is fittingly expressed by a *duet*. The relationship is considerably less antagonistic, as the adaptor stresses the union of creative visions in producing a play that underscores synthesis. The participants' duet produces a new work of art, something esthetically beautiful and thematically profound, and the jointly produced text highlights the collaboration of the source author and adaptor. Rivera's metaphors provide a unique type of analytical instrument for investigating the evolving relationship between the original playwright and the 21st-century adaptor, between the source and the new play, between the duel and the duet. The *Relationship Model* allows those who analyze adaptation, both theoretically and in response to specific plays, to approach the adaptor and his or her adaptation as a response to the original source of inspiration; it then takes the analysis forward by examining the various ways in which that response is realized onstage. Ultimately, Rivera's "dance with Calderón" offers a way of approaching adaptation that foregrounds the evolutionary process of transforming a classical play into a new text for new audiences.

These models for examining the process and product of adaption for the theater suggest the range of possibilities available for ongoing discussions of the topic. As we address the "afterlife of plays" and "subsequent performances" to which Jonathan Miller refers,[13] such approaches (or others yet to be offered) can help take the conversation forward as we explore the multiple levels of adaptation that occur when a classical drama is "translated" for modern audiences. We are not yet on the same page—or stage—with regard to boundary-pushing: how much creative freedom does/can/should the adaptor of the classics have? What constraints affect the creative process involved? How do interpretation and esthetics intersect with—or play off—one another? How do audiences participate in determining the outcome of the newly created text and performance(s) of it? Questions such as these and the criteria for evaluation that I have offered above may help us better "come to terms" with the adaptation of the Spanish classics for modern, English-speaking audiences. In the end, the final product, the staged adaptation, no matter where it lies along the continuum of transformed texts, becomes the site from which future adaptations and performances will emerge and from which future performance histories will be created. The adaptor's dance with the original dramatic poet and his or her drama metamorphoses into the inspiration for new interpretations in which the future is always, necessarily, mediated on at least some level by the past.

Notes

1. Nonetheless, scholars have expressed a growing interest in describing and theorizing this sub-field. In Hispanic studies, see Louise and Peter Fothergill-Payne, Catherine Boyle and David Johnston, Susan Paun de García and Donald R. Larson, Susan L. Fischer, Charles Ganelin, and Harley Erdman and Paun de García, as well as the *Out of the Wings* database and the work of the Association for Hispanic Classical Theater and its journal, *Comedia Performance*; more generally, see Linda Hutcheon, W. B. Worthen and Julie Sanders. See also my "Calderón's *La vida es sueño*" and "Terms and Concepts."

2. I list almost thirty terms in the adaptation lexicon (most of which are used interchangeably) in "Calderón's *La vida es sueño*" and provide a much-shortened version of that list in "Terms and Concepts." The vocabulary tends to focus on describing adaptations that differ greatly from the original ("reimagining," "re-writing," "reinvention," "interpretation," "appropriation"), those that take into account the temporal distance between the classic and the new version ("updating," "modernization"), adaptations that more closely resemble the source text ("imitation," "paraphrasing," "approximation") or those combining separate, but related, actions ("tradaptation").

3. Fischer emphasizes this argument: "The universalizing belief in a stable and authoritative text is turned on its ear by the mere fact of contemporary performance" ("Aspectuality" 35).

4. See *The Spanish Golden Age in English* for its explication of this process.

5. Mountjoy draws attention to the cutting of lines for performance: "as rehearsals progressed, more and more requests made [of the translator] were for cuts. This is because once the play became the cast's own, their questions were often no longer expressed in the need for a rewritten or reinstated line, but instead they worked harder for a change in blocking or even a cut to make room for their developing stage language" (80). See also Matthew D. Stroud's "The Director's Cut."

6. See, for example, Stam, Hutcheon (and Bortolotti and Hutcheon), Sanders, Worthen and Connor, as well as my "Terms and Concepts."

7. It is fair to state that not everyone will agree with this position. David Johnston's interview with Spanish playwright and adaptor Juan Mayorga illuminates an opposing view; Mayorga states: "You have an identity, your own independence, *vis à vis* the text, but you still have to enter the text with a fundamentally humble attitude, as though you are going into a cathedral. You go in with respect … I'm not saying that plays don't develop different meanings as contexts change around them. But respect for the original strikes me as being crucial." (Johnston "Interview," 147).

8. Although we agree on many points, Ganelin takes particular issue with one of the terms I use here: he eschews the use of "update," which, he believes, connotes "a superficial redressing, light touches to language or costume or plot with little concern for artistic integrity" ("*Refundición* Redux" 2).

9. As I have noted previously, André Lefevere and Willis Barnstone offer related ways of dealing with the topic. In both cases, the adaptation/translation is measured against specific categories that may or may not reflect the original text. Lefevere analyzes how theatrical adaptations re-write texts to give them new life for new audiences, whether the original is modified a great deal or very little. The re-writing is measured in terms of changes in language (including its socio-cultural context); ideology or world view, broadly speaking; and poetics ("Refraction" 192). Barnstone, discussing the related practice of translation, posits three similar categories that could serve as useful models for analyzing the elements of an adaptation: register, or translation level; structure, or degree of source text in translation; and authorship, or dominant voice (*Poetics* 25). Like Lefevere's model, Barnstone's categories promote a structured view of adaptation, offering audience members, academics, and reviewers a discrete set of tools for describing what the adaptor has done, without attaching any sort of value judgment to those actions.

10. In a related discussion of translation for the theater, Jean-Michel Déprats treats three issues related to the new, target text: "*theatricality* (are these translations meant to be read, or performed on stage?), *historicity of the language* (should the translation be deliberately archaic or modern?), and *the question of verse* (should the translation be in metered verse, free verse, or prose?)" ("Translation" 12). See also the perspective of translator/actor/director/playwright Dakin Matthews ("Translating *Comedias*"), in particular, the discussion of poetry and modern audiences.

11. I cite the metaphor previously but expand here on its potential application in approaching adaptation from a more theoretical perspective.

12. Rivera describes his evolving relationship with Calderón: "As the months went by, I found my relationship to Calderón changing. Someone once told me that to write an adaptation is to serve an apprenticeship with a master. Like any good apprentice, I approached the Old Man with awe mixed with fear. This was followed by familiarity as I chipped away at the many translations of this play in pursuit of its beating heart. This was followed by a strange irritation at Calderón's repetitions, his limited vocabulary, his recycled metaphors, his slavish devotion to the conventions of his time, his unwieldy subplot, and his obstinate championing of the status quo. This was followed by a truly oedipal desire to kill the old bastard. But eventually, when it was all said and done, I returned to a newborn respect and came back full circle to true awe, that is, awe *without* the fear" (8).

13. Miller reminds us that the theater "producers and performers bring into the field of the fine arts"; it "depends on successive reproduction for its existence, where mutation and change are built into it, whether you like it or not. Those of us who are often accused of ravaging these works are, I believe, by our ravages, guaranteeing their immortality" (*Afterlife* 35).

Works Cited

Barnstone, Willis. *The Poetics of Translation: History, Theory, Practice*. New Haven, CT: Yale UP, 1993. Print.

Boyle, Catherine, and David Johnston, eds., with Janet Morris. *The Spanish Golden Age in English: Perspectives on Performance*. London: Oberon, 2007. Print.

Bortolotti, Gary R., and Linda Hutcheon. "On the Origin of Adaptations: Rethinking Fidelity Discourse and 'Success'—Biologically." *New Literary History* 38 (2007): 443–58. Print.

Connor, J. D. "The Persistence of Fidelity: Adaptation Theory Today." *M/C Journal* 10.2 (2007): n. p. *Open Journal Systems*. Web. 11 Jan. 2013. <http://journal.media-culture.org.au/0705/15-connor.php>.

Déprats, Jean-Michel. "Translation at the Intersections of History." *Shakespeare and Modern Theatre*. Ed. Michael Bristol and Kathleen McLuskie, with Christopher Holmes. London: Routledge, 2001. 73–92. Print.

Erdman, Harley, and Susan Paun de García, eds. *Remaking the Comedia: Spanish Classical Theater in Adaptation*. Woodbridge, UK: Tamesis, 2015. Print.

Fischer, Susan L. "Aspectuality, Performativity and 'Foreign' *Comedia*." Boyle and Johnston 31–48. Print.

———. *Reading Performance: Spanish Golden Age Theatre and Shakespeare on the Modern Stage*. Woodbridge, UK: Tamesis, 2009. Print.

Fothergill-Payne, Louise, and Peter Fothergill-Payne, eds. *Prologue to Performance: Spanish Classical Theater Today*. Lewisburg, PA: Bucknell UP, 1991. Print.

Ganelin, Charles. "The Art of Adaptation: Building the Hermeneutical Bridge." Fothergill Payne 36–48. Print.

———. "*Refundición* Redux: Revisiting the Rewritten *Comedia*." Erdman and García, in press. Print.

García, Susan Paun de, and Donald R. Larson, eds. *The Comedia in English: Translation and Performance*. Woodridge, UK: Tamesis, 2008. Print.

Hutcheon, Linda. *A Theory of Adaptation*. 2nd ed. New York: Routledge, 2006. Print.

Johnston, David. "Historicizing the Spanish Golden Age: Lope's *El perro del hortelano* and *El caballero de Olmedo* in English." Boyle and Johnston 49–60. Print.

———. "Interview with Juan Mayorga." Boyle and Johnston 141–47. Print.

Larson, Catherine. "Calderon's *La vida es sueño* meets Callaghan's *Fever/Dream*: Adaptation and Performance." *Comedia Performance* 10 (2013): 19–58. Print.

———. "Found in Translation: María de Zayas's *Friendship Betrayed* and the English-Speaking Stage." García and Larson 83–94. Print.

———. "Terms and Concepts: The Adaptation of Classical Texts for the Stage. Erdman and García, in press. Print.

———. "Zayas's *La traición en la amistad* in English: Translation and Adaptation in a New Era." *Comedia Performance* 11 (2014): 1–36. Print.

Lefevere, André. "Refraction: Some Observations on the Occasion of Wole Soyinka's *Opera Wonyosi*." *Page to Stage: Theatre as Translation*. Ed. Ortrun Zuber-Skerritt. Amsterdam: Rodopi, 1984. 191–98. Print.

Matthews, Dakin. "Translating Comedias into English Verse for Modern Audiences." García and Larson 37–53. Print.

Miller, Jonathan. *The Afterlife of Plays*. San Diego: San Diego State UP, 1992. Print. University Distinguisehd Graduate Research Lecture 5.

———. *Subsequent Performances.* New York: E. Sifton/Viking, 1986. Print.

Mountjoy, Kathleen. "Literal and Performative Text." Boyle and Johnston 75–88. Print.

Out of the Wings. Web. 12 Dec. 2012. <http://outofthewings.org>.

Rivera, José. "A Dance with Calderón." *Sueño.* Woodstock, IL: Dramatic Publishing, 1999. 5–8. Print.

Sanders, Julie. *Adaptation and Appropriation.* London: Routledge, 2006. Print.

Stam, Robert. "Introduction: The Theory and Practice of Adaptation." *Literature and Film: A Guide to the Theory and Practice of Adaptation.* Ed. Robert Stam and Alessandra Raengo. New York: Blackwell, 2005. 1–52. Print.

Stroud, Matthew D. "The Director's Cut: Baroque Aesthetics and Modern Stagings of the *Comedia.*" *Comedia Performance* 1.1 (2004): 77–94. Print.

Worthen, W. B. *Shakespeare and the Authority of Performance.* Cambridge, UK: Cambridge UP, 1997. Print.

Act Five

Contours and Contexts: Crossing (Temporal/Spatial/Political) Boundaries

The Contours of Self-Representation: Why Call Himself Tirso de Molina?

HENRY W. SULLIVAN
Tulane University

In a career spanning almost five decades, Matt Stroud has enriched the field of Spanish Classical theater studies constantly. I first heard his name in 1981 when he single-handedly rescued Calderón and Juan Hidalgo's three-act Court opera *Celos aun del aire matan* [*Even Baseless Jealousy Can Kill*] (1660) from oblivion, staged it in Texas, and subsequently created a color film version of the modern revival. Colleagues will recall his study of uxoricide, *Fatal Union* (1990); also, the first thorough-going Lacanian monograph on the Spanish drama, *The Play in the Mirror* (1996); as well as his most recent book *Plot Twists and Critical Turns* (2007), which uses queer theory as an approach to the same body of literature. But in his prolific production Matt has returned again and again to the world of Tirso de Molina (1579–1648). He took up the theme of uxoricide once more in his 1983 article on Tirso's *La vida y muerte de Herodes* [*The Life and Death of Herod*]. He pursued the ambiguities of gender identity in Tirso's *Don Gil de las calzas verdes* [*Don Gil of the Green Breeches*] in 1991; published on sainthood and psychoanalysis in Tirso's trilogy *La Santa Juana* [*Saint Juana*] in 1996; edited a web adaptation of Jean Chittenden's lengthy study *Characters and Plots of Tirso's Comedias* in 2002; and, most recently, contributed an article in 2012 on the Biblical Ruth as *dama principal* of Tirso's *La mejor espigadera* [*The Best Gleaner*]. Readers of these pages need hardly be reminded that Tirso de Molina was also the nom de plume of Fray Gabriel Jusepe Téllez, O. de M., a friar of the Mercedarian Order. But no one to my knowledge has systematically or satisfactorily proposed reasons for Téllez's choice—or coinage—of the nom de plume for his second career as dramatist. In this homage, I therefore convey my admiration and respect for Matt Stroud's achievements by taking up this very question in greater detail: Why, indeed, did Tirso de Molina call himself Tirso de Molina?

Why Tirso?

The first feature to note in addressing this issue is that—while pseudonyms are not uncommon in other literatures or periods (Stendhal, George Eliot, Mark Twain, Lewis Carroll, Gabriela Mistral, John le Carré)—Fray Gabriel Téllez was rare among Golden Age writers in attempting to hide his identity behind a literary double. One common-sense explanation for this is the Mercedarian's wish not to compromise the reputation of his religious Order by bandying his real identity about the *corrales* [public theaters] of Madrid when so much ecclesiastical opinion of the time regarded the theater as a sinful place. The main bone of contention here was the "lascivious example" it presented to the public and to young people, the disorderly moral life of the actors and, more especially, the actresses; the scandal of their quasi-marital intimacy or sexual liaisons when not actually married; male actors watching scantily clad women changing in the dressing-rooms, and the like. Critics did not normally accuse actors of mortal sin, but some argued that actors employed for money were well on the way to it. Other theologians maintained that lay people committed a venial sin by attending such spectacles or allowing their wives and children to do so, while sectors of the Church and staid persons were repelled by the sexual emphasis of almost all secular plays, to say nothing of their exaggerated cult of honor and vengeance (Mori; Sullivan 13–32). According to this theory, Fray Gabriel would have wished to avoid the disgrace of being the perverse example of a priest in orders indulging an avocation which other churchmen found improper.

One major weakness in this argument, however, may be detected in the close parallel with Tirso's fellow dramatist—himself a Mercedarian and eighteen years Tirso's senior—Fray Alonso Remón, O. de M. (1561–1632). Remón had a major reputation in his lifetime as prose writer, orator and chronicler. As playwright, he cultivated historical dramas (notably *El señor Don Juan de Austria en Flandes* [*Don Juan of Austria in Flanders*] of 1604), and also comedies such as *¿De cuándo acá nos vino?* [*From Whence Did We Receive This?*] (1610–1615), co-authored with Lope de Vega, or *Las tres mujeres en una* [*Three Women in One*] (1609). But despite such fame and distinction (and being in religious orders), Fray Alonso Remón did not feel it necessary to write under a pseudonym. Nevertheless, the issue of respect for decorum under discussion here may lie behind the disconnect between the claims for Remón's overall productivity—in his *Tratado de los reinos de*

Indias [*Treatise on the Kingdoms of the Indies*] it is said he wrote two hundred plays—and the scanty score-odd of his stage-works, which have actually come down to us. Cervantes, in the *Viaje del Parnaso* [*Journey to Parnassus*] (composed before 1613), names Remón among a group of "seis personas ... en sacra religión constituídas" [six people ... established in Holy Orders] who, for that reason, found praise tiresome ("tienen las alabanzas por molestas") and so they preferred to dissimulate their celebrity as writers. But even this consideration, if true, did not lead Remón actually to adopt a pseudonym as did Fray Gabriel Téllez. In which case, what was the "extra" factor which drove Tirso to invent a literary double?

The next question to ask is when Tirso first used his pseudonym. This is an even harder conundrum to solve. The Mercedarian signed himself "Fr. Gabriel Téllez" his whole life long, as we know from the very many notarial and conventual chapter documents—in monasteries of the Order in Guadalajara, Toledo, Soria, Segovia, Madrid and elsewhere—which have been preserved for us. On the other hand, most authorities would place Tirso's beginnings in the quinquennium 1606–1610, when we first hear of his reputation as poet and dramatist. For instance, the Mercedarian chronicler P. Bernardo de Vargas—writing in Latin in 1622—recalled the year 1606 in the following terms:

> 1606. Por estos tiempos floreció gran número de varones, celebrados entre los seglares, que ilustraron nuestra Religion con la santidad de su vida y la excelencia de las letras. Sumamente prolijo sería mencionarlos a todos, pero para no silenciarlos totalmente, apuntamos, entre muchos, a estos pocos: ... Fr. Gabriel Téllez y Fr. Alonso Remón, poetas famosísimos.

> [1606. Around this time there flourished a large number of men, famous among lay people, who lent glory to our Order by the holiness of their lives and their excellence in literature. It would be extremely tedious to mention them all, but so as not to omit them entirely, we note—among the many—these few: ... Fray Gabriel Téllez, Fray Alonso Remón, poets of great renown].[1]

The first non-ecclesiastical reference to Tirso as a dramatist is that of the second-rank playwright and actor-manager Andrés de Claramonte y Monroy in his *Letanía moral* [*Moral Litany*] (1610), where he mentions: "Padre fray Gabriel Téllez, mercedario, poeta cómico" [Father Fr. Gabriel Téllez, Mercedarian and comic dramatist].[2]

In the third place, we may document the odd circumstance that Tirso's change of name seems *not* actually to have been very effective. Indeed by the early 1620s his veiled identity was an open secret. In the *Tasa* ["Tax"] to the *Cigarrales de Toledo* [*Toledan Country Houses*], dated 1624, Hernando de

Vallejo fixes the book's price at 292 maravedís and states it was composed by "el Maestro don Gabriel Tirso de Molina," a combination which Luis Vázquez termed "a strange hybrid of name and pseudonym." Vázquez also noted that from this period onwards "El Maestro Tirso de Molina" would be his pseudonym (93n2). The royal privilege to the *Cigarrales* volume signed by Pedro de Contreras repeats this formula: "Por cuanto por parte de vos, el M[aestro]. D[on]. Gabriel Tirso de Molina, nos fue fecha relación ..." (Vázquez, *Cigarrales* 95) [When we learned from you, Maestro Don Gabriel Tirso de Molina ...].[3] And when the politically motivated *Junta de Reformación* [Reformation Council] condemned Tirso on trumped up charges of scandal on March 6, 1625, they repeated this equivalence, stating: "Tratóse del escándalo que causa un fraile mercedario, que se llama el Maestro Téllez, por otro nombre, Tirso ..." (qtd. in Penedo 143) [The case concerned the scandal caused by a Mercedarian friar who is called Maestro Téllez, or by another name, Tirso ...]. Final confirmation is provided by Tirso's nephew Francisco Lucas de Ávila writing in the prefatory sections to the *Tercera parte* [*Third Part* (*Of Tirso's Comedias*)] (1634). There he refers to the "*primera parte de Comedias del Maestro Tirso de Molina* mi Tío" and in the Prologue itself to "el Alarife mi Tío el Maestro" ["the Architect my Uncle the Maestro"] (emphasis added).[4]

So our dramatist endeavored via the literary double to spare his Order embarrassment or draw unsavory attention to his other self-as-friar. He seems to have decided on the use of this disguise formula towards 1610 (and was one of very few Golden Age writers to do so), but nevertheless, despite his efforts, the theater-going public and Madrid civil administration later came to know his real identity. But in making his original decision—to push the hermeneutical envelope a little further—why did Téllez pick out the name Tirso? And to what or to whom precisely was he referring when he did so? The River Tirso, for example, is the main waterway on the island of Sardinia. It also reappears as a real name during the 17th century in the person of the Jesuit theologian, the Rev. Thyrsus (or Tirso) González de Santalla (1624–1705). Thus far at least three theories have been advanced to solve the riddle, theories which we may respectively term: 1) the hagiographical, 2) the pastoral, and 3) the Dionysiac. In good logic, one must also concede these possibilities could be mutually reinforcing rather than mutually exclusive. But let us begin with the hagiographical theory.

St. Thyrsus (or San Tirso) was a Christian martyr put to death in Apollonia, Phrygia (modern Turkey) in 251 AD, in the persecutions of Emperor Decius. He was first tortured for his faith and then sentenced to be cut in two, but the teeth of the saw could not pierce his skin (which finally became so heavy the executioners could not lift it). After his martyrdom, the relics of Thyrsus were transferred to Constantinople. During the Middle Ages, his cult became popular in Spain, particularly in the ancient Kingdom of Leon. He had an entire office in the Mozarabic liturgy, for example. Several towns in Leon and Asturias bear his name (San Tirso de Cabarcos, San Tirso de Abres, San Tirso Margolles) and even in France we find a 12th-century church dedicated to him at Châteauponsac in the Limousin, as well as the Cathédrale de Notre Dame et Saint Thyrse at Sisteron in the Alps of Upper Provence ("Tirso"). The interest of this cult for us, however, lies in the connections between San Tirso, our Tirso, and the city of Toledo.

We know Tirso studied theology in Toledo between 1603 and 1607, and his later intimate relationship with the city is most manifest in the *Cigarrales de Toledo* of reference (Penedo 45; Vázquez, *Cigarrales* 104n16).[5] A decade before his residence there, in the course of excavating near the main square of Toledo where the Royal Hospital was to be built, diggers in 1595 uncovered the ruins of an ancient temple together with many human bones and other relics (García-Arenal and Rodríguez 204–08). One Jerónimo Román de la Higuera then claimed to have found a Visigothic letter in manuscript sent by King Silus of Asturias (reigned 774–783 AD) to Archbishop Cixila (and supposedly housed in the Cathedral Library), where the monarch described his difficulties in building a shrine to the martyred St. Thyrsus because the Moors ruled Toledo at the time. The modern townspeople of Toledo were delighted thus to learn of the unshakeable faith of their Mozarab forebears under Islam—now that they found an Apostolic Man in their midst—and the cult around him grew feverishly. Román de la Higuera even followed up his forgery with a treatise on whether San Tirso was a native of Toledo (García-Arenal and Rodríguez 208). Did the 1595 "discovery" of San Tirso's legacy and the new fervor abroad in Toledo move Fray Gabriel Téllez to adopt the martyr's name as nom de plume some fifteen years later?

Our second—pastoral—theory traces the name Tirso back to the *Idylls* of Theocritus. The Doric poet lived in the third century B.C. and is credited with inventing bucolic verse set in the Edenic rural landscape of Arcadia. Of these poems, the First *Idyll* entitled, in Greek, Θύρσις or *Thyrsis* is among the most famous. Here the shepherd Thyrsis sings to a goatherd about how Daphnis, the mythical herdsman, defied the power of the goddess Aphrodite, who had rendered him lovesick. Despite the quizzing of mythological divinities (Hermes, Priapus, Aphrodite) or shepherds and goatherds, Daphnis dies rather than giving in to the passion inflicted on him. The lack of any sympathy shown for the dying man reflects the Greek view that it was madness for humans to challenge the gods. Virgil later used the character

Thyrsis in his "Seventh Eclogue" as a shepherd who lost a singing match to Corydon. The pastoral resurfaced in Renaissance Italy (Castiglione reworked Theocritus' first bucolic tale as *Il Tirsi* [*The Thyrsis*] in 1508, for example) and the genre was taken up in Spain by Juan del Encina in his dramatic *Eclogues* (1496), by Garcilaso de la Vega (1501–1536) in his poetry, and by Jorge de Montemayor in his novel *La Diana* [*The Diana*] (1559). Tirso de Molina partly spoofed the pastoral conventions in his comedy *La fingida Arcadia* [*The False Arcadia*] (1621) and the hero, a knight called Don Felipe, hides his identity behind the rustic Tirso. The Spanish (and Italian) rendering of Thyrsis, however, was not Tirso but Tirsi. And while these poetic and literary traditions open up the pastoral theory as a plausible one, Gabriel Téllez's exact pseudonym derived from the Greek word Θύρσος (Thyrsos) and not from Θύρσις (Thyrsis).

But the word *thyrsos* (or thyrsus) had indirect literary associations of its own. The *thyrsos* was actually the roughly meter-long, fennel staff of Bacchic revels, wound with vine-leaves and ivy and topped with a pine cone (or sometimes ribbons), which the Maenads carried in orgies associated with Dionysus, the god of wine and the patron of drama. Greek vases have survived portraying a Maenad (or Bacchante) bearing this *thyrsos*. Various authorities also note the phallic character of the symbol and one Portuguese website sees the pine cone as a more specific symbol for semen ("Tirso").[6] This symbolism was not lost on the Spanish Golden Age, since Sebastián de Covarrubias gives a detailed account of the Bacchic *tirso* and *tirsígeros* [bearers of the rod] in his encyclopedic *Tesoro* (1611). The mythic wand seems to have originated in Ancient Egypt and in Phoenicia, then been assimilated by Thracian populations on the mainland, and thence transmitted to the whole Hellenistic world.

So Tirso, the stage, and Dionysus can be connected. The god himself was believed by some ancients to have constructed the Theater of Dionysus Eleuthereus on the south slope of the Athenian Acropolis, while the origins of Greek drama itself go back to the religious and communal life of the *polis*, which was intimately connected with the worship of this deity. Barbara F. McManus notes Patricia Easterling's work "A Show for Dionysus" and the associations of Greek tragedy with major characteristics of the god such as wine and intoxication, positive or self-destructive release of passions, wild nature outside the civilized city, half-animal satyrs and unbounded sexuality, ecstatic possession and loss of the individual's conscious identity, frenzied and trance-like states, dancing as a celebration of freedom, otherness, and also mystic initiation into cults like the Eleusinian mysteries of Demeter and Persephone (Easterling 36–53).[7] The god is thus the protector of those who do not belong to conventional society and he symbolizes everything which is chaotic, dangerous and unexpected—the Liberator (*Eleutherios*) freeing his followers from self-conscious fear and care ("Dionysus"). We need not belabor the appropriateness of *thyrsos* as a word to describe a tragic and comic dramatist—or a wizard of chaos—like Gabriel Téllez. But beyond that, many of the other attributes and symbols of the god remind us to an uncanny degree of our Spanish Golden Age playwright.

Almost all critics of Tirso de Molina feel the exuberant, even subversive sexuality of his theater as a topsy-turvy world suffused in *jouissance* [joy] and desire of which Don Juan Tenorio would be the most famous expression (Sullivan and Galoppe). Don Juan's priapism could be linked to Dionysus' divine son Priapus, the god of vegetable gardens (often portrayed as a garden statue with penis in a permanent state of erection). The political and political-sexual anarchy which quickly develops in so many of his comedies also seems Dionysiac, his driven women overwhelm his men, and highly influential women scholars—in a strange, indirect acknowledgment of Tirso de Molina's fascination with female sexual and intellectual power—have been drawn to the study of his theater in droves (his editor Teresa de Guzmán in the 18th century, Doña Blanca de los Ríos y Lampérez, Alice H. Bushee, Ruth Lee Kennedy, Ivy McClelland, Margaret Wilson, Carmen Bravo-Villasante, María del Pilar Palomo, Berta de Pallares de R. Arias, Melveena McKendrick, Laura Dolfi, and many others). Raúl A. Galoppe has even made the case that, from a Lacanian psychoanalytic point of view, the flesh-and-blood Tirso de Molina could be construed as a *male* in the biological sense of the term, but *feminine* in terms of subject position and sexuation (Galoppe 59–98).

One more parallel between Dionysus and Tirso de Molina deserves mention in this context. I refer to the status of Bacchus as the god of homosexuality. In a collection called "Summary of the Olympian God" he is termed the patron of homosexuality, effeminacy, and cross-dressing ("DIONYSUS"). One myth tells of Dionysus' love for a handsome young satyr named Ampelos who was gored to death while trying to ride a wild bull. From his blood Dionysus created the first grapevine. Another story tells of the birth of Dionysus from the thigh of Zeus and how Hermes—entrusted with the child—took him to Ino and Athamas and persuaded them to bring him up as a girl. We hardly need to emphasize how prominent a role cross-dressing, effeminacy, and suggestions of both lesbianism and homosexuality play in the Mercedarian's theater. These themes have been the subject of articles and books too numerous to mention. But if the Dionysiac theory holds water, then how well Gabriel Téllez knew himself to pick this second persona of sexual anarchy for carrying his vision to the world!

Why de Molina?

There are as many as four theories known to me which try and explain the
second half of Gabriel Téllez's pseudonym. These may be expressed as: 1) the
Molina de Aragón theory, 2) the Luis de Molina theory, 3) the Queen María
de Molina theory, and 4) the Conde de Molina de Herrera theory. The first line
of argument supposes a connection between our playwright and the historic
Señorío [Seigneury] de Molina de Aragón (90 miles north-east of Madrid in
the province of Guadalajara). This theory has been most elaborately developed
by Fray Manuel Penedo Rey O. de M. In his long Introduction to the *Historia
General* [*General History*], Penedo cites a 1908 edition of Tirso's *Vida de la
Santa María de Cervellón* [*Life of Saint Mary of Cervellón*], where the Mercedarian author claims to be of royal blood and a descendant of the Principality
of Catalonia. Penedo adduces further material from genealogies concerning
the house of the Manrique de Lara family, the first Manrique of whom was
"Conde e Señor de Molina" (38). In this connection he invokes Tirso's early
play *Cómo han de ser los amigos* [*How Friends Should Be*], which has as its subject the foundation of the Señorío of Molina de Aragón by the Don Manrique
Pérez de Lara in question (d. 1164). Penedo even points to rough doodles
from Téllez's pen on pages of the *Historia General* manuscript describing large
millwheel circles which could be construed as recalling the coat-of-arms of the
Molinas with its half mill-wheel at the foot of the escutcheon beneath a tower
argent on an azure field. One might say of these various claims that Penedo
makes an intriguing and tolerably strong circumstantial case here, but even he
admits that: "Los indicios que poseo no son todavía decisivos ..." (37) [The
pieces of evidence which I possess are not yet conclusive ...].

The next two theories have in common their notion of a putative gesture of self-baptism based on Tirso's admiration for a real person. In the
first hypothesis the admired person would be the outstanding 16th-century
theologian and author of the *Concordia liberi arbitrii cum gratiae donis*
[*The Harmony of Free Will with Gifts of Grace*] (1588), P. Luis de Molina
S. J. (1535–1600). This was the work that set out most thoroughly the
Jesuit case for the freedom of the human will in harmony or "concord" with
the gifts of grace and God's ability to know or foresee human actions. It
was immensely controversial in its day and precipitated a theological civil
war with the Dominicans in Spain. Defenders of this theory, however, see
Tirso's theological positions in dramas dealing with grace, salvation and damnation (such as *El condenado por desconfiado* [*Damned By Despair*]) as being
quite in tune with Molinist optimism and opposed to the neo-Augustinian
or crypto-Calvinist doctrines of predestination such as those advertised by

Tirso's fellow Mercedarian, P. Pedro Franco de Guzmán (a close relative of the royal favorite, Gaspar de Guzmán y Pimentel, Count-Duke of Olivares). Franco de Guzmán saw himself, doubtless correctly, as the person being condemned by *El condenado por desconfiado* in the figure of the devout hermit Paulo who, misreading an ambiguous message from the Devil in disguise, despairs of God's salvific grace and is consigned to Hell in the play's ending. It was through Guzmán's machinations that the *Primera parte* of Tirso's plays printed in Madrid in 1626 was destroyed, because it contained the offending play as twelfth in sequence. *El condenado* did not appear in print till 1635 in the *Segunda* [Second] *parte*.

The second person supposedly admired by Tirso to the point of taking her name as his own is the Medieval Queen, Doña María de Molina (1265–1321). In her edition of 1958, Blanca de los Ríos expressed boundless praise for Téllez's historical saga dramatizing the career of Queen María de Molina as Regent for her small son Fernando IV—*La prudencia en la mujer* [*Prudence in a Woman*]—but she did not suggest this admiration affected Tirso's choice of name. Writing in 1948, however, Ruth Lee Kennedy made exactly this claim. Commenting on the pseudonym Tirso de Molina, she surmised:

> And the form his nom de plume took may possibly be related to the protagonist of *La prudencia*, with whom he shared the name of Téllez. For it must not be forgotten that María de Molina was descended on her mother's side from a Téllez. She was the daughter of Don Alfonso *de Molina* (son of the union of Alfonso IX of León and Doña Berenguela the Great) and of his third wife, Doña Mayor Alfonso de Meneses, who was the granddaughter (on the maternal side) of don Alfonso *Téllez* de Meneses. (Kennedy 1131–90, 1179n86; emphasis original)[8]

While intriguing, this hypothesis—so heavily dependent on remote medieval genealogies and a single play—comes across as a little like grasping at straws.

The fourth theory is to be inferred from the text on the death certificate of Gabriel's father Andrés López, reported on and transcribed by Luis Vázquez Fernández in 1987. In the Madrid church of Santa Cruz's parish registers we may read:

> En 24 de agosto de 1618 falleció Andrés López, criado de Don Pedro de Mexía de Tobar. Recibió los Sa[n]ctos Sacramentos de mano de Don Xptoval D'Olmos, teniente de Cura de la dicha yglesia. No hiço testamento, que no hubo de qué. Enterrólo de limosna el dicho Don Pedro. Dio a la fábrica quinçe Reales" (Vázquez, "Apuntes" 18)

> [On August 24, 1618 the servant of Don Pedro Mexía de Tovar, Andrés López, passed away. He received the Holy Sacraments from the hands of the parish priest of said church, Don Cristóbal de Olmos. He did not make a will since he had

no estate [to bequeath]. He was buried by the charity of said Don Pedro who
donated fifteen Reals to the church maintenance fund].

The employer and benefactor of Gabriel's deceased father was, then, a scion of
the Mexía de Tovar family, previously Lord of Molina de Herrera and—as of
June 29, 1627 and by the grace of King Philip IV—first Count of Molina de
Herrera. Writing in an electronic mail on May 2, 2012, the expert on Spanish
peerage Alfonso Ceballos-Escalera described Don Pedro as first Count of
Molina de Herrera, Lord of the towns of Monterrubio and Tovar by purchase
of the jurisdiction in 1627, Lord of Molina de Herrera, Santo Domingo de las
Posadas and Pozancos, alderman *in perpetuum* of Ávila and Toro, knight of
the Order of Santiago (1599), of the Council of the Treasury and the Council
of Indies, and principal majordomo of Cardinal-Prince Ferdinand of Austria
(the younger brother of Philip IV) [Ceballos-Escalera].

The strength of the Molina de Herrera theory lies not only in the employer-
employee relationship between the Count and Gabriel's father Andrés López,
but in the wider family's connections with the mature Fray Gabriel Téllez.
For example, the second wife of Don Pedro Mexía de Tovar (as of 1613)—a
witness on his baptismal certificate—was Doña Elvira Clara de Paz y Pacheco
from a distinguished family in Salamanca. She was related to Alonso Antonio de Paz, alderman (*regidor*) of Salamanca (as of April 26, 1618) and the
dedicatee of Tirso's *Doze comedias nuevas* [*Twelve New Comedias*] (Seville,
1627). Tirso thanks him effusively in the Prologue, puns gratefully on his
name meaning "Peace" (since the recent years had been politically stormy for
Gabriel) and makes it clear he had often shared the *regidor's* bounteous table
when Paz stayed in Madrid. The godmother on Gabriel's baptismal certificate was Doña Francisca de Aguilar, the mother of the Francisco López de
Aguilar y Coutiño who defended Lope de Vega's writings in the *Expostulatio
spongiae* [*The Repudiation of* The Sponge] of 1618 (as did Tirso throughout
his career). Gabriel Téllez thus emerges as a man well-placed in the arena of
politics and family patronage in Spain, as well as in the literary life of Madrid.

Conclusion

It is impossible in the final instance to be dogmatic in answering the questions
posed at the beginning of this piece, because it is impossible posthumously or
even a priori to get inside Fray Gabriel Téllez's head. But we have said that
some theories may be mutually reinforcing and, in the case of St. Thyrsus (San
Tirso) and the Bacchic Thyrsos (Tirso), we have a seductive instance of this.
By this I mean that the two dimensions of the word Θύρσος (Thyrsos): 1) the
Christian martyr and 2) the god of drama, wine and revels—etymologically

of identical Greek origin—actually fit our dramatist like a glove. In the first place, the Spanish cult of San Tirso represents both the explicitly Christian and ecclesiastical side of the man and—after 1595—the strong apostolic associations with Fray Gabriel's beloved Toledo (where, as he tells us in the *Cigarrales*, he had a warmer welcome than in his native Madrid) (Vázquez, *Cigarrales* 200).[9] The rod of the drama-god Dionysus represents Téllez as Lord of Misrule and conjures up a world of contravention, liberation, anarchy (*La república al revés* [*The World Upside-down*]), and of polymorphous sexual inversion in the Golden Age theater. We may imagine the surge of elation when Gabriel first hit on this semantic crux for his chosen persona.

As regards the choice of the bogus *apellido* [surname] de Molina, it is hard, in the light of Luis Vázquez's archival discoveries (and his irrefutable documentation of Fray Gabriel's family, alliances and patrons), to contest the idea that Tirso chose the title of his father's longtime employer Don Pedro Mexía de Tovar as his inspiration—Lord and (after 1627) first Count of Molina de Herrera. This was after all the man who thought so highly of Gabriel's father that he paid the funeral expenses of Andrés López on the penniless man's death in 1618. P. Vázquez even proposes Gabriel worked as a shepherd on the extensive Molina de Herrera grazing-lands of the Mexía de Tovar as a boy (amid the fighting-bulls bred in Jarama 20 miles southeast of Madrid), a suggestion which may not be too far-fetched (Vázquez, "Apuntes" 20). In the sense that Gabriel Téllez was connected with the earldom of Molina de Herrera via his father—and his father's protective overlord and benefactor Don Pedro Mexía de Tovar—we may say that "de Molina" had virtually the force of a true patronymic.

Notes

1. Quoted by Luis Vázquez Fernández, ed., *Cigarrales de Toledo* 15. The Spanish translation is that of P. Manuel Penedo Rey. The Mercedarians had three houses in Italy with publishing facilities during this period: at Naples, Palermo (the capital of Sicily), and Cagliari (the capital of Sardinia).

2. Quoted by Vázquez (*Cigarrales* 15–16). Cervantes praised two Mercedarian playwrights in his *Viaje del Parnaso* (1613), one by name—Alonso Remón—and the second (by implication) Gabriel Téllez. Cervantes's probable reference to Tirso is confirmed by the line: "Sus glorias tiene en Alcalá esculpidas" ("He has his glories carved in Alcalá"), since we know Tirso was studying theology in Alcalá de Henares at that time. For Tirso's residence in Alcalá and the citation by Cervantes, see Penedo Rey 47n29, 48n31.

3. The same formula appears in the *Aprobación* 99.

4. The respective quotations are from folio 3r and folio 3v of the volume. The *Tercera parte* came out on the Tortosa presses of Francisco Martorell in 1634. For a thorough

discussion of the controverted nephew's collaboration and real existence, see Henry W. Sullivan and Luciana da Cunha Monteiro 101–36, especially n16 and n17.
5. For some real historical acquaintances of Tirso in Toledo, see Gerald E. Wade.
6. This website also provides a reproduction of a Greek vase showing the Maenad holding a *thyrsos*. For the pine cone as semen, see also <http:// pt.wikipedia.org/wiki/ Tirso>.
7. Quoted in McManus.
8. The article was translated and reprinted without changes as "'La prudencia en la mujer' y el ambiente que la produjo" ["'Prudence in a Woman' and the Ambient That Brought It Forth"].
9. Describing his own boat's entry into the poetry competition on the Tagus, our playwright wrote the following: "Tirso, que, aunque humilde pastor de Manzanares, halló en la llaneza generosa de Toledo mejor acogida que en su patria – tan apoderada de la envidia extranjera …" (Cf. Vázquez, *Cigarrales* 200).

Works Cited

Ceballos-Escalera, Alfonso. "Re: LOS MESSIA Y MESSIA DE TOVAR DE VILLAC-ASTÍN." Web log comment. *Heraldria.com.* 25 Oct. 2009. Web. 24 May 2013. <http://www.heraldaria.com/phorum5/read.php?3,2710,3317>.

Cervantes Saavedra, Miguel de. Capítulo 4. *El viaje del Parnaso. Obras completas.* Comp. Ángel Valbuena Prat. Vol. 1. Madrid: Aguilar, 1967. 84a–84b. Print.

Cotarelo y Mori, Emilio. *Bibliografía de las controversias sobre la licitud del teatro en España.* Madrid: Estudios de la "Revista de archivos, bibliotecas y museos," 1904. Print.

Covarrubias y Orozco, Sebastián de. *Tesoro de la lengua castellana o española.* Madrid: Luis Sánchez, 1611. Print.

"DIONYSUS: Greek God of Wine & Festivity." *DIONYSUS: Greek God of Wine & Festivity.* Web. 23 May 2014. <http://www.theoi.com/Olympios/Dionysos.html>.

"Dionysus." *Wikipedia.* Wikimedia Foundation. Web. 23 May 2013. <http://en.wikipedia.org/wiki/Dionysus>.

Easterling, P. E. "A Show for Dionysus." *The Cambridge Companion to Greek Tragedy.* Cambridge, UK: Cambridge UP, 1997. 36–53. Print.

Galoppe, Raúl A. "Género y confusión." *Género y confusión en el teatro de Tirso de Molina.* Madrid: Pliegos, 2001. 58–98. Print.

García-Arenal, Mercedes, and Fernando Rodríguez Mediano. Trans. Consuelo López-Morillas. *The Orient in Spain: Converted Muslims, the Forged Lead Books of Granada, and the Rise of Orientalism.* Leiden, Neth.: Brill, 2013. Print.

Hartzenbusch, Juan Eungenio, ed. "Tercera parte." *Comedias escogidas de Fray Gabriel Téllez (el Maestro Tirso de Molina).* Madrid: Hernando, 1930. Print.

Kennedy, Ruth L. *"La prudencia en la mujer" and the Ambient That Brought It Forth.* New York: MLA, 1948. Print.

———. "'La prudencia en la mujer' y el ambiente que la produjo." *Tirso de Molina: Ensayos sobre la biografía y la obra del Padre Maestro Fray Gabriel Téllez.* Madrid: Revista "Estudios," 1949: 223–93. Print.

McManus, Barbara F. "Dionysus and Greek Drama." Web. 23 May 2014. <http://www2. cnr.edu/home/bmcmanus/tragedy/dion.html>.

Menédez y Pelayo, Marcelino, ed. "Una obra inédita de Tirso de Molina: *Vida de la Santa María de Cervellón.*" *Revista de archivos, bibliotecas y museos* 3a. época 18 (1908): 1–17, 243–56. Print.

Penedo Rey, Manuel. *Historia general de la orden de Nuestra Señora de Las Mercedes.* Madrid: Provincia de la Merced de Castilla, 1973. Print.

Stroud, Matthew D. *Fatal Union: A Pluralistic Approach to the Spanish Wife-Murder Comedias.* Lewisburg, PA: Bucknell UP, 1990. Print.

———. *Plot Twists and Critical Turns: Queer Approaches to Early Modern Spanish Theater.* Lewisburg, PA: Bucknell UP, 2007. Print.

———. *The Play in the Mirror: Lacanian Perspectives on Spanish Baroque Theater.* Lewisburg, PA: Bucknell UP, 1996. Print.

Sullivan, Henry W. "Ecclesiastical Controversy over Calderón." *Two Hundred Years of Calderonian Criticism.* Diss. Harvard U, 1970. 13–32. Print.

———, and Luciana da Cunha Monteiro. "Tirso de Molina and His Nephew: The Case for the Real Existence of Francisco Lucas de Ávila." *Bulletin of the Comediantes* 64.2 (1965): 246–72. Print.

———, and Raúl A. Galoppe. Introduction. *Tirso de Molina: His Originality Then and Now.* Ottawa: Dovehouse Editions Canada, 1996. 9–14. Print.

"Tirso." *Wikipedia.* Web. 24 May 2014. <http://en.wikipedi.org/wiki/Tirso>.

Vargas, Bernardo. *Chronica Sacri Et Militaris Ordinis B. Mariae De Mercede Redemptionis Captivorvm.* Panormi [Palermo]: Ioannes Baptista Maringus, 1619. Print.

Vázquez Fernández, Luis. "Apuntes para una nueva biografía de Tirso." *Tirso de Molina, vida y obra: Actas del I simposio internacional sobre Tirso, Washington, noviembre 1984.* Ed. Josep María Solá-Solè and Juan Vázquez Fernández. Madrid: Revista "Estudios," 1987. 9–50. Print.

———. Ed. *Cigarrales de Toledo.* By Tirso de Molina. Madrid: Clásicos Castalia, 1996. Print.

Wade, Gerald E. "Tirso's *Cigarrales de Toledo*: Some Clarifications and Identifications." *Hispanic Review* 33 (1965): 246–72. Print.

Inquisitorial Pressures: Honour as Metaphor on the Boards

ISAAC BENABU
The Hebrew University of Jerusalem

In any discussion about the relationship between art and reality oftentimes we will hear quoted what Shakespeare wrote in *Hamlet* about the aim of theatre "both at first and now, was and is as, to hold as 'twere the mirror up to nature" (III.2). But Shakespeare's remark is all too general because it does not specify the angle at which that mirror is to be held: in other words, what aspect of nature is to be reflected and from what angle, distortions included. These remarks are pertinent to the subject under discussion here: the honour theme on the boards and its relation to life in 17th-century Spain. For the concept of honour in Spanish literature as a whole, and in the 17th-century Spanish comedia in particular, differs from European treatments of honour, which are often related to moral questions and questions of integrity.

The public theatre in 16th-and 17th-century Spain, or even the Court theatre for that matter, would have been hard put to compete with the spectacles staged by the Inquisition itself. I am thinking of the *autos de fe* [acts of faith]. When we say Inquisition we think for instance of racial prejudice, laws which circumscribe individual freedom, public spectacles of cruelty such as the *auto de fe*. However, we think less of the constricting atmosphere created within Spanish society from the 15th century onwards, the years in which the Inquisition held sway over the lives of the man in the street, and the permutations which this restrictiveness went through in successive years. Referring to this limiting phenomenon, Domínguez Ortiz has written:

> ... the Spanish people lived for centuries haunted by the phantom which they themselves conjured up. Commissaries, responsible for "proofs", trod relentlessly across the land, interrogating witnesses and collating documents in the

home towns of those who aspired to a position governed by statute. All who were candidates for posts of this kind wondered anxiously whether the investigations would uncover, or enemies would invent, some unknown Jewish great-grandfather. There is no doubt that this specifically Spanish environment ... contributed to the pathos enveloping the Spaniard of the Golden Century ... (220)

Some background remarks: the *comedias de corral* [of the public theatre], plays in which the honour theme figures prominently, were presented in the public theatres of the day. In his treatise on the *comedia* of 1609, Lope de Vega recommends honour as a powerful motif "porque mueven con fuerza ..." (18) [because it moves (spectators) deeply], but he doesn't explain why this should be so. These plays work on the stage largely through action and the medium of utterance: not the word as it appears in the playscript but the word performed. Other forms of theatre may express their theatricality in different ways: the three-dimensional quality of the artform allows for many transformations. Yet a theatrical form which draws heavily on the spoken word in performance necessarily looks to factors like the vocalization of speech, physiognomic expression, physical gesture and movement to communicate theatrical effect. This is not to say that other theatrical means are not used to produce effect. Silent theatrical transmitters like costume, props, stage-space, stage levels, and the positioning points of access to and exit from the stage clearly play important functions. But they do so in service to the utterance. It may explain why stage-directions in the comedia are largely incorporated into what the actors say. The playwright "speaks" to the actor and audience alike by transcending the playtext: this is also how he must speak to the reader (Benabu, *Reading* 70). All the foregoing is relevant when considering the way honour appears in a theatrical context, what stage mood it creates, and how it influences the world of the play. For we shall not find many direct references to the Inquisition in the theatre of Golden Age Spain, understandably so since the censor present at every performance would have been quick to exercise his powers.

I am by no means the first to consider the relation the theme of honour as represented on the stage had to the value of honour in real-life in 17th-century Spain. A long list of scholars (some are quoted below) have pondered the question, and they include Américo Castro, Antony van Beysterveldt, Cyril Jones and Melveena MacKendrick. And we do well to question its application when discussing the relation between history (more specifically, the Inquisition) and the way honour is used by playwrights, which is what I shall attempt to do in this paper. But some historico-sociological considerations first as well as some background on the *comedia*.

Many have tried to explain the frequency with which the honour theme occurs in 17th-century theatre and the strong feelings it evokes, both on and offstage, as reflecting the concern of the age with purity of blood (*limpieza de sangre*). Américo Castro, for example, in his book *De la edad conflictiva* [*Of the Conflicted Age*] distinguishes between contemporary European and Spanish concepts of honour, where honour is not a moral attribute but a status conferred and confirmed by others, i.e., how others see you. In 1966 van Beysterveldt published a book which links the concern for purity of blood with the honour theme on the *comedia* stage. Cyril Jones, in an article entitled "Honor in the Spanish Golden Age Drama: Its Relation to Real Life and to Morals" wrote:

> There is no doubt that the theme of honour in the plays is not a complete fiction, and that there were cases in real life similar to those which occurred in the theatre, where we know them as cases of honour. But it is perhaps worth noting that the feature which the cases found in the records had in common was that they were sensational, and that they were sensational because, although perhaps not very rare, they were at least not normal ... Honour was used as a theme in literary types other than the drama, and the fact that honour was frequently condemned by moralists and didactic writers is evidence that it must have had some importance in real life as well as in the drama. (200)

But after considering the aims of drama, Jones concludes "the justification of the honour theme in Spanish drama of the Golden Age is to be found where the dramatists themselves found it, in its success as a motive" ("Honor" 209)—which recalls Lope de Vega's recommendation quoted earlier.

The well-known historian of 17th-century Spain, Domínguez Ortiz, also conceives of Spanish society at the time as being obsessed with the question of *limpieza de sangre*, and the honour theme on the stage as a reflection of this social obsession. In an article published in 1984, Melveena McKendrick comes close to the line of argument pursued in this paper. She writes:

> My contention is, briefly, that the obsessional energy is in both cases one and the same, that the honour/vengeance motif in the wife/murder plays and others mimics not the sexual mores of the age ... but the psychology of the age's obsession with *limpieza de sangre* ... What seems to me to have been at work here is largely intuitive translation of obsessional energy from one area of experience to another, a process of mimetic transference. ("Honour" 322)

And she concludes:

> A conscious transposition of the obsession with immaculacy and pollution from one ideological framework to another was scarcely necessary, for both were different manifestations of the same compulsion to see oneself only through the eyes of other people, to define oneself in relation to the social norms of the day. ("Honour" 335)

It is necessary to highlight some aspects of society in 17ᵗʰ-century Spain in order to understand what may lie behind the popularity of the honour theme on the boards. I shall cite some of the arguments advanced by McKendrick because they provide essential background to my reading of *El médico de su honra* [*The Physician of His Honour*] that follows:

> In the fifteenth, sixteenth and seventeenth centuries the gradual loss of func-
> tion and the accelerating emergence of a social climbing middle class made other
> forms of self-definition essential, and central to these was the *limpieza de sangre*,
> by which the others stood or fell. Restrictive barriers had to be erected where
> before none had been necessary, and the respect society owed its nobles had to
> be jealously guarded. This respect, however, was not man's to take but society's
> to give. What really mattered was not whether a man was noble and *limpio* and
> therefore honourable, but whether he was considered to be so by his fellows, and
> recourse to *ejecutorias* (patents of nobility), witnesses, and even the law, was insuf-
> ficient compensation for a sullied social reputation. Thus the possibility of dis-
> grace was an ever-present spectre that haunted all but the inviolate minority. The
> noble, particularly the *caballero* without a title, was condemned to a life of eternal
> vigilance over something over which he himself exercised little control, to a life,
> in other words, that was a permanent crisis of social identity. ("Honour" 330–31)

To conclude this first part of the article: I have sought to provide different scholarly evaluations of the climate of oppression at work in 17ᵗʰ-century
Spain, which I have termed "inquisitorial pressures." These are the pressures
I shall be analysing in my reading of Calderón's *El médico*. I close this section
by quoting from a later article by McKendrick, in which she explores the
changes undergone by Spanish society with regard to honour in the period
under discussion:

> The view that the very suspicion or articulated possibility of dishonour constitutes
> dishonour itself, is predicated, of course, upon the idea that honour is both a
> man's estimation of his own worth and society's acknowledgement of that claim.
> Dishonour or its possibility therefore involves a loss of authority and control
> inseparable in a patriarchal society from manhood ... [I]n societies based on the
> assumption of social inequality and hierarchy ... the man who loses his honour
> loses his place in the hierarchy and therefore his identity. ("Calderón" 139–40)

* * *

It is true enough to observe, as Stroud has done, that "an interesting murder has always provided good dramatic plot material" (13). For there can
be no doubt that honour seems to have provided contemporary playwrights
with the potential for high drama. It supplied plots with powerful conflictive-
ness, plots which generate strong theatrical tensions in countless plays. What
is more, the honour theme provided the Spanish playwrights with all the

permutations for moving an audience that Fate had in classical tragedy. All of this, together with what was discussed in the first part of this article suggests that honour as a theme could have had some metaphorical function too.

These remarks provide background for the theatrical considerations underlying the use of the honour theme in 17th-century Spain; the example I have chosen to illustrate my analysis constitutes one of the leading plays of the period, Calderón de la Barca's *El médico de su honra*. I have studied this play in great detail elsewhere (Benabu, *Reading* 36–52): what I propose to do here is to analyse the world of the play so as to consider the nature of the pressures exercised, which may reflect the social pressures alluded to in the first half of this article.

Turning to *El médico*, I shall first try to determine the mood at the opening. Mood at the opening of any play is a theatrical device of singular importance since it will determine how the audience is engaged in the action. From the start the mood created in this play is one where suspicion reigns, where a character's actions are conditioned by what others will think of him. From the start the mood created on stage is one where rumour and suspicion are dominant: "si oyen las paredes, / los troncos, don Arias, ven" (I.33–34) [Walls have ears, Don Arias /and trees have eyes to see]. Very soon we find that we are in a world where a concern for honour, in the peculiarly Spanish sense outlined earlier, overrides all other nobler pursuits, where emotions must be painfully repressed to protect honour, and where suffering for honour's sake knows no limit. Gutierre, the tragic protagonist, plays a very small part in the introduction of these themes; it is Mencía his wife who is involved in these actions at the outset when she is unexpectedly confronted by her former lover.

At the end of Act I, Gutierre is imprisoned for challenging another before the King: however he regrets, not imprisonment, but the fact he will not be able to see the wife he loves:

> No siento en desdicha tal
> ver riguroso y cruel
> al Rey; sólo siento que hoy,
> Mencía, no te he de ver. (I.997–1000)

> [I am not by half so vexed / by the fierce rigour of the King / as that today / I shall not see Mencía.]

Calderón has shown here that though honour carries much weight with Gutierre, his love for his wife is very powerful too. And this is the first intimate impression we gain of Gutierre by the end of Act I.

In Act II, however, accident rather than design arouses Gutierre's suspicions about his wife's fidelity. I say accident because he misjudges the evidence of what he sees. But in the world of honour, it is impossible to ask questions to ascertain whether his perceptions are correct. Instead he must observe what he calls "una dieta de silencio" (II.1674–75) [a diet of silence]: the parallel with the social obsession outlined before is very clear. As the play progresses, Gutierre undergoes a growing isolation. Even when he thinks he has ascertained his wife's guilt, he judges or rather misjudges what he sees; yet, there is no blame which attaches to Gutierre since he cannot but help arrive at the conclusions he does. The world of the play presents a reality which conspires against the individual. In a moving soliloquy midway through the second act, Gutierre tries to apply logic to dispel the doubts which have invaded him. But in so doing the protagonist expresses his concern with identity: as has already been mentioned, honour and identity are closely aligned. For it is when the character feels his honour is compromised, that he tries to assert his identity. The ironic use of the phrase "soy quien soy" (II.1650) [I am who I am] (which is of Biblical origin and attributed to God), is uttered by Gutierre in this case as he struggles to convince himself that his honour is intact. Doubts torment him well before he gives expression to them, for a nagging sense that his honour has been compromised lurks behind his vain attempt to suppress his doubts. Pathetically, therefore, he tries to weigh the evidence to clear Mencía of any wrongdoing, against a much stronger sense of doubt and suspicion:

> Y así acortemos discursos,
> pues todos juntos se cierran
> en que Mencía es quien es,
> y soy quien soy; no hay quien pueda
> borrar de tanto esplendor
> la hermosura y la pureza. (II.1647–52)

> [But now / Our arguments must be cut shorter since / They [proofs] all concur in this—that she's Mencía / And I am who I am. No one alive / Can cast a slur upon the bright effulgence / Of so much beauty and such purity. (Trans. Campbell 45)]

Before continuing with the soliloquy, the actor should pause to mark the transition as doubts override the logical process:

> Pero sí puede, mal digo;
> que al sol una nube negra
> si no la mancha, la turba …
> A peligro estáis, honor … (II.1653–59)

> [And yet—yes! it can be, I speak wrongly / For a black cloud can dim the sun, although / It cannot blot it out … / You are in peril, Honour … (Trans. Campbell 45)]

In the first part of this article this mental state was described as obsessive. What the play shows, as one might expect of theatre, is the pathology of an obsession which grows steadily. And from the start of the soliloquy, the audience is sensible to Gutierre's isolation, and the fact that honour condemns him to silence his doubts. Herein lies the irony of one who strives to judge a situation impartially, when the extent of his emotional involvement impedes any objective appreciation of the situation.

As Act III progresses we see time and again that the demands that Honour places on Gutierre only compel him to arrive at the wrong conclusion (Mencía is entirely innocent throughout). Only the all-knowing spectator possesses the necessary detachment to appreciate the inexorability of Gutierre's plight.

A single image, of unusually poetic poignancy and originality, and which is evoked by both Gutierre and Mencía, underscores the play's tragic mood. Upon realizing that the words they speak when they are alone could compromise their honour, both husband and wife invoke the air with which those words were exhaled to return to their mouths: an impossibility of course, which is caught in this tragic image.

Gutierre goes on the evidence of what he sees, but isn't human vision similarly condemned to this limitation, as shown in the earliest classical tragedies? Herein lies the tragic focus Calderón has given the action of this play, and it recalls the isolation, the tragic plight of those who suffered from the dictates of *limpieza* and who lived under its threatening shadow. This is precisely the picture Calderón paints of his protagonist at the plays' end. Gutierre is tragic because he is the victim not of any supernatural force, nor of any evil individual, like the heroes of so many Greek and Renaissance tragedies, but of a reality which conspires against him from the start: it misleads him and it condemns him to silence.

The desperate off-stage cries at the end are but a hint of Gutierre's silent anagnorisis: killing his wife only increases the burden of his pain, for the world he inhabits condemns him to suffer his guilt by the very means with which he executed his crime, that is, in silence. The sense of total isolation at the end (he is left alone on the stage), where Gutierre is left with no exit, is what undeniably confers the status of tragedy on the play.

On the stage then, the price paid for observing the demands of the honour code at the end of Calderón's play, on the one hand, and in the society of 17th-century Spain, the threat posed by the concern with *limpieza*, on the other hand, focus on the individual caught in a web which constricts and ultimately defeats him: this is the stuff of tragedy on the stage, and an expression of a phenomenon which contributed to a disintegration of the social fabric and to the decline of Imperial Spain.

Works Cited

Benabu, Isaac. *Reading for the Stage: Calderón and his Contemporaries*. Woodbridge, UK: Tamesis, 2003. Print.

———. *On the Boards and in the Press: Calderón's* Las tres justicias en una. Kassel, Ger.: Reichenberger, 1991. Print.

Calderón de la Barca, Pedro. *El médico de su honra*. Ed. Don Cruickshank. Madrid: Castalia, 1987. Print.

———. *The Surgeon of his Honour*. Trans. Roy Campbell. Madison: U of Wisconsin P, 1960. Print.

Castro, Américo. *De la edad conflictiva*. Madrid: Taurus, 1961. Print.

Domínguez Ortiz, Antonio. *La sociedad española en el Siglo XVII*. Madrid: Consejo Superior de Investigaciones Científicas, 1963. Print.

———. *The Golden Age of Spain*. Trans. James Casey. London: Weidenfeld and Nicolson, 1971. Print.

Jones, Cyril A. "Honor in the Spanish Golden Age Drama: Its Relation to Real Life and to Morals." *Bulletin of Hispanic Studies* 35 (1958): 199–210. Print.

———. "Spanish Honour as Historical Phenomenon, Convention and Artistic Motif." *Hispanic Review* (1965): 32–39. Print.

McKendrick, Melveena. "Honour/Vengeance in the Spanish comedia: a Case of Mimetic Transference." *Modern Language Review* 79 (1984): 313–35. Print.

———. "Calderón and the Politics of Honour." *Bulletin of Hispanic Studies* 52 (1993): 135–46. Print.

Stroud, Matthew D. *Fatal Union: A Pluralistic Approach to the Spanish Wife-Murder Comedias*. Lewisburg, PA: Bucknell UP, 1990. Print.

van Beysterveldt, Antony A. *Répercussions du souci de la pureté de sang sur la conception de l'honneur dans la "comedia nueva" espagnole*. Leiden, Neth.: Brill, 1966. Print.

Vega Carpio, Lope Félix de. *Arte nuevo de hacer comedias en este tiempo*. Madrid: Espasa Calpe, 1967. Print.

Staging the Fall in 16th-Century Spain: *The* Aucto del peccado de Adán

RONALD E. SURTZ
Princeton University

Para Matt Stroud, maestro de la ciencia del bien y del mal

The anonymous *Aucto del peccado de Adán* [*Play of Adam's Sin*] is one of 96 religious plays found in the so-called *Códice de autos viejos* [*Codex of Old Plays*] that was compiled in the 16th century, probably between 1570 and 1578. In this essay I discuss the play's staging and the idiosyncratic features of its dramatization of Genesis. I give special attention to the twin motifs of clothing and nakedness, speculating on the role that costumes or their lack may have performed in the work's staging and reception. Finally, I examine how in performance the *Aucto* uses two contrasting modes of music, harmonious for Adam and Eve, raucous and demonic for Lucifer and his diabolic henchmen.

At first glance, the play appears to be a fairly straightforward dramatization of the account of the Fall in Genesis, and that is fundamentally the case. There are moments, however, when the work distances itself from the Bible. While Genesis offers no reason for the serpent's initiative, the Spanish play motivates Lucifer's conduct by making him envious of the favor that God has shown to Adam and Eve because they are destined to occupy the heavenly thrones left empty by his fellow fallen angels.[1] According to Medieval theologians, Adam and Eve sinned out of pride, for they aspired to possess God's knowledge of good and evil (St. Thomas Aquinas, *Summa Theologica* 2a 2ae, Q.163 [IV.1858]). However, in the Castilian play pride is not an issue; rather, it is Gula [Gluttony] and Avariçia [Greed], Lucifer's two allegorical companions, who collaborate with him in leading Adam and Eve into sin.[2] The Fall itself is not dramatized until lines 137–224. However, in a preliminary scene (I.89–111), Gula and Avariçia hatch their plot to bring about Adam and Eve's downfall by inducing them to eat the forbidden fruit. However rudimentary, this initial episode anticipates Calderón's far more sophisticated technique in his *autos sacramentales* [allegorical Eucharist plays] of having a character—often the Devil—on the stage conceive a scheme that will later be put into practice, thus generating the action of the play (Parker 83–84, 90).

When Lucifer, disguised as a serpent, enters hissing, he affirms that he will attempt to overcome the woman, for she is the weaker vessel (I.137–41). However, unlike in Genesis, in the *Aucto* Eve creates dramatic tension when she initially resists the serpent's flattering words.[3] Finding the apple delicious, she encourages Adam to taste its sweetness. As Eve had done previously, Adam initially resists—thus creating further dramatic tension—, but ends up tasting the fruit, not out of pride, but rather in order to please Eve and to avoid offending her (I.217–24; cf. Muir 69). When God confronts Adam and Eve, as in Genesis, Adam puts the blame on Eve, but in the Castilian play he adds that he only ate the apple to please her (I.346). Thus, in a sense the *Aucto del peccado de Adán* attributes the Fall to Adam and Eve's love for one another.

It was common for Medieval plays based on the Fall to mention its theological implications and especially to anticipate the atonement (Muir 68; cf. *Teatre bíblic* 117). The *Aucto del peccado de Adán* is no exception, for its doctrinal meaning is incorporated into the text from the moment Adam and Eve sin. For example, the promise of the Redemption is implicit in Lucifer's narration of the parable of the Good Samaritan when he recounts that Adam sought to occupy the very throne that the demon once held (I.274–75). The Devil's first-person narrative goes on to say that as a result of his encounter in the guise of a robber (here not several robbers as in the Gospel of Luke) with Adam on the road to Jericho, he left the traveler wounded and despoiled of his garment of innocence. When Lucifer, still identified with the robber from the gospel parable, brags about his victory over the unfortunate traveler, identified with Adam, he unwittingly gives the play theological density and dramatic irony. If the audience was familiar with both the biblical parable and with standard medieval interpretations of it, it would know that the Adam-figure would be redeemed, for "Christ is the good Samaritan who places man upon his own body and brings him to the Church" (Wailes 210).

Later, when God sentences the serpent to crawl upon its belly, as in Genesis, he adds that since the serpent led a woman to sin, another woman, a virgin, will crush its head (I.382–86). Thanks to the Eva/Ave anagram, the audience would understand that the Virgin Mary, the Second Eve, was to remedy the First Eve's sin by giving birth to the Redeemer, the Second Adam.

Finally, the last pages of the play greatly amplify the Genesis narrative. In the Bible, it is God himself who casts Adam and Eve out of Paradise. Here, as in certain other European dramatizations of the Fall, it is an angel that expels them (Muir 70; cf. *Teatre bíblic* 116–17). Moreover, in the Spanish play, the angel consoles Adam with the promise of humankind's future redemption, thus evoking the doctrine of the atonement. When Adam and Eve are condemned to toil, Adam offers the shame he is suffering as satisfaction for his wickedness (I.424–26). Thus, Adam's repentance begins even before he is cast out of the Garden. And when the pair is about to be expelled from the earthly paradise, Adam recognizes his error and asks the angel for solace; specifically, he seeks to know if he will eventually achieve God's pardon. The angel tells him not to despair of divine goodness, for he will find mercy if he and Eve do penance (I.467–76). And indeed, their exit song implores God's clemency: "Pues nos despedistes vos, / mi Dios, porque os ofendimos, / misericordia pedimos" (I.507–09) [Inasmuch as you threw us out, / oh my God, because we offended you, / we beg for your mercy].

The use of music in the play contributes to the foreshadowing of the eventual, albeit extratextual, happy ending of the atonement, for the musical trajectory of the *Aucto del peccado de Adán* moves from harmony, to harmony shattered, to harmony restored. The play has scarcely begun before Adam and Eve sing a duet in which they give thanks to God (I.21–23). Their literal harmony in song echoes the initial harmony of their blessed state, because, as Aquinas explains, their lower powers were subjected to reason, which in turn was subjected to God (*Light of Faith* I.217–19). Thus, the union of Adam and Eve's voices in song indicates their state of grace, their harmony with God's will. Later, the music and other sound effects turn demonic, for after the Fall, Lucifer orders infernal music to resound and commands his demons to howl (I.242–51). In addition, after the segment in which Lucifer recounts his version of the parable of the Good Samaritan, the demon Asmodeo orders the infernal instruments and the diabolic howls to resound once again. The demon himself explicitly contrasts that hellish cacophony with the previous harmonious music of Adam and Eve's duet, when he commands: "las çelestes cançiones / buelvan en triste clamor" (I.305–06) [let the heavenly songs / become mournful clamor]. It is not difficult to imagine that such a din was intended to be raucous and harsh-sounding, for it has been suggested that "hellish music" on the Medieval stage was characterized by the arrhythmic and out-of-tune shouting of semantically meaningless words (Rastall 111, 116).

Moreover, in the pictorial arts, the soldiers who accompanied Christ during his arrest and the carrying of the cross were sometimes depicted with horns or trumpets in accordance with the use of musical instruments in the

Old Testament during animal sacrifices (Marrow 153–61). For members of the audience who were aware of this musical connection, the diabolic trumpet sounds emanating from Hell would have established yet another association between the Fall and Christ's atoning sacrifice.[4] Finally, when Adam and Eve sing together the song that ends the play (I.507–09), their musical harmony foreshadows the eventual restoration of harmony between God and man, thanks to the future redemption prophesied by the angel.

The *Aucto del peccado de Adán* offers sparse stage directions, few of which refer to costumes. However, it is possible to speculate as to how the actors were dressed by considering the conventions of 15th- and 16th-century stagecraft and by analogy with other Adam and Eve plays. In Medieval Iberia it was normal for demons to wear masks as, for example, in the case of the Corpus Christi plays performed in late 15th-century Toledo (Torroja Menéndez and Rivas Palá 188). The probable ugliness of the masks worn by such evil characters would underscore their diabolical nature, given the close association between ugliness and sin in the symbolic world of the Middle Ages (Surtz 85). Angels too were represented in highly conventionalized terms. In the late Medieval Valencian Adam and Eve play the angel wore a white robe and scarlet gloves, and its wings were attached to a corselet (*Teatre bíblic* 101). For the Feast of Corpus Christi in early 15th-century Valencia angels wore masks (*Staging of Religious Drama* 188), and this may have been so later in the Valencian Adam and Eve play and likewise in Toledo (Torroja Menéndez and Riveras Palá 50). Thus, in late Medieval Spain masks were worn by the otherworldly characters, both the supergood (the angels) and the superevil (the devils). This may have also been the case in staging the *Aucto del peccado de Adán*. In Toledo God wore a crown of tin plate, while in Valencia he wore an alb, a rochet, and a scarlet cope, and displayed rays of light made of tin. The serpent in Toledo wore a wig, a garment of flesh-colored cloth, and a tail stuffed with coarse wool, while in Valencia the serpent had a tail attached to its wide britches (*Teatro en Toledo* 54; *Teatre bíblic* 101). In Toledo the holy protagonists (Christ, the prophets, and the apostles) normally wore diadems or wigs in imitation of the halos that surrounded the heads of sacred characters in Medieval painting.[5] There is some ambiguity, and perhaps a bit of iconographic kinkiness here, for in Toledo not only Adam and Eve, but also the serpent, wore wigs of dyed hemp (Torroja Menéndez and Riveras Palá 54–55).[6] In any case, it is probable that, as suggested above, in the *Aucto del peccado de Adán* Lucifer wore a grotesque mask.[7]

It is not clear if in the staging of the *Aucto del peccado de Adán* the serpent— or its mask—had the human face of a maiden or a matron as it often did in late Medieval iconography (Gussenhoven; Kelly).[8] Since the serpent was probably played by the same actor who played Lucifer, the use of a mask, whether to indicate femaleness or not, was almost unavoidable. Hybridity is often disturbing, so the male actor disguised as a female serpent cuts across and upsets the boundaries between such categories as male and female, natural and supernatural, and human and animal. In addition, such monstrous interspecies cross-dressing would have contributed to the gendering of evil, for at the crucial moment of the temptation of Eve, Avariçia, Gula, and the possibly female-faced serpent, although played by male actors, all played roles gendered "female."[9] No specific costumes are indicated for Avariçia or Gula, but it is possible that they carried such traditional attributes as a purse for Avariçia or foodstuffs for Gula.

The motif of nakedness figures prominently in the Genesis account of the Fall and likewise in the staging of the *Aucto del peccado de Adán*. Although the Bible explicitly states that Adam and Eve were naked before the Fall, it is unlikely that in the Spanish play the two characters actually appeared without clothing in the acting area, for since Eve was probably played by a young boy, his visible male genitalia would have prevented any sort of verisimilitude (cf. Muir 69).[10] What is more likely is that nakedness was simulated by some kind of body stocking. In Toledo, Adam and Eve wore garments made of flesh-colored cloth (Torroja Menéndez and Riveras Palá 54). Likewise, in Lucerne in 1583 and 1597, Adam and Eve wore body stockings over their bare bodies (*Staging of Religious Drama* 130). At the beginning of the *Aucto del peccado de Adán* it is said that Adam and Eve are wearing "vestiduras de orijinal ynoçençia" (I.31–32) [garments of original justice], which, I assume, was some sort of white clothing that denoted their prelapsarian innocence. After the episode of the Fall, Adam and Eve state that they have been stripped of their garments of original justice, and this bit of stage business is explicitly evoked in the play's dialogue when Avariçia tells Lucifer to reach out with his hook, saying: "llevemosles el vestido" (I.234) [let us remove their clothing]. It is worth noting that even as modern representations of the Devil depict him with a pitchfork, in Medieval representations he wielded a crook or hook (*Staging of Religious Drama* 210). Adam and Eve call further attention to their lack of clothing when, as in Genesis, after the Fall they state that they are ashamed of their nakedness and that they still feel naked even after covering themselves with fig leaves (I.309–16).

Nakedness is also relevant to the parable of the Good Samaritan, for the traveler that the Samaritan helped had been stripped naked by the robbers. And as we have seen, the *Aucto*'s rewriting of that parable adds theological density to the Genesis plot by associating the traveler with Adam's Fall and the Samaritan with Christ's redeeming mercy. Then, when God is about to

confront the guilty pair, Adam and Eve hide out of shame for their nakedness (I.335–36), which has come to symbolize their guilt in sinning, for as in
Genesis, God observes that they would not feel shame unless they had sinned
by eating the forbidden fruit (I.337–41). Further wordplay with the concept
of nakedness serves to connect Lucifer's motivation and Adam and Eve's sin
and eventual reward. When Adam and Eve are stripped of their garments,
Lucifer orders their clothing to be hung over the gates of Hell as his spoils
("despojo" [I.237]) of victory.[11] But "despojo" comes from the same verb
despojar that means "to strip." Likewise, it is highly relevant that Lucifer uses
the verb "despojó" when he complains that he was "stripped" of his throne
in Heaven (I.276), for Christ's sacrifice will enable the just to occupy those
very same thrones.

The performance of the *Aucto del peccado de Adán* required a minimal
number of stage properties. We can assume the presence of an apple, and at
one point God refers to "… this tree" (I.46). While the tree could have been
merely evoked by his words, its centrality to the plot of the play would have
made its actual presence a plus.[12] In addition to Lucifer's hook mentioned
above, the text also refers to Eve's distaff and spindle, Adam's spade, and the
angel's sword. The fig leaves Adam and Eve wear to cover their nakedness
were probably visible to the audience, for Adam uses the deictic "estas hojas
de higuera" (I.313) [these fig leaves]. It seems that such props were commonly used in other Medieval Adam and Eve plays. For example, in Valencia
the angel was given a sword and a spade, and it presumably passed the latter
on to Adam at the moment of the Expulsion (*Teatre bíblic* 101).

It is likely that the *Aucto del peccado de Adán* used the simultaneous
staging characteristic of Medieval stagecraft, that is, several locations were
simultaneously visible to the audience. In the Castilian play the two visible
locations would have been the earthly paradise, probably with its emblematic
Tree of the Knowledge of Good and Evil, and the space occupied by Lucifer,
possibly indicated by the entrance to Hell in the form of the gaping jaws of a
monster. It was not usual in 16th-century Spanish plays to actually represent
Hell on stage; rather, the place was merely suggested by the presence of its
entrance (Mateo Alcalá, "Espacio y figuras" 451). This may have been the
case for the *Aucto del peccado de Adán*, since the passage in which Lucifer
declares that he is going to have Adam and Eve's garments of original justice
hung above the gate of Hell (I.259–61) would have greater impact if that
entrance were actually visible to the spectators. And the raucous music said
to emanate from Hell would call attention to some sort of representation of
its entrance if it was likewise manifest to the audience. On the other hand, it
could have sufficed for Hell to be heard, if not seen.

What might the performance of the play have meant to its audience? Here it is useful to return to the particular orientation that the anonymous author of the *Aucto del peccado de Adán* gives to his version of the story. Of course, the episode of the Fall depicts the entry of evil into the world. But the references to the coming atonement that dot the *Aucto del peccado de Adán* call attention to the doctrine of the *félix culpa*, the "fortunate fall," that is, the notion that God sometimes permits evil in order to allow a higher good to come out of it. In the case of the Fall, that greater good is Christ's atonement through the crucifixion. In a sense, the consequences of Adam and Eve's sin continued to be relevant for the play's audience, an audience understood to be obsessed with its own salvation. Adam and Eve's repentance, which begins even before the Expulsion, is a model for the spectators, who learn that they too can find mercy, no matter how great their sins. In their daily lives the spectators were constantly called upon to choose between good and evil, a choice whose consequences are emblematized by the play's staging with its twin poles of the earthly paradise and Hell. By thematizing that notion of space—Paradise or Hell, empty or occupied thrones—the *Aucto* invites, or even compels, its audience to consider its own place on the axis of good and evil and to literally confront such spatial reminders of the choices in front of them. Significantly, in Lucifer's retelling of the parable of the Good Samaritan, the Devil expresses his regret that he was unable to rob the traveler/Adam of his free will (I.287–90). The spectators in turn must exercise their free will. Will they choose good over evil? Will they occupy heavenly thrones or will they be cast out of Paradise and consigned to Hell?

Notes

1. *Colección de autos* 136, 84–86. Subsequent references to the *Aucto del peccado de Adán* will be indicated by the single Act and verse number in parentheses. When God confronts the serpent after the Fall, he accuses it of envy (I.362–66).
2. The relation between gluttony and the Fall is self-evident. In his commentary on Genesis, Ephrem the Syrian (fl. 363–73) argued that it was avarice that led Adam and Eve to follow the serpent's counsel (*Ancient Christian Commentary* 77).
3. This was also the case in the late Medieval Valencian *Misteri de Adam y Eva* (*Teatre bíblic* 106–07).
4. Lucifer's speech specifically evokes the presence of trumpets ("boçinas" [I.248]) in the infernal din.
5. Twycross and Carpenter (17–18), quoting Durandus of Mende, observe that long, flowing hair was an iconographic convention denoting sanctity.
6. Perhaps Lucifer's wig was dyed red in accordance with the flaming hair—symbolizing evil—that he was often given in Medieval iconography (Link 67).

7. It is not clear if Lucifer had feathered or bat-like wings as he often did in the visual arts (Link 67). For the use of masks by diabolic figures in other plays from the same manuscript that contains the *Aucto del peccado de Adán*, see Mateo Alcalá, "Máscaras y tocados."

8. It is also worth recalling that serpent is feminine in Spanish (cf. I.355).

9. However, an extreme misogynist reading of the play is prevented by the fact that it is titled the *Aucto del peccado de Adán*, the "Play of *Adam*'s Sin."

10. Although Lucifer was often depicted naked or wearing a loincloth in Medieval iconography (Link 52–56), it is unlikely that he appeared naked in the staging of the Spanish play.

11. The play also uses "despojo" to refer to the ultimate despoliation, the future consignment of Adam's moral remains to the earth (I.410–11).

12. In contrast, the flowers and the flowing stream, while possibly visible to the audience, could also have been merely evoked by Adam's word painting (I.117–34).

Works Cited

Ancient Christian Commentary on Scripture: Old Testament, I. Ed. Andrew Louth. Downers Grove, IL: InterVarsity P, 2001. Print.

Colección de autos, farsas, y coloquios del siglo XVI. Ed. Léo Rouanet.Vol. 2. Barcelona: "L'Avenç," and Madrid: M. Murillo, 1901. Print.

Gussenhoven, Frances. "The Serpent with a Matron's Face: Medieval Iconography of Satan in the Garden of Eden." *European Medieval Drama* 4 (2001): 207–30. Print.

Kelly, Henry Ansgar. "The Metamorphoses of the Eden Serpent during the Middle Ages and Renaissance." *Viator* 2 (1972): 301–28. Print.

Link, Luther. *The Devil: The Archfiend in Art from the Sixth to the Sixteenth Century.* New York: Abrams, 1995. Print.

Marrow, James H. *Passion Iconography in Northern European Art of the Late Middle Ages and Early Renaissance: A Study of the Transformation of Sacred Metaphor into Descriptive Narrative.* Kortrijk, Belg.: Van Ghemmert, 1979. Print.

Mateo Alcalá, María Luisa. "Espacio y figuras infernales en el *Códice de autos viejos.*" *Actas del VII Congreso de la Asociación Internacional del Siglo de Oro.* Ed. Anthony Close. Vigo, Sp.: Asociación Internacional Siglo de Oro, 2006. 449–54. Print.

———. "Máscaras y tocados para las figuras infernales del Códice de autos viejos." *Teatro de palabras* 5 (2011): 163–95. Print.

Muir, Lynette R. *The Biblical Drama of Medieval Europe.* Cambridge, UK: Cambridge UP, 1995. Print.

Parker, Alexander A. *The Allegorical Drama of Calderón: An Introduction to the Autos Sacramentales.* Oxford: Dolphin, 1968. Print.

Rastall, Richard. "The Sounds of Hell." *The Iconography of Hell.* Ed. Clifford Davidson and Thomas H. Seiler. Kalamazoo, MI: Medieval Institute Publications, 1992. 102–31. Print.

The Staging of Religious Drama in Europe in the Later Middle Ages: Texts and Documents in English Translation. Ed. Peter Meredith and John E. Tailby. Kalamazoo, MI: Medieval Institute Publications, 1983. Print.

Surtz, Ronald E. "Masks in the Medieval Peninsular Theatre." *Festive Drama.* Ed. Meg Twycross. Cambridge, UK: D. S. Brewer, 1996. 80–87. Print.

Teatre bíblic: Antic testament. Ed. Ferran Huerta Viñas. Barcelona: Barcino, 1976. Print.

Thomas Aquinas, St. *Light of Faith: The Compendium of Theology.* Manchester, NH: Sophia Institute P, 1993. Print.

———. *Summa Theologica.* Trans. Fathers of the English Dominican Province. 5 vols. 1948. Westminster, MD: Christian Classics, 1981. Print.

Torroja Menéndez, Carmen, and María Rivas Palá. *Teatro en Toledo en el siglo XV:* Auto de la Pasión *de Alonso del Campo. Boletín de la Real Academia Española*, Anejo 35. Madrid, 1977. Print.

Twycross, Meg, and Sarah Carpenter. "Masks in Medieval English Theatre: The Mystery Plays." *Medieval English Theatre* 3.1 (1981): 7–44. Print.

Wailes, Stephen L. *Medieval Allegories of Jesus' Parables.* Berkeley: U of California P, 1987. Print.

Baltasar Funes y Villalpando's El golfo de las sirenas: An Homage to Calderón?

KERRY WILKS
Wichita State University

The history for the late 17th-century Aragonese courtier and playwright Baltasar Funes de Villalpando is primarily found in the research of 19th-century scholars with few references from contemporary scholars. Nevertheless, the extant record contains multiple contradictions, perhaps owing to the fact that Funes took his name from the more prominent side of his family tree, which had long dedicated itself to both "armas y letras" [arms and letters] in Aragón.[1] This essay will illuminate the bibliographical record and characteristics of this minor playwright by focusing on a play contained in a manuscript housed in the Biblioteca Nacional de España (MSS 4.085), *El golfo de las sirenas* [*The Sirens' Abyss*].[2] Though the essay is expository in nature, it is important to detail the author's work since this has yet to be published with complete accuracy. One of the errors that frequently occurs is the attribution of Funes's work to Francisco Jacinto Funes y Villalpando, including his plays *El mártir antes de nacer, San Mamés* [*The Martyr Before Birth, Saint Mamés*] and *El vencedor de sí mismo* [*His Own Conqueror*] (a re-working of *El golfo*).[3] In addition to these three plays, (Baltasar) Funes also published poetry in various collections, including: a sonnet in López de Gurrea's 1663 *Clases poéticas* [*Poetry Classes*] (n.p., frontal material) and two poems in Boneta's 1687 *Vida ejemplar* [*Exemplary Life*] (166–69).

Funes's play, *El golfo*, is part of a 766-folio manuscript that includes an extensive collection of poetry and theater. The spine of the book is labeled by hand and says "Funes y Calderón," but it appears that Funes's play was a later edition to the volume of poetry/short plays. This is evidenced by the handwriting, dual pagination, dates and biographical information contained within the second part.[4] With this, Funes's portion of this extensive manuscript consists of only 97 folios. As one may surmise, the play is a *refundición* [adaptation] of Calderón de la Barca's *égloga piscatoria* [piscatory eclogue] with the same title.[5] Calderón's play was first performed for Philip IV at El Pardo in January of 1657. The entire spectacle was Calderón's work – *loa* [prelude], the one-act *zarzuela* [Spanish lyric-dramatic genre] (*El golfo de las sirenas*) and a *mojiganga* [farce] for the finale.[6] Funes's *refundición* was performed in 1685 and, similar to Calderón, the manuscript includes a complete *fiesta* [celebration]: preface, *loa*, introduction, *jornada I* [Act I], *entremés* [interlude], *jornada* II and a *fin de fiesta (fábula)* [finale]. The *teatro breve* [short theatrical pieces] of the *fiesta* represents Funes's original work, since the *loas*, *entremés* and *fábula* are not based on Calderón's play.[7] Within this framework we see that Funes not only appropriates Calderón's verses for the new *zarzuela*, but he also imitates the unique structure of the *fiesta*.

With respect to the "play proper," Funes does not alter any of Calderón's text from the one-act *zarzuela* in the expansion to his two-act play. The only variances are minor misreadings of Calderón's text and small changes to accommodate the expanded plotline. The fundamental difference in the play is Funes's addition of Circe as a major protagonist in the work who motivates the plotline.[8] Calderón begins his play after Ulises [Ulysses] has left Circe's island. Her name is mentioned, but she has no importance to the plot of the work. In Funes's new version, the play begins as Ulises is fleeing Circe's island. She chastises the Greek for departing and thereby betraying her: "¡No huyas, tirano griego / vil huésped, traidor Ulises ..." (19) [Do not flee Greek tyrant, / vile guest, traitor Ulysses! ...].[9] Circe laments the ineffectiveness of her beauty and charm to prevent Ulises from departing. However, she realizes that her tears and sighs are in vain and decides to use her other powers to avenge the affront to her beauty: "Pero, ¿vanas son mis quejas? / ¿No tiembla el mundo de Circe? / Y puedo vengarme ..." (21) [But are my complaints in vain? / Does the world not tremble at Circe? / I can take revenge ...]. Circe sends a storm as punishment, but Ulises invokes the help of Juno, who sends her messenger, Iris, to assist him. Iris calms the storm and Ulises is able to escape from the island. Circe then vows revenge and enlists the help of Caribdis and Escila [Charybdis and Scylla] to help her in this end.[10] As seen in this brief description, Funes's new play takes many of the elements found in one of Calderón's previous plays, *El mayor encanto, amor* [*Love, The Greatest Enchantment*]. Thus, even when Funes deviates from his source material, *El golfo*, he still seeks inspiration from Calderón.[11] The *refundición*, then, takes on multiple layers as Funes appropriates both Calderón's verses and themes from multiple plays to create this expanded piece.[12]

The dialogue between Circe, Escila, and Caribdis flows naturally into Calderón's original opening of *El golfo*, since Calderón has Ulises arrive at Escila's island during a storm—the same storm that Circe creates in the Funes version. One could argue that Funes, seeing the relationship between *El mayor encanto* and *El golfo*, decides to create one work that combines the themes found in both plays. After Ulises arrives on the island, the remainder of the play closely follows Calderón's story found in *El golfo*. The only major changes made are those in which Circe enters the plot. For example, Circe appears immediately after Caribdis and Escila decide to hold their competition to gain Ulises's favor. By postponing Circe's entrance, Funes is able to incorporate the entire scene between Caribdis and Escila as they work out the details of their competition between *vista* and *oído*. However, before Escila and Caribdis have even begun the competition, Circe rapidly descends to the stage to tell the story of her encounter with Ulises. Her account is similar to Calderón's version of the myth as told in *El mayor encanto*, except she solicits the help of both women to achieve her vengeance on Ulises to which they both agree:

> ¡Oh, cómo gusto de ver
> que hagáis de esta competencia,
> pues tomáis cada una así
> mi injuria por vuestra cuenta! (37)

> [I'm delighted to see / that you both participate in this contest / and in this way each one of you / takes on my affront as your own.]

The competition between Escila and Caribdis continues, but the purpose is no longer simply to see which of their attributes will conquer Ulises. Instead, their seduction attempts are contrived to help Circe achieve her vengeance.

The play returns to Calderón's plot line as both women attempt to seduce Ulises with their individual charms. However, in the second act we return to Funes's invention as Circe becomes jealous and impatient during the course of the competition and she therefore decides to take matters into her own hands to punish the Greek.[13] To do this she actually takes over Escila's body—speaking to Ulises as if she were Escila, allowing the element of spectacle to enter the piece. The staging in this scene is carefully detailed and is found in the marginalia of the manuscript: "Ojo. Sube Escila por delante de Circe en un escotillón rápido como que se transforma en ella y todos los apartes los dice Circe detrás del paño haciendo Escila las acciones como si los dijera" (67) [Look! Escila quickly rises in front of Circe through the trapdoor as if Circe is transformed into her. Circe says all of the asides from behind the curtain and Escila moves as if she were saying the lines]. Ulises's companions rescue him soon after this dialogue and the Greeks board their ship to continue their journey. The last scenes of the play are a wonderful example of Funes's ability to intersperse Calderón's dialogue within the context of his newly created plotline. With Funes, Ulises flees as all three women watch and announce their plans for revenge. Caribdis calls on the sirens to prevent him from fleeing, but Ulises escapes the sirens with the help of his crew (as seen in Calderón). Recognizing their defeat, the three women lament their fate through metamorphosis—Escila and Caribdis are transformed into two reefs and Circe is changed into a fiery volcano, reminiscent of Calderón's ending of *El mayor encanto*.

The play text itself provides for a fascinating study on the nature of *refundiciones*, yet, there are further elements to explore that elucidate the performance history and help us better understand the author who has remained shrouded in mystery. These elements are not found within the body of the play, but are instead in the frontal material of the manuscript. Funes included three separate introductions for distinct purposes with this *fiesta*. The first of these appears to be designed for a printed edition of the play ("Al que leyere" ["To the Reader"]). The author's use of the past tense within the prose description seems to indicate that this portion of the manuscript was written after the performance of the play; however, there is no indication that it was published during his lifetime. In the preface, Funes states his intention of presenting Calderón's work with his own additions to form a new play. He is careful in his wording so as not to imply that Calderón's original one act *zarzuela* needs improvement and even evokes the characteristic tone of *humilitas* that is often found in prefaces to describe his own contributions:

> [y] pues mis versos suenan graznidos en los conceptos de esos otros, bástame este conocimiento por disculpa y el ver que feos lunares son relieves de la perfección, y más cuando el intento es dilatar la historia … como el engaste de una joya que aunque la aumenta lo añadido, no la quilata lo precioso por ser de inferior materia; pues los diamantes chispean más luces en el contraste de la oposición. (1–2)

> [and though my verses, among his, may sound like squawking, this knowledge will be punishment enough, knowing that my ugly imitations, whose only purpose is story expansion, only showcase his perfection … like a jewel's setting in that even though it may add to the piece, it doesn't take away from it with its inferior materials since diamonds sparkle more when contrasted with their opposite.]

After this brief prose introduction, Calderón includes his second introductory piece, which is a *loa*. With this, we also learn details as to the performance history of the *refundición*, since the title page indicates that the fiesta was performed to honor the marriage of Doña Constanza de Eril and Don Faustino Cavero: "Fiesta que se representó en el desposorio de Don Faustino Cavero [Conde de Sobradiel], con mi señora Doña Constanza de Eril compuesto por Don Balthasar de Funes y Villalpando: Loas, sainetes y la mitad de la comedia y la otra mitad de Don Pedro Calderón de la Barca año de mil seiscientos y ochenta y cinco" (2) [Celebration performed at the wedding of Don Faustino Cavero [Count of Sobradiel] with my Lady, Doña Constanza of Eril, composed by Don Balthasar de Funes y Villalpando: Prologues, farces, and one half of the *comedia* with the other half from Don Pedro Calderón de la Barca, in the year 1685].[14] On the first page of the *loa* we also find information as to the company, Escamilla, who performed the fiesta. The piece uses the bride and bridegroom in the play, represented by Fausto and Constancia, joined by Cupido, Anteros and La Fortuna. The work opens with Fausto boasting of his many attributes, yet Cupido quickly enters to teach him about divine and honest love that cannot be achieved without "constancia" [constancy]. The god warns him that his *gusto* [pleasure] will soon turn to *pesar* [sadness], and in the end Fausto happily accepts Constancia as his wife.

In addition to the *loa* created for the bridal couple, Funes also includes a second "*loa*" that immediately follows the first in the manuscript, labeled "Introducción a la zarzuela del golfo de las sirenas." While there is no date associated with this piece, there is a note added to the top of the page indicating it was created for the patio ("Hízose para el patio"). This short piece follows the more traditional format of a *loa* and is similar in tone to the prose introduction. The allegory has four characters, Fama, Envidia, Aplauso and Respeto [Fame, Envy, Applause and Respect], which Funes uses to invoke the trope of *humilitas* to introduce the audience to his respectful borrowing of Calderón's work. While discussing the work that is about to be performed and extolling its virtues, Fama responds to an inquiry concerning the identity of the play's author:

> Dicen que es de dos ingenios,
> uno es Calderón, por quien
> yo por ser la Fama vengo
> como tan acostumbrada
> a celebrar sus conceptos ... (15)

> [They say it's by two clever authors, / one is Calderón, whose work / I celebrate, / as usual, / because I'm Fame ...]

Funes's name, however, escapes Fama:

> No tiene nombre y así,
> para decirlo enmudezco,
> porque sin nombre no es fácil
> por la Fama conocerlo. (15)

> [I'll stay mute / as he doesn't have a name / and thus I'm silent / since it isn't
> easy for Fame / to know someone who has no name.]

Envidia then immediately steps in to clarify the identity of the second author
(Funes):

> Por esotro vengo yo
> y no como envidia, viendo
> que será razón tacharle,
> culpando el atrevimiento
> de ver que haya quien, sin ser
> loco, temerario o necio,
> mezclar sus versos intente
> de Calderón con los versos ... (15)

> [I've come for this other one, / but not as envy, / seeing how it would be logical
> to criticize him / after seeing someone who tries to blend / their verses with
> Calderón's / without being mad, reckless or foolish ...]

Considering the fact that *comedia* authors frequently "borrowed" each other's works – Calderón, for example, appropriated an entire act from Tirso's
La venganza de Tamar [*Tamar's Revenge*] to create the second act of *Los
cabellos de Absalón* [*Absalom's Hair*]—it is interesting to note Funes's focus
on this exercise in the introduction. It seems reasonable to imagine that Funes
chose Calderón for the same reasons that many late 17th-century playwrights
sought his texts as models and why companies continued to use his plays for
their performances—Calderón was *the* Baroque dramatist par excellence to be
imitated. But the question remains as to whether Funes's use of the familiar
trope of *humilitas* functions as his own form of *captatio benevolentiae*. Funes
lulls the reader/spectator into a Baroque game of *engaño* [deceit] in which
he asserts that his verses cannot compare to Calderón's to prove the opposite.
His writing style during his additions to the play consists of extremely Baroque
poetry that makes even the most complex of Calderón's verses seem transparent. Perhaps Funes uses the trope in the hopes that his work would rise to or
above that of Calderón's. This assertion could be supported by the author's
second *refundición* of the play—*El vencedor de sí mismo*. It appears that Funes
was no longer satisfied with the work he appropriated from Calderón as he
eliminates the majority of Calderón's lines in the play and he also heavily

edits his own work from the first play. Nonetheless, many of the changes he made from the former Calderonian sections do not significantly alter the play's meaning. And although Funes altered Calderón's words, the tone and connotations of the passages remain the same and *El golfo* still serves as the basis of the work. Funes removes all of the direct appropriations from the first version and replaces it with reworkings or paraphrasing for *El vencedor*. There is, though, one other significant change—he does not mention Calderón's name in any part of the manuscript.

We will never know the precise reason why Funes decided to write his new version of Ulises's tale with *El vencedor*. The answer, though, would appear to be related to the author's own pride in his craft. Perhaps Funes was tired of walking in Calderón's shadow, or he might have felt jealous of the continued attention paid to Calderón's plays rather than the plays of current dramatists, himself included. Even though Funes modestly offered his share of verses in *El golfo de las sirenas*, he certainly hoped to be considered on a level, if not equal to, at least comparable to Calderón—as seen by his decision to combine their writings. It is conceivable that the public, or perhaps worse, his peers at Court, neglected to applaud his efforts with the first play. A man who is tired of always following "Envidia" when he longs to be paired with "Fama," would have good reason to rework his play. These questions, though, are just a few of the intrigues that surround Baltasar Funes y Villalpando. One can only hope that the discussion of these manuscripts will inspire further investigation into this neglected courtier, poet and playwright.

Notes

1. Bibliographers and critics appear to have followed Félix Latassa's initial identification of this author being Melchor Funes y Villalpando's brother (211–12). This name, along with Francisco Jacinto Funes y Villalpando (Melchor's half-brother), are the ones most often linked to the author. Latassa's initial assessment, though, was erroneous, as the author pertains to a separate branch of the family tree. Thus, in addition to a lack of critical studies pertaining to his work, the small, extant historical record is also inaccurate. See my upcoming article for more information on the Funes Villalpando family tree.

2. The majority of the research done for this essay has occurred during my work to publish a critical edition of the play. With this essay I hope to honor Professor Stroud's work at the beginning of his career with his groundbreaking edition of Calderón's *Celos aun del aire matan* [*Even Baseless Jealousy Can Kill*]. In the more recent past, Stroud returned to *comedia* editing with a pedagogical focus, providing annotated *comedias* on The Association for Hispanic Classical Theater's website that were created by his students at Trinity University.

3. Both of these play manuscripts can be found in the Biblioteca Nacional de Madrid, MS 15.161 and MS 14.071(5). The library's digitalization project from the last few

years allows current researchers a much better platform from which to conduct this research and therefore eliminate future erroneous attributions.

4. See also Antonia María Ortiz Ballesteros, who has studied the manuscript.

5. As Matt Stroud indicates in his introduction to *Celos aun del aire matan*, Calderón's *El golfo* has received the label of Spain's first *zarzuela* (8).

6. As evidenced in Sandra Nielsen's complete edition of the play, it is critical to see the complete *fiesta* for a thorough understanding of the work. Unlike the traditional theatrical practice of including "stand-alone" works for the short pieces that were performed with the plays, Calderón's *fiesta* weaves the three components together to create a work where there is meaning between the three parts. Unfortunately, the one-act play has been published without the *loa* and *mojiganga* in the past. Nielsen's arguments seem to have taken root among scholars since Neumeister's latest edition of *El golfo*, found in *Comedias IV*, includes each of these elements.

7. The scope of the paper does not allow for a discussion of Funes's *entremés* and *fábula*, yet a brief description of the two may be useful. The entremés is entitled *Baile de zagalejos* [*Dance of the Shepherd Boys*], which, as the titles suggests, is pastoral in nature. *Fábula del juicio de Paris* [*Fable of the Judgment of Paris*], which Funes labels a "fin de fiesta," tells the story of Paris's judgment of Juno, Pallas and Venus. As Urzáis noted, this piece is essentially the same one that was published with Clavijo's *Las Belides* [*The Belides*] (published in 1687 with performance in 1686), but some parts were changed to suit the specific staging of this play. Funes's name does not appear in the publication, but Clavijo states that the short pieces included with his play were written by a friend, and the *Baile* includes the abbreviation "D.B.F.V." To date, Urzáis's article is the sole piece that has analyzed Funes's *fiesta* with detail.

8. In addition to Circe, Funes also changes the presentation of the *graciosos*. Funes's modification of Celfa and Alfeo is quite logical since a significant portion of the plot line between the two occurs in Calderón's *loa* and *mojiganga*. Funes keeps the highly comical tone introduced by Calderón and uses portions of both the *loa* and *mojiganga* within the adaptation of the *zarzuela*. Funes expands Calderón's introduction of the couple in the *loa* into a comical scene between the two at the beginning of his first act. Elements of the *mojiganga* are included at the end of Funes's second act when Alfeo reappears on the island by means of the whale's belly. Funes's appropriation of this material for the "play proper" reinforces the concept that Calderón's *fiesta* functions as a complete unit, as argued by Nielsen.

9. All citations to the work note the folio number, but the text has been modernized and punctuation marks have been included.

10. In both plays, Caribdis and Escila initially decide to spare Ulises's life in an effort to determine which of their attributes is best (*vista* [sight] versus *oído* [hearing]). Escila hopes to win Ulises with her beauty, while Caribdis hopes to lure him with her singing (her face is covered). As Nielsen states, the competition between *vista* and *oído* represents "the usual message of the Baroque period...don't trust your senses" (40).

11. There is also borrowing from a third play, *Polifemo y Circe* [*Polyphemus and Circe*], in which Calderón was the author of the third act. In terms of chronology, *Polifemo y Circe* was written first, followed by *El mayor* and then *El golfo*. Each of these plays includes Ulises as one of the protagonists. With this, we can consider Funes's adaptation to be one of three plays, though the base text is *El golfo*.

12. It is worth noting here that these layers become even more complicated when one considers Funes's later manuscript, *El vencedor de sí mismo*, a *refundición* of the *refundición*. According to the manuscript, it was performed before the King and Queen at the Retiro. The manuscript does not include a date but in *Representaciones palaciegas* [*Palace Performances*] Shergold and Varey include a document that references an earlier performance of *El vencedor de sí mismo*. The document is dated December 2, 1688, which could leave us with a performance of the second play between 1685 (the date listed with *El golfo*, the base text for *El vencedor*) and December 2, 1688.
13. Circe's jealous response to the competition is similar to the response that Circe had in *El mayor encanto*, when she asked Flérida to feign her attraction for Ulises.
14. The couple was related to Funes by marriage. See my upcoming article to further explain the Funes Villalpando family history.

Works Cited

Boneta, José. *Vida ejemplar del venerable padre M. Fr. Raymundo Lumbier de el Orden de N. S. del Carmen de la Antigua Observancia*. Zaragoza, Sp.: Domingo Gascón, 1687. Print.

Calderón de la Barca, Pedro. *Comedias IV*. Ed. Sebastian Neumeister. Madrid: Biblioteca Castro, 2010. Print.

Funes y Villalpando, Baltasar. *El golfo de las sirenas*. MS 4.085. Biblioteca Nacional, Madrid.

———. *El mártir antes de nacer, San Mamés*. MS 15.161. Biblioteca Nacional, Madrid.

———. *El vencedor de sí mismo*. MS 14.071–5. Biblioteca Nacional, Madrid.

Latassa y Ortín, Félix. *Biblioteca nueva de los autores aragoneses que florecieron desde el año 150 hasta el de 1802*. 6 vols. Pamplona, Sp.: Joaquín de Domingo, 1798–1802. Print.

López de Gurrea, Baltasar. *Clases poéticas*. Zaragoza, Sp.: Ivan de Ybar, 1663. Print.

Nielsen, Sandra. Introduction. *El golfo de las sirenas*. By Pedro Calderón de la Barca. Kassel, Sp.: Reichenberger, 1989. 1–64. Print.

Ortiz Ballesteros, Antonia María. "El MS. 4.085 de la BNM: Variedad de sonetos y otras Cuestiones." *Manuscrt. Cao* 5 (1993): 57–65. Print.

Shergold, N. D., and J. E. Varey. *Representaciones palaciegas: 1603–1699: Estudio y documentos*. London: Tamesis, 1982. Print.

Stroud, Matthew. Introduction. *Celos aun del aire matan*. By Pedro Calderón de la Barca. San Antonio, TX: Trinity UP, 1981. 3–55. Print.

Urzáiz Tortajada, Héctor. "Más sobre reescritura teatral: *El golfo de las sirenas*, de Calderón ¿y Funes?" *Calderón 2000*. Ed. Ignacio Arellano. Vol. 2. Kassel, Ger.: Reichenberger, 2002. 369–82. Print.

The Transformation of a Baroque Zarzuela *into an 18th-Century Opera: The Case of Salazar y Torres's* Los juegos olímpicos

THOMAS A. O'CONNOR
Binghamton University

In the introduction to my edition of Agustín de Salazar y Torres's *También se ama en el Abismo* [*You Also Love in Hell*, 1670] and *Tetis y Peleo* [*Thetis and Peleus*, 1671], I underscored the influence on Salazar's writing of the opera *Il pomo d'oro* [*The Golden Apple*], which was first performed in Vienna in 1668, although it had originally been planned to celebrate the 1666 marriage of the Spanish Princess Margaret Theresa of Austria (1651–1673) and Emperor Leopold of Austria (1640–1705). Salazar had accompanied the Duke of Albuquerque, the head of the entourage that escorted the Princess to Austria. *Il pomo d'oro* begins with the complaints of Proserpina, Pluto's wife and Queen of the Underworld (Scenes 1–3). In *También se ama en el abismo,* Salazar dramatizes Proserpina's abduction by Pluto, thus explaining how she became Queen of Hades. In *Tetis and Peleo*, Salazar dramatizes how the mortal Peleus became the goddess Thetis's husband; their son (Achilles) would, according to the Fates, surpass his father in power and strength. After the passage of a year when Salazar did not produce any new *fiestas* [grand royal celebrations], he wrote a play to celebrate the birthday of the Queen Mother, Mariana of Austria, *Los juegos olímpicos* [*The Olympian Games*, first staged on December 22, 1673]. *Los juegos olímpicos* treats Paris of Troy's youth and marriage to Oenone. The third and fourth scenes from *Il pomo d'oro* celebrate the wedding of Thetis and Peleus, during which *Discordia* [*Discord*] tossed into the feast the golden apple of discord, destined "for the most beautiful goddess."

It is clear that themes related to the Trojan War and the myths associated with it drew Salazar's attention, especially the introductory episodes of the main conflict. The playwright concluded his contribution to the topic with *Los juegos olímpicos*, because the audience knew well that following the weddings at the end of the *zarzuela* [light opera], Paris would settle the dispute among the goddesses, which would eventually guarantee him the abduction and possession of Helen and as a result would trigger the prophecy foretold by the Fates, the Trojan War. It should be noted that this *zarzuela* by Salazar is the only Spanish dramatic work that deals with the romantic relationship between Paris and Oenone (O'Connor 597).

At the end of *También se ama en el abismo*, Jupiter declares that "lo que los hados ordenan, / cumplir el cielo es preciso" (II.2624–25) [That which the Fates ordain, / Heaven must carry out]. In *Tetis y Peleo*, when Prometheus encourages Peleus to undertake his courtship of the disdainful sea nymph Thetis, he assures him that the Fates have decreed that the Nereid's beauty be surrendered to a mortal, affirming, "... así lo quieren / los hados inevitables" (II.1301–02) [... the inevitable Fates / thus desire it]. At the end of the play, when Deiphobus, Thetis's other suitor, despairs over losing the nymph, Prometheus proclaims:

> Detente, Deifobo invicto,
> que esto los hados ordenan,
> y querer contradecirlo
> es en vano, que no hay fuerza
> contra preceptos divinos. (II.2800–04)

> [You're wasting your time, / distinguished Deiphobus, / for the Fates ordain this, / and to try to dispute it / would be to act in vain, as there is no force / that can stop divine precepts].

Such pronouncements are fatalistic, in spite of their insistence on a Catholic position vis-à-vis old-world determinism or Calvinist theological predestination. For example, Peleus asserts "... que las esferas / en el humano albedrío / inclinan pero no por fuerza" (II.2182–84) [... that the realms / in human agency / can bend, but not by force]. Despite this, the repetition of a fatalistic posture in Salazar's writing forces us to examine the topic carefully and with clarity and to face the possibility of a superior force that, at the very least, may affect our free will in a serious and negative manner, even if it does not completely dominate it.

Salazar dramatizes yet again—although more subtly this time—the influence of the Fates on human affairs in *Los juegos olímpicos*. At the beginning of the *zarzuela*, young Paris asks his father to reveal the truth about his odd upbringing, which was shaped by something mysterious that had never been clearly explained. Something is threatening the young man, but he does not know what it might be, since Nicteo's [Nycteus's] warnings are always vague and confusing, Paris implores him:

> Declárate, y, si es desgracia
> la que me previene el hado,
> mejor es averiguarla
> que temerla ... (I.107–10)

> [Speak up, and if misfortune / is what Fate is warning me about / it is better to find out / than to fear it ...]

Almost immediately he insists on the orthodox position: "Y pues es cierto que manda / el albedrío en los astros" (I.113–14) [And so it is true that / free will rules in the stars]. Nevertheless, Salazar joins battle by expressing opposing and irreconcilable positions from the beginning of the *zarzuela*.

The topic is also addressed extensively in Príamo's [Priam's] long narration. As a general principle, the King observes that the wheel of Fortune can bring abrupt changes that could transform the joy of Hecuba's pregnancy into sadness, a result of the Queen's ill-fated dream. Priam observes "que aquesto no es acaso, / es superior providencia" (II.2000–01) [this is not chance; / it is high-ranking providence]. The dream foretells the destruction of Asia and Troy, whose basis lies in the birth of Paris:

> si conociese que era
> Príncipe del Asia, el Asia
> reduciría a sangrienta,
> fatal ruina, introduciendo
> infausta, trágica guerra,
> causada de una hermosura. (II.2071–76)

> [If he were to know that he was / the Prince of Asia, Asia / would be reduced to bloody, / fatal ruin, introducing / infamous, tragic war, / caused by beauty.]

The audience members are well acquainted with the story of the Trojan War, and due precisely to this foreknowledge, they now recognize that the eventual resolution of the dramatic conflicts is merely provisional, since a greater force governs everyone's fate. Priam does not leave room for doubt when he states, "que siempre suele la adversa / fortuna infalible" (II.2101–02) [bad fortune always / seems infallible]. Free will is the consoling dream of philosophers and theologians, which future events will contradict, in this case, at least. Maybe because of a higher power, Salazar has Priam repeat the orthodox perspective at the end of the *zarzuela* when he declares that:

... los decretos
perdonen de las estrellas,
pues que no siempre son ciertos,
cuando manda el albedrío. (II.2786–89)

[May the stars's decrees / be excused, / as they are never certain / when free will rules].

Paris, up to a point another Segismundo, will not fulfill the destiny that Priam glimpses here. Human passions are treacherous, and the classic Spanish model of the character who conquered them, because he conquered himself, is Segismundo from *La vida es sueño* [*Life is a Dream*]; the one who would not or could not do so is Salazar y Torres's Paris. The joyful weddings at the play's conclusion are but a momentary interval in a much longer story, in which Fortune's wheel keeps spinning, and in a not so remote future, the sad misfortune of Troy's total destruction will inevitably come to pass.

In the second act of the *zarzuela*, the themes of fate and the succession to the throne of Troy converge. In *Los juegos olímpicos*, if Hecuba and Priam's son had known he was the Prince of Troy, according to the prediction, he would reduce Asia to mortal ruin because of beauty. In the play's conclusion, Priam reveals Paris's identity as Troy's heir, although he also expresses reservations with respect to the future that is awaiting all the Trojans (II.2876–79). Can the hopes of the Trojan king be justified after all? For the play's spectators and readers who know what will inevitably happen in the Trojan War, the conclusive answer is definitely negative. How can the playwright reconcile and harmonize the classical fatal destiny of the Trojan people, foretold by Hecuba's dream and interpreted and confirmed by the king's prophets, with the Christian concept of free will? Salazar's only alternative is to develop Paris's fickle and impatient character, which would explain, to a certain extent, his future participation in fulfilling destiny.

In another Salazar play, performed at the beginning of the 1673–1674 theatrical season, Rosolea's fate (as Queen of Sicily or wife of Jesus Christ) was the central axis of *La mejor flor de Sicilia, Santa Rosalea* [*The Best Flower of Sicily, Saint Rosalia*, 1673], a saints's play that chronologically follows *Tetis and Peleo*. *La mejor flor de Sicilia, Santa Rosolea* provides another perspective on this theme. In the plot, the force that acts upon and influences the actions of men and women is referred to as Divine Providence, which suggests that predestination operates more effectively than does the will of the dramatic characters. Nonetheless, perhaps as a result of the issues that the plot of *Tetis y Peleo* raised for Salazar, the dramatist emphasizes the important role of Rosolea's will, which unites with the divine plan for her and her kingdom. This *comedia de santos* [Saints' play] was staged in a *corral* [popular, open-air theater] in Madrid, where censors would scrutinize, with penetrating judgment, the play's theological orthodoxy or heterodoxy, and as a result, would either approve or prohibit its representation onstage. For this reason, the conditions of its performance differed from those related to his previous grand royal celebrations.

How was *La mejor flor de Sicilia, Santa Rosolea* interpreted in the Court in Madrid? In this play, the successor to the Sicilian throne abandoned the capital and fled to the mountains to live as a hermit. Political customs and traditions related to succession to the Sicilian throne did not mesh with the intervention of Divine Providence that was highlighted in the play. This also allows us to question the presumption of divine will in the selection of royal heirs by virtue of their birth. Is there any connection to the figure of the regent Queen who, as is widely known, dressed like a nun after the death of Philip IV on September 17, 1665? The succession issue would become the fundamental institutional problem in the reign of Charles II, but at this moment in time, the feeble and sickly figure of the prince and heir worried in particular those who exercised power in the royal house.

As I have shown in the introduction to *La mejor flor de Sicilia, Santa Rosolea*, one can observe increasing numbers of musical performances in Salazar's plays, although there are fewer in *Tetis y Peleo*. The following verses are sung either completely or partially:

1° *Elegir al enemigo* [*To Choose One's Foe*]	142 vv. of 3039 vv. = 4.67%
2° *El amor más desgraciado, Céfalo y Pocris* [*The Most Ill-fated Love: Cephalus and Procris*]	119 vv. of 2270 vv. = 5.24%
3° *También se ama en el abismo*	411 vv. of 2633 vv. = 15.61%
4° *Tetis y Peleo*	96 vv. of 2837 vv. = 3.38%
5° *La mejor flor de Sicilia, Santa Rosolea*	454 vv. of 3722 vv. = 12.18%
6° *Los juegos olímpicos*	497 vv. of 2934 vv. = 16.94%

The structural principle consists of presenting the drama's theme through lyrics sung across a string of verses. This system functions as the *leitmotiv* of each part of the *zarzuela*. The playwright masterfully weaves together the poetic structure, intertwining the musical elements in such a manner that they illuminate the different parts of the plot. The high percentage of sung verses in Salazar's *zarzuelas*, in addition to the musical flow of those that were spoken, contributed to the opinion that Baroque plays would be appropriate for adaptation to 18th-century operatic style.

Judith Farré Vidal provides a summary of palace stagings of Salazar's *zarzuelas* (I.18n13). After the December 22, 1673 premiere of *Los juegos olímpicos,* the play was also performed in 1677, 1680, 1683, 1686 (twice), 1688, 1694, 1695, and 1698 (twice), as well as in 1678 in the Viceroyalty of New Spain. The data provided by René Andioc and Mireille Coulon regarding 18th-century productions are indeed impressive; *Los juegos olímpicos* was staged in 1711, 1714, 1716, 1719, 1720, 1722, 1723, 1724, 1725, 1728, 1729, 1730, 1731, 1735, and 1752. That year marks the first adaptation of the play: Josef de Parra's theater company performed the text "embellished by Nicolás Martínez" [I.229]; we may infer that the productions from that time on relied on Martínez's modifications in 1762, 1766, 1772 (Eusebio Ribera's theater company staged the play from November 4–9), and 1777 (Ribera again produced the play, July 7–12).

René Martín summarizes the events that Salazar used as the foundation for his version of the protagonist:

> En una ocasión, París acudió a Troya para participar en unos juegos fúnebres, donde pronto destacó al salir victorioso de todas las pruebas. El joven fue reconocido por su hermana, la profetisa Casandra, y Príamo, feliz por recobrar al hijo que creía perdido, le restituyó su lugar en la mansión real. (338)

> [On one occasion, Paris came to Troy to participate in some funeral games, where he soon stood out for having won all the athletic trials. The young man was recognized by his sister, the prophetess Cassandra, and Priam, happy to recover the son he had thought lost, restored him to his place in the royal mansion.]

In *Los juegos olímpicos,* Salazar characterizes Paris as an impetuous young man dominated by his passions, always ready to compete against other men, and who knows how to deceive women.[1] It is possible that the issue of Fate predicting Paris's and Troy's futures had its repercussions among 17th-century Court audiences, who faced their own futures under the leadership of Prince Charles, "The Bewitched." Perhaps the best explanation of the *zarzuela*'s success as a theatrical work may have to do with Salazar's writing style, in which the declamatory flow and inherent musicality of the play's verses harmonize naturally and gracefully.

With Nicolás Martinez's adaptation of *Los juegos olímpicos,* the play took on another dimension. Fortunately, we now have access to manuscripts located in the Institut del Teatre de Barcelona [Theater Institute of Barcelona (B)][2] and the Biblioteca Histórica Municipal del Ayuntamiento de Madrid [Municipal Historical Library of the Madrid City Council (M)]. The documents in B refer to a performance earlier than those of 1772 and 1777, while the sources in M bear witness to the productions taking place in 1772 and 1777.

It was observed that in 1777, the play did not please the audience because of its timing in relation to the San Fermín festival.[3] The chronological order of the prompter's notes for the 1777 staging is: M 2°, M 3°, and M 1°. There is also a 1777 musical score, MUS-24–1, from the composer Blas de Laserna, which contains all the music for this production. M 1° belonged to the first prompter and contains a clean copy of the play. M 3° belonged to the stagehand and matched M 2°. M 2° has information about the scenery and the actors' movement onstage. It details their entrances and exits and the exact place where they have to be, and it includes their names at the moment the prompter must warn them that they will soon need to come onstage to perform.[4]

The documents dealing with the 18th century only refer to theaters in Madrid, but as we know, there were numerous other theaters across the Peninsula at that time.[5] What might have caused Madrid's audiences to react so negatively to the adaptation in 1777, aside from its conflict with the entertainment of the San Fermín festivals? Andioc notes that in the evolution of the mythological *zarzuela*: "si bien se representa alguna que otra en los primeros años del reinado de Carlos III (1746–88), las zarzuelas con que se celebraron en 1764 los esponsales de la infanta pertenecen ya a un género nuevo" (59) [Even though one or two are staged in the first years of Carlos III's (1746–1788) reign, the *zarzuelas* that celebrated Princess María Luisa's 1764 wedding belonged to a new genre].

To further answer the question with accuracy, we need only dissect the existing manuscripts. The verses in B and M that are reduced in number, cut, or added may be summarized as follows.[6] First, as one might expect, the number of Baroque musical performances has been greatly reduced or eliminated so that the new operatic forms of the 18th century would fit well in the adaptation. Second, elements of the lengthy rhetorical accounts that 17th-century audiences had enjoyed so much were also reduced or cut. This is the case of the long and detailed explanation of Paris and Cassandra's background, recounted by Priam at the beginning of the third act of the adaptation, which was totally cut in the 1777 staging as a result of the play's excessive length.[7] Third, almost all the eliminated verses were part of the Baroque songs or lyrics from the original manuscript or from the adaptation's source text, a *suelta* [a play published singly in pamphlet format] dated 1729, in Madrid.

The text from B appears to be the second prompter's script of stagings of *Los juegos olímpicos* from 1752, 1762, or 1766.[8] In order to adapt the Baroque *zarzuela* to the operatic forms then in force, several musical changes were made. In the first act, after v. 690a, the recitative [9] "Suelta, villano" ["Let Go, Peasant"] was introduced, followed by the duet, "Mi bien" ["My Dearest"].

From that point on, the manuscript follows v. 701 of the original text. In the second act, two new musical pieces are introduced. First, vv. 1564–1615 are deleted, and in its place Oenone and Paris sing a duet that begins after v. 1563. The second change is that after v. 1881, there are new introductory verses, and then Paris sings the recitative "¿Qué es esto, Amor?" ["What is This, Love?"] and a simpler melodic form of the aria,[10] a *cavatina*,[11] "Detén el golpe airado" ["Stop the Angry Blow"]. In the third act, there is only one new musical performance: after v. 2846, there are two new introductory verses, after which Paris sings "Monarca invicto" ["Undefeated Monarch"] and the *copla* [song or verses] that follows. The text continues with v. 2867. Although the musical changes might be considered extensive, in accordance with the intent to modernize the Salazarian *zarzuela* they do not significantly change the development of the dramatic text, despite the removal of many of the original text's verses.

In the Madrid productions of 1772 and 1777, the comprehensive adaptation of the text to operatic style and the resultant textual rewriting produced profound modifications that affected the dramatic nature of the work.[12] It is also possible that the M manuscript originally referred to a staging prior to 1772, due to the fact that the last name, Lavenan, of the actress who played the role of Paris, is found on all three manuscripts, but she did not appear in subsequent performances. This indicates that the modifications made on the M manuscripts mainly refer to the two different stagings that took place in 1772 and 1777.

The 1777 production adds three new musical pieces, which are only found in MUS 24–1. The first musical performance in the adaptation is a new text, occurring after v. 493 to v. 541, when Oenone laments Paris's absence. B reproduces almost all the original verses, but it cuts vv. 500–523 and then indicates that all the verses remaining from the original text should be trimmed. There is evidence of the two different stagings in M 2°. In the performance prior to that of 1777, "señora Paca" had sung a rather lengthy *cavatina*, "Pura fuente" ["Pure Fountain"], and in 1777, "señora Mayora" sang it. Nonetheless, the entire *cavatina* was later cut and was replaced by the aria "Dejadme aquí un momento" ["Leave Me Here a Moment"], the text of which only appears in the score MUS 24–1 and was originally sung in the second act of the 1772 staging. It is not known when these substitutions were made, but we can infer that after discovering that the play was too long, the changes were made during the rehearsals or after the first performance. This illustrates the difficulties that Eusebio Ribera's company faced due to the complexity of the new grand-scale adaptation. Although the aria was musically successful for the audience, as a consequence of the many alterations made to the dramatic text, it was transformed into a mere platform for displaying "la señora Mayora's" vocal talent and the current operatic style.

The second musical performance of the first act takes place after v. 690. B includes Paris and Oenone's recitative, which introduces the aria duet that follows. M reproduces the recitative and aria, but later M 1° trims all the other verses up to "¡Ah, errada voluntad!" ["Ah, Mistaken Will!"] and in their place substitutes a recitative duet by Paris and Oenone, employing the same verses found in B. After the recitative there had been an aria duet, "¡Mi bien!," but in 1777 this aria was deleted, and a duet by "señora Mayora" and "señor Robles" took its place. In MUS 24–1 another last name appears under that of "señor Robles." Does this suggest a case of "musical recycling" in the sense of recovering usable material? The original duet was eliminated, and the substitution only exists in the musical score. Only by combining M 1° and MUS 24–1 can the reconstruction of the 1777 performance and the admirable efforts to preserve the text be clearly seen. Only the prompter's notes, however, show all the changes made at different times and for a variety of reasons.

In the second act of the adaptation, we can see many changes are initially difficult to follow because they refer to the 1772 and 1777 stagings. First, in M, new verses introduce Oenone's aria, "Déjadme aquí un momento," which was sung in the 1772 performance, but subsequently was moved to the first act. Even later, it seems, another aria, "Amor … amor," ["Love … love"] was introduced; it only appears in the score of the 1777 performance.[13] It is a new aria, replacing the verses formerly sung after v. 1563. In all the manuscripts we find Oenone and Paris's duet after v. 1563, which begins with "De Casandra las luces" ["The Lights of Cassandra"], but M 2° and M 1° shorten the duet. M 2° and M 1° later write again the action that follows, and the substitution for the shortened verses, which appears in four and five pages, respectively, is added to the two manuscripts; it is in a different hand from the rest of the manuscript, representing the changes made to the 1777 performance.

The second change occurs after v. 1881. In all the manuscripts, Paris sings a recitative, "¿Qué es esto, Amor?," which introduces the aria *cavatina*, "Detén el golpe airado." M introduces more verses to the version of the aria, whose original text is also in B. In a performance prior to 1772, "señora Lavenan" had played the role of Paris, and her last name appeared on M. M 2° crosses out her last name and replaces it with the last name of "señora Figueras," who had played the role in 1772. On the other hand, in the 1777 staging, M 2° and M 1° shortened the recitative and aria and only added "Aria" to indicate that a substitution appears in MUS 24–1, sung by "señor Robles." The Ribera company staged the play in both 1772 and 1777, but curiously, during the 1772 performance, "señora Figueras" played the role of Paris, and in the other one that M refers to, the role was played by "señora Lavenan." In 1777, "señora Figuras" played the role of Cassandra. At the end of the third act, Paris, now desperate, tries to commit suicide after losing to Corebo in their competition over Cassandra. The verses he sings appear in all the manuscripts, but MUS 24–1 specifies that Robles sings a recitative, followed by a *copla* [rhyming couplet]. The effects of all these changes can only be identified and better understood when we can connect them to the musical performances described in MUS 24–1.

As this brief examination of adaptations and performances of *Los juegos olímpicos* reveals, the evolution from Baroque *zarzuela* to 18th-century opera responds to diverse factors from the talents of the players to the tastes of the audiences. With careful comparison of existing sources, we can gain many insights into these oft-neglected works whose performance history, complete with prompter's notes, provides glimpses into the history of musical theater.

Notes

1. Topics such as "la promoción del individuo" [advancement of the individual] and "el casamiento desigual" [unevenly matched marriages] were, Andioc notes, of interest to 18th-century audiences (104). Up to a certain point, these topics help shape the plot of the *zarzuela*.
2. This manuscript seems to have been the second prompter's script for a version of the opera performed before 1772 and 1777. See the commentary on M 2° that follows to understand its role in the prompters' distribution of tasks.
3. Due to the appearance of the giants, M 2° states: "No gustó [en blanco] días por salir los gigantes" [They did not like (at all) having to wait days for the giants to leave]; this appears to refer to the parades featuring giant figures, which were held each morning of the week-long San Fermín festival. We now know that the play was produced at the Teatro del Príncipe [The Prince's Theater] from July 7–12, and the festival of San Fermín lasts from July 7–14, so the festival celebration in Madrid in 1777 contributed to the frustration referred to in the text. Andioc observes that the "fines de junio y principio de julio" [end of June and the beginning of July] was "una de las peores épocas del año teatral" (38) [one of the worst times of the theatrical year].
4. I draw on Ascención Aguerri Martínez's research and her important contributions on the Madrid manuscripts, specifically, her descriptions of the prompters' notes.
5. Andioc refers to the theaters in Seville, Barcelona, Valencia, Zaragoza, Cádiz, and Valladolid during the 18th century (7).
6. In a study of the rewritings of two 17th-century Calderonian comedies, Alejandra Pacheco summarized the musical practices of the time: "el acercamiento más libre al texto cantado, con supresiones, adiciones e incluso grandes añadidos al texto, o la superposición de distintas variantes musicales y añadidos a lo largo del tiempo" (388)

[the freest approach to the sung text, with cuts, additions, and even more extensive augmentations to the text, or the overlapping of different musical variants and additions over time].

7. Andioc correctly observes with regard to Clavijo y Fajardo's *Briseida* [*Briseis*] that "la mitología se reducía […] a una mera fachada tras la que se [ocultaba] a duras penas el 'petrimetre' Aquiles" (59) [the mythology was reduced (…) to a mere facade behind which the 'fop' Aquiles was hiding with great difficulty].

8. It is important to remember that these dates refer only to the stagings of *Los juegos olímpicos* that were performed in Madrid; we do not have data on those that might have taken place in other cities.

9. *Recitado*: "Usado como substantivo, se llama en la música moderna aquella parte de composición que antecede a la Aria. Llámase así porque se canta como cuando se recita" (Real Academia Española, *Diccionario de Autoridades*) [Used as a noun, in modern music this is the part of the composition that precedes the Aria. It is called that because it is sung like being recited aloud].

10. *Arieta*: "Composición, música que consta de dos estancias, que la segunda se contiene en la misma clave de la primera, que es solo la que se repite … Es voz italiana y nuevamente introducida. Llámase también aria" [Composition, music, that consists of two stanzas, with the second one in the same key as the first, which is the only one repeated … It is a newly introduced Italian term, also called an aria].

11. *Cavatina*: "Aria de cortas dimensiones, que a veces consta de dos tiempos o partes" (Real Academia Española, *Diccionario de Autoridades*) [A brief aria, which at times consists of two tempos or parts].

12. With regard to the following, Andioc advises: "suele ocurrir con cierta frecuencia que el texto original de una obra esté más o menos podado de orden de la censura o por necesidades de la puesta en escena" (28) [With relative frequency, it happens that the original text of a work is to a greater or lesser extent trimmed by order of the censors or because of staging needs].

13. Andioc refers to what he calls "un factor de rejuvenecimiento y […] de éxito" (53) [a factor of rejuvenation and (…) of success] when a composer such as Laserna "podía añadir, años más tarde, varias partituras de factura más conforme a la moda del día, o incluso modificarlas con el fin de adaptarlas a otra obra" (53) [could add, years later, various scores made more in accordance with the style of the day, or even modified with the goal of adapting them to another work].

Works Cited

Aguerri Martínez, Asención. "La catalogación de los apuntes de teatro en la Biblioteca Histórica Municipal." *Revista general de información y documentación* 17 (2007): 133–64. Print.

Andioc, René. *Teatro y sociedad en el Madrid del siglo XVIII*. Madrid: Castalia, 1987. Print.

———. y Mireille Coulon. *Cartelera teatral madrileña del siglo XVIII (1708–1808)*. 2 vols. Toulouse, Fr.: Presses Universitaires du Mirail, 1996. Print.

Farré Vidal, Judith. *Dramaturgia y espectáculo del elogio. Loas completas de Agustín de Salazar y Torres*. 2 vols. Kassel, Ger.: Reichenberger, 2002. Print.

Martín, René, ed. *Diccionario de la mitología griega y romana*. Madrid: Espasa-Calpe, 1996. Print.

O'Connor, Thomas Austin. "Bibliografía de mitos dramatizados en la literatura española (del siglo XVI a principios del XIX)." *La mitología clásica en la literatura española: Panorama diacrónico*. Ed. J. A. López Férez. Madrid: Ediciones Clásicas, 2006. 569–99. Print.

Pacheco, Alejandra. "Versiones musicales sobre Calderón en el siglo XVIII: la reescritura musical para *Los tres afectos de amor* y *Eco y Narciso*." *Calderón y su escuela: Variaciones e innovación de un modelo teatral. XV Coloquio Anglogermano sobre Calderón*. Ed. Manfred Tietz and Gero Arnscheidt, with Beata Baczyńska. Stuttgart: Franz Steiner, 2011. 379–402. Print.

Real Academia Española. *Diccionario de autoridades*. Madrid: Gredos, 1990. Print.

———. *Diccionario de la lengua española*. Madrid: Gredos, 2001. Print.

Salazar y Torres, Agustín de. *Fiestas reales en torno a los años de la Reina, 1670–1672. También se ama en el abismo. Tetis y Peleo*. Ed. Thomas Austin O'Connor. Kassel, Ger.: Reichenberger, 2006. Print.

———. *Dos comedias sobre herederas del trono y la política matrimonial dinástica. Elegir al enemigo. La mejor flor de Sicilia, Santa Rosolea*. Ed. Thomas Austin O'Connor. Kassel, Ger.: Reichenberger, 2012. Print.

———. *Una zarzuela barroca y su refundición operática en el siglo XVIII, con la partitura dieciochesca de Blas de Laserna. Los Juegos Olímpicos*. Ed. Thomas Austin O'Connor. Kassel, Ger.: Reichenberger, in press. Print.

Two Visions of Brotherhood: Calderón and Richard Strauss

DONALD R. LARSON
The Ohio State University

In the spring of 1934, the German composer Richard Strauss was putting the finishing touches on his opera *Die schweigsame Frau* [*The Silent Woman*], and in his spare moments casting about for ideas for his next project. Resolutely anti-militarist, he had for some time wanted to create a work dealing with the theme of universal peace. His first thought was to focus such a work on the Peace of Konstanz, signed by the Emperor Frederick Barbarrosa with the Lombard states in 1183, but he soon concluded that an opera set in Medieval times would inevitably invite comparison with those of Richard Wagner, a comparison that he logically wished to avoid. Then, while perusing a history of world theater by the Austrian cultural historian Joseph Gregor, he came across a discussion of Calderón's *El sitio de Bredá* [*The Siege of Breda*] (1625), accompanied by a reproduction of Velázquez's painting, *La rendición de Bredá* [*The Surrender of Breda*] (1635), which is generally accepted as deriving in part from Calderón's play.[1] Both of these works, of course, took as their subject a signal event in the protracted struggle between the Spaniards and the insurgents in the Low Lands, the surrender by the rebels in June, 1625, of the Dutch town of Breda. Perceiving that the play might be reworked into the kind of opera he had in mind, Strauss arranged a meeting at that summer's Salzburg Festival with Stefan Zweig, the Austrian Jewish writer who had been the librettist of *Die Schweigsame Frau*, and during the ensuing conversation he broached the possibility of a new collaboration, based on *El sitio de Bredá*.[2]

A lifelong humanist and pacifist, Zweig was immediately taken with the idea of an opera centered on the spirit of reconciliation and brotherhood found both in Calderón's drama and Velázquez's famous painting. However, in order to give the projected work greater impact in those German-speaking lands then being overtaken by Nazi militarist ideology, he suggested a transposition of the action of the play, lifting it from the Netherlands and the context of the hostilities between the Spanish and the Dutch and placing it instead in Germany at the conclusion of the Thirty Years' War. Finding Strauss receptive to this notion, Zweig wrote to him a few weeks after their meeting, proposing a one-act work to take place on the day on which the Peace of Westphalia was concluded, and to be entitled, perhaps, *24 October 1648*. What the opera might be like was already clear to him. "In it," he wrote, "I want to embrace three elements: the tragic, the heroic, and the humane, merging into that Hymn to the Reconciliation of the People, to the Grace of the work of Reconstruction" (Del Mar 55).

In this same letter, Zweig set forth a synopsis which is remarkably similar to the plot of the completed opera. As a Jew, however, Zweig was finding his position in Austria and Germany increasingly precarious, and he indicated to Strauss that it would be dangerous for both of them to undertake further collaboration. Although understanding of his friend's position, Strauss was very disappointed, and attempted to persuade him that they could work together secretly. Zweig, naturally, was opposed to such an unrealistic plan, and by way of counter-suggestion he proposed several other possible librettists to Strauss, one of whom was Joseph Gregor himself. After first extracting from Zweig a promise that he could still be called upon for advice, Strauss eventually agreed to work with Gregor. He did so, however, with extreme reluctance, for he considered Gregor's artistic talents to be greatly inferior, both to those of Zweig and to his own.

The opera that Strauss wrote to Gregor's libretto came in time to be called *Friedenstag*, that is, *Day of Peace*, and it was first performed in Munich on the night of July 24, 1938. Later that year the opera was performed in seven other cities, and in 1939 it was mounted in fourteen additional cities, including Vienna. Shortly after that, the work dropped from sight, and it was not presented again in Germany until 1956.

Discussions of *Friedenstag* sometimes, although not always, mention its connection to Calderón's play. None of the commentaries, however, insofar as I am aware, explores in depth the relationship of the two works. Indeed, the one study that might especially be expected to do so, Kenneth Birkin's *Friedenstag and Daphne: An Interpretive Study of the Literary and Dramatic Sources of Two Operas by Richard Strauss*, implies that the matter is not worth extended discussion, stating that "close examination of Calderón's work confirms that despite the obvious 'reconciliation' *motif*, its impact upon the 1648 project was minimal in the extreme" (102). As I hope to show, however, *El sitio de Bredá* exercised a clear influence on the conception and writing of the opera, although it is obvious that there are important differences between the two. *Friedenstag* is not merely an adaptation of Calderón's play but a loose one, as is always the case when a work is transposed from one medium to another, each of which has its own strengths and limitations. Thus, *Friedenstag* is highly selective in what it chooses to borrow from *El sitio* and what it opts to leave aside. Moreover, even those elements that *are* adopted are reshaped in order to better engage with the historical and cultural experiences of the opera's intended audience, as well as to reflect the interests and sensibilities of its three creators: Strauss, Gregor, and—not to be forgotten—Zweig.[3]

One of a relatively small number of Spanish Golden Age plays that deal with contemporary history, *El sitio de Bredá* focuses primarily on the final days of the famous siege, which had been laid on August 28, 1624, and which was to last over nine months.[4] It took place at a critical time in Spain's military fortunes. The Twelve Years' Truce with the Dutch had expired in 1621, and despite a few successes, the Army of Flanders seemed unable for a few years thereafter to make substantial progress against the Dutch rebels, to the great frustration of the young King, Philip IV, and his Prime Minister, the Count-Duke of Olivares. What was needed, everyone agreed, was a resounding victory that would restore morale among the soldiers and repair Spain's damaged prestige among the nations of Europe.[5] This, then, was the charge given to the commander of the army in the Netherlands, the renowned Genoese general, Ambrogio Spinola.

Spinola's choice of Breda as the site of an operation was a controversial one. On the one hand it made sense, because Breda was the ancestral home of the Orange-Nassau family, the leaders of the revolt in the Low Countries, and thus of great symbolic importance; at the same time, it was also strategically important for it lay on the confluence of the Mark and Aa rivers and on the main road between Antwerp and Utrecht. On the other hand, taking Breda would be extremely difficult. Not only was it guarded by high, thick walls within which stood an unusually well-fortified citadel, outside the walls it was surrounded by a series of three concentric moats, the attempted crossing of which would open the attackers to deadly fire from within the town.

Spinola's solution, of course, was not to attack Breda directly, but rather to encircle it and starve it into submission. This he was able to do, because his army, made up not just of Spaniards but also Italians, Germans, Burgundians, Walloons, and others, was one of the largest ever assembled in Europe to that time, with estimates of its size ranging from 18,000 to 23,000. In contrast, the number of defenders of Breda, also a multinational force, is thought to have been about 7,000. Both besiegers and those besieged displayed great ingenuity and bravery during the blockade, and observers came from all over to view the brilliantly executed manoeuvers and counter-manoeuvers. Both sides also endured great deprivation, with the Spanish forces suffering almost as much as their opponents. The long ordeal finally came to end on June 2, 1625, when the governor of Breda, Justin of Nassau, surrendered under famously generous terms to Spinola.[6] Three days later, with banners flying and drums beating, the defenders of the town marched out of the citadel, "looking in better shape," Anthony Bailey has written, "than those they were surrendering to" (65). At this point, Justin and Spinola met and saluted, and the latter formally took possession of the town. Whether the brief ceremony included the handing over of keys, as is portrayed both in Calderón's play and in Velázquez's painting, has never been verified with certainty.

The occasion of *El sitio de Bredá*'s first performance has been a matter of some dispute. Simon A. Vosters supposed that it occurred in a public theatre sometime in 1628–29 (*La rendición* 8–47 and "Again"), but in an article of 1978 Shirley B. Whitaker argued, convincingly in my opinion, that there had been a presentation at Court in the fall of 1625. Then, in a paper delivered at the annual symposium of the Association for Hispanic Classical Theater in 1999, she cited newly uncovered evidence of earlier *corral* [public theater] performances in Madrid in August of 1625, that is to say, less than three months after the fall of Breda. What one concludes from this is that Calderón wished to put his play before the public while the news from abroad was still fresh, and that it was written with great speed. Unfortunately, insofar as I know, Whitaker's paper has not yet been published.

As might be anticipated, given the patriotic audience for whom it was created, *El sitio de Bredá* is primarily epic in tone. It celebrates the bravery and fortitude of Spinola (called Espínola in the play), his Captains, and their forces, but perhaps somewhat surprisingly, it also gives considerable, and fundamentally favorable, attention to their staunch opponents, the defenders of Breda, led by the governor of the town, Justin of Nassau. In this regard, as John Loftis has pointed out (191–94), it is quite unlike the play that probably served in some sense as a model for Calderón, Lope's *El asalto de Mastrique* [*The Assault of Maastricht*], which is far more one-sided in its depiction of the conflict in the Netherlands. Also unexpected in a work seemingly written to glorify military success is its focus on the suffering brought about by warfare. With the same bifurcated vision that characterizes many of his later plays, Calderón shows here that while faith, country, and honor may be values worth fighting for, their defense exacts a price, and that price often entails vast misery on the part of those caught up in the fighting, combatants and non-combatants alike. Spinola's troops, camped outside the walls of Breda, are forced to endure lack of food and adequate shelter, but if their travails are great, still greater are the travails visited upon the townspeople, and it is notable that Calderón does not shy from recognizing this. Although Protestants, and thus, in the eyes of Spinola and his men, heretics, the people of Breda are nevertheless human beings, and in his play Calderón treats their misfortune with pronounced sympathy.[7]

There are two scenes that are especially revealing in this regard, each of which centers on the play's principal female character, Madama Flora, one of the women of the town. The first occurs toward the end of Act II, when, in order to conserve the dwindling food supply, Justin orders that all those who are not essential to the defense of Breda, that is, the very young and the very old, must leave forthwith. Flora has both an elderly father and a young son, and knowing that they face death if they leave the security of the city, she pleads with Justin to spare them from the edict. He relents only to the extent of declaring that one of the two may stay, and Flora is then faced with the horrific decision of determining which of her kinsmen shall remain. Agonizing pitifully over the choice, she concludes that her greater responsibility is to her father, and then, as the scene comes to an end, she bids a heart-rending farewell to her son.

Equally affecting is the scene with which Act III opens. Haggard, exhausted, and starving, the townspeople come to Justin and entreat him to surrender the city. Flora acts as their spokesperson, and in a long monologue evokes the ways in which her friends and neighbors are struggling piteously toward their tragic, foreseeable ends; Breda, she says, is a sepulcher filled with still-living bodies. Justin is moved by the desperation of the townspeople, but exhorts them to endure for one more day because he expects a relieving force to appear at any moment. Mollified by Justin's words, Flora and the others withdraw, only to find their hopes of salvation dashed shortly afterward with the news that the troops sent to break the siege have been turned back.

In El *sitio de Bredá*, then, Flora is the emblem of the suffering victims of warfare. But she has another function as well, and that is to represent the dream of peace, reconciliation, and concord. In his illuminating discussion of the play, Frederick A. de Armas aptly relates Flora to her namesake, the Roman goddess Flora, the goddess of flowers and perpetual spring, and also to Venus, the goddess of love, harmony, and abundance. As a kind of avatar of the latter, Flora is identified throughout the work with different kinds of love: the love of her husband, who has been killed in the conflict with the besieging army, the love of her son, and the love of her elderly father. But significantly, she comes to represent another sort of love as well, the love that one can experience for one's supposed enemy, for during the course of the action she finds herself strongly attracted to Don Fadrique Bazán, who had treated her with great kindness when he encountered her, helpless and alone, in the fields outside Breda.

The scene in which Flora meets the Spanish combatant is preceded by another, equally important. In the earlier scene, Flora is watching the enemy army passing by in the distance, and as she relates to others what she has seen, images that at first suggest contrary notions appear to fuse: winter and summer become one; the weapons of the soldiers, likened to ice, shade into the plumes of their helmets, suggestive of flowers; the forward motion of the troops, marching to war, yields to an evocation of tranquilly undulating fields of wheat. As de Armas writes, "Flora's beautiful vision … seems to transform the horrors of war, of a war that had already killed her husband, into a radiant vision of the possibilities of world peace and perfection" (439).[8]

The progression in Flora's speech, like the development in the somewhat later scene where Flora encounters Don Fadrique for the first time, clearly suggests a movement from an outbreak of aggression and violence to the blossoming of harmony and accord. As de Armas shows, this is the same movement that one finds in Sandro Botticelli's famous painting, "Primavera" ["Allegory of Spring"], and Calderón's play does, indeed, seem to contain conscious references to Botticelli's painting. In *El sitio de Bredá*; the culmination of the movement occurs, as one would expect, in the final scenes of the play. At this point, with no help on the way, Justin of Nassau has come to realize that he has no choice but to surrender Breda to the besiegers. He is determined to do so on *his* terms, however, which will preserve not just the lives of the defenders, but their dignity, their property, and their religion as well. These terms are in large part accepted by Spinola, and his decision to be magnanimous in victory is supported enthusiastically by the soldiers from Spain, if not by those from other nations.

With this, the gates of the city are opened, and as the weary townspeople begin to appear from one direction, the equally weary besieging forces converge from the other. Then, Justin and Spinola meet in the center of the stage. Handing the keys to the city to Spinola, a somewhat defiant Justin explains that the defenders have surrendered, not through fear or lack of heart, but because it was clear that fortune was against them. The consoling phrases with which Spinola accepts the keys have become famous. "Justino," he says, "yo las recibo, / y conozco que valiente sois; / que el valor del vencido / hace famoso al que vence" (III.1008–11, 130) [Justin, I receive them, / and acknowledge that you are valiant; / for the valor of the vanquished / confers fame on the victor]. And with these words of understanding and brotherhood *El sitio de Bredá* comes to an end.

It was almost precisely three hundred years after the premiere of *El sitio de Bredá* that Richard Strauss commenced work on *Friedenstag*, prompted by the generous and inclusive vision that Calderón's play and Velázquez's *La rendición de Bredá* together offer. The music that he came to write is quite different from that of any of his other operas. It depends for much of its effect on the use of massed choruses, and, in keeping with the primary subject matter of the work, the horror of warfare; it is, until the final scenes, predominantly stark and somber. Furthermore, its score is dominated by male voices, there being but one principal female role, something which makes it unique among the composer's works for the stage.

The notably concentrated action of the opera takes place, as Zweig had originally envisioned, in a citadel somewhere in that part of Germany that had remained loyal to the Holy Roman Emperor and to the Catholic faith during the Thirty Years' War. In obvious parallel to the story of *El sitio de Bredá*, the fortress, and the unnamed town that it guards have been besieged for months, and the citizens are exhausted, starving, and mutinous. Forcing their way into the citadel, they beg the Commandant to surrender to the opposing Protestant forces in words that are reminiscent of their counterparts in Calderón's play. The Commandant, however, is unswerving in his devotion to the Emperor and to his own military creed, and he will not hear of capitulation. Instead, he devises secretly to blow up the stronghold and all those who remain within. Learning of this plan, the Commandant's wife, Maria, who like Flora in *El sitio* stands for both peace and love, urges him to reconsider and to flee with her to safety. The Commandant, who seems to combine qualities of both Spinola and Justin of Nassau, remains obdurate, however, and Maria comes to the decision that her love for her husband demands that she die with him. But before the Commandant's terrible plan can be put into effect, a cannon shot is heard in the distance and then, one by one, all the bells in the town begin to peal. News has arrived of the agreements of the Peace of Westphalia, and three decades of harrowing warfare have come to an end. At this point, the stage fills with jubilant townspeople, who are shortly after followed by the Protestant commander and his forces. At first, the Commandant rejects the handshake of reconciliation offered him by his opponent, preferring the honor and glory to be found in war to the friendship to be found in peace, but after the impassioned intervention of his wife, Maria, who sings ecstatically of the superiority of love, hope, and brotherhood, he throws down his sword and embraces his counterpart. The work then comes to a close with an exultant chorale, sung by all the principals and the massed choruses.

As Norman del Mar has observed (62), *Friedenstag* divides into three different sections. The first of these spans the period from the opening moments, as dawn breaks over the fortress, to the entrance of Maria, a little over a third of the way through. This section centers on the irruption of the townspeople into the citadel, their pleas for surrender, and the Commandant's unyielding response. Both literally and figuratively its atmosphere is very dark. Appropriately, then, the music that Strauss composed for it is prevailingly bleak and foreboding. Minor keys predominate throughout, and there is frequent use of harsh dissonance.

The score of the second section of the work, in which Maria and her husband are the only characters onstage, consists of a long aria for her and an equally long duet for her and the Commandant. In both of these pieces, so different from the music heard previously, Strauss gives full rein to his gift for sustained lyricism. Maria's aria, a soliloquy, focuses on her love for the Commandant and her fears for their future. Gradually, as she sings, her doubts give way to a feeling that peace is at hand. The vocal line rises ever higher, and her thoughts turn rhapsodically toward images of the rising sun that promises to put an end to darkness and suffering.

Maria's reverie is interrupted by the sudden entrance of her husband, and the duet that follows moves through a series of contrasting passages in different keys, as Maria refuses to give up her vision of sunlight and concord, and the Commandant holds fast to his sense of duty and honor. The conclusion of the duet is particularly memorable. The Commandant evokes the oath that he has taken to the Emperor, and then he and Maria voice simultaneously totally opposed views of war, noble and glorious for the Commandant, cursed and dreadful for Maria.

The duet of Maria and the Commandant constitutes the thematic center of *Friedenstag*, and its termination signals the end of the second section of the work. The third and final section begins with the muffled sound of the distant cannon and the tolling of the bells. It centers on the transformation of the Commandant from a man dominated by a militarist ethic to one who accepts sincerely, if belatedly, Maria's vision of peace and understanding. The completion of the transformation is signaled by the clasp of brotherhood, as implied in Calderón's play and depicted in Velázquez's painting. Following the embrace of the two commanders comes the mighty final chorus, clearly inspired by the finale of Beethoven's Ninth Symphony. Over the chorus one hears Maria's proclaiming her dream for humanity in a melodic line that rises higher and higher until it culminates, thrillingly, in a series of high Cs. With these joyous notes, the work comes to a stirring and unforgettable conclusion, and the curtain slowly descends.

Similar as they are in affirming the need for brotherhood and reconciliation, the two works examined here are nevertheless different in their emphases.

In his play, written while patriotic fervor gripped Madrid in the summer of 1625, Calderón recognizes unflinchingly the suffering and devastation that war brings, but he also extols, seemingly without irony, the honor and glory that a courageous and loyal soldier may find in warfare. It is because they have both endured bravely that Justin and Spinola are able to meet as brothers at the end of the work. Strauss's opera, on the other hand, presents with great consistency the view that war is an unmitigated evil and that spiritual salvation is only to be found in love, peace, and universal understanding.

Given the pacifistic theme of *Friedenstag*, it is astonishing to learn that in the audience the night of its premiere in Munich in 1938 were several high-ranking members of the Nazi party, including Joseph Goebbels. Because of this, the work has been attacked by some as a work of propaganda on behalf of the National Socialists, eager at the time to foster the illusion that they were a party dedicated to preserving peace in Europe. But that is obviously wrong.[9] Although in the past Strauss had been willing on various occasions to accommodate himself to the dictates of the party, it is clear that his personal ideology was quite different, as was, of course, that of Stefan Zweig, the man responsible for the original outline of *Friedenstag*. Let us, then, approach the opera with an open mind, accepting it for what it is, an admirable work that, like *La rendición de Bredá* and *El sitio de Bredá*, suggests that even in the face of conflict the notion of brotherhood is an ideal to be prized and pursued.

Notes

1. See, for example, Brown and Elliott 182.
2. My account of the circumstances surrounding the creation of *Friedenstag* derives principally from the studies of Birkin (9–161), Del Mar (52–83), and Kennedy (287–319).
3. Given the freedom demonstrated by the opera's borrowings from Calderón's play, many contemporary theorists would probably prefer to categorize it as an "appropriation," rather than adaptation. Cf. Sanders: "An adaptation signals a relationship with an informing sourcetext or original ... On the other hand, appropriation frequently affects [sic] a more decisive journey away from the informing source into a wholly new cultural product and domain" (26).
4. The siege of Breda has been extremely well documented. See, for example, the accounts in Bailey, Wagner-Pacifici, and Vosters (*La rendición*), with their attendant bibliographies. And for a wider historical context, see, among others, Parker.
5. The intense desire on the part of Philip and Olivares at this time to reassert Spain's prominence and recover its reputation has been the subject of numerous studies, including several by Elliott. See, for example, the essay entitled "Power and Propaganda in the Spain of Philip IV," contained in *Spain and Its World*.
6. For a summary of the terms, see Wagner-Pacifici 31.

7. On Calderón's sympathetic treatment of the Dutch, as well as the possibility that he may have participated in the siege of Breda, see, among others, Sullivan 34–36.
8. For a somewhat different perspective on this transformation, see the article of McKim-Smith and Welles.
9. For a discussion of this sensitive matter, see, particularly, Potter.

Works Cited

Armas, Frederick A. de "At War with Primavera: Botticelli and Calderón's *El sitio de Bredá.*" *Hispania* 82.3 (1999): 436–47. Print.

Bailey, Anthony. *Velázquez and the Surrender of Breda.* New York: Henry Holt, 2011. Print.

Birkin, Kenneth. *Friedenstag and Daphne: An Interpretive Study of the Literary and Dramatic Sources of Two Operas by Richard Strauss.* New York: Garland, 1989. Print.

Brown, Jonathan, and J. H. Elliott. *A Palace for a King: The Buen Retiro and the Court of Philip IV.* New Haven, CT: Yale UP, 1980. Print.

Calderón de la Barca, Pedro. *El sitio de Bredá.* Barcelona: Linkgua, 2012. Print.

Del Mar, Norman. *Richard Strauss: A Critical Commentary on his Life and Works.* III. London: Barrie & Jenkins, 1972. Print.

Elliott, J. H. *Spain and Its World: 1500–1700.* New Haven, CT: Yale UP, 1989. Print.

Kennedy, Michael. *Richard Strauss: Man, Musician, Enigma.* Cambridge, UK: Cambridge UP, 1999. Print.

Loftis, John. *Renaissance Drama in England & Spain: Topical Allusion and History Plays.* Princeton: Princeton UP, 1987. Print.

McKim Smith, Gridley, and Marcia L. Welles. "Topographical Tropes: The Mapping of Bredá in Calderón, Callot and Velázquez." *Indiana Journal of Hispanic Literature* 1 (1992): 184–212 Print.

Parker, Geoffrey. *The Army of Flanders and the Spanish Road, 1567–1659.* Cambridge, UK: Cambridge UP, 1972. Print.

Potter, Pamela M. "Strauss's *Friedenstag*: A Pacifist Attempt at Political Resistance." *The Musical Quarterly* 69.3 (1983): 408–24. Print.

Sanders, Julie. *Adaptation and Appropriation.* London: Routledge, 2006. Print.

Sullivan, Henry W. *Calderón in the German Lands and the Low Countries: His Reception and Influence, 1654–1980.* Cambridge, UK: Cambridge UP, 1983. Print.

Vosters, Simon A. "Again the First Performance of Calderón's *El sitio de Bredá.*" *Revista Canadiense de Estudios Hispánicos* 6.1 (1981): 117–34. Print.

———. *La rendición de Bredá en la literatura y el arte de España.* London: Tamesis, 1973. Print.

Wagner-Pacifici, Robin. *The Art of Surrender: Decomposing Sovereignty at Conflict's End.* Chicago: U of Chicago P, 2005. Print.

Whitaker, Shirley B. "The First Performance of Calderón's *El sitio de Bredá.*" *Renaissance Quarterly* 31.4 (1978): 515–31. Print.

Curtain Calls

Fin de Fiesta

And now, to close our most Prismatic Reflections,
Our curtain falling on sincere genuflections,
We hope our public does savor these confections,
Inspired by the genius, in each of the sections,
Of our "autor"'s true scholarly predilections.
To those who wish to raise censure or objections,
We humbly beg your pardon for imperfections.

Tabula Gratulatoria

Ellen M. Anderson
Alan Astro
Carl Atlee
J. C. & Violeta Berbiglia
Larry Jay Bivins
William R. Blue
Robert V. Blystone
Bruce R. Burningham
Richard V. Butler
Joan F. Cammarata
Gwyn E. Campbell
John P. Colhouer
Catherine Connor-Swietlicki
Tom Davis
Manuel Delgado
María José Delgado
Donald T. Dietz
Ralph A. Di Franco
Nina Ekstein
Ezra S. Engling
Edward H. Friedman
Charles Victor Ganelin
David Gitlitz
Margaret R. Greer
Ken Harvey & Jane Armstrong
Valerie Hegstrom & Dale Pratt
Katrina M. Heil
David J. Hildner

John H. Huston
Robert M. Johnston
Mary Jane & Raymond Judd
Patricia Kenworthy
Catherine Larson
Donald R. Larson
Maryrica Ortiz Lottman
Arturo Madrid
Barbara Mujica
Thomas A. O'Connor
James & Patricia Parr
Susan Paun de García
Daniel E. Salcido
Diane Saphire
Barbara Simerka
Louise K. Stein
Gwen H. Stickney
Henry Wells Sullivan
Ronald E. Surtz
Peter E. Thompson
Trinity University,
    English Department
Sharon D. Voros
William O. Walker, Jr.
Barbara F. Weissberger
Kerry K. Wilks
Amy R. Williamsen

Index